# NEW METHODS IN THE STUDY OF ISLAM

**Advances in the Study of Islam**

**Series Editors:** Abbas Aghdassi, Ferdowsi University of Mashhad, Iran, and Aaron W. Hughes, University of Rochester, USA

*Advances in the Study of Islam* publishes cutting-edge research that reflects the long history and geographic breadth of Islam. It rethinks traditional literary canons while simultaneously offering innovative and alternative approaches to push beyond traditional understandings of Islam. The series provides a platform for creative studies spanning:

- Disciplines including religious studies, legal studies, archaeology and anthropology
- Theoretical questions including historical, philological, ethnographic, comparative and redescriptive
- Time periods from late antiquity to the present
- Geographical regions including the so-called Arab World, South Asia, Africa, Iran and the Persian World, Europe and North America



edinburghuniversitypress.com/series/asi

# NEW METHODS IN THE STUDY OF ISLAM

Edited by Abbas Aghdassi
and Aaron W. Hughes

EDINBURGH
University Press

Edinburgh University Press is one of the leading university presses in the UK. We publish academic books and journals in our selected subject areas across the humanities and social sciences, combining cutting-edge scholarship with high editorial and production values to produce academic works of lasting importance. For more information visit our website: edinburghuniversitypress.com



Edinburgh University Press Ltd
The Tun – Holyrood Road
12 (2f) Jackson's Entry
Edinburgh EH8 8PJ

First published in hardback by Edinburgh University Press 2022

Typeset in 11/15 Adobe Garamond by
IDSUK (DataConnection) Ltd, and
printed and bound by CPI Group (UK) Ltd,
Croydon, CR0 4YY

A CIP record for this book is available from the British Library

ISBN 978 1 3995 0349 5 (hardback)
ISBN 978 1 3995 0350 1 (paperback)
ISBN 978 1 3995 0351 8 (webready PDF)
ISBN 978 1 3995 0352 5 (epub)

# CONTENTS

# FIGURES

# SERIES EDITORS' FOREWORD

We tend to work on the assumption that the world around us simply self-categorises, and that it is our task to describe it accurately or at least as accurately as possible. In the world of scholarship this often translates into the idea that it is our job to read more and more texts, accumulate greater amounts of data, all with an eye towards better understanding our subject matter, which are believed to simply await uncovering through what we imagine to be objective description. This is not the case, however. The world does not present itself to us tidily or in a manner that our recountings and narrations either reflect correctly or exactly what it is that we encounter. Far from it. We instead bring our data into existence through a variety of methods and theories, subdivided into numerous sub-methodologies and sub-theories, all of which have lengthy genealogies, complete with tacit assumptions, uses and abuses, in addition to covert (and even overt) political and ideological connotations. We choose, for example, what texts to read, what countries or villages in which to do field work, what to compare with something else (or not). None of these are natural acts, however; they are instead all based on choice and selection. We need to reflect – well aware of the limits of reflexivity – on these matters because they are what ultimately make scholarship possible and bring the numerous worlds we create into active existence.

The goal of the present series is to encourage reflection on how we bring these worlds – fields, disciplines, texts, historical narratives and so on – into existence with our scholarly acts. We want to encourage greater contemplation on how we imagine data, locate its existence, bring it into clearer focus and, just as importantly, in a manner that does not simply assume that if we squint hard enough we can describe it both simply and accurately. Such contemplation is not meant to occur at the expense of our data. Method without theory becomes rudderless and simply spins theoretical wheels for the sake of spinning them. It would also seem appropriate to add that some methods seem to be better suited than others because they conform more accurately to what we perceive. Yet surely all this needs to be discussed in the light of day and, for this reason, we present this venue wherein such issues can be discussed as they relate directly to the study of Islam. For how we decide between methods and methodologies might not simply be a natural decision, but informed by a host of other, perhaps even non-scholarly, decision-making processes.

We hope the reader can see how these issues relate to the study of Islam. This tradition has been studied, examined and re-examined for many purposes over the past few centuries (and even longer if we include various Indigenous methods). Constructed as Europe's inverse, Islam has been made to contort into a variety of positions and for a variety of purposes. While of late it has become in vogue to critique the excesses of Orientalism, reflection on other methods, we maintain, is often sorely lacking. Very few works, for example, venture beyond the binary Oriental versus Indigenous in search of new and creative intellectual spaces. It is for this reason that we have created this series to offer one of the first venues wherein scholars working with Islam can think about, discuss and otherwise reflect on what it means to study Muslim data – and, just as importantly, how we might continue to do so moving forward.

Within this context, the present volume that inaugurates this series, *New Methods in the Study of Islam*, co-edited by us, attempts to advance these methodological conversations by showcasing a set of, as the title notes, 'new methods'. These involve everything from examining how aspects of the Islamic past have been used for present political purposes to prosopography to comparative theology to what is now often referred to as 'lived Islam' in a variety of local contexts. The results of these approaches move the study of Islam beyond traditional philological and historical scholarship with the aim of opening the tradition to a set of fresh methods in conversation with other fields and disciplines in the Humanities and Social Sciences.

# ACKNOWLEDGEMENTS

The editors of the volume would like to express their gratitude to all the scholars who contributed to our volume. It was because of their patience and dedication to the idea of this work that the current volume exists. Special thanks go to Nicola Ramsey of Edinburgh University Press, who introduced us to Emma House, Commissioning Editor for Islamic and Middle Eastern Studies, who also kindly welcomed the idea of our volume and the series. We are also grateful to the Press Committee at EUP, who analysed our proposals, commented on them and approved them. Two anonymous reviewers read our proposals and provided very constructive comments and positive feedback. We appreciate their views.

Aaron: I would like to thank my co-editor, Abbas Aghdassi, for his perseverance and good-nature. What was supposed to be a volume seems to have turned into a book series! As always, I thank my friends in the field and my family, especially my mum, and my life-partner, Liliana Leopardi.

Abbas: I would like to express my deepest thanks to Prof. Aaron W. Hughes for his welcoming and supporting the early idea of a volume on new methods and methodologies in the study of Islam, in the early days of June 2020 – when he probably did not know that I would burden him with an exchange of over 200 emails! I highly appreciate your help, Aaron. I would also like to express my gratitude to Prof. M. Samiei (University of Tehran), who was the first professor to kindle concepts of neo-/orientalism in my mind and how post-colonial frameworks could (and could not) shape the study of Islam. I am forever grateful for my parents and in-laws – particularly Mr Seyed Hossein Saffari, who is a brilliant source of critical thinking. I remain very much indebted to my wife for all she did and does in my life.

# NOTES ON CONTRIBUTORS

**Eyad Abuali** received his PhD in the study of Sufism from SOAS in 2017. His previous research has focused on the intellectual and cultural history of the senses at Utrecht University in the framework of the European Research Council funded SENSIS project. He is currently a postdoctoral researcher at the Humboldt Institute of Islamic Studies, focusing on the history of emotions in Sufism.

**Dauda Abubakar** is a senior lecturer in the Department of Religion and Philosophy, University of Jos, Nigeria. He holds a PhD from the Freie Universität Berlin, Germany. He teaches undergraduate and postgraduate courses in Comparative Religion, African Traditional Religion, Islam and Social Anthropology of Religion. Abubakar has published many articles in local and international journals as well as chapters in books. He is the author of *They Love Us because We Give Them Zakāt: The Distribution of Wealth and the Making of Social Relations in Northern Nigeria* (2020). His upcoming book is titled *Stateless Citizens in Nigeria: Entanglement of Ethnicity, Politics and Religion*. Abubakar has participated in many local and international research collaborations with scholars within and outside Nigeria. His current research is on returning migrants from Europe to Nigeria. Abubakar is presently supervising undergraduate and postgraduate (MA and PhD) students. His areas of specialisation include: Muslim–Christian relations and anthropology of Islam with interest in West Africa.

**Abbas Aghdassi** serves as an Assistant Professor in the Department of History and Civilisation of Muslim Societies, Ferdowsi University of Mashhad (FUM), Iran. He teaches courses on Methods and Methodologies in Islamic Studies, Contemporary Muslim World, and Islam and/in the West. His publications include: *Islām va Musalmānān dar Birītānīyā* (2015); *Persian Academic Reading* (2018); *Tashayyu' dar Āmrīkā* (2020); and *Perspectives on Academic Persian* (2021). He focused on Twelver minorities in New York, particularly, African American and Khoja Shi'as in his fieldwork studies. He was a visiting research scholar in the Graduate Center (New York). Abbas is the managing editor of *Tārīkh va Farhang*, a journal in Persian on pre-Safavid Iran and Islam. He has recently started a curated page with Oxford Bibliographies Online: *Spotlight in Iranian and Persian Studies*. His fields of interest include methods in Islamic studies, Muslim minorities, academic Persian, bibliography and bibliometrics, (humanising) Orientalism, and socio-historical study of Greater Khorasan.

**Esra Akay Dağ** is a Research Assistant at the Department of History of Religions, Faculty of Theology, Sakarya University, Turkey. She holds a PhD from the University of Bristol, UK. Her primary research areas are Christian–Muslim Relations, Comparative Theology and Contemporary Approaches to Religious Diversity. She is the author of *Christian and Islamic Theology of Religions: A Critical Appraisal* (2017), and some other articles.

**Ayşe Almila Akca** heads the Junior research group 'Islamic Theology in context: science and society' at the Berlin Institute for Islamic Theology at Humboldt-University Berlin. She received her PhD from the Institute of Islamic Studies/Freie Universität Berlin in 2018. Her ethnographic study on negotiations of Islamic knowledge, tradition and religious authority in mosques in Germany was awarded with the DAVO Dissertation Award 2019: *Moscheeleben in Deutschland. Eine Ethnographie zu Islamischen Wissen, Tradition und religiöser Autorität* (transcript publishing Bielefeld, 2020). She was a research fellow at the Catholic Academy of Rottenburg-Stuttgart and at the Georg-Eckert-Institute for International Textbook Research in Braunschweig. She conducted researches on Christian–Muslim relations, gender issues, Islamic fields in Europe and Near East, Islamic knowledge in modernity, and religious authority and canonisation processes. Following a practice–theory approach her recent research projects include various religious practices of Muslims in western societies such as fasting, celebrating religious festivities and ecological practices.

**Johanne Louise Christiansen** is Professor in the Department of the Study of Religions, University of Southern Denmark. Her research focuses on the application of theoretical perspectives from other research fields, such as the study of religions, to the Qurʾān. Among Christiansen's recent work are the articles '"Stay Up during the Night, Except for a Little" (Q 73:2): The Qurʾānic Vigils as Ascetic Training Programs', *Religion* 49(4) (2019): 614–35; and 'God Loves not the Wrongdoers (*ẓālimūn*): Formulaic Repetition as a Rhetorical Strategy in the Qurʾān', *Journal of Qurʾānic Studies* 22(1) (2020): 92–132); and her new book *The Exceptional Qurʾān: Flexible and Exceptive Rhetoric in Islam's Holy Book* (2021).

**Housamedden Darwish** is a senior research fellow at the Centre for Advanced Studies in the Humanities and Social Sciences, University of Leipzig, and lecturer at the Department of Oriental Studies, University of Cologne. His papers, lectures and seminars are on topics related to modern and contemporary Arab intellectual thought and the question of democracy and secularism in the Arab and Islamicate world. He holds a PhD from the Department of Philosophy at the University of Bordeaux3/Montaigne, France, with a specialisation in Hermeneutics. He is the author of three books in French, three in Arabic, and dozens of refereed research papers and studies, in both Arabic and English. He has held visiting positions at the Department of Philosophy, University of Duisburg-Essen, the Department of Oriental Studies, University of Cologne, and University of Leipzig. His work has been supported by the German Research Foundation (DFG) and the Volkswagen Foundation.

**Maribel Fierro** is Research Professor at the Institute for the Languages and Cultures of the Mediterranean – Consejo Superior de Investigaciones Científicas (CSIC). She has published on the political and intellectual history of the pre-modern Islamic West (al-Andalus and North Africa) with books such as *Al-Andalus: saberes e intercambios culturales* (2001;

trans. into French and Arabic); *ʿAbd al-Rahman III: The First Cordoban Caliph* (2005); *The Almohad Revolution* (2012); and *ʿAbd al-Muʾmin: Mahdism and Caliphate in the Islamic West* (2021). She has edited *The Western Islamic World, vol. II: Eleventh–Eighteenth Centuries*, the *New Cambridge History of Islam* (2010); *Orthodoxy and Heresy in Islam: Critical Concepts in Religious Studies* (2013); and *The Routledge Handbook on Muslim Iberia* (2020). She has held visiting positions at Leiden University, Exeter University and EHESS (Paris). Her work has been supported by the Spanish Ministry of Education, the European Research Council and the Alexander von Humboldt Foundation.

**Alejandro García-Sanjuán** is Professor of Medieval History at the University of Huelva, Spain. His major publications include *Till God Inherits the Earth: Islamic Pious Endowments in al-Andalus* (2007); *Coexistence and Conflict: Religious Minorities in Medieval Iberia* (2015, in Spanish); and *The Islamic Conquest of Iberia and the Misrepresentation of the Past* (2019, 2nd edn, in Spanish). More recently, he published *Jihad: The Rules of War in Classical Islamic Doctrine* (2020, in Spanish); and co-edited with Hussein Fancy the collective volume *What Was the Islamic Conquest of Iberia? Understanding the New Debate* (2021). His ongoing research addresses the reception of al-Andalus and medieval Iberia in modern Spanish culture and scholarship, with a special focus on the notion of *Reconquista* and its current ideological re-engineering among conservative and far-right academic and political outlets.

**Ateeb Gul** is a PhD student in Islamic Studies at the Graduate Program in Religion, Boston University. He studied for a BSc (hons) in Social Sciences at Lahore University of Management Sciences (LUMS) and for an MA in Editorial Studies at Boston University's Editorial Institute. He is also a professional editor, writer, poet and translator. His graduate paper titled 'Early Muslim Responses to the Child Marriage Restraint Act 1929' was awarded the GCWS Motherboard Writing Prize 2020.

**Aaron W. Hughes** holds the Dean's Professorship of the Humanities and the Philip S. Bernstein Professorship of Religious Studies in the Department of Religion and Classics at the University of Rochester, New York. He is the author of over twenty books with diverse titles, including *Shared Identities: Medieval and Modern Imaginings of Judeo-Islam* (2017); *From Seminary to University: An Institutional History of the Study of Religion in Canada* (2020); and *An Anxious Inheritance: Religious Minorities and the Shaping of Sunnī Orthodoxy* (2022). He has held visiting positions at the Hebrew University of Jerusalem, McMaster University (Hamilton, Ontario) and the Faculty of Oriental Studies at the University of Oxford. His work has been supported by the Social Sciences and Humanities Research Council of Canada (SSHRC), the Lady Davis Fellowship Trust (Jerusalem), the Killam Foundation, and the National Endowment for the Humanities (NEH).

**Abdul Jaleel P.K.M.** is currently associated with Muhammad Al Agil Chair at the Asia Research Institute, National University of Singapore. He has taught West Asian Studies at the University of Kerala and was a visiting fellow at Berlin Graduate School of Muslim Cultures and Societies, Free University, Berlin. He has been awarded a PhD for his thesis, 'Hadrami Sayyid Diaspora in Kerala and Singapore: A Comparative Study', from Jawaharlal Nehru University, New Delhi. His publications include: 'Religious Rivalries in Eighteenth Century Malabar: The Diasporic Writings of a Hadrami Scholar', in Michael N. Pearson and Mahmood Kooria (eds), *Malabar in the Indian Ocean: Cosmopolitanism in a Maritime Historical Region* (2018); and 'Arab Immigrants under Hindu Kings in Malabar: Ethical Pluralities of "Naturalization" in Islam', in Ray Jureidini and Said Fares Hassan (eds), *Migration and Islamic Ethics* (2020).

**Georg Leube** (Dr Habil) is Akademischer Rat (Assistant Professor/ Adjunct Lecturer) at the Chair of Islamic Studies, University of Bayreuth, Germany. Between October 2020 and September 2022, he represented 50 per cent of a professorship in Islamic Studies at the University of Hamburg. He completed his PhD on early Islamic history and historiography from a prosopographical perspective in 2014 (*Kinda in der frühislamischen Geschichte*, published Berlin 2017). His current research engages with the representational culture at the *Qara-* and *Aqquyunlu* courts (Habilitationsschrift positively evaluated 2021.6, to be published in two separate monographs).

**Claudia Seise** obtained her PhD in Southeast Asian Studies from Humboldt University, Berlin. During her PhD, she conducted extensive qualitative research in Indonesia; her dissertation is titled 'Religioscapes in Muslim Indonesia: Personalities, Institutions and Practices'. Her research interests include Islam and Muslim practices in southeast Asia, especially in Indonesia; Muslim minorities; Inter-religious dialogue; modern art in southeast Asia; and research methodology. She was an academic fellow at Humboldt University, Berlin, in 2017, and worked as an assistant professor at the International Islamic University Malaysia from April 2018 until August 2019. She has published several articles and one main monograph. Besides her academic writing, Claudia has contributed to the German Islamic newspaper since 2008. In 2019, she published a collection of essays about Islam in southeast Asia in German. Claudia joined the Berlin Institute of Islamic Theology at Humboldt University in September 2020.

**Aydın Süer** is a member of the Junior Research Group *Islamic Theology in Context: Science and Society* at the Berlin Institute for Islamic Theology, Humboldt University of Berlin. He holds a PhD in sociology and is an alumni of the Berlin Graduate School of Social Sciences (BGSS). He was an affiliated researcher at the Zentrum Moderner Orient (ZMO) Berlin in 2009. Currently he is working on his postdoctoral project on *Art as a Form of Islamic Religious Practice*. His other major fields of interest are social theory, practice theory, sociology of religion, historical sociology and Islam in Germany. His dissertation on the topic of Ottoman and Turkish discourses of decline was published in 2019.

# NOTE ON TRANSLITERATION

This volume follows the transliteration guidelines of *IJMES* for Arabic, Persian and Turkish terms. Although *EI* and *EIr* provide more accurate systems of transliteration and transcription for Arabic and Persian languages accordingly, *IJMES* remains a more accessible and user-friendly system to both authors and readers – regardless of some of its technical shortcomings for publishing and indexing services. For all other local languages, the transliterations are those of the LOC.

To every self-reliant person,
academic or not,
for whom discovering *a place betwixt*
matters;
and
for whom any human-constructed duality
– Oriental vs Occidental,
Eastern vs Western,
Colonial vs Decolonial –
shatters.

# 1

# INTRODUCTION: WHY NEW METHODS IN THE STUDY OF ISLAM?

ABBAS AGHDASSI AND AARON W. HUGHES

> Arts, crafts, and most human activities always have more or less well-developed methods. Experience teaches us that following such methods, developed in the course of experience, leads to desired results. There is no need for further critical reflections.[1]

> Most of the research and studies on prevailing scientific practice adhere to customs, traditions and procedures that researchers have not traced back to their origins, and the authoritative point of reference for which they have not attempted to identify. Rather, they content themselves with the knowledge that these methods are familiar and widely practiced.[2]

## Introduction

With this volume, we, the editors, inaugurate a new series devoted to the methods and methodologies that have defined the academic study of Islam in the past, and that inevitably will continue to do so moving forward into the future. What is novel about this emphasis is that, too often, we tend to focus overwhelmingly on data, oftentimes at the expense of

[1] Thomas M. Seebohm, *Hermeneutics: Method and Methodology* (Dordrecht: Springer, 2007), 153.

[2] Fathi Hasan Malkaw, *Epistemological Integration: Essentials of an Islamic Methodology* (London: International Institute of Islamic Thought, 2014), 86.

the methods that conjure said data into existence. Such privileging risks the assumption that our data is all that is important and we just have to discover more and more of it in order to reach some Archimedean position of repose. We argue, however, that this is not the case and instead is itself a position that emerges out of its own methodological assumptions that elevate philology to the level of a divine science. Change the interpreter, however, and the interpretation will also change. While so-called Muslim data – texts, beliefs, rituals, historical events – are seemingly available to scholars from a wide array of disciplinary perspectives, we duly note the manifold ways that such data have been and continue to be interpreted.

Do not get us wrong. Manifold interpretations are certainly richer and theoretically more nuanced than monolithic or monothetic ones. There can, after all, be no singular let alone definitive interpretation of human behaviour and institutions. Political scientists who deal with Islam, for example, approach their material using the methods supplied by their larger field; ditto for sociologists and anthropologists of Islam. While there is a plethora of methods used to study Islam, there is not a confusion of such methods, but there most certainly is a need to sort them out, classify them and reflect on their utility. This is precisely what this volume seeks to undertake. We, as editors, work on the assumption that there exists a healthy mix of methods and methodologies, but currently no one venue where scholars can come together to think about how methodological reflection pertains both to their own work and, just as importantly, to that of others. This is precisely the goal of this volume and the series it inaugurates.

Islam is, after all, first and foremost, a way of being human, and Islamic studies deal with the richness and the creativity of Muslims as they have tried to understand their social and religious worlds over the past millennium and a half. Yet, and this is our point, as scholars of Islam we ought to focus more of our collective attention on what we are doing and how we are doing it, as opposed to simply doing it. A reflection on method certainly cannot come at the expense of our data. We are not encouraging everyone to drop what they are doing and suddenly become 'theory heads'. Far from it. We are instead providing an oft-ignored and much-needed venue for scholars to come together in order to offer, test out and convince others of new ways – not *the* way – to study Islam the religion and Muslims as social actors.

We all engage in method, whether we admit it or not. Perhaps rather than leave the term 'method' ambiguous, we should define the term, to the best of our abilities. Methods are those sets of scholarly conventions that enable scholars to bring what they study into focus. Political scientists, to reiterate the example used above, use the methods that the discipline of political science has bequeathed to them. Sociologists do the same with the methods of sociology; anthropologists with those of anthropology; and historians with those of history. Things get a little more complex outside disciplines, in, for example, fields such as religious studies or literary studies. Religious studies, for instance, witnesses no dominant methodology, and some scholars are certainly more critical than others, whereas others are more reverential.[3] In like manner, even when there are entrenched disciplines, we should note that there are different kinds of sociologists, anthropologists, historians and so on. In terms of the latter, for example, there are social historians, intellectual historians, economic historians, Marxist historians and so on. They would certainly all disagree on the nature of their data, especially if they were all interpreting the same dataset.

Methods and methodologies, it should be increasingly clear, are anything but natural or value-neutral, though they are often presented as such. In what follows, we attempt to address these, and related issues pertaining to methods, by focusing simultaneously on some of the shortcomings of previous methods and the need for new methods to understand Islam, all the while realising that we cannot chart a future without a realisation of where we have been. Before elaborating on this volume's structure, allow us to continue to reflect a little more on methods and methodologies.

While, on one level, we might all certainly agree that there can be no knowledge without implicit sets of descriptions, juxtapositions and comparisons. She is taller than him, for example, or this is darker than that. Such statements may well seem obvious enough as we go about our daily lives, deciding, for example, which batch of apples look better or what colour of car is sportier, but when used as an academic method, problems inevitably arise because we often forget or overlook the fact that our decision-making is now employed as a theoretical or heuristic construct. Items in the world, in other words, do not self-arrange or

[3] See, for example, Russell T. McCutcheon, *Critics Not Caretakers: Redescribing the Public Study of Religion* (Albany, NY: State University of New York Press, 2001), 3–20.

self-classify. On the contrary, things encountered about which we claim to know something are placed into their various relationships of similarity and difference by curious and invested observers proactively arranging their worlds – —social, academic or the like. Scholars of Islam, for example, have no problem using categories like myth, ritual, pilgrimage, prayer, text, etc., to name and organise different things and actions, from different contexts, *as if* they are members of the same class, all for purposes of making claims about the world.

Methods, in sum, provide us with frameworks. But frameworks, if not understood as such, condition us to see certain things and not others, and to see them, moreover, as if they were a natural outcome of our cognitive processes simply awaiting our descriptions. We must acknowledge that our frameworks possess countless blind spots, assumptions and problematic assertions, which structure, frame and otherwise bring data into focus or, alternatively, obscure it. However, and despite these shortcomings, we cannot get around the fact that we rely on these frameworks to think about, comprehend, argue and formulate – either consciously or not – our data, regardless of disciplinary background. This is why methods should also ideally force us to think about these blind spots and assumptions, which, alternatively, illumine and obnubilate, minimise and magnify, unify and alienate the things we encounter as we go about our daily academic lives. Habituation or familiarity often plays a bigger role in this process than we perhaps give it credit for. We are, after all, conditioned to reject or distance ourselves from that which is unfamiliar, while gravitating towards that which is familiar to us. Again, this familiarity/unfamiliarity means that we potentially miss certain features just as we simultaneously gravitate towards others.

To cite a few examples. A study of the Qurʾān that emphasises explanation of its contents (e.g., *tafsīr* or commentary) will result in analyses and conclusions that would be considerably different from, for instance, a method that emphasises comparison with other religious texts (either Islamic or non-Islamic). The habituation of each approach – each with its own academic, political and ideological genealogy – often translates into a resistance to the other. In like manner, a method that applies a historical approach to some aspect of Islamic history – say the *miḥna* (Inquisition) of the Abbāsid Caliph al-Mahdī – would look considerably different than one that relies on a methodology derived from political science. The point, of course, is that we need both methods, in addition to others, to understand the event in question, or the Qur'ān using the earlier example.

This is precisely where this volume, and the series that it inaugurates, comes into play. In the summer of 2020, we circulated an international call for a volume devoted to 'New Methods in the Study of Islam'. The response was overwhelming, and we received many excellent abstracts from Europe, North America, the so-called Islamic world and Africa. Our call revolved around asking a series of broad questions: what are (the) new methods in the study of Islam? Can newer approaches to methods and methodologies provide different lenses to examine *Islam* and *Islamic Studies*? Can technology revolutionise our method and methodological preferences? Should textuality, once the dominant method, be replaced by non-textual methods to understand Islam and its relations with other religions?

Upon closer examination, we now realise that the positive response to our call reveals a much larger interest in the methods used to study Islam, Islamic traditions and Muslim communities, both in the past and the present. The question that illumines this volume, as it does the series as a whole, is how do we, as scholars relate our amalgamated data to existing or even new methods? It has, for example, become fashionable, at least since the publication of Said's *Orientalism* (1978), to focus on the excesses of Orientalism as a scholarly tradition.[4] While some have tried to reclaim certain aspects of the tradition,[5] the current default methodological position seems to be one of decoloniality.[6] But these are all methodological debates, despite the fact that they are often presented in the angriest of tones, and it behooves us to understand these methods, in addition of course to others.

[4] Edward W. Said, *Orientalism* (New York: Vintage, 1978). A more recent attempt at reformulation, arguing that Said simultaneously went too far and not far enough, is Wael B. Hallaq, *Restating Orientalism: A Critique of Modern Knowledge* (New York: Columbia University Press, 2018).

[5] Majid Daneshgar, 'I Want to Become an Orientalist Not a Colonizer or a "De-Colonizer"', *Method and Theory in the Study of Religion* 33(2) (2021): 173–85.

[6] See, for example, Sajjad Rizvi's response to Daneshgar titled 'Reversing the Gaze?: Or Decolonizing the Study of the Qur'an', *Method and Theory in the Study of Religion* 33(2) (2021): 122–38. For a shift from Orientalism to decoloniality, what the editors call 'cosmopolitanism', see Carl Ernst and Richard C. Martin (eds), *Rethinking Islamic Studies: From Orientalism to Cosmopolitanism* (Chapel Hill, NC: University of North Carolina Press, 2010).

It would, however, be incorrect to reduce all methodological impulses in Islamic studies today to the antagonism between (neo-)Orientalism and decoloniality. There currently exists, as the chapters that follow reveal, a wide array of methodological approaches that help us to illumine Islamic data from new and different perspectives.

## Breakdown of Chapters

What follows is devoted, as indicated by the title, to methods and methodologies in the study of Islam. It presents a structured, contemporary and timely contribution to the very broad field of Islamic studies. The volume is divided into five distinct, yet overlapping sections.

Part I, Methods: Old and New, is devoted to a reflection on method – what it has done, and what it continues to do – as it relates specifically to the study of Islam. This includes the introduction of new methods and using such methods to look at traditional topics (e.g., al-Andalus).

Aaron W. Hughes, in Chapter 2, 'New Methods, Old Methods in the Study of Islam: On the Importance of Translation', seeks to put Orientalism into counterpoint with those claims that seek to decolonise the study of Islam by returning to what are now often referred to as 'Indigenous' methods. Neither of these approaches, he argues, are natural. He instead suggests that we investigate them, seeing whence they emerge, and what and whose interests (ideological, social, economic, etc.) they advance and uphold.

In Chapter 3, 'The Reception of al-Andalus (1821–2021): Two Hundred Years of Study and Debate', Maribel Fierro and Alejandro García-Sanjuán review the case of al-Andalus, now imagined as an integral part of the so-called West, but something that, of course, was not always so. While Muslim communities continued living in the region under Christian rule, this was far from a *convivencia* and has created problems for the present, including issues of integration, minoritian traditions, forms of nationalism and so forth. All of these issues, they argue, has made al-Andalus into a convenient site to examine the promotion of specific methods and methodologies.

Part II, Textual Studies, switches focus to the traditional mainstay of Islamic studies, the study of classical texts (e.g., the Qur'ān), and seeks to provide new ways of understanding them.

Georg Leube, in Chapter 4, 'Subversive Philology? Prosopography as a Relational and Corpus-based Approach to Early Islamic History', suggests a prosopographic engagement with the formative period of Islam. Such an approach, based on a systematic and corpus-based approach, aids in overcoming the lingering influence of colonialist and (self-)orientalising paradigms.

In Chapter 5, 'Juxtaposition, Tension, Play: The Development of Islamic Law and Legal Theory', Ateeb Gul shows how various trends in Islamic textual hermeneutics are best understood using terms and categories (e.g., juxtaposition, tension and play) as developed by J. Z. Smith and Sam Gill. Following their model, Gul analyses the key developments in Islamic legal history: the development of classical *fiqh* literature, especially al-Shāfiʿī's *Risāla*; the development and use of the *siyāsa-sharʿiyya* model in the medieval period; and the interplay between the authority of the *ʿulamāʾ*, on the one hand, and, on the other, the influence of colonialism in modern South Asia. He concludes by showing how the element of play has had a formative role in shaping the Islamic legal tradition.

In Chapter 6, 'New Theoretical Approaches to the Qurʾān and Qurʾānic Studies: An Analysis of the Qurʾānic (Disabled) Body in Light of Conceptual Metaphor and Conceptual Blending Theory', Johanne Louise Christiansen seeks to apply the theoretical frameworks supplied by conceptual metaphors and conceptual blending as formulated within the sub-field of Cognitive Linguistics. Using a comparative method, she discusses the Qurʾānic use of the body, body parts and disabilities by placing the Qurʾān's 'metaphoricity' in terms of the broader academic debates over its historical context, its relations to other traditions, and how this functions in the academic study of religion more broadly.

Part III, Islam and/as Critique, examines the ways in which Islam offers an alternative to western and European forms of secular liberalism.

In Chapter 7, 'On the Relationship between Culture/Religion and Politics: A Critique of the Culturalist Approach to Islam', Housamedden Darwish has examined some features of what he calls 'the culturalist approach to Islam as an ideal type'. Referring to some Muslim countries, particularly Syria, he argues that a culturalist approach to Islam (so-called Islamicate) reduces culture to a religious dimension, and that this becomes a means of autocracy or political despotism in the Arab and Islamicate worlds. Phrases such 'Islam is the problem' and 'Islam as the solution' are thus based on a culturalist understanding.

Part IV, New Comparisons, invokes, critiques and reframes the traditional method in the Humanities writ large, and the study of Islam writ small – that of comparison.

In Chapter 8, 'Can Comparative Theology Help Muslims to a Better Understanding of Religious Diversity?', Esra Akay Dağ discusses various academic approaches to religious diversity. Reviewing the development of theology of religions and comparative theology, she shows how Muslims have contributed to the discourses associated with religious diversity, though in a limited fashion. She suggests that through comparative theology Muslim theologians ought to be able to gain a better understanding of religious others.

Finally, Part V, Local Islams, examines geographical religions and religious beliefs and practices that are traditionally left out of the main narratives of Islamic studies.

Chapter 9, 'Eastern or Western Paradigm: The Struggle for Methodological Dominance in the Study of Islam in Universities in Northern Nigeria', sees Dauda Abubakar showcase how universities in Nigeria struggle over how to study Islam. This results in a confusion over methods, which include local academics with some levels of local training, traditional clerics and graduates from Arab countries. This raises for the author a key question: should the academic study of Islam be theological with an eastern inflection or based on a scientific method embedded within the West?

In Chapter 10, 'Narratives from the Peripheries: An Indian Ocean Perspective for the Study of Islam', Abdul Jaleel P.K.M. argues that studies on Islam and Muslims have traditionally focused on the Middle East, despite the fact that the majority of Muslim societies exists in the far-flung regions of Asia and Africa. Focusing on the significance of what he calls 'the littoral societies of the Indian Ocean', he shows how such communities play a role in the development of Islamic studies by offering contributions that echo the dynamicity of Islam in the non-Arab socio-political and maritime ecological contexts. He argues that an Indian Ocean perspective on Sufi experiences as opposed to legalistic textual traditions reveals a much different understanding of Islam, one that was conveyed by traders, Sufis and scholars.

Claudia Seise, in Chapter 11, 'Including Localized Islamic Concepts in the Study of Islam', makes the case for the inclusion of localised Islamic concepts in the study of Islam. She argues that the application of ethnography, in addition to mastering local languages, aid us in better understanding 'localized concepts'. She then elaborates on this by focusing on a set of localised Islamic concepts (e.g., *silaturahmi* and *barokah*) in present-day Indonesia.

Finally, in Chapter 12, 'Bodies, Things, Doings: A Practice Theory Approach to the Study of Islam', Ayşe Almıla Akca, Eyad Abuali and Aydın Süer highlight the importance of understanding and appreciating the rich material cultures in the study of Islam. They argue that an appropriate methodology has to account for the local and the material. They develop an interdisciplinary approach to show how lived Islam, both in the past and the present, can be examined through the lenses of practice theories that include embodiment and material religion.

Taken together, these chapters seek to push the study of Islam forward by focusing on the methods that have been used to study Islam in the past, that are currently used to study it in the present, with an eye towards future analysis. When these chapters are read together, they reveal the complexity of Islam as a religious system, as a political discourse and as a lived tradition that can – indeed ought to – be studied using a variety of new methods and methodologies.

## Bibliography

Daneshgar, Majid, 'I Want to Become an Orientalist Not a Colonizer or a "De-Colonizer"', *Method and Theory in the Study of Religion* 33(2) (2021): 173–85.

Ernst, Carl and Richard C. Martin (eds), *Rethinking Islamic Studies: From Orientalism to Cosmopolitanism*. Chapel Hill, NC: University of North Carolina Press, 2010.

Hallaq, Wael B., *Restating Orientalism: A Critique of Modern Knowledge*. New York: Columbia University Press, 2018.

Malkaw, Fathi Hasan, *Epistemological Integration: Essentials of an Islamic Methodology*. London: International Institute of Islamic Thought, 2014.

McCutcheon, Russell T., *Critics Not Caretakers: Redescribing the Public Study of Religion*. Albany: State University of New York Press, 2001.

Rizvi, Sajjad, 'Reversing the Gaze?: Or Decolonizing the Study of the Qur'an', *Method and Theory in the Study of Religion* 33(2) (2021): 122–38.

Said, Edward W., *Orientalism*. New York: Vintage, 1978.

Seebohm, Thomas M., *Hermeneutics: Method and Methodology*. Dordrecht: Springer, 2007.

# Part I

## METHODS: OLD AND NEW

# 2

# NEW METHODS, OLD METHODS IN THE STUDY OF ISLAM: ON THE IMPORTANCE OF TRANSLATION

AARON W. HUGHES

## Introduction

The field of Islamic studies, in both western and non-western contexts, is certainly alive and well in both its methods and its output. We see Islamic data approached from various perspectives, from everything that includes – for lack of better terms – the 'Orientalist' and the 'Indigenous'.[1] Many of these methods should be familiar enough to the reader, and they have consisted of, among others, the historical, textual, theological, legal, anthropological, sociological, political and so on. Taken together, all of these

[1] Unlike many, I do not use the term 'Orientalist' or 'Orientalism' in a pejorative sense here. While certainly aware of its historical excesses, including its involvement in the colonialist project, I prefer to characterise it here as an academic tradition, one invested in a host of Euro-Christian assumptions to be sure, interested in documenting the textual and historical tradition of Islam. In the words of my colleague, Majid Daneshgar, we must remember that the Orientalist tradition is 'replete with thousands of unknown scholars who have largely been forgotten in our top-down approach to Islamic studies: these include travel reports, periodicals, translations, and often times provocative hypotheses. Most of these are largely ignored, forgotten, and buried. An entire network of knowledge, passion and innovation has disappeared alongside these works.' See Majid Daneshgar, 'I Want to Become an Orientalist Not a Colonizer or a "De-Colonizer"', *Method and Theory in the Study of Religion* 33(2) (2021): 173–85, at 179.

methodological approaches have done a great deal to represent the myriad of historical and contemporary expressions of Muslim actors and the social worlds they have created and continue to create. What is worth pointing out, however, is that the overwhelming emphasis of these methodological focuses have gone into actual representations, as indeed should be the case. However, we must also be sensitive to the fact that when we focus solely on the data, the various acts that make such representations possible in the first place often recede into the background, if they are not ignored altogether. The present chapter focuses less on Islam, then, than it does on the various lenses that bring it into focus. These lenses are, of course, nothing more nor less than the various methods invoked to encounter and ultimately represent Islam to colleagues, to students and, more generally, to the public at large.

What I wish to emphasise here is that none of these methodological acts are natural, let alone value-neutral, nor do they take place from some Archimedean ground. Nevertheless, they are more often than not presented precisely as such. Instead, they all take that gargantuan and unwieldy thing we all too neatly refer to as 'Islam' and then simplify and reduce it into something that can presumably be meaningfully studied. The simplification and reduction, however, is what I am most interested in here. What are the imaginative and other acts that permit us to frame some aspect of Islam by delimiting it and subsequently bringing it into conversation with something else? This is often done to such an extent that it is never some pure or essentialised 'Islam' that is refined and articulated – though it can often be presented in such a manner – so much as it is the understanding or definition of that tradition as understood and put forth by the interpreter.[2]

Methods, framed somewhat differently, all come from somewhere and, unfortunately, far too little intellectual energy is expended in tracing both their genealogies *and* examining how they potentially distort as much as they potentially illumine. This strikes me as one of the reasons why Shahab Ahmed's *What Is Islam?* (2015) was so critically acclaimed on account of the fact that it was among one of the first books to think about methodological

[2] See my comments in ': Thinking about Islam Through the Act of Comparison', in Frank Peter, Paula Schrode, and Ricarda Stegmann (eds), *Conceptualizing 'Islam*[working title] (London: Routledge, forthcoming).

frames. In his review essay of the volume, Michael Pregill remarked, 'despite this methodological diversity and the overall flourishing of the field in the last decades, attempts at conceptualizing the subject of inquiry, of reappraising it in critical terms, are rather rare.'[3] While I certainly do not want what follows simply to be an engagement with Ahmed's work, I do after all find it deeply problematic, it is nevertheless important to look at it briefly given that it proposes to offer both a new theory and a new method. That it ultimately ends up reinforcing a certain normativity only proves my point: an emphasis on data over method, and of representation over the acts of representation, is potentially problematic. And, unfortunately, the uses and abuses of such representative acts receive far too little attention.

The need to develop new methods to study Islam, then, cannot simply replace the need to interrogate just what method is and does. For this reason, the goal of this chapter is to get us to reflect more theoretically, and simultaneously more concretely, on just what method is (and is not), what it does (and does not), and, in the process, how such reflection can ultimately help us in our study of the diversity and complexity of Islamic data.

## What is Method? How Does it Relate to Theory?

In the Humanities in general, and the study of religion in particular, there are a rather limited number of methods in operation. If we are to reflect on 'new methods' for the study of Islam, it is incumbent upon us both to clarify what the term 'method' means and then to try to ascertain what sorts of intellectual work it is supposed to perform. Unless there is such clarification, then method – and, by extension, methodology – can mean anything, something that one could argue is all too common in the secondary literature. If a term can mean anything, after all, then it can also simultaneously mean nothing. Like other critical terms, method and methodology are ultimately equivocal, meaning different things to different people, and, because of this, they are often used in ways that are often diametrically opposed to one another.

The word 'method' signifies the approach one takes to a topic of study. Derived from the Latin *methodus*, itself from the ancient Greek μέθοδος, the

[3] In this regard, see the comments in Michael Pregill, 'I Hear Islam Singing: Shahab Ahmed's *What Is Islam? The Importance of Being Islamic*', *Harvard Theological Review* 110(1) (2017): 149–65.

term denotes a way of investigating a topic or the procedure and approach one adopts before engaging in such an investigation. Apart from such generic uses as the plan of action to attain some particular end, by the early seventeenth century the term came to refer to a system of classification. It is within this latter sense that we encounter what may well be one of the most famous uses of the term as a scholarly mode of analysis. I refer, in particular, to *Discours de la Méthode pour bien conduire sa raison, et chercher la vérité dans les sciences* (1637).[4] In this work, René Descartes (1596–1640) seeks to ascertain a non-theological foundation upon which a system of human knowledge could be built, something that he claimed to have found in his ability to doubt everything but his own existence as a thinking subject. Hence, his famous declaration *cogito ergo sum* or, in French translation, 'Je pense, donc je suis'.

In the so-called hard sciences, method refers to the ideal of studying data systematically and as part of a replicable step-by-step procedure, in such a manner that the analysis is the same regardless of where or by whom it is carried out. Method, in that context, is meant to be repeatable and thus an essential or characteristic feature of any scientific pursuit. Without a repeatable and time-tested method, in other words, there can be no advancement in knowledge. In the Humanities, however, method would seem to mean something entirely different. Now it becomes some vague and just as often highly idiosyncratic – and thus potentially unrepeatable – understanding of some idiosyncratic datum (e.g., a person or a text). Indeed, the Canadian scholar of Islam, Wilfrid Cantwell Smith (1916–2000) once famously characterised what he considered to be his 'revolutionary' methodological rule for the field: 'that no statement about a religion is valid unless it can be acknowledged by that religion's believers'.[5] Such a locution, of course, begs the question as to what believers, and assumes, of course, that all believers believe the same things. There would seem to be two types of methods, then: one for scientists and another for humanists. This, of course, is fine as long as we are aware of the difference and acknowledge it. Words nor categories need be monolithic,

[4] English translation: *Discourse on the Method of Rightly Conducting One's Reason and of Seeking Truth in the Sciences*, trans. Ian Maclean (Oxford: Oxford University Press, 2006).

[5] 'Comparative Religion: Whither – and Why?', in The History of Religions: Essays in Methodology, eds Mircea Eliade and Joseph Kitagawa (Chicago: University of Chicago Press, 1959), 31–58.

after all, let alone static. However, we must certainly take note of the fact that there is much potential for confusion when meanings, and their intents, are not properly clarified, and it is simply assumed that they mean the same thing in different domains.

In like manner there can be no method without theory, with the latter denoting an idea (or, in some cases, a hunch) of the way things came to be the way that they are, an activity that is often accomplished through the application of method. Theory and method, then, though similar in scope, must certainly be qualified and perhaps differentiated from one another. What they share, however, is the act or set of acts that we use to focus on our data, including what we deem significant and thus worthy of scholarly attention. Theory, like method, is far from a natural act, as many unfortunately presuppose, and primarily refers to the way we bring data into focus and then how we go about subjecting said data to analysis. Theory forces us to ask questions, perhaps even uncomfortable ones. Not unlike method, the term theory signifies too many things to too many people and, for this reason, often remains vague, muted or hidden in the margins – all of this despite the fact that it is omnipresent. Indeed, theory, as I use the term here, refers to those discourses responsible for establishing a network of signifiers that casts its web over meanings, objects and practices. To engage in theory thus means an interrogation of authority and the status quo.[6]

In order to get at this clarification, what follows is divided into several parts. In the first part, I examine some of the main methods used in the Humanities in general and the study of Islam in particular. These consist of: comparison, explanation, interpretation and description. Following this, I examine how these methods play out in the study of Islam, with a primary focus on what have increasingly been referred to as issues of 'Indigeneity'. This segues into the issue of 'decoloniality', and whether or not this concept can salvage the study of Islam from previous Orientalist excesses. Using Shahab Ahmed's *What Is Islam?* as my case study, I argue that we need to find appropriate methods for the study of Islam that combine the best of Orientalist – including post-Orientalist – scholarship and more Indigenous methods that inform and are, in

[6] Here I follow the lead of the English scholar Terry Eagleton, *Literary Theory: An Introduction* (Minneapolis: University of Minnesota Press, [1983] 2008), 169–89.

turn, informed by it. It suggests the translation of Orientalist and Indigenous methods into one another becomes a reminder that neither are natural, nor, claims to the contrary, value-free. We should also be aware that, although the Orientalist and the Indigenous are often constructed as binaries, they are, in many ways, two sides of the same coin, with both being the product of human creativity and, by extension, fallibility.

All of this meandering leads to my conclusion that too great of a focus on our data (e.g., Islam, Muslims) at the expense of the methods used to bring said data into focus is potentially problematic. It means that we all tend to work in our own silos, which often means that we think our data is self-evident and thus it is not necessary to connect it to larger questions and issues in the Humanities or even the Social Sciences.

## Methods: A Brief Subdivision

There are, for all intents and purposes, relatively very few methods in the Humanities, or at least the academic study of religion, the field wherein I ply my trade. They can be reduced and categorised to the following: comparison, explanation, interpretation and description.[7] Allow me to spend a little time defining the pros and cons of each. A *description* involves the attempt to portray the essence of someone or something whether though providing a partial list of attributes or the sum of qualities that the person engaged in the description decides to be representative or characteristic. The problem with such a method, as should already be clear, is that it is prone to essentialism and, thus, either unable or unwilling to attend to the incongruous, the liminal or the marginal.

The second major method in the Humanities is *interpretation*. This names the attempt to decode the meaning of a text, an action, or an artefact, often with an eye towards identifying or clarifying its meaning or purpose. This is often predicated on the assumption that the claims of an actor or a group are comprised of symbols whose associations and settings need to be uncovered and closely examined in order to arrive at that which is customarily called

[7] These are on full display in Brad Stoddard (ed.), *Method Today: Redescribing Approaches to the Study of Religion* (Sheffield: Equinox, 2018).

their meaning. The goal of interpretation, especially in early usages of the term – where it was primarily employed with the Bible – was to exposit contents for the faithful.[8] Once again, problems arise, especially when there are no criteria for what counts as a proper interpretation. As a result, this method can be as denominational (e.g., a Protestant interpretation is different from a Catholic one, and both, of course, are different from a Muslim or a Jewish one) as it is idiosyncratic. Also problematic is the fact that there is an assumption that texts (or acts or beliefs) inherently contain that which is interpreted *out of* them, and that the interpreter somehow neutrally conveys that meaning to an audience.[9]

An *explanation*, not infrequently juxtaposed with interpretation, is the act that identifies the cause or function of something. If the latter pulls meaning out of a text or practice, an explanation seeks to offer an account of what something does. Though certainly open to debate and contention, in the study of religion a method that seeks to explain a religious phenomenon by recourse to something else (e.g., something social, psychological or cognitive) is often treated with suspicion.[10] Not unlike the previous two methods, however, we once again see just how idiosyncratic an explanation can be. A Marxist, for example, might explain something one way, whereas a psychoanalyst or a sociologist might explain the same phenomenon in a radically different manner.

Finally, *comparison* refers to the act of grouping together two or more items because they are somehow imagined to be equivalent or, at the very least, somehow or in some manner similar to one another.[11] As a method, comparison is an activity that selects, juxtaposes and manipulates two or more

[8] Even today, for example, we still have academic journals with titles such as *Interpretation* and *Biblical Interpretation* (founded 1993), both of which are devoted to biblical study and, as the titles suggest biblical interpretation.

[9] Bruce Lincoln, *Authority: Construction and Corrosion* (Chicago: University of Chicago Press, 1994), 1–13.

[10] Perhaps the most important articulation of the so-called irreducibility of the sacred is the work of Mircea Eliade. See, in particular, his *The Sacred and the Profane: The Nature of Religion*, trans. Willard R. Trask (New York: Harvest, 1957).

[11] More generally, see my *Comparison: A Critical Primer* (Sheffield: Equinox, 2017), esp. 8–24.

unrelated objects that an individual perceives to share one or more similar or overlapping characteristics.[12] Comparison habitually finds itself gravitating towards two ends of an ideological continuum: either (1) to show how two or more things are either entirely different or (2) to demonstrate how they are essentially the same. Like the previous methods, however, comparison has been used to for all sorts of ideological and political ends. It has protected, it has undermined and it has elevated.[13]

What is common to all of these methods, of course, is choice and, just as often, suppressed or hidden agendas, that can lead to unintended results. In terms of the former, in all four of these methods we witness idiosyncratic commentators determine what is of significance or what is not, what is relevant or irrelevant, and what is important or unimportant. However, this is often done with absolutely no objective criteria other that what the interpreter deems, supposes or otherwise suspects to be of relevance. All of these methods are presented by those who engage in them – whether consciously or unconsciously – as natural and, by extension, as value-neutral. Such determinations are also related to the latter issue, that of hidden or suppressed agendas, since we might not always be honest and/or upfront about why or how we engage in such studies in the first place precisely on account of the fact that we imagine our activities to be natural. Yet nothing could be further from the truth since most studies in the Humanities – of which we most certainly must include the academic study of Islam, in all of its many branches – are idiosyncratic, non-repeatable and just as often non-theorised. Instead, they are simply presented as part of the natural world that the commentator in question simply engages or activates. Since the worlds we inhabit do not self-classify or self-taxonomise, there has to be an awareness that it is we who do this. To repeat my point from earlier: while new

[12] Good work on comparison includes the likes of Jonathan Z. Smith, 'In Comparison a Magic Dwells', in *Imagining Religion* (Chicago: University of Chicago Press, 1982), 19–35; J. Z. Smith, *Drudgery Divine: On the Comparison of Early Christianities and the Religions of Late Antiquity* (Chicago: University of Chicago Press, 1990), 36–53; Bruce Lincoln, *Apples and Oranges: Explorations In, On, and With Comparison* (Chicago: University of Chicago Press, 2018), 3–24; Oliver Freiburger, *Considering Comparison: A Method for Religious Studies* (Oxford: Oxford University Press, 2019), 20–44.

[13] See, for example J. Z. Smith, *Drudgery Divine*, 1–35.

methods are important, equally important is the method of reflecting on methodologies. New methodologies, thus, have to be self-reflective.

This, of course, is not to argue that there exists much variation or even sub-methods beneath all of the methods surveyed in this section. On the contrary, it is to say that there are four basic methodological paradigms in the Humanities, all of which seem to be predicated on some notion of what the German historian, Wilhelm Dilthey (1833–1911), called *Verstehen* or 'understanding'. According to this principle, humanistic study, in all of its many dimensions, is primarily a hermeneutical affair since human behaviour, including the systems within which humans live and interact, are imagined by the interpreter as inherently meaningful. This implies that their proper study requires scholars to understand that meaning – both in the sense of comprehending it and, more often than not, in the sense of empathetically re-experiencing and potentially appreciating it for themselves.

## Muslim Methods

To the aforementioned, we would be remiss if we did not acknowledge that there also exist many Indigenous methods for studying Muslim data, as presumably there are for any religious tradition or civilisation.[14] Though, of course, we should note that the claim that someone, something or some mode of knowing as 'Indigenous' immediately marks a contest over identity, place and resources, one that is derived from sorting and subsequently classifying people by means of such binary alternatives as natural or unnatural, simple or complex, primary or derivative, local or imported, safe or dangerous and, finally, us or them. Despite this, or indeed perhaps because of this, 'Indigenous' can be neatly differentiated from the 'European', the 'colonial' or the 'Orientalist'. Though, we should also note that every method is ultimately Indigenous with the difference that the European has been sublimated to the level of the universal or the trans-Indigenous.

[14] Indigenous, not unlike 'Orientalist', is also a difficult word. The former term is frequently employed to name something thought to be shared in common by those considered to be local to, or the original or perhaps even natural inhabitants of a region or a land. More specifically, it is often used in a descriptive sense (as mentioned above under methods) as it names a particular way of thinking.

When we use the phrase 'Indigenous methods', then, we would seem to refer to a set of local, historical – perhaps even romantic or at least wistful, in the sense that they are imagined to be untouched by European domination – approaches to the study of Islamic religious texts. The *ulūm islāmiyya* ('Islamic sciences'), as they are called by devout Muslims, refer to those methodological acts that, among other things, provide commentary on scripture (through *tafsīr*), elucidate the law through *fiqh*, establish truth claims through *kalām* or create a body of literary expression known as *adab*. These all refer to internal modes of knowing based on the elucidation of the unknown from the known (e.g., Qur'ān and *sunna*). Such methods were developed in the early Islamic period and subsequently expanded upon in the subsequent centuries to create – not unlike the case in the West and as surveyed above – Islamic data by bringing it into focus by, among other things, deciding to focus on certain things and not others.

It cannot simply be the case, as some want to maintain, that 'Orientalist' methods are bad and 'Indigenous' ones are good. They both operate on similar systems of privileging and marginalisation, and of inclusion and omission. Once again, we see the importance of choice and the fact that such choice is often simply assumed to be uncovering that which exists naturally in the world. This, of course, is where the tensions emerge. Some scholars associated with the Orientalist tradition imagine the work produced in Islamic contexts as naive, outmoded or not 'rational' enough. In like manner, some of those in Islamic contexts envisage the Orientalist tradition as based on a set of political and ideological motives grounded in racism and colonialism. The point here is not to wade into this debate, something that many have already documented,[15] but it is to say that Indigenous modes of knowing are

[15] The classic study remains, of course, Edward W. Said, *Orientalism* (New York: Vintage, 1978). For a more recent expression, one that argues that Said simultaneously went too far and not far enough, see Wael B. Hallaq, *Restating Orientalism: A Critique of Modern Knowledge* (New York: Columbia University Press, 2018). To this list, we could also add Roger Owen, 'Studying Islamic History', *Journal of Interdisciplinary History* 4(2) (1973): 287–98; Talal Asad (ed.), *Anthropology and the Cultural Encounter* (Amherst, NY: Humanity Books, 1973); Abdallah Laroui, *The Crisis of the Arab Intellectual: Traditionalism and Historicism*, trans. Diarmid Cammell (Berkeley, CA: University of California Press, 1976); and more recently Suzanne L Marchand, *German Orientalism in the Age of Empire: Religion, Race, and Scholarship* (Cambridge: Cambridge University Press, 2009).

no less invested in politics or ideologies than western ones. Claims that one is superior, more objective, or based less in the colonialist enterprise – including the concomitant call simply to replace one with the other – would seem to miss the major point that all methods – so-called eastern and so-called western, so-called Islamic and so-call Orientalist – all emerge from the same epistemological space. This space is grounded in choice (often in an unreflective manner), mistaking the part for the whole (and vice versa), and the existence of hidden or suppressed agendas about the correct ordering of one's social world.

Both sets of methods, western/Orientalist and Islamic/Indigenous, are assumed to reflect accurately the natural world as opposed to being a set of manufactured categories that are projected onto it. Like all methods, then, methods used to study Islam tend not to be theorised as a set of folk *taxa*, which they ultimately are, but instead are largely taken for granted and assumed to be natural and discrete categories waiting to be uncovered. We, thus, run into the same situation with both non-Muslim and Muslim categories, including the methods that bring them into existence.[16] Occasionally, we witness the attempt to translate them into one another, when we define, for example, *taʾrīkh* as history, *kalām* as theology, *sharīʿa* as law, *taṣawwuf* as mysticism, or the Qurʾān as scripture. While on one level helpful since such translation tries to bring the two categories – and, by extension, modes of knowing – into conversation with one another, such translations invite as many problems as they attempt to solve. For one thing, while such translations attempt to redescribe traditional Muslim terms and methods into ostensibly western ones, the redescription never goes the other way. That is, we never attempt to understand, say, mysticism as *taṣawwuf* or theology as *kalām*, which might be even more interesting than in the opposite translation. Indeed, the translation of Arabic terms and categories – including the methodologies that are associated with them – might well open up the study of western Humanities in a more interesting manner.

[16] Of course, I am not even considering all those studies grounded in Islamophobia that unfortunately populate so many generalist bookshops in the current moment.

## Can We Decolonialise and Re-Indigenise the Study of Islam?

The question now becomes: how can we engage in a mutually beneficial translation of western terms, categories and methods into Islamic ones and vice versa, especially in such a manner that involves neither appropriation nor violence? Now, of course, is an opportune moment to engage in such translation since many academic disciplines and fields in the West – in response to a host of external events that include everything from colonialism to Black Lives Matter (BLM) to land claims of First Nations communities to Israel's treatment of Palestinians – are currently interested in both dismantling their first principles and expanding (if not outright demolishing) their canons. More often than not, this is associated with the call to 'decolonise the curriculum', though unfortunately with little thought about what such decolonisation might entail or even look like.

We, thus, stand at an interesting crossroads in redefining the Humanities, something that, I imagine, has necessarily precipitated this volume's quest for ascertaining new methods. This quest, however, demands thoughtful attention and not the simple throwing out the proverbial baby with the proverbial bathwater. While canons should always be expanded and the status quo consistently interrogated (if not actually overturned), we have to be cautious of dismantling an entire intellectual edifice in the service of what may well prove to be a set of interests defined and reinforced by identity politics, which by definition are neither inclusive nor methodologically repeatable, let alone verifiable.[17]

The first, and most basic, issue that arises comes in the form of a question: can a decolonial approach to the study of Islam be critical? Now, by 'critical' I do not necessarily mean deconstructive or one that employs a set of methods that work on the assumption that Muslims are somehow rendered incapable of understanding their own traditions because they are so inside their traditions that they cannot possibly stand on the outside and analyse it objectively. On the contrary, I instead only want to raise the issue here that we have to be

[17] See my *Theorizing Islam: Disciplinary Deconstruction and Reconstruction* (Sheffield: Equinox, 2012); and further *Islam and the Tyranny of Authenticity: An Inquiry into Disciplinary Apologetics and Self-Deception* (Sheffield: Equinox, 2015), esp. 15–36.

cautious of simply taking insider accounts at face value and thus being in no need of either critical analysis or explanation (to return us to the above section on methodological frameworks). Such methods, using the western ones described above, are largely descriptive or interpretive, but rarely explanatory or comparative in orientation. Even if we want to call such methods 'decolonial', it should be duly noted that, for the most part, the former two methodologies largely function as the operative methodologies of the status quo in much of Islamic studies, especially as practiced in North America, at the current moment. What, in other words, would change?

I certainly understand – and indeed here try to promote – the need for a so-called decolonial approach, something that seeks to undo at least some of the logic of colonialism, especially the latter's concomitant notions of hegemony. Since colonialism is often associated with the enlightenment project, we must also realise that its roots go to the heart of the modern university.[18] It was universities, after all, that trained administrators for colonial outposts, received goods and commodities (read: texts and artefacts), and produced systems of knowledge based on it. The latter often involved artificial distinctions between us and them, civilised and barbaric, and Christian and primitive. The goal of decolonial approaches, it seems to me, is to replace this logic, one that continues to structure our knowledge production, including the erection of parameters beyond which it is difficult to see, with a set of critical Indigenous methodologies.[19] Or, if not actually replace them, then at the very least to call our attention to the fact that there are other ways of classifying the world around us. In what follows I am more interested in the latter approach, which exposes the artificiality of our systems, as opposed to the former, which strikes me as having the potential to lead to a highly non-critical and non-analytic set of frameworks, one no less invested in ideology, wherein no one can critique anyone else on account of the injustices they have suffered under

[18] One of the best accounts of this approach may be found in Mallory Nye, 'Decolonizing the Study of Religion', *Open Library of Humanities* 5(1) (2019), available at: https://olh.openlibhums.org/articles/10.16995/olh.421.

[19] For example, Linda Tuhiwai Smith, *Decolonizing Methodologies: Research and Indigenous Peoples*, 2nd edn (London: Zed Books, 2012), 1–19.

the Euro-West's hegemony. This strikes me as little more than identity politics, something that currently besets Humanistic scholarship.

Without wanting to undermine the desire for some sort of mutual reinforcement between critical and Indigenous methodologies, one that still needs to be worked out in detail, I will say that there is an inevitable tension in their mutual pairing. Much of this revolves the equivocal term 'critical'. Obviously, everyone imagines themselves as engaging in critical work – everyone from the Sunni cleric, the western apologist, or the Islamophobe regards him- or herself as engaging in some sort of value-neutral or 'objective' scholarly activity. If critical is such a relative adjective here, deployed in such contradictory ways, then what are we expected to do with so-called 'critical' methodologies? We can, and indeed do, thus, ostensibly have critical methodologies that are, in fact, anything but.

Even if we were to develop a set of decolonial methods, however, we would still face an equally difficult question. I refer, in particular, to the subsequent critiquing of such methodologies. After all, methodologies do not – assumptions of some to the contrary – fall from heaven or emerge *ab novo*. Instead, they develop slowly as more and more data is accumulated and others offer modification to original formulations. Yet if decolonial approaches are seen as somehow Indigenous to particular times and places, if we engage in a critique of them, we are then imagined to undermine someone else's identity. That is, is such critique imagined as silencing others? There is an implicit danger, then, that such a decolonial approach might become – this, of course, is not to say that it has to – little more than a description using a set of Indigenous categories. This may well be just the other side of the coin where 'other' local traditions are understood in terms of western (and thus themselves local) categories that are assumed to be universal in both nature and scope.

Within this context, there is a danger that decolonial methodologies, and the approaches that either follow in their wake or are produced by them, might mean little more than taking an insider or non-critical approach to the beliefs of others, something one could argue is little different from the status quo in the field already. A decolonial approach, in other words, need not necessarily be a critical one. We thus have to be cautious of adopting a set of methodologies grounded in the project of decolonialism. While I shall spend some time in the next section discussing how we might move forward, it is certainly worth reiterating in the present context that new methods cannot simply be created overnight. On the contrary, they need to build upon existing ones, can account for our datasets, and in such a manner that we are able to move forward in creative and dynamic ways. Paradigm shifts, in other words, are long-term processes.

What might all of this mean for the academic study of Islam? Within this context, I think we need to be cautious of simply bypassing the western academic tradition of studying the tradition – though, of course we need to be aware of its excesses – and simply reverting to a study of that tradition that simply reintroduces Indigenous terms and categories. The risk of such an endeavour is twofold. First, as mentioned above, it risks being either uncritical or not subject to criticism. Secondly, and equally important, it risks making all of the ideas, beliefs and practices associated with the manifold traditions of Islam largely untranslatable to the modern Academy. This would mean that Islam – or perhaps other traditions, as well – might appear as somehow different from the West, thus reinforcing traditional Orientalist assumptions.

A decolonial approach also might mean that only those who are part of the tradition – and, in the case of Islamic studies, this would include converts to the tradition as well – are permitted by the guild to have a voice. Non-Muslims, in other words, would then simply have to refrain from entering the conversation, and function simply as cheerleaders to the competing voices of their Muslim colleagues. There is also the risk that the boundary between the academic study of Islam and Islamic perspectives on a particular topic might blur so that one does not know where the one begins and the other ends.[20] There is a danger, in my view, that a decolonial approach to the study of religion might default to a set of largely non-critical, non-sceptical and insider approaches. There are, of course, those who might argue that this is little different from the manner in which the academic study of religion is currently carried out in the North American Academy.

[20] See, for example, the essays in Carl Ernst and Richard C. Martin (eds), *Rethinking Islamic Studies: From Orientalism to Cosmopolitanism* (Chapel Hill, NC: University of North Carolina Press, 2010).

## Orientalist and Indigenous: Mutually Reinforcing Methods

So how do we proceed? For me, it would make most sense to take pre-existing methods, ones developed in Orientalist ateliers and subsequently developed in the post-Orientalist period, and then allow them to inform and be informed with more Indigenous methods. Such an approach would seem to offer a much better alternative than simply dismantling the Orientalist (or European or western, or whatever else we decide to call it – they are all, after all, used interchangeably with one another) and replacing them with those imagined to be Indigenous under the guise of 'decolonialism' or the 'decolonial' project. Both the Orientalist and the Indigenous, after all, begin with the same basic premise that takes texts seriously, and both put a premium on being able to read them and interpret them. They are also similar in the assumptive manner in which they present their findings as natural, objective or otherwise value-neutral. Where they differ, of course, is in the status of such texts. Whereas Indigenous methodologies imagine them as sacred and divinely given or interpreted, the Orientalist tradition tends to regard them as the products of human creation. This difference, however, need not be terminal to some sort of mutual reconciliation or, at the very least, translation.

The huge question remains, of course, and that is: how exactly to do this? How, in other words, is it possible to engage in a mutually beneficial project of methodological translation? One of the more recent and celebrated attempts to move such conversations forward is the work of the late Shahab Ahmed. In his *What is Islam?*, for example, he begins with the premise that that which we refer to as the study of Islam must not simply be an insider club, something in which Muslims – whether in the so-called Islamic world or the liberal modern Academy – engage to work out their own fears and desires, to make the tradition either more or less inclusive dependent, of course, on their own particular agendas. What is so refreshing about Ahmed's work is that he argues, and also shows, how the academic study of Islam must illumine and be illumined by relevant cognate fields. As he states near the beginning of his work, 'a valid concept of "Islam" must denote and connote all possible "Islams" whether abstract or "real" mental or social'.[21] Or, as he

[21] Shahab Ahmed, *What is Islam?: The Importance of Being Islamic* (Princeton, NJ: Princeton University Press, 2016), 104.

states in his conclusion, 'this book has sought to locate the logic of difference and contradiction as coherent with and internal to Islam – that is, to provide a coherent account of contradiction in and as Islam'.[22]

All of this sounds good, of course, until we confront the methodological repercussions of going about this business. Most importantly for my purposes here, is the fact that everything risks becoming 'Islamic' on Ahmed's reading, indeed, to such an extent that, methodologically speaking, there is no way either to process or analyse one's data. The result is that Islam can mean everything and, because of this, it can concomitantly mean nothing. He is certainly correct in his assessment that to call something 'Islamic' is an act of authorisation, just as when we opt to label something as 'un-Islamic' we somehow de-authorise it.[23] Methodologically, this creates all sorts of problems, however. If Islam is everywhere, then it is concomitantly nowhere. If everything is Islamic, then nothing is Islamic. If both of these equations are correct, then how can we possibly develop a set of methods to understand this overwrought complexity.

Some have argued, as Michael Pregill does, that 'one of the critical methodological maneuvers Ahmed makes here is reorienting the definition discussion not only to enfranchise different types of evidence, but to relocate it to a [different] chronological and geographical frame'.[24] While the shift from classical to post-classical Islam, from the Arabo-Iranian context to the 'Balkans–Bengal complex', and elites to non-elites is certainly appreciated, attendant methodological problems remain. Despite Pregill's comment that perhaps the most significant methodological advance that Ahmed offers here is 'the shift from the historical and still endemic emphasis in the field on early and classical Islam and its predominantly Arabic literary remains to a more holistic view of the development of Islam',[25] we are still left with the same problem. Namely, how do we study this? It is in this respect that we witness a confusion in Ahmed's work between theory – that is, articulating the complexity of Islam, something that he does very well – and method, that is, how

[22] Ahmed, *What is Islam?*, 542.

[23] Ahmed, *What is Islam?*, 107.

[24] Pregill, 'I Hear Islam Singing', 153.

[25] Pregill, 'I Hear Islam Singing', 161.

can we appropriately or adequately study this complexity, in such a manner that we are self-reflexive of our own agendas and biases?

While Ahmed is certainly to be praised for his desire to move beyond prescriptive and normative accounts in the study of Islam, he ultimately, and paradoxically, falls into the same problem of trying to develop something no less normative. Indeed, as Pregill does well to note, 'the line between a purely analytical project and a constructive-normative project appears at times very blurry in his work'.[26] In a move that would please any classic phenomenologist, Ahmed argues that what connects Muslims together – both temporally and geographically – is the idea that, what he calls the rupture of *the* ultimate Truth of the Unseen reality occurred in seventh-century Arabia, something that is now believed to be canonised within the Qurʾān.[27]

I began this chapter lamenting the paucity of theorising when it comes to the academic study of Islam. Certainly, Islamic data can be, and indeed is, approached in any number of ways: textually, ethnographically, sociologically, and with attention to gender, race, and increasingly, to what has more recently been called 'lived' or 'material' religion. The latter, in particular, represents a new sub-field developed within the study of religion, that seeks to correct what was seen as a traditional over-emphasis on the interpretation of texts and a preoccupation with studying male elites – indeed, we see several examples of this at play in the present volume. Emphasis is accordingly placed on how religion is instead experienced 'on the ground'.[28]

All of these diverse methods should, at least on one level, be regarded as a general sign of the health of the field and shows clearly that it has not remained static in its traditional Orientalist stage of development. Reflective of the Humanities more generally, we increasingly see a movement away from traditional texts. We witness, instead, a rather wide array of methods that seek to demonstrate the variety of historical and contemporary expressions of

[26] Pregill, 'I Hear Islam Singing', 163.

[27] Ahmed, *What is Islam?*, 345–50.

[28] On the latter, see the essays in David D. Hall (ed.), *Lived Religion in America: Toward a History of Practice* (Princeton, NJ: Princeton University Press, 1997). For a sustained study, see Nancy T. Ammerman, *Everyday Religion: Observing Modern Religious Lives* (Oxford: Oxford University Press, 2007).

Islam. Yet, despite this variety – or, indeed, perhaps because of it – we have largely failed in the much bigger task of reflecting upon, or reconceptualising, just what it is we are doing. We see a lot of description and interpretation, but very little critical reflection on just what and how it means to engage in such methodological acts. We, for the most part, just keep on keeping on with our various studies and examinations, often assuming that the methods we use and the data we choose to focus on (or not) is a natural process that simply mirrors the natural world with which we interact in our scholarly and other endeavours. Lost in Ahmed's otherwise impressive analysis was a reflection of how it brings Islamic 'things' (e.g., beliefs, practices, customs) into existence in the first place.

## New Methods, Old Methods: Translation

It would be inappropriate to move to a conclusion of this chapter with the suggestion that there should only be one method to study Islam. The title of this volume is, after all, devoted to new *methods*, that is, in the plural. One cannot, after all, engage in a set of ethnographic methods to read, say, a twelfth-century legal text. In like manner, one cannot take a new method that stresses codicology and the taxonomy of medieval manuscripts and apply it to the anthropological study of a Nigerian village. However, as we move forward, perhaps the theoretical and methodological insights that ethnography provides might prove – in some way, shape or form – useful to our understanding of medieval textuality. It is this interplay of methods, in the final analysis, that might well provide us with the newness with which to understand Islamic data in all of its rich diversity and complexity.

The 'new' that this chapter wishes to emphasise, then, might not be on the actual development of a method hitherto unheard of or one that has never before been developed, one that simply awaits our discovery. No, the tenor of this chapter has been that perhaps the most novel type of methodology is one that emphasises self-reflexivity and forces us to confront what, when, where, why and how we engage in methodological questions. The newness that this chapter emphasises, then, is not the accumulation of more data, but an emphasis on a proper attunement to the genealogy of the terms, categories and discourses we use, on the one hand, and a critical self-reflexivity, on the other.

This, however, is not nearly as easy as it sounds. Genealogy is not simple history, ascertaining where things come from. It is, instead, much more, the understanding that we do not necessarily find Islam out there, but that we conjure it into existence by the theoretical choices, methodological moves and rhetorical flourishes *we* chose. This is what the late Jonathan Z. Smith meant in his famous and oft-cited introduction to his *Imagining Religion*: 'there is no data for religion. Religion is solely the creation of the scholar's study'[29] – to which we could just as easily substitute 'Islam' for 'religion'.[30] Since the secular and academic study of Islam is, at most, 200 years old, and it was preceded by a millennia or so of internal Islamic theological speculation, we need to be cautious of how each set of intellectual traditions can potentially create distortion.

Self-reflexivity and genealogy, I submit, needs to begin from a point of translation. How, for example, can we use Indigenous terms and concepts as way to translate those produced from within the context of the modern academy? To translate the Qur'ān as scripture or *kalām* as theology, for example (or even vice versa), creates as many problems as it solves. *Kalām* is not theology, at least as developed and understood in the context of the Christian West, where it refers to a particular type of thinking about God and Christology specific to Christian universities and seminaries. As a result, the sense the word has in English depends in large part on the sense the Latin and Greek equivalents had acquired in patristic and medieval Christian usage. This is, of course, radically different from the way in which it is understood in Islam, where *kalām* refers to a different set of discourses developed in the Islamic world at the end of late antiquity to address the problem of correct belief that wracked the burgeoning caliphate. *Kalām*'s stating point is thus different, both conceptually and historically, than that found in the largely Christian tradition of theology. *Kalām*'s methods of

[29] Jonathan Z. Smith, *Imaging Religion: From Babylon to Jonestown* (Chicago: University of Chicago Press, 1982), xi.

[30] See my 'There is No Data For Islam: Testing the Utility of a Category', in Leif Stenberg and Philip Wood (eds), *What is Islamic Studies?: European and North American Approaches to a Contested Field* (Edinburgh: Edinburgh University Press, 2022), 32–41.

argumentation, its concerns, its conclusions and its debates are all different from its Christian predecessor.[31]

This certainly does not mean that we should not engage in the task of such translation, however. On the contrary, it seems to me that it is incumbent upon us to do so, but we should do so only insofar as we are aware of the potential for slippage and distortion. It seems to me that not nearly enough reflection has been done on bringing these two scholarly traditions together. Ultimately this is what we are doing. We are not using 'superior' western or European methods or theories to understand an 'inferior' Islam, including its own Indigenous modes and methods of analysis. We are, instead, bringing two traditions together with the aim of mutual translation and in such a manner that each tradition is better understood in the process.

This is why the call to 'decolonise' the study of Islam – or, the Humanities more generally – are doomed to fail. Such endeavours fail to wrestle with genealogies. In this latter sense, Indigenous methods are just as invested in their own ideologies and political wills to power as those found in anything produced in the classic tradition of Orientalism. The replacement of one for the other, in other words, will not get us very far. If anything, they will succeed – at least in the case of Islam – in making that tradition unknowable to the secular western academy. While some might say that this has always been the problem, it seems to me that making things less knowable as opposed to more knowable is not a desideratum, especially at this present moment of history.

In the final analysis, it is also important for us to understand that Indigenous categories can also help us to better understand our own intellectual shortcomings. This involves not realising that our own terms, categories and base narratives are somehow universal or universalising. If anything, they are just as contingent as those of any other set of folk *taxa*. It is only for a host of political and economic reasons that we have decided to elevate them to the level of the natural. If we are to develop new methods for the study of Islam and Muslims, we thus have to move beyond our traditional categories.

[31] See further my 'Kalām: Constructing Divinity', in Majid Daneshgar and Aaron. W. Hughes (eds), *Deconstructing Islamic Studies* (Cambridge, MA: Harvard University Press, 2020), 124–44.

This can occur only after we come to the realisation that they are constructed categories and not natural markers.

## Bibliography

Ahmed, Shahab, *What is Islam?: The Importance of Being Islamic*. Princeton, NJ: Princeton University Press, 2016.

Ammerman, Nancy T., *Everyday Religion: Observing Modern Religious Lives*. Oxford: Oxford University Press, 2007.

Asad, Talal (ed.), *Anthropology and the Cultural Encounter*. Amherst, NY: Humanity Books, 1973.

Daneshgar, Majid, 'I Want to Become an Orientalist Not a Colonizer or a "De-Colonizer"', *Method and Theory in the Study of Religion* 33(2) (2021): 173–85.

Descartes, René, *Discourse on the Method of Rightly Conducting One's Reason and of Seeking Truth in the Sciences*, trans. Ian Maclean. Oxford: Oxford University Press, 2006.

Eagleton, Terry, *Literary Theory: An Introduction*. Minneapolis: University of Minnesota Press, [1983] 2008.

Eliade, Mircea, *The Sacred and the Profane: The Nature of Religion*, trans. Willard R. Trask. New York: Harvest, 1957.

Ernst, Carl and Richard C. Martin (eds), *Rethinking Islamic Studies: From Orientalism to Cosmopolitanism*. Chapel Hill, NC: University of North Carolina Press, 2010.

Freiburger, Oliver, *Considering Comparison: A Method for Religious Studies*. Oxford: Oxford University Press, 2019.

Hall, David D. (ed.), *Lived Religion in America: Toward a History of Practice*. Princeton, NJ: Princeton University Press, 1997.

Hallaq, Wael B., *Restating Orientalism: A Critique of Modern Knowledge*. New York: Columbia University Press, 2018.

Hughes, Aaron W., *Theorizing Islam: Disciplinary Deconstruction and Reconstruction*. Sheffield: Equinox, 2012.

Hughes, Aaron W., *Islam and the Tyranny of Authenticity: An Inquiry into Disciplinary Apologetics and Self-Deception*. Sheffield: Equinox, 2015.

Hughes, Aaron W., *Comparison: A Critical Primer*. Sheffield: Equinox, 2017.

Hughes, Aaron W., 'Kalām: Constructing Divinity', in Majid Daneshgar and Aaron W. Hughes (eds), *Deconstructing Islamic Studies*. Cambridge, MA: Harvard University Press, 2020, 124–44.

Hughes, Aaron W., 'There is No Data For Islam: Testing the Utility of a Category', in Leif Stenberg and Philip Wood (eds), *What is Islamic Studies?: European and*

*North American Approaches to a Contested Field.* Edinburgh: Edinburgh University Press, 2022, 32–41.

Hughes, Aaron W., 'Islam *and* . . . : Thinking about Islam Through the Act of Comparison', in Frank Peter, Paula Schroder and Ricarda Stegmann (eds), *Conceptualizing 'Islam'.* London: Routledge, forthcoming.

Laroui, Abdallah, *The Crisis of the Arab Intellectual: Traditionalism and Historicism*, trans. Diarmid Cammell. Berkeley, CA: University of California Press, 1976.

Lincoln, Bruce, *Authority: Construction and Corrosion.* Chicago: University of Chicago Press, 1994.

Lincoln, Bruce, *Apples and Oranges: Explorations In, On, and With Comparison.* Chicago: University of Chicago Press, 2018.

Marchand, Suzanne L., *German Orientalism in the Age of Empire: Religion, Race, and Scholarship.* Cambridge: Cambridge University Press, 2009.

Nye, Mallory, 'Decolonizing the Study of Religion', *Open Library of Humanities* 5(1) (2019), available at: https://olh.openlibhums.org/articles/10.16995/olh.421.

Owen, Roger, 'Studying Islamic History', *Journal of Interdisciplinary History* 4(2) (1973): 287–98.

Pregill, Michael, 'I Hear Islam Singing: Shahab Ahmed's *What Is Islam? The Importance of Being Islamic*', *Harvard Theological Review* 110(1) (2017): 149–65.

Said, Edward W., *Orientalism.* New York: Vintage, 1978.

Smith, Jonathan Z., *Imagining Religion: From Babylon to Jonestown.* Chicago: University of Chicago Press, 1982.

Smith, Jonathan Z., 'In Comparison a Magic Dwells', in *Imagining Religion: From Babylon to Jonestown.* Chicago: University of Chicago Press, 1982, 19–35.

Smith, Jonathan Z., *Drudgery Divine: On the Comparison of Early Christianities and the Religions of Late Antiquity.* Chicago: University of Chicago Press, 1990.

Smith, Linda Tuhiwai, *Decolonizing Methodologies: Research and Indigenous Peoples*, 2nd edn. London: Zed Books, 2012.

Smith, Wilfred Cantwell, 1959 essay, 'Comparative Religion: Whither – and Why?' in Mircea Elaide and Joseph M. Kitagawa (eds), *The History of Religions: Essays In Methodology.* Chicago: University of Chicago Press, 1959, 31–58.

Stoddard, Brad (ed.), *Method Today: Redescribing Approaches to the Study of Religion.* Sheffield: Equinox, 2018.

# 3

# THE RECEPTION OF AL-ANDALUS, 1821–2021: TWO HUNDRED YEARS OF STUDY AND DEBATE

MARIBEL FIERRO AND
ALEJANDRO GARCÍA-SANJUÁN

## Introduction

Al-Andalus was the term used by Muslims to refer to the Iberian Peninsula, and from it comes the name Andalucía, the southern region of Spain where Muslim rule lasted the longest.

The Visigothic kingdom that succeeded Roman rule in the region of Hispania collapsed with the Muslim conquest of 711, led by Arab and Berber troops. Direct Muslim control was established over the majority of the Iberian Peninsula, except for the mountainous areas in the north and northwest, where Christian kingdoms were eventually formed. A process of Arabisation and Islamisation ensued, such that by the eleventh century the majority of the population were Arabic-speaking Muslims. The number of Christians living in al-Andalus diminished through emigration, deportation and conversion, while the Jewish communities flourished, except during the early Almohad period when forced conversion to Islam took place.

In 756, following the Umayyads' defeat at the hands of the Abbasids, an Umayyad prince from Syria arrived in the Iberian Peninsula. His arrival signalled the beginning of autonomous Muslim rule in al-Andalus, with Cordoba as the capital, first of the Umayyad emirate (756–929) and then of the Umayyad caliphate (929–1031). Cordoba became then the largest, most populated and richest city in Latin Europe due to the flourishing of agriculture and trade that went together with cultural splendour, epitomised by the rich caliphal library.

By the end of the tenth century, internal tensions caused by the legacy of the powerful chamberlain al-Manṣūr b. Abī ʿĀmir, who had become the de facto ruler, erupted in civil wars that led to the abolishment of the Umayyad caliphate in 1031 and the appearance of the short-lived caliphate of the Ḥammūdids, descendants of the Prophet Muḥammad. Al-Andalus was then divided into a number of petty (Taifa) kingdoms ruled by local notables from different backgrounds. Because of their military weakness, they eventually had to pay tribute to the Christian kingdoms to stop the latter's territorial advance. The fall of Toledo to the Christians in 1085 led the Taifa kings to seek the military aid of the Almoravids, Berber camel-drivers from the Sahara who had conquered the far Maghreb (present-day Morocco) and founded Marrakech.

The Almoravids defeated the Christians at the battle of Zallāqa in 1086 and eventually banished or killed the Taifa kings in order to incorporate al-Andalus into their empire. Their legitimacy was based on the acknowledgement of the Abbasid caliphate in Baghdad, on their jihad against the Christians, and on the legality of their taxes. But after they proved unable to hold back the Christian advance and began instituting illegal taxes of their own; around the year 1141 anti-Almoravid rebellions erupted in the main towns, under the leadership of local judges and military commanders. In the Algarve (Portugal) the mystic Ibn Qasī raised an army among his novices and fought the Almoravids, eventually seeking the help of the Almohads.

The Almohad movement had started among the Berber (Maṣmūda) population of the Atlas Mountains (Morocco), led by a mahdi (messiah) of their own who claimed to be infallible, and whose successor – a Zanāta Berber – adopted the title of caliph. The Almohads defeated the Almoravids, conquered the whole of North Africa from Tripoli (Libya) to the Atlantic Ocean, and also incorporated al-Andalus into their empire once they had quashed the local Muslim polities that had formed in the wake of the collapse of the Almoravid empire. Some Andalusis rejected the Almohads because of their mahdism and their initial anti-Maliki stance. Others, such as Ibn Ṭufayl and Ibn Rushd al-Ḥafīd (Averroes), were recruited into the Almohad scholarly elite, and influenced seminal doctrinal and intellectual developments. Other luminaries educated under the Almohads were Maimonides and Muḥyī l-dīn Ibn ʿArabī.

The fall of the Almohad empire, brought on by internal causes, was furthered along by decisive military defeats at the hands of the Christians, such as the battle of Las Navas de Tolosa (1212). A number of local leaders attempted to found viable independent Muslim polities within a context of Christian military and political superiority that saw the loss of major towns such as Cordoba in 1236, Valencia in 1238, Jaen in 1246 and Seville in 1248. Only the region around Granada remained in Muslim control. The Nasrid kingdom managed to survive through vassalage to the Christian rulers, diplomacy, commerce and military ingenuity when hostilities erupted, but in 1492 it was finally conquered by the so-called Catholic monarchs, who had united the Christian kingdoms of Castile and Aragon. That same year, the Jews were forced to convert to Christianity. By then communities of Muslims, known as Mudéjares, had a long history of openly maintaining their faith under Christian rule. In 1502, however, edicts of forced conversion against them were promulgated in Castile, and in 1525 in Aragon. These Muslim converts to Christianity were known as Moriscos, and many continued to live in Spain as crypto-Muslims. Between 1609 and 1613, the Moriscos, suspect in their religion and feared as a possible fifth-column in the fight against the Ottomans, were expelled from the Iberian Peninsula.[1]

This brief overview of the history of al-Andalus is meant to highlight its potential for addressing crucial issues in the study of Islam: the processes of Islamisation and Arabisation, and how they took place according to the diverse ethnic groups involved (Berbers, Hispano-Romans and Visigoths); the emergence of the group of Muslim religious scholars; the interplay between the local and the global (pilgrimage to Mecca, eastward travel for study, emigration); how the political structure – with the presence of locally grounded caliphates (Cordoban Umayyads, Hammudids, Almohads) – both reflected and influenced the conception of religious authority; the place of religious charisma in messianic and mystical movements; the resilience of Muslim communities having to live under non-Muslim rule and the ways

[1] Maribel Fierro (ed.), *The Routledge Handbook of Muslim Iberia* (London: Routledge, 2020).

in which this situation was justified; how the expelled Moriscos adapted to a fully Muslim religious context after having lived as Christians; the legacy of al-Andalus in the Iberian Peninsula and beyond the Pyrenees, among many others. It also raises questions of how the Muslim past of the Iberian Peninsula has been integrated into the national historical narratives of Spain and Portugal, as well as the history of Europe, and how this past is dealt with differently by Muslim authors depending on whether the target audience is Muslims in general, or more particularly those who also claim the legacy of al-Andalus on the basis of common history, as is the case with modern nation-states such as Morocco, Algeria or Tunisia.

## Literature

In the western academic world, the study of the Muslim presence in the Iberian Peninsula has by no means been limited to scholars working in Spain and Portugal, and thus reflects a diversity of approaches in both methods and content. Three main focuses can be detected: the history of al-Andalus in connection with both Christendom and the Islamic world; the role of al-Andalus in the transmission of Arabic and Islamic knowledge to Europe and in cultural processes of cross-pollination among different religious communities; and, lastly, its use for dealing with contemporary issues. In the overview that follows, the main focus will be on developments that have taken place in Spain.

### *History*

The wealth of information found in Arabic sources regarding the history of the Iberian Peninsula since the Muslim conquest aroused the interest of non-Muslim historians from very early on. Thus, the bishop of Toledo, Rodrigo Jiménez de Rada (d. 1247) and the king of Castile, Alfonso X (r. 1252–84) made use of such sources, integrating this information into their own chronicles.[2] Later, from the sixteenth century onwards, the forced conversion of the

[2] Lucy Pick, *Conflict and Coexistence: Archbishop Rodrigo and the Muslims and Jews in Medieval Spain* (Ann Arbor: University of Michigan, 2004); Rodrigo Jiménez de Rada, *Estoria de los árabes. Traducción castellana del siglo XIV de la Historia Arabum*, ed. Fernando Bravo López (Córdoba: Editorial de la Universidad de Córdoba, 2019); Francisco Márquez Villanueva, *El concepto cultural Alfonsí* (Madrid: Mapfre, 1994).

Moriscos and their eventual expulsion was accompanied by intense debates inside Spain regarding the legality and consequences of such measures, spawning many books that reflected underlying social and religious anxieties, and also intellectual curiosity and admiration.[3]

A renewed interest in the Arabic sources arose in Spain during the nineteenth century, when the writing of 'national history' became imperative in the context of the modern nation-state. The main trend was to conceive of Spanish national history as marked by an ongoing war against Islam. The Muslim presence was construed as an interlude that had temporarily interrupted Spain's essential adherence to Christianity, and thus the medieval history of Spain was the history of the 'Reconquista', the recovery of the territory lost to the Muslims by Christian kings who claimed the legacy of the defeated Visigoths. This understanding became entrenched in history books aimed at school pupils and other audiences.[4]

During the nineteenth and twentieth centuries, much progress was made in the edition and translation of the Arabic primary sources thanks to the efforts of Arab and European scholars. Inside Spain, the need to produce such editions and translations made it possible to formally integrate Arabic studies into the academic system, thanks to the pioneering efforts of Pascual de Gayangos (1809–97) and Francisco Codera (1836–1917).[5] The liberal Pascual de Gayangos – the first holder of a chair in Arabic (Central University of Madrid) – during his exile in Great Britain wrote a selected English

[3] Barbara Fuchs, *Exotic Nation: Maurophilia and the Construction of Early Modern Spain* (Philadelphia: University of Pennsylvania Press, 2011); Mercedes García-Arenal and Fernando Rodríguez Mediano, *The Orient in Spain: Converted Muslims, the Forged Lead Books of Granada, and the Rise of Orientalism* (Leiden: Brill, 2013); Antonio Urquízar-Herrera, *Admiration and Awe: Morisco Buildings and Identity Negotiations in Early Modern Spanish Historiography* (Oxford: Oxford University Press, 2017).

[4] Martín Ríos Saloma, *La Reconquista. Una construcción historiográfica, siglos XVI–XIX* (Madrid and Mexico: Marcial Pons and Universidad Nacional Autónoma de México, 2011); Alejandro García-Sanjuán, 'Rejecting al-Andalus, Exalting the Reconquista: Historical Memory in Contemporary Spain', *Journal of Medieval Iberian Studies* 10(1) (2018): 127–45.

[5] Cristina Alvarez Millán and Claudia Heide, *Pascual de Gayangos: A Nineteenth-Century Spanish Arabist* (Edinburgh: Edinburgh University Press, 2008); María Jesús Viguera, Introduction to Francisco Codera y Zaidín, *Decadencia y desaparición de los almorávides en España* (Pamplona: Urigoiti, 2004).

translation of *Nafḥ al-ṭīb*, the monumental compilation on Andalusi history written by the seventeenth-century North African author al-Maqqarī.[6] The most systematic endeavour regarding the edition of Arabic sources corresponds to Gayangos' main pupil, Francisco Codera, holder of the Arabic-language chair at the University of Zaragoza. He is considered the 'father' of the Spanish school of Arabic studies; internally referred to as the 'Banu Codera', made up of Codera, Codera's pupil Julián Ribera (1858–1934), Ribera's pupil Miguel Asín Palacios (1871–1944) and Asín Palacios' pupil Emilio García Gómez (1905–95). Codera launched the *Biblioteca arabico-hispana* series (1882–95) that made available the main Arabic biographical dictionaries dealing with religious scholars (*ʿulamāʾ*). Starting from the 1930s, Arabic studies scholars began to explore new sources, including legal and doctrinal texts, a tendency that, however, would not be consolidated until decades later. Codera's endeavour likewise opened up new methodological approaches with his pioneering work in the field of Islamic numismatics. A. Prieto y Vives (1870–1939) then produced his classical study on eleventh-century coinage, thus paving the way for the study of economic issues, as well a better grasp of the different resources used by the rulers in their political and religious efforts at legitimisation.[7]

Outside Spain, and mostly drawing on nineteenth-century Romanticism, a largely exotic envisioning of al-Andalus developed, as shown specially in some works by American writer Washington Irving (1783–1859) and British traveller Richard Ford (1796–1858), among others. Taking a much more scholarly approach and thanks to his profound mastery of the source materials, the Dutch scholar Reinhart Dozy (1820–83) wrote a history of al-Andalus that for years would remain hugely influential.[8] He was later followed by the

[6] Under the title *The History of the Mohammedan Dynasties in Spain*, 2 vols (London: Oriental Translation Fund of Great Britain and Ireland, 1840–3).

[7] Francisco Codera, *Tratado de numismática arábigo-española* (Madrid: Lib. de M. Murillo, 1879); A. Prieto y Vives, *Los Reyes de Taifas. Estudio histórico-numismático de los musulmanes españoles en el siglo V de la Hégira (XI d. de J.C.)* (Madrid: Junta de Ampliación de Estudios e Investigaciones Científicas, 1926).

[8] Reinhart Dozy, *Histoire des musulmans d'Espagne jusqu'à la conquête de l'Andalousie par les Almoravides* (Leiden: Brill, 1861). On Dozy, see Arnoud Vrolijk and Richard Van Leeuwen, *Arabic Studies in the Netherlands: A Short History in Portraits 1580–1950* (Leiden: Brill, 2014), 95–100.

French scholar Évariste Lévi-Provençal (1894–1956), by far the most outstanding scholarly personality in the study of al-Andalus throughout the first half of the twentieth century.[9] Both authors likewise worked intensely on editing and translating Arabic source materials.

The first three decades of the twentieth century witnessed a great effort to support the development of science and scholarship in Spain, with the founding in 1907 of an institution for the promotion of research (the Junta para la Ampliación de Estudios e Investigaciones Científicas) that was indebted to the movement known as the Institución Libre de Enseñanza, whose main aim was the promotion of an education independent of the Catholic Church.[10] The Junta offered opportunities for the convergence of the research carried out by both historians and Arabists, but the latter eventually left the institution after the scandal that followed their support for a conservative candidate for a chair in sociology – a priest and a friend of Miguel Asín Palacios, himself a priest.[11]

The Arabists Miguel Asín Palacios and Emilio García Gómez adapted well to the Franco dictatorship (1939–75) that followed the Spanish Civil War (1936–9) and put an end to the Spanish Republic (1931–6). The dictatorship was inspired by fascist and especially National Catholic ideologies. Within both, the backbone of medieval Spanish history was considered to be the 'Reconquista'. However, this conception transcended the political divide, and can also be found in the extensive oeuvre of historian Claudio Sánchez Albornoz

[9] Evariste Lévi-Provençal, *Histoire de l'Espagne musulmane*, 3 vols (Paris: Maisonneuve et Larose, 1950–67, repr. 1999); Spanish translation by E. García Gómez. *España musulmana hasta la caída del Califato de Córdoba (711–1031 de J.C.), Historia de España Menéndez Pidal*, vols IV–V, 4th edn (Madrid: Espasa-Calpe, 1976). On Lévi-Provençal, see David J. Wasserstein, 'Nota Biographica: Makhlouf Levi and Evariste Lévi-Provençal', *Al-Qantara* 21(1) (2000): 211–14.

[10] Antonio Jiménez-Landi, *La Institución Libre de Enseñanza*, 4 vols (Madrid: Taurus, 1987).

[11] Manuela Marín, Cristina de la Puente, Fernando Rodríguez Mediano and Juan Ignacio Pérez Alcalde, *Los epistolarios de Julián Ribera Tarragó y Miguel Asín Palacios. Introducción, catálogo e índices* (Madrid: CSIC, 2009), 107–38; Patrick Henriet, 'Miguel Asín Palacios (1871–1944), le christianisme et l'islam: thèses, idéologie, réception', in Jean-Luc Fournet, Jean-Michel Mouton and Jacques Paviot (eds), *Civilisations en transition (III). Sociétés multiconfessionnelles à travers l'histoire du Proche Orient* (Byblos, 2017), 181–211.

(1893–1984), a staunch Republican who, in exile, settled in Argentina.[12] While in exile in the United States, his contemporary, literary historian Américo Castro (1885–1972), developed a vision of Spain not as an essence that transcended historical time, but as the result of the 'living together' (in Spanish, *convivencia*) of the different religious groups present on Iberian soil: Jews, Christians and Muslims. Hugely influential in the American academic context, where he taught at prestigious universities and came to have an important following, Castro's proposal had much less impact in Franco's Spain.[13]

Conversely, the work of French historian Pierre Guichard (1939–2021) was largely ignored in the United States, but became seminal for both French and Spanish researchers. His book on the anthropological structure of Andalusi society assigned a central role to the ways in which the Arab and Berber tribal components that carried out the Muslim conquest influenced the ensuing history of the Iberian Peninsula. It corrected the almost exclusive 'Hispanic' focus of Spanish Arabic studies, bringing to the fore what he called the 'Oriental' make-up of Andalusi society, for example, in terms of marriage practices. His work was also instrumental in highlighting the Berber element and in paying attention to the convergence of Sufism and political activism, especially in the last centuries of Andalusi history.[14] Pierre Guichard and the French and Spanish historians who were influenced by his ideas – such as Miquel Barceló (1939–2013) and Manuel Acién Almansa (1950–2013) – combined the study of written sources with archaeological data, fostering new understandings of the social, economic and cultural history of al-Andalus.[15]

[12] Alejandro García-Sanjuán, 'Al-Andalus en la historiografía nacionalcatólica española: Claudio Sánchez-Albornoz', *eHumanista* 37 (2017): 305–28.

[13] Américo Castro, *The Structure of Spanish History* (Princeton, NJ: Princeton University Press, 1954). On the reception of Castro in Spain, see Eugenio Asensio, *La España imaginada de Américo Castro* (Barcelona: Ediciones El Albir, 1976).

[14] Pierre Guichard, *Al-Andalus. Estructura antropológica de una sociedad islámica en Occidente* (Barcelona: Barral, 1976; repr. Granada: Universidad de Granada, 1998, with Introduction by Antonio Malpica detailing its impact); *Les musulmans de Valence et la Reconquête (XIe–XIIIe siècles)*, 2 vols (Damascus: IFAO, 1990–1; Spanish translation Madrid-Valencia: Universidad de Valencia, 2001).

[15] Miquel Barceló, *Arqueología medieval. En las afueras del medievalismo* (Barcelona: Crítica, 1988). On Acién's work, see below.

Aside from these academic developments, another approach to the Muslim conquest that arose in this period was the 'negationist' stance of Ignacio Olagüe (1903–74), a self-taught writer with fascist convictions, who found it problematic that the cultural and artistic splendour of al-Andalus was attributed to foreign 'Semitic' invaders. He thus decided to 'indigenise' al-Andalus, proposing that the Arabs had never invaded the Iberian Peninsula and that 'Muslim Spain' was in fact the product of local anti-Trinitarian trends that eventually converged with Islam. His book on the topic was the subject of scathing reviews by, among others, the American scholar and student of Castro, James T. Monroe, but was much later championed by Emilio González Ferrín, an Arabist from the University of Seville who endorsed Olagüe's proposal in a book published in 2006 that aroused some interest among American scholars.[16]

*Transmission, Translation, Cross-pollination*

For nineteenth-century European Jewish thinkers involved in the process of integrating their communities into the wider societies in which they lived, the history of Sepharad (the Hebrew name for the Iberian Peninsula) became a crucial site for promoting the view that such integration did not involve a loss of identity but, on the contrary, opened new avenues for intellectual and cultural prosperity. According to these scholars, the Jews living in pluri-ethnic and pluri-lingual medieval Iberia set in motion a 'Golden Age' – a conception now subject to debate – for the study and production of the religious sciences, poetry, literature, philosophy, mysticism, medicine and so on. The Iberian Jews likewise acted as decisive mediators in the transmission of

[16] Maribel Fierro, 'Al-Andalus en el pensamiento fascista español: La *Revolución islámica en Occidente* de Ignacio Olagüe', in Manuela Marín (ed.), *Al-Andalus / España. Historiografías en contraste, siglos XVII–XXI* (Madrid: Casa de Velázquez, 2009), 325–49; Alejandro García-Sanjuán, *La conquista islámica de la península ibérica y la tergiversación del pasado. Del catastrofismo al negacionismo*. 2nd edn (Madrid: Marcial Pons, 2019); Alejandro García-Sanjuán, 'Denying the Islamic Conquest of Iberia: A Historiographical Fraud', *Journal of Medieval Iberian Studies* 11(3) (2019): 306–22.

knowledge written in Arabic towards Europe, and thus had a seminal role in the process that gave rise to the Renaissance.[17]

The role of Spain in European intellectual history was a debated issue. Spain had famously been considered to be part of Africa and not of Europe by the French, with the encyclopaedist Masson de Morvilliers (d. 1789) asking the provocative question 'Que doit-on à l'Espagne?'[18] The Spanish Jesuit Juan Andrés (d. 1817) answered with a book in which he aimed at proving that the intellectual development of Europe was indebted to the process of reception of both the legacy of Greek learning and of Arab contributions that took place in the southern Mediterranean region during the period of Muslim domination.[19] Spanish Arabists promoted this view with studies of their own, as reflected in the French title of Juan Vernet's (1923–2011) book *Ce que la culture doit aux Arabes d'Espagne* (*What Culture Owes to the Arabs of Spain*).[20] Special attention was paid to issues such as the reception of Averroes' Aristotelianism in Christendom, for example, in the writings of St Thomas Aquinas,[21] and the influence of Islamic eschatology in Dante's *Divine Comedy* and that of Sufism in Christian mystical writings such as those of St John of the Cross. The work of

[17] Menahem Ben-Sasson, 'Al-Andalus: the So-called "Golden Age" of Spanish Jewry – a Critical View', in C. Cluse (ed.), *The Jews of Europe in the Middle Ages (Tenth to Fifteenth Centuries)* (Turnhout: Brepols, 2004), 123–37; Mark R. Cohen, 'The "Golden Age" of Jewish–Muslim Relations: Myth and Reality', in Jane Marie Todd et al. (eds), *A History of Jewish–Muslim Relations: From the Origins to the Present Day* (Princeton, NJ: Princeton University Press, 2013).

[18] Miguel Ángel Ladero Quesada, 'La "Decadencia" española como argumento historiográfico', in Miguel Ángel Ladero Quesada, *Lecturas sobre la España histórica* (Madrid: Real Academia de la Historia, 1998), 213–85, at 232.

[19] Roberto M. Dainotto, 'The Discreet Charm of the Arabist Theory: Juan Andrés, Historicism, and the De-centering of Montesquieu's Europe', *European History Quarterly* 36(1) (2006): 7–29.

[20] French translation by Gabriel Martinez-Gros (Paris: Sindbad, 1985) of Juan Vernet, *La Cultura hispano-árabe en Oriente y Occidente* (Barcelona: Ariel, 1978). A later edition of the Spanish version appeared as Juan Vernet, *Lo que Europa debe al Islam de España* (Barcelona: El Acantilado, 1999).

[21] Aquinas and 'the Arabs' International Working Group, directed by Richard Taylor (Marquette University), available at: http://richardctaylor.info/aaiwg.

Arabist Miguel Asín Palacios concentrated on the last two themes,[22] while his student Emilio García Gómez studied hybrid poetic forms such as the *muwashshaḥāt*, written in Arabic but including verses in Romance and also in Hebrew, as analysed by Samuel S. Stern (1920–69).[23]

These topics that are related to Castro's conception of *convivencia* have great appeal for cultural historians and scholars of the religious sciences, who form the bulk of those who have devoted themselves to Andalusi matters in the American academic milieu,[24] but are also studied by scholars associated with specific institutions, such as Charles Burnett at the Warburg Institute,[25] and with projects such as *Islamolatina* at the University of Barcelona,[26] and the German-funded *Digital Averroes Research Environment*.[27] Projects funded by the European Research Council have also been instrumental in advancing our knowledge in this area, as in the case of *The European Qur'ān*.[28]

The intellectual and religious impact that al-Andalus had on the rest of the Islamic world has been an object of interest mostly for scholars based in Muslim-majority countries, who are also the ones who have produced the most studies related to the Islamic sciences, such as Qur'ānic exegesis and readings, hadith, law, theology and grammar.[29] Islamic law has also been studied by scholars in the Western academic world, with an initial

[22] Miguel Asín Palacios, *Islam and the Divine Comedy* (London: H. Watson, 1926); Miguel Asín Palacios, *Huellas del Islam. Santo Tomás de Aquino, Turmeda, Pascal, San Juan de la Cruz* (Madrid: Espasa Calpe, 1941).

[23] Otto Zwartjes, *Love Songs from al-Andalus: History, Structure and Meaning of the Kharja* (Leiden: Brill, 1997).

[24] See below for examples.

[25] Charles Burnett, *Arabic into Latin in the Middle Ages: The Translators and their Intellectual and Social Context* (Farnham: Variorum Collected Studies Series, 2009).

[26] See at: https://grupsderecerca.uab.cat/islamolatina.

[27] See at: https://dare.uni-koeln.de.

[28] Directed by Mercedes García-Arenal, Jan Loop, John Tolan and Roberto Tottoli, available at: https://euqu.eu.

[29] As can be verified through the online database *Historia de los Autores y Transmisores de al-Andalus (HATA)*, directed by Maribel Fierro, available at: https://www.eea.csic.es/red/hata.

interest that can be located in the colonial expansion of France and Spain in Morocco, as its legal history is closely linked to that of al-Andalus.[30]

*Using al-Andalus to Talk about the Present*

José-Antonio Conde's (1766–1820) *Historia de la dominación de los árabes en España*, was published in 1820–1. Conde was a liberal and *afrancesado* (supporter of the French occupation of Spain by Napoleon) scholar who had gone into exile in 1813, and, after his return, decided to give voice to the Muslims who had been expelled from the Iberian Peninsula. Conde seems to have connected his own plight to that of the Moriscos, as did other liberal writers and thinkers who suffered exile and persecution in the political turmoil characteristic of nineteenth-century Spain.[31]

Américo Castro's ideas on *convivencia* have been linked with the trauma caused by the Spanish Civil War: if Spain had been formed by different religious and ethnic groups 'living together', the existence of a plurality of ideas and of voices – as quashed by Franco's dictatorship – could be vindicated. Castro's ideas that fit well with local concerns and interests in the United States (the 'melting pot', the frontier, cultural identities, post-colonialism) flourished there with scholars such as James T. Monroe, Samuel G. Armistead (1927–2013) and Francisco Márquez Villanueva (1931–2013). They were further developed later on by a new generation of scholars, such as Luce López Baralt (b. 1944), from Puerto Rico. and Cuban-born María Rosa Menocal (1953–2012). Menocal's *The Ornament of the World: How Muslims, Jews and Christians Created a Culture of Tolerance in Medieval Spain* (2003), was used as a scholarly weapon in the fight against Islamophobia after 11 September 2001. By concentrating on a rather selective representation of al-Andalus, Menocal's work opened the door for the virulent reaction of Darío Fernández-Morera who, following the path set out years earlier in Spain by

30 Amalia Zomeño Rodríguez, 'El derecho islámico a través de su imagen colonial durante el Protectorado español en Marruecos', in Fernando Rodríguez Mediano and Elena de Felipe Rodríguez (eds), *El protectorado español en Marruecos. Gestión colonial e identidades* (Madrid: CSIC, 2002), 307–37.

31 Jesús Torrecilla, *España al revés. Los mitos del pensamiento progresista (1790–1840)* (Madrid: Marcial Pons, 2016).

Serafín Fanjul,[32] wrote a book with the exclusive intention of demonising Muslim Iberia.[33] For Fernández-Morera and like-minded writers, the notion of 'Reconquista' is still the prism through which to approach the Islamic phase of Iberian history. At the same time, the usefulness of the concept of *convivencia* has also been subject to debate from a variety of viewpoints.[34]

## Discussion

The history of al-Andalus, and in particular how it fits into the Spanish national narrative, has consistently remained a highly conflictive topic in Spanish historiography, and has given rise to radically opposing approaches.[35]

In what follows, we will focus on the methodological evolution in the study of al-Andalus that has taken place in Spain roughly between 1821 and 2021, a time span in which two sharply different periods can be clearly distinguished. Before the 1970s, the study of al-Andalus developed in a social and political context largely influenced by nationalism, while most scholarly approaches drew on a largely positivist methodology. Following the liberal revolutions which brought about the new political notion of national sovereignty, the nineteenth century saw the all-pervasive outbreak of a radically new form of historical narrative in which the nation played the leading role, taking the place previously occupied by the monarchy and the Church. In Spain, the Catholic tradition heavily influenced the nation-building process and decisively conditioned the reception of al-Andalus. The nineteenth century also saw, as we have seen, the academic institutionalisation of Arabic

[32] Serafín Fanjul, *Al-Andalus contra España. La forja del mito* (Madrid: Siglo XXI, 2000).

[33] Darío Fernández-Morera, *The Myth of the Andalusian Paradise: Muslims, Christians, and Jews under Islamic rule in Medieval Spain* (Wilmington, DE: ISI Books, 2016): cf. the critical review by Sarah J. Pearce, available at: https://wp.nyu.edu/sjpearce/2017/03/17/paradise-lost.

[34] Jonathan Ray, 'Beyond Tolerance and Persecution: Reassessing Our Approach to Medieval *Convivencia*', *Jewish Social Studies* 11(2) (2005): 1–18; Maya Soifer, 'Beyond Convivencia: Critical Reflections on the Historiography of Interfaith Relations in Christian Spain', *Journal of Medieval Iberian Studies* 1(1) (2009): 19–36; Eduardo Manzano Moreno, 'Qurtuba: Some Critical Considerations of the Caliphate of Cordoba and the Myth of Convivencia', *Reflections on Qurtuba in the 21st Century*, 2013, 111–34, available at: http://www.awraq.es.

[35] Maribel Fierro and Alejandro García-Sanjuán (eds), *Hispania, al-Ándalus y España: Identidad y nacionalismo en la historia peninsular* (Madrid: Marcial Pons, 2020).

studies. The focus of the Arabists active in the Spanish universities was on the Arabic language, and they were trained to read, edit and translate Arabic source texts in order to study them, as well as to make them available to specialists in other disciplines. In order to secure their academic survival, they had a vested interest in insisting that the authors they studied were 'Spanish', and that al-Andalus was best referred to as 'Arab Spain' or 'Muslim Spain'.[36] As Julián Ribera explained, in the same way that throwing red aniline in a lake will dye the water but will not affect its composition, Islam had merely altered the colour of a reality that was essentially 'Spanish'. Thus, he reasoned, the cultural traces left by the local Muslims could be legitimately studied as having been the product, after all, of 'Hispano-Arabs' or 'Hispano-Muslims'.[37] Nationalistic by definition, nineteenth-century historical writing largely misrepresented al-Andalus through a two-pronged approach. Developed mostly by the Spanish Arabists, the notion of 'Arab Spain' or 'Muslim Spain', on the one hand, provided an integrative framework in which al-Andalus' most iconic literary, scientific, artistic and intellectual achievements were considered part of Spain's own national heritage. On the other hand, within the 'Reconquista' paradigm, al-Andalus represented the anti-Spain: after the Visigothic kingdom (considered to be the earliest Spanish state) was destroyed by the 711 Islamic conquest, the eight-century-long process of Christian territorial conquest – presented as a 're-conquest' – enabled the reunification of Spain and the definitive shaping of the Spanish nation.[38] While in the first approach the Muslims were largely considered as 'Spaniards', in the second they merely played the degrading role of invaders and interlopers, regardless of the local origins of the vast majority of them.

Caught in the middle of these two contradicting approaches, the study of al-Andalus became extremely problematic and controversial. After being

[36] James T. Monroe, *Islam and the Arabs in Spanish Scholarship (Sixteenth Century to the Present)* (Leiden: Brill, 1970); Fernando Rodríguez Mediano, 'Culture, Identity and Civilisation: The Arabs and Islam in the History of Spain', in Frank Peter, Sarah Dornhof and Elena Arigita (eds), *Islam and the Politics of Culture in Europe. Memory, Aesthetics, Art* (Bielefeld: Verlag, 2013), 41–60.

[37] Julián Ribera y Tarragó, *Disertaciones y opúsculos* (Madrid: Impr. de E. Maestre, 1928), I, 26.

[38] Alejandro García-Sanjuán, 'Weaponizing Historical Knowledge: The Notion of *Reconquista* in Spanish Nationalism', *Imago temporis. Medium Aevum* 14 (2020): 133–62.

almost entirely demolished by Pierre Guichard's devastating criticism in the 1970s, the integrative approach nearly became extinct. The fate of the 'Reconquista', as mentioned, has been rather different. The Spanish philosopher José Ortega y Gasset (1883–1955) famously said in 1921 that he could not see how a process that lasted eight centuries could be framed as a 'reconquest'.[39] However, under the Franco dictatorship, the heyday of the National Catholic movement, the ideology of the 'Reconquista' reached its all-time high. Later, although it fell into some degree of disrepute in the democratic period following Franco's death (1975), it has by no means become a thing of the past. Far from vanishing, it has survived nearly intact into the present. In fact, the notion of the 'Reconquista' has been dramatically bolstered over the past several years within the conceptual framework of the 'Clash of Civilisations', feeding on the anxieties and fears raised by Muslim immigration and jihadist terrorism. Its appeal is not limited to Spain, as shown by the reference to Pelayo – the Christian king who allegedly set in motion the 'Reconquista' – found among the weapons of the far-right attacker in the 2019 Christchurch mosque shootings in New Zealand.[40] While the nineteenth-century national framework has been largely overcome in academia, it is still very much alive and well in the public consciousness.

## The Traditional Approach, 1821–1976

Over the last two centuries, the study of al-Andalus has experienced a radical methodological shift, moving from a classical philological approach mostly drawing on chronicles and literary sources and aimed at highlighting – from a nationalistic perspective – its intellectual achievements, to historical-based studies relying on archaeology and written legal sources.

In the nineteenth century, the nascent discipline of Arabic studies carried out, as already mentioned, extensive work editing, translating and studying Arabic historical texts (chronicles, bio-bibliographical dictionaries, geographical

[39] José Ortega y Gasset, *España invertebrada. Bosquejo de algunos pensamientos históricos*, 2nd edn (Madrid: Calpe, 1921), 159.

[40] 'New Zealand mosque shooter names his "idols" on weapons he used in massacre', *Daily Sabah*, 15 March 2019, available at: https://www.dailysabah.com/asia/2019/03/15/new-zealand-mosque-shooter-names-his-idols-on-weapons-he-used-in-massacre.

works), also producing studies on numismatics. In general, the Spanish Arabic studies school focused primarily on literary and cultural aspects, and refrained from offering general syntheses, as they seem to have aimed at first establishing a comprehensive appraisal of the available sources. The result of this was that the earliest histories of what was then called 'Muslim Spain' were carried out by non-Spanish scholars, first Reinhart Dozy, from the Netherlands, and then Évariste Lévi-Provençal, from France. Over the second half of the twentieth century, a more solid historiographical tendency took root in Spanish Arabic studies, with relevant contributions by scholars such as Jacinto Bosch Vilá (1922–85) on the Almoravids, and Ambrosio Huici Miranda (1880–1973) on the Almohads.[41] In both cases, they had been trained as historians and did not belong to the tradition of the 'Banu Codera'. Moreover, Huici Miranda worked extensively on the translation of Arabic sources, especially chronicles, into Spanish.

In the early twentieth century Spain underwent a process of political and intellectual modernisation, as seen in the efforts to secularise education and promote scientific development, and in the 1931 proclamation of the Second Republic. In this context, the country witnessed relevant changes in methodologies and research projects which profoundly contributed to expanding the available knowledge on Iberian Islamic culture. Although Islamic archaeology did not fully develop as a discipline of its own until the 1980s, profoundly impacting the study of al-Andalus, the most outstanding pioneer in this field of research, Félix Hernández (1889–1975), carried out excavations in the caliphal palatine city of Madīnat al-Zahrāʾ throughout the 1920s, and in the Great Mosque of Cordoba during the 1930s. In this second case, Hernández sought to unearth the church of St Vincent, mentioned in Arabic texts from the time of the caliphate as the immediate architectural predecessor over which the first Umayyad emir of Cordoba built the mosque in the eighth century. However, he eventually reached the conclusion that the archaeological record did not support its existence. Today, this has turned into a highly polemical issue. In 2006, the Catholic Church became the legal owner of the building,

[41] Jacinto Bosch Vilá, *Los Almorávides* (Tétouan: Editora Marroquí, 1956); Ambrosio Huici Miranda, *Historia política del Imperio almohade*, 2 vols (Tétouan: Editora Marroquí, 1956–7).

and under the pressure from a citizen movement demanding public ownership, the bishop of Cordoba has consistently promoted the pre-existence of St Vincent's church in order to deflate this pressure.[42]

Starting in 1923, architect Leopoldo Torres-Balbás (1888–1960) likewise played a key role in the restoration of the Alhambra in Granada.[43] Just as in the case of Hernández, a good part of his numerous publications on Islamic art appeared in the journal *Al-Andalus*, first published in 1933 as an organ of expression of the Escuela de Estudios Árabes, founded a year earlier within the project of scientific and cultural renewal undertaken by the Republic in 1931 and that was shaken by the military *coup d'état* of 1936 that led to the Spanish Civil War.

The most intense and influential academic debate prior to 1976 regarding the medieval Iberian past and involving the Islamic period took place within a conceptual framework overwhelmingly influenced by nationalist perspectives. In his 1948 *España en su historia, cristianos, moros y judíos*, Hispanist and philologist Américo Castro made the earliest in-depth revision of nineteenth-century Spanish scholarship, although rather than a true breakup, it merely represented an original reformulation. Castro called into question both the notion of 'Muslim Spain', based on the notion of the deeply Hispanic character of Iberian Muslims, and that of the 'Reconquista', which rejected any role of Arab and Islamic culture in the shaping of Spanish national identity. Largely relying on a methodology that drew mostly on literary sources, Castro turned upside-down the Hispanicisation of the Iberian Muslims and claimed, instead, that Semitic influences (both Arab and Jewish) heavily impacted the formation of Spanish culture. Rather than Hispanicising the Muslims, Castro Semiticised the Spaniards.

In his view, therefore, Spanish national identity largely developed as a process of cultural blending involving the three Abrahamic religions, a process

[42] Fernando Arce-Sainz, 'La supuesta basílica de San Vicente en Córdoba: de mito histórico a obstinación historiográfica', *Al-Qanṭara* 36(1) (2015): 11–44. The most comprehensive study is Antonio Fernández Puertas, *Mezquita de Córdoba: su estudio arqueológico en el siglo XX* (Granada: Editorial Universidad de Granada, 2009).

[43] Alfonso Muñoz Cosme, *La vida y la obra de Leopoldo Torres Balbás* (Seville: Junta de Andalucía, 2005).

accomplished thanks to widespread *convivencia*, Castro's second major conceptual contribution. Accordingly, far from the product of a drawn-out confrontation ultimately leading to the triumph of Catholicism, Spanish national identity would have resulted from cultural cross-pollination between local components and Semitic influences. Although Castro considerably drifted away from the most traditional historiography of his time, the focal point of his contribution consisted of defining the historical origin of the Spanish national identity, very much in line with the rest of his contemporaries. Arguably, rather than breaking completely away from the pervasive nationalist approach, Castro simply gave it his own twist.

While Francoism turned the 'Reconquista' into a highly effective ideological weapon to fight the Republic and legitimate Franco's leadership, its most vocal academic representative was in fact a Republican. After holding relevant positions in the Republican government, Claudio Sánchez-Albornoz fled Spain in 1936 and in Argentina published what amounted to a fierce rebuttal of Américo Castro, under the title *España, un enigma histórico* (later translated into English as *Spain: A Historical Enigma*).

Castro and Sánchez-Albornoz belonged to the same generation and, as members of the Centro de Estudios Históricos (part of the Junta para Ampliación de Estudios), shared the same scholarly environment until the outbreak of the Civil War.[44] What is more, they held a very similar commitment to the Republican government, and were thus forced to leave the country, together with many of the most outstanding intellectuals and scientists of the time. And yet, no matter how much they had in common, they not only represented radically opposite visions about the meaning of the medieval period in Iberia, but openly and bitterly disagreed with one another in a harsh controversy that was to leave a deep imprint on the evolution of Spanish medieval studies up to the present day.

While Castro's model, based on multiculturalism, was quick to detect Arab, Islamic and Jewish ingredients within the chemical formula of Spanish nationhood, Sánchez-Albornoz, by contrast, excluded al-Andalus from the national narrative, labelling it as an 'anti-Spain', instead touting Catholicism as the core component of Spanish identity. He consistently extolled the 'Reconquista' and

[44] José-María López Sánchez, *Heterodoxos españoles. El Centro de Estudios Históricos, 1910–1936* (Madrid: Marcial Pons, 2006).

brought it to the height of its prestige, branding it as 'the key concept of the history of Spain'. At the end of his life, he most brazenly reworked this notion into a National Catholic framework. Released in 1983, *De la Andalucía islámica a la de hoy* (*From Islamic Andalusia to that of Today*) represented the outraged, acrimonious and unapologetic reaction of a 90-year-old historian against the Andalusian nationalist movement in southern Spain. This movement gave rise to the Partido Andalucista – active 1976–2015, with its peak immediately after the end of the Franco regime – which looked to the Arab and Islamic past in order to find the deepest roots of the Andalusian nation.

'Andalusian' (referring to Andalucía, one of the autonomous communities that makes up post-1978 Spain) should not be confused with 'Andalusi' (referring to al-Andalus). Confusing such terms and inventing an *andalucismo* of his own, a book recently published –very much in the vein of Fernández-Morera, although going to the opposite direction – promotes an 'emotional' reading of history in which ideological concerns related to the present overrun historical accuracy and promote a falsified representation of the past.[45] Emotions also loom large in the writings about al-Andalus – the lost paradise (*al-firdaws al-mafqūd*) – in the Arab and Islamic worlds.[46]

## Scholarly Renewal, 1976–2021

The second period of scholarship covers the last forty-five years, which, although much shorter than the first period, have witnessed substantial

[45] Charles Hirschkind, *The Feeling of History: Islam, Romanticism, and Andalusia* (Chicago: University of Chicago Press, 2020). This book is representative of a more general trend that we may call 'the emotional approach to al-Andalus', as discussed by Maribel Fierro, 'The Tales of Feeling: Looking for Emotions in Andalusia', *Al-Qanṭara* 42(1) (2021); Fernando Rodríguez Mediano, 'Fernando Rodríguez Mediano, 'The Feeling of History. Islam, Romanticism, and Andalusia', *Medieval Encounters* 27(3) (2021), 267–84; and Alejandro García-Sanjuán, 'Feeling Bad about Emotional History: The Case of *Andalucismo. Al-ʿUṣūr al-Wusṭā* 29 (2021): 303–22. This 'emotional' approach to al-Andalus was previously explored by the Spanish anthropologist José Antonio González Alcantud, *El mito de al-Andalus. Orígenes y actualidad de un ideal cultural* (Córdoba: Almuzara. 2014).

[46] Pedro Martínez Montávez, *Al-Andalus y España en la literatura árabe contemporánea* (Malaga: Arguval, 1992); Cristina Civantos, *The Afterlife of al-Andalus: Muslim Iberia in Contemporary Arab and Hispanic Narratives* (Albany, NY: State University of New York Press, 2017).

methodological transformations that have greatly contributed to radical changes to how we approach the study of al-Andalus.

The publication of *Al-Andalus. Estructura antropológica de una sociedad islámica en Occidente*, the ground-breaking book by the French historian Pierre Guichard, made 1976 the most decisive theoretical and methodological turning point in the study of the Arab and Islamic period in Iberia.[47] Largely drawing on anthropological structuralism, Guichard's insightful work focused on two main topics – tribal kinship and women's social status during the Umayyad period (eighth–eleventh centuries) – clearly pointing to a full assimilation of al-Andalus within the rest of the Arab and Islamic societies of that time. Above all, his contribution stands as the definitive breakaway from the nationalist paradigm, ushering in a new methodological era in the study of al-Andalus. Ever since Guichard, the traditional approach according to which the Iberian Islamic society merely represented the continuation of local 'Hispanic' or pre-Islamic tendencies fell into deep disrepute, and even the name 'Muslim Spain' itself largely fell into oblivion, although it still survives, for example, in the American academic milieu.[48] At any rate, when used today, it no longer conveys the same meaning that it held prior to 1976.

Over the 1960s and the 1970s, historical materialism represented a pervasive and highly influential theoretical framework, and it certainly had a major impact on the study of al-Andalus, especially with regard to the notion of tributary societies, coined by Egyptian Marxist economist Samir Amin (1931–2018). First introduced in Spain by Majorcan medievalist Miquel Barceló, Guichard later developed it in his second major contribution, focused on the territory of the Levant or Sharq al-Andalus (*Les musulmans de Valence et la Reconquīte, XIe–XIIIe siècles*), which remains the most comprehensive study of Muslim society in al-Andalus to date. In this book, Guichard developed a methodology largely based on a three-pronged approach: the Arabic literary sources, documents and texts written by the Christians after the conquest, and archaeology.

[47] Eduardo Manzano, 'Al-Andalus: un balance crítico', in Philippe Sénac (ed.), *Villa 4. Histoire et archéologie de l'Occident Musulman. Al-Andalus, Maghreb, Sicile* (Toulouse: Presses universitaires du Midi, 2012), 19–31.

[48] Jessica A. Coope, *The Most Noble of People: Religious, Ethnic, and Gender Identity in Muslim Spain* (Ann Arbor: University Michigan Press, 2017).

Historical materialism likewise inspired historian Manuel Acién, whose contribution points to the increasing role played by medieval studies in refining our understanding of al-Andalus. In his path-breaking 1994 book on ʿUmar ibn Ḥafṣūn, Acién offered a fresh reading of the sources regarding the revolts that took place in the second half of the third/ninth century. Dismissing the ethnic and religious rivalries as a cliché used by the sources in order to describe the causes leading to the widespread rebellion against Umayyad rule, Acién pointed instead to social and economic causes associated with a period of transition in which different social formations – feudal, tribal and Islamic – confronted each other, the last of them ultimately winning out over the rest.[49] According to Acién, while feudalism largely draws on the indistinctness between the private and public spheres, Islamic social formation is based on two main elements: the hegemony of the private and the pre-eminence of urban life.[50]

Acién's remarkable insights sparked a burgeoning historiographical debate, in all likelihood the broadest and most relevant since 1976, including comments and critiques from authors such as M. Fierro, E. Manzano and P. Guichard, among others. Acién carefully and meticulously responded to all the criticism in the prologue to the second edition of his book, which allowed him to refine and nuance some of his positions and correct certain approaches. To a large extent, the discussion focused on methodological problems related to the reading of Arab sources raised by Acién, for example, regarding the alleged Visigothic origins of the rebel aristocracy characterised in the sources as *muwalladūn*.[51]

A historian by training, Guichard likewise represented another relevant methodological breakthrough. Because of the largely nonsensical academic split between Arabic and medieval studies in Spain, historians had traditionally

[49] Manuel Acién Almansa, *Entre el feudalismo y el islam. Umar ibn Ḥafṣūn en los historiadores, en las fuentes y en la historia*, 2nd edn (Jaen: Universidad de Jaén, 1997).

[50] Manuel Acién Almansa, 'On the Role of Ideology in the Characterization of Social Formations: The Islamic Social Formation', in *Manuel Acién. Obras escogidas, I* (Jaén: Universidad de Jaén, 2020), 171–222.

[51] Alejandro García-Sanjuán, 'Manuel Acién Almansa, medievalista pionero y renovador de la historia de al-Andalus', *Medievalismo* 26 (2016): 135–53.

focused on the study of Christian society, becoming entirely oblivious to al-Andalus, with a few outstanding exceptions, Sánchez-Albornoz among them. Starting in the 1980s, however, contributions by archaeologists and medievalists dramatically increased, to the point that today Arabic studies have ceased to monopolise the study of al-Andalus. In fact, the number of Spanish Arabists who focus on the local Iberian Arab and Islamic past has substantially declined over the last two decades.

Arabic studies, however, have not only remained a highly influential scholarly field of expertise throughout the last forty-five years, but have developed new and highly productive methodological endeavours. Along with the increasing role of Arab scholars in the edition of Arabic texts – in connection with the widespread interest in *turāth* – perhaps one of the most significant strides has been the increasing interest in legal and doctrinal sources.

Framed in the context of growing attention to social and economic history, this interest very much corresponds, on the one hand, with the richness and variety of Islamic doctrinal literature, and, on the other, with the almost complete non-existence of Arabic archival documents. The work by Pedro Chalmeta over the 1970s and 1980s represents an essential point of reference in this regard, producing the most substantial study so far on the institution of *ḥisba* (urban markets administration).[52] He also paid attention to the Arabic legal sources, such as the tenth-century notarial treatise by Ibn al-ʿAṭṭār.[53] His very recent *Historia socioeconómica de Alandalús* (2021) stands as a paramount and much-needed contribution that fills a long-neglected scholarly gap.

Approaching socio-economic issues through the study of Islamic legal and doctrinal materials has been consolidated over the last decades as one of

[52] Pedro Chalmeta, *El señor del zoco en España. Edades media y moderna, Contribución al estudio de la historia del mercado* (Madrid: Instituto Hispano-Árabe de Cultura, 1973). See likewise Pedro Chalmeta, *El zoco medieval. Contribución al estudio de la historia del mercado* (Almería: Fundación Ibn Tufayl, 2010).

[53] Pedro Chalmeta and Federico Corriente, *Formulario notarial hispano-árabe. Por el alfaquí y notario cordobés Ibn al-ʿAṭṭār (s. X)* (Madrid: Instituto Hispano-Árabe de Cultura, 1983); Spanish trans. P. Chalmeta and Marina Marugán, *Formulario notarial y judicial andalusí del alfaquí y notario cordobés m. 399/1009 Ibn al-ʿAṭṭār* (Madrid: Fundación Matritense del Notariado, 2000).

the most relevant methodological trends, proving extremely productive with regard to a range of different topics, such as pious endowments[54] and religious minorities, among others.[55] Within Islamic legal sources, *fatāwà* literature represents a particularly fruitful genre, basically made up of jurisprudential rulings by the *ʿulamāʾ* relating to all kinds of issues, from marriages and sales to divorces and rentals, among many other topics. In this regard, the work carried out over the 1980s and 1990s by French scholar Vincent Lagardère with texts belonging to the great collection of the Maghrebi al-Wansharīsī (d. 1508) stands out.[56]

Similarly, the study of Islamic doctrinal literature made possible a much broader understanding of aspects related to the evolution of Maliki doctrine, the backbone of the identity of al-Andalus.[57] By the same token, the combined study of biographical and doctrinal sources and the application of quantitative methodologies have made it possible to gain knowledge of an unprecedented depth on the religious scholars of al-Andalus.[58]

Along with innovative methodologies, Arabic studies have likewise continued to contribute to the more purely philological work, in particular the translation of Arabic sources. The work of F. Maíllo is particularly relevant in this regard.[59] The classical philological approach is still being applied, for example, by L. Molina in his historiographical studies.[60]

54 Alejandro García-Sanjuán, *Till God Inherits the Earth: Islamic Pious Endowments in al-Andalus (9–15th Centuries)* (Leiden: Brill, 2007).

55 Maribel Fierro and John Tolan (eds), *The Legal Status of* Dhimmi-*s in the Islamic West (Second/Eighth-Ninth/Fifteenth Centuries)* (Turnout: Brepols, 2013).

56 Vincent Lagardère, *Histoire et société en Occident musulman au Moyen âge. Analyse du Miʿyār d'al-Wanšarisī* (Madrid: Casa de Velázquez-CSIC, 1995).

57 Maribel Fierro, 'Spanish Scholarship on Islamic Law', *Islamic Law and Society* 2(1) (1995): 43–70.

58 As shown by the database *Prosopografía de los ulemas de al-Andalus (PUA)*, available at: https://www.eea.csic.es/pua; and the series *Estudios onomástico-biográficos de al-Andalus*.

59 Felipe Maíllo, *Historia de al-Andalus* (Madrid: Akal, 1986); Felipe Maíllo, *La caída del califato de Córdoba y los reyes de taifas* (Salamanca: Universidad de Salamanca, 1993). See also the series *Fuentes Arabico-Hispanas* of the Editorial CSIC.

60 Luis Molina, 'Técnicas de *amplificatio* en el *Muqtabis* de Ibn Hayyān', *Talia Dixit. Revista interdisciplinar de retórica e historiografía* 1 (2006): 55–79.

Together with the contributions inspired by historical materialism, the consolidation of Islamic archaeology since the early 1980s arguably represents the most radical methodological breakthrough of the past forty-five years, with pioneering scholars such as Juan Zozaya (1939–2017) and Guillem Roselló-Bordoy (b. 1932). The most powerful boost came hand in hand with the intense activity of French scholars associated with the Casa de Velázquez (Madrid), Guichard himself among them, together with A. Bazzana, P. Cressier, Ph. Sénac and S. Gillotte among others. The articulation of rural spaces and, in particular, the different roles played by fortifications in the Islamic and Christian Iberian societies, are among the most substantial achievements of this scholarship.[61] Similarly, the work of T. F. Glick has contributed substantially to the comparative study of peninsular societies.[62] The scholarly group gathered around M. Barceló has consistently developed the so-called 'hydraulic archaeology', especially in the Balearic Islands, shedding light on the organisation and functioning of peasant work among rural Islamic communities, on which the Arabic written sources provide hardly any information.[63] Over the last two decades, archaeology has extensively and decisively contributed to the study of al-Andalus in a wide range of areas,[64] from urban spaces[65] to funerary

[61] André Bazzana, Patrice Cressier and Pierre Guichard, *Les Châteaux ruraux d'Al-Andalus. Histoire et archéologie des Husun du Sud-est de l'Espagne* (Madrid: Casa Velázquez, 1988).

[62] Thomas F. Glick, *Islamic and Christian Spain in the early Middle Ages: Comparative Perspectives on Social and Cultural Formation* (Princeton, NJ: Princeton University Press, 1979).

[63] Miquel Barceló, *El agua que no duerme. Fundamentos de la arqueología hidráulica andalusí* (Granada: Fundación El legado andalusí, 1996). On Barceló's contribution, see Pierre Guichard, 'Miquel Barceló et la Casa de Velázquez', *Mélanges de la Casa de Velázquez* 45(1) (2015): 245–52.

[64] José C. Carvajal López, 'The Archaeology of Al-Andalus: Past, Present and Future', *Medieval Archaeology* 58(1) (2014): 318–39.

[65] María-Teresa Casal García, 'The Rabaḍ of Šaqunda in Umayyad Córdoba (750–818 AD)', in Sabine Panzram and Laurent Callegarin (eds), *Entre civitas y madīna. El mundo de las ciudades en la península ibérica y en el norte de África (siglos IV–IX)* (Madrid: Casa de Velázquez, 2018), 119–32.

archaeology,[66] material culture[67] and zooarchaeology,[68] among others, to the point that it currently holds the highest level of methodological influence, together with the study of written sources.

Gender studies have also made inroads with the pioneering work of, among others, Manuela Marín,[69] who also has paid special attention to food culture within the Spanish academy's long-standing interest in Andalusi developments in agronomy, botany and diet,[70] and more generally in the 'sciences of the ancients'. Julio Samsó has not only written a comprehensive monograph on this topic, but more recently has deepened our understanding of the social context in which such sciences developed, and how the Andalusi case cannot be studied in isolation from North Africa.[71]

The end of the Muslim presence in the Iberian Peninsula was subject to intense study and debate by scholars of late medieval and early modern history, with questions such as: was religious homogenisation inevitable? How can it be conceptualised? What was the impact of forced conversion on Spanish society in religious, social and economic terms, among others?[72]

[66] María Paz de Miguel, '*La maqbara de Pamplona (s. VIII). Aportes de la osteoarqueología al conocimiento de la islamización en la marca superior*', PhD, Universidad de Alicante, 2016.

[67] José C. Carvajal López, 'After the Conquest: Ceramics and Migrations', *Journal of Medieval Iberian Studies* 11(3) (2019): 323–41.

[68] Marcos García, 'Archaeozoology's Contribution to the Knowledge of al-Andalus', in J. C. Carvajal (ed.), *Al-Andalus: Archaeology, History and Memory* (Edinburgh: Akkadia Press, 2016), 33–8.

[69] Manuela Marín, *Mujeres en al-Ándalus* (Madrid: CSIC, 2000); Simon Barton, *Conquerors, Brides and Concubines: Interfaith Relations and Social Power in Medieval Iberia* (Philadelphia: University of Pennsylvania Press, 2015).

[70] See, for example, the publications by Expiración García Sánchez, available at: https://www.eea.csic.es/publicaciones/garcia-sanchez-expiracion.

[71] Julio Samsó, *Las ciencias de los antiguos en al-Andalus*, addenda and corrigenda by J. Samsó and M. Forcada, 2nd edn (Almería: Fundación Ibn Tufayl-Fundación Cajamar, 2011); Julio Samsó, *On Both Sides of the Strait of Gibraltar: Studies on the History of Medieval Astronomy in the Iberian Peninsula and the Maghrib* (Leiden: Brill, 2020).

[72] Mercedes García-Arenal and Gerard Wiegers (eds), *The Expulsion of the Moriscos from Spain: A Mediterranean Diaspora* (Leiden: Brill, 2014).

## Conclusion

Over the last forty-five years, as the most traditional scholarship was finally overcome, studies on al-Andalus were able to grow into the extraordinarily complex, varied and burgeoning academic field we find today, with an increasing connection with medieval studies, despite the considerable obstacles that still separate the two disciplines. While in the first period examined here, studies on al-Andalus appeared almost exclusively in specialised journals such as *Al-Andalus*, today they can be found in journals devoted to a range of disciplines (archaeology, history, literary studies, religious sciences, cultural studies and more).

As we have seen, major advances have been made in the study of the political, social and economic history of al-Andalus. Of late, the new methodologies associated with the so-called digital humanities have likewise begun to have an impact, including, for instance, the use of geographic information systems. The intellectual and religious history of al-Andalus is already profiting from ambitious projects such as the *Biblioteca de al-Andalus*[73] and the *Prosopography of the 'Ulamā' of al-Andalus*. As with other regions of the Islamic world, there is renewed interest in studying the sources from a variety of perspectives, such as palaeography and codicology, and paying attention to reading practices and reception processes.

The sustained use of al-Andalus to talk about present concerns has placed it between the Scylla of idealisation and the Charybdis of demonisation.[74] Notwithstanding the wide range and broad scope of the methodological developments analysed here, popular perceptions widely disseminated among

[73] *Biblioteca de al-Andalus*, ed. J. Lirola Delgado and J. M. Puerta Vílchez, 7 vols + vol. A (Apéndices) + vol. B (Balance de resultados e índices) (Almería: Fundación Ibn Tufayl de Estudios Árabes, 2004–13). Other volumes are planned.

[74] Idealisation is mostly found in books written for the general public, such as Chris Lowney, *A Vanished World: Christians, Muslims and Jews in Medieval Spain* (New York: Oxford University Press, 2006), while academics are responsible for some demonising views such as Fernández-Morera and Rafael Sánchez Saus, *Al-Andalus y la cruz. La invasión musulmana de Hispania* (Barcelona: Stella Maris, 2016). On the latter, see Alejandro García-Sanjuán, 'La persistencia del discurso nacionalcatólico sobre el medievo peninsular en la historiografía española actual', *Historiografías* 12 (2016): 132–53.

non-specialised audiences remain heavily burdened by ideological prejudices, stereotypes and falsehoods, a major challenge to be taken up by scholarship in the years to come.

## Bibliography

Acién Almansa, Manuel, *Entre el feudalismo y el islam. Umar ibn Ḥafṣūn en los historiadores, en las fuentes y en la historia*, 2nd edn. Jaén: Universidad de Jaén, 1997.

Acién Almansa, Manuel, 'On the Role of Ideology in the Characterization of Social Formations: The Islamic Social Formation', in *Manuel Acién. Obras escogidas, I*. Jaén: Universidad de Jaén, 2020, 171–222.

Álvarez Millán, Cristina and Heide, Claudia, *Pascual de Gayangos: A Nineteenth-Century Spanish Arabist*. Edinburgh: Edinburgh University Press, 2008.

Aquinas and 'the Arabs' International Working Group, directed by Richard Taylor (Marquette University), available at: http://richardctaylor.info/aaiwg.

Arce-Sainz, Fernando, 'La supuesta basílica de San Vicente en Córdoba: de mito histórico a obstinación historiográfica', *Al-Qanṭara* 36(1) (2015): 11–44.

Asensio, Eugenio, *La España imaginada de Américo Castro*. Barcelona: Ediciones El Albir, 1976.

Asín Palacios, Miguel, *Islam and the Divine Comedy*. London: H. Watson, 1926.

Asín Palacios, Miguel, *Huellas del Islam. Santo Tomás de Aquino, Turmeda, Pascal, San Juan de la Cruz*. Madrid: Espasa Calpe, 1941.

Barceló, Miquel, *Arqueología medieval. En las afueras del medievalismo*. Barcelona: Crítica, 1988.

Barceló, Miquel, *El agua que no duerme. Fundamentos de la arqueología hidráulica andalusí*. Granada: Fundación El legado andalusí, 1996.

Barton, Simon, *Conquerors, Brides and Concubines: Interfaith Relations and Social Power in Medieval Iberia*. Philadelphia: University of Pennsylvania Press, 2015.

Bazzana, André, Cressier, Patrice and Guichard, Pierre, *Les Châteaux ruraux d'Al-Andalus. Histoire et archéologie des Husun du Sud-est de l'Espagne*. Madrid: Casa Velázquez, 1988.

Ben-Sasson, Menahem, 'Al-Andalus: the So-called "Golden Age" of Spanish Jewry – a Critical View', in C. Cluse (ed.), *The Jews of Europe in the Middle Ages (Tenth to Fifteenth Centuries)*. Turnhout: Brepols, 2004, 123–37.

*Biblioteca de al-Andalus*, ed. J. Lirola Delgado and J. M. Puerta Vílchez, 7 vols + vol. A (Apéndices) + vol. B (Balance de resultados e índices). Almería: Fundación Ibn Tufayl de Estudios Árabes, 2004–13.

Bosch Vilá, Jacinto, *Los Almorávides*. Tétouan: Editora Marroquí, 1956.

Burnett, Charles, *Arabic into Latin in the Middle Ages: The Translators and their Intellectual and Social Context*. Farnham: Variorum Collected Studies Series, 2009.

Carvajal López, José C., 'The Archaeology of Al-Andalus: Past, Present and Future', *Medieval Archaeology* 58(1) (2014): 318–39.

Carvajal López, José C., 'After the Conquest: Ceramics and Migrations', *Journal of Medieval Iberian Studies* 11(3) (2019): 323–41.

Casal García, María-Teresa, 'The Rabaḍ of Šaqunda in Umayyad Córdoba (750–818 AD)', in Sabine Panzram and Laurent Callegarin (eds), *Entre civitas y madīna. El mundo de las ciudades en la península ibérica y en el norte de África (siglos IV–IX)*. Madrid: Casa de Velázquez, 2018, 119–32.

Castro, Américo, *The Structure of Spanish History*. Princeton, NJ: Princeton University Press, 1954.

Chalmeta, Pedro, *El señor del zoco en España. Edades media y moderna, Contribución al estudio de la historia del mercado*. Madrid: Instituto Hispano-Árabe de Cultura, 1973.

Chalmeta, Pedro, *El zoco medieval. Contribución al estudio de la historia del mercado*. Almería: Fundación Ibn Tufayl, 2010.

Chalmeta, Pedro and Corriente, Federico, *Formulario notarial hispano-árabe. Por el alfaquí y notario cordobés Ibn al-ʿAṭṭār (s. X)*. Madrid: Instituto Hispano-Árabe de Cultura, 1983.

Chalmeta, Pedro and Marugán, Marina, *Formulario notarial y judicial andalusí del alfaquí y notario cordobés m. 399/1009 Ibn al-ʿAṭṭār*. Madrid: Fundación Matritense del Notariado, 2000.

Civantos, Cristina, *The Afterlife of al-Andalus: Muslim Iberia in Contemporary Arab and Hispanic Narratives*. Albany, NY: State University of New York Press, 2017.

Codera, Francisco, *Tratado de numismática arábigo-española*. Madrid: Lib. de M. Murillo, 1879.

Cohen, Mark R., 'The "Golden Age" of Jewish–Muslim Relations: Myth and Reality', in Jane Marie Todd et al. (eds), *A History of Jewish–Muslim Relations: From the Origins to the Present Day*. Princeton, NJ: Princeton University Press, 2013.

Coope, Jessica A., *The Most Noble of People: Religious, Ethnic, and Gender Identity in Muslim Spain*. Ann Arbor: University Michigan Press, 2017.

Dainotto, Roberto M., 'The Discreet Charm of the Arabist Theory: Juan Andrés, Historicism, and the De-centering of Montesquieu's Europe', *European History Quarterly* 36(1) (2006): 7–29.

de Miguel, María Paz, 'La maqbara de Pamplona (s. VIII). Aportes de la osteoarqueología al conocimiento de la islamización en la marca superior', PhD, Universidad de Alicante, 2016.

Dozy, Reinhart, *Histoire des musulmans d'Espagne jusqu'à la conquīte de l'Andalousie par les Almoravides*. Leiden: Brill, 1861.

Fanjul, Serafín, *Al-Andalus contra España. La forja del mito*. Madrid: Siglo XXI, 2000.

Fernández-Morera, Darío, *The Myth of the Andalusian Paradise: Muslims, Christians, and Jews under Islamic rule in Medieval Spain*. Wilmington, DE: ISI Books, 2016.

Fernández Puertas, Antonio, *Mezquita de Córdoba: su estudio arqueológico en el siglo XX*. Granada: Editorial Universidad de Granada, 2009.

Fierro, Maribel, 'Spanish Scholarship on Islamic Law', *Islamic Law and Society* 2(1) (1995): 43–70.

Fierro, Maribel, 'Al-Andalus en el pensamiento fascista español: La *Revolución islámica en Occidente* de Ignacio Olagüe', in Manuela Marín (ed.), *Al-Andalus / España. Historiografías en contraste, siglos XVII–XXI*. Madrid: Casa de Velázquez, 2009, 325–49.

Fierro, Maribel and Tolan, John (eds), *The Legal Status of* Dhimmi-*s in the Islamic West (Second/Eighth-Ninth/Fifteenth Centuries)*. Turnout: Brepols, 2013.

Fierro Maribel (ed.), *The Routledge Handbook of Muslim Iberia*. London: Routledge, 2020.

Fierro, Maribel, 'The Tales of Feeling: Looking for Emotions in Andalusia', *Al-Qanṭara* 42(1) (2021).

Fierro, Maribel, *'Abd al-Mu'min. Mahdism and Caliphate in the Islamic West*. London: Oneworld, 2021.

Fierro, Maribel and García-Sanjuán, Alejandro (eds), *Hispania, al-Ándalus y España: Identidad y nacionalismo en la historia peninsular*. Madrid: Marcial Pons, 2020.

Fuchs, Barbara, *Exotic Nation: Maurophilia and the Construction of Early Modern Spain*, Philadelphia: University of Pennsylvania Press, 2011.

García, Marcos, 'Archaeozoology's Contribution to the Knowledge of al-Andalus', in J. C. Carvajal (ed.), *Al-Andalus: Archaeology, History and Memory*. Edinburgh: Akkadia Press, 2016), 33–8.

García-Arenal, Mercedes and Mediano, Fernando Rodríguez, *The Orient in Spain: Converted Muslims, the Forged Lead Books of Granada, and the Rise of Orientalism*. Leiden: Brill, 2013.

García-Arenal, Mercedes and Wiegers, Gerard (eds), *The Expulsion of the Moriscos from Spain: A Mediterranean Diaspora*. Leiden: Brill, 2014.

García-Sanjuán, Alejandro, *Till God Inherits the Earth: Islamic Pious Endowments in al-Andalus (9–15th Centuries)*. Leiden: Brill, 2007.

García-Sanjuán, Alejandro, 'La persistencia del discurso nacionalcatólico sobre el medievo peninsular en la historiografía española actual', *Historiografías* 12 (2016): 132–53.

García-Sanjuán, Alejandro, 'Manuel Acién Almansa, medievalista pionero y renovador de la historia de al-Andalus', *Medievalismo* 26 (2016): 135–53.

García-Sanjuán, Alejandro, 'Al-Andalus en la historiografía nacionalcatólica española: Claudio Sánchez-Albornoz', *eHumanista* 37 (2017): 305–28.

García-Sanjuán, Alejandro, 'Rejecting al-Andalus, Exalting the Reconquista: Historical Memory in Contemporary Spain', *Journal of Medieval Iberian Studies* 10(1) (2018): 127–45.

García-Sanjuán, Alejandro, 'Denying the Islamic Conquest of Iberia: A Historiographical Fraud', *Journal of Medieval Iberian Studies* 11(3) (2019): 306–22.

García-Sanjuán, Alejandro, *La conquista islámica de la península ibérica y la tergiversación del pasado. Del catastrofismo al negacionismo*, 2nd edn, Madrid: Marcial Pons, 2019.

García-Sanjuán, Alejandro, 'Weaponizing Historical Knowledge: The Notion of *Reconquista* in Spanish Nationalism', *Imago temporis. Medium Aevum* 14 (2020): 133–62.

García-Sanjuán, Alejandro, 'Feeling Bad about Emotional History: The Case of *Andalucismo*. *Al-ʿUṣūr al-Wusṭā* 29 (2021): 303–22.

Gayangos, Pascual (trans.), *The History of the Mohammedan Dynasties in Spain*, 2 vols. London: Oriental Translation Fund of Great Britain and Ireland, 1840–3.

Glick, Thomas F., *Islamic and Christian Spain in the Early Middle Ages: Comparative Perspectives on Social and Cultural Formation*. Princeton, NJ: Princeton University Press, 197).

González Alcantud, José Antonio, *El mito de al-Andalus. Orígenes y actualidad de un ideal cultural*. Córdoba: Almuzara. 2014.

Guichard, Pierre, *Al-Andalus. Estructura antropológica de una sociedad islámica en Occidente*. Barcelona: Barral, 1976; repr. Granada: Universidad de Granada, 1998, with Introduction by Antonio Malpica.

Guichard, Pierre, *Les musulmans de Valence et la Reconquête (XIe–XIIIe siècles)*, 2 vols. Damascus: IFAO, 1990–1; Spanish translation Madrid-Valencia: Universidad de Valencia, 2001.

Guichard, Pierre, 'Miquel Barceló et la Casa de Velázquez', *Mélanges de la Casa de Velázquez* 45(1) (2015): 245–52.

Henriet, Patrick, 'Miguel Asín Palacios (1871–1944), le christianisme et l'islam: thèses, idéologie, réception', in Jean-Luc Fournet, Jean-Michel Mouton and Jacques Paviot (eds), *Civilisations en transition (III). Sociétés multiconfessionnelles à travers l'histoire du Proche Orient*. Byblos, 2017, 181–211.

Hirschkind, Charles, *The Feeling of History: Islam, Romanticism, and Andalusia*. Chicago: University of Chicago Press, 2020.

*Historia de los Autores y Transmisores de al-Andalus (HATA)*, directed by Maribel Fierro, available at: https://www.eea.csic.es/red/hata.

Huici Miranda, Ambrosio, *Historia política del Imperio almohade*, 2 vols, Tétouan: Editora Marroquí, 1956–7.

Jiménez-Landi, Antonio, *La Institución Libre de Enseñanza*, 4 vols. Madrid: Taurus, 1987.

Jiménez de Rada, Rodrigo, *Estoria de los árabes. Traducción castellana del siglo XIV de la Historia Arabum*, ed. Fernando Bravo López. Córdoba: Editorial de la Universidad de Córdoba, 2019.

Ladero Quesada, Miguel Ángel, 'La "Decadencia" española como argumento historiográfico', in Miguel Ángel Ladero Quesada, *Lecturas sobre la España histórica* (Madrid: Real Academia de la Historia, 1998), 213–85.

Lagardère, Vincent, *Histoire et société en Occident musulman au Moyen âge. Analyse du Miʿyār d'al-Wanšarisī*. Madrid: Casa de Velázquez-CSIC, 1995.

Lévi-Provençal, Evariste, *Histoire de l'Espagne musulmane*, 3 vols. Paris: Maisonneuve et Larose, 1950–67, repr. 1999; Spanish trans. E. García Gómez, *España musulmana hasta la caída del Califato de Córdoba (711–1031 de J.C.), Historia de España Menéndez Pidal*, vols IV–V, 4th edn. Madrid: Espasa-Calpe, 1976.

López Sánchez, José-María, *Heterodoxos españoles. El Centro de Estudios Históricos, 1910–1936*. Madrid: Marcial Pons, 2006.

Lowney, Chris, *A Vanished World: Christians, Muslims and Jews in Medieval Spain*. New York: Oxford University Press, 2006.

Maíllo, Felipe, *Historia de al-Andalus*. Madrid: Akal, 1986.

Maíllo, Felipe, *La caída del califato de Córdoba y los reyes de taifas*. Salamanca: Universidad de Salamanca, 1993.

Manzano Moreno, Eduardo, 'Al-Andalus: un balance crítico', in Philippe Sénac (ed.), *Villa 4. Histoire et archéologie de l'Occident Musulman. Al-Andalus, Maghreb, Sicile*. Toulouse: Presses universitaires du Midi, 2012, 19–31.

Manzano Moreno, Eduardo, 'Qurtuba: Some Critical Considerations of the Caliphate of Cordoba and the Myth of Convivencia', *Reflections on Qurtuba in the 21st Century*, 2013, 111–34, available at: http://www.awraq.es.

Marín, Manuela, *Mujeres en al-Ándalus*. Madrid: CSIC, 2000.

Marín, Manuela, de la Puente, Cristina, Rodríguez Mediano, Fernando and Pérez Alcalde, Juan Ignacio, *Los epistolarios de Julián Ribera Tarragó y Miguel Asín Palacios. Introducción, catálogo e índices*. Madrid: CSIC, 2009.

Márquez Villanueva, Francisco, *El concepto cultural alfonsí*. Madrid: Mapfre, 1994.

Martínez Montávez, Pedro, *Al-Andalus y España en la literatura árabe contemporánea*. Malaga: Arguval, 1992.

Molina, Luis, 'Técnicas de *amplificatio* en el *Muqtabis* de Ibn Hayyān', *Talia Dixit. Revista interdisciplinar de retórica e historiografía* 1 (2006): 55–79.

Monroe, James T., *Islam and the Arabs in Spanish Scholarship (Sixteenth Century to the Present)*. Leiden: Brill, 1970.

Muñoz Cosme, Alfonso, *La vida y la obra de Leopoldo Torres Balbás*. Seville: Junta de Andalucía, 2005.

Ortega y Gasset, José, *España invertebrada. Bosquejo de algunos pensamientos históricos*, 2nd edn. Madrid: Calpe, 1921.

Pick, Lucy, *Conflict and Coexistence: Archbishop Rodrigo and the Muslims and Jews in Medieval Spain*. Ann Arbor: University of Michigan, 2004.

Prieto y Vives, Antonio, *Los Reyes de Taifas. Estudio histórico-numismático de los musulmanes españoles en el siglo V de la Hégira (XI d. de J.C.)*. Madrid: Junta de Ampliación de Estudios e Investigaciones Científicas, 1926.

*Prosopografía de los ulemas de al-Andalus (PUA)*, available at: https://www.eea.csic.es/pua.

Ray, Jonathan, 'Beyond Tolerance and Persecution: Reassessing Our Approach to Medieval *Convivencia*', *Jewish Social Studies* 11(2) (2005): 1–18.

Ribera y Tarragó, Julián, *Disertaciones y opúsculos*. Madrid: Impr. de E. Maestre, 1928.

Ríos Saloma, Martín, *La Reconquista. Una construcción historiográfica, siglos XVI–XIX*. Madrid and Mexico: Marcial Pons and Universidad Nacional Autónoma de México, 2011.

Rodríguez-Mediano, Fernando, 'Culture, Identity and Civilisation: The Arabs and Islam in the History of Spain', in Frank Peter, Sarah Dornhof and Elena Arigita (eds), *Islam and the Politics of Culture in Europe: Memory, Aesthetics, Art*. Bielefeld: Verlag, 2013, 41–60.

Rodríguez Mediano, Fernando, 'The Feeling of History. Islam, Romanticism, and Andalusia', *Medieval Encounters* 27(3) (2021), 267–84. doi: https://doi.org/10.1163/15700674-12340105.

Samsó, Julio, *Las ciencias de los antiguos en al-Andalus*, addenda and corrigenda by J. Samsó and M. Forcada, 2nd edn. Almería: Fundación Ibn Tufayl-Fundación Cajamar, 2011.

Samsó, Julio, *On Both Sides of the Strait of Gibraltar: Studies on the History of Medieval Astronomy in the Iberian Peninsula and the Maghrib*. Leiden: Brill, 2020.

Sánchez Saus, Rafael, *Al-Andalus y la cruz. La invasión musulmana de Hispania*. Barcelona: Stella Maris, 2016.

Soifer, Maya, 'Beyond Convivencia: Critical Reflections on the Historiography of Interfaith Relations in Christian Spain', *Journal of Medieval Iberian Studies* 1(1) (2009): 19–36.

Torrecilla, Jesús, *España al revés. Los mitos del pensamiento progresista (1790–1840)*. Madrid: Marcial Pons, 2016.

Urquízar-Herrera, Antonio, *Admiration and Awe: Morisco Buildings and Identity Negotiations in Early Modern Spanish Historiography*. Oxford: Oxford University Press, 2017.

Vernet, Juan, *La Cultura hispano-árabe en Oriente y Occidente*. Barcelona: Ariel, 1978; French translation by Gabriel Martinez-Gros. Paris: Sindbad, 1985.

Vernet, Juan, *Lo que Europa debe al Islam de España*. Barcelona: El Acantilado, 1999.

Viguera, María Jesús, Introduction to Francisco Codera y Zaidín, *Decadencia y desaparición de los almorávides en España*. Pamplona: Urigoiti, 2004.

Vrolijk, Arnoud and Van Leeuwen, Richard, *Arabic Studies in the Netherlands: A Short History in Portraits 1580–1950*. Leiden: Brill, 2014.

Wasserstein, David J., 'Nota Biographica: Makhlouf Levi and Evariste Lévi-Provençal', *Al-Qantara* 21(1) (2000): 211–14.

Zomeño Rodríguez, Amalia, 'El derecho islámico a través de su imagen colonial durante el Protectorado español en Marruecos', in Fernando Rodríguez Mediano and Elena de Felipe Rodríguez (eds), *El protectorado español en Marruecos: gestión colonial e identidades*. Madrid: CSIC, 2002, 307–37.

Zwartjes, Otto, *Love Songs from al-Andalus: History, Structure and Meaning of the Kharja*. Leiden: Brill, 1997.

# Part II

## TEXTUAL STUDIES

# 4

# SUBVERSIVE PHILOLOGY? PROSOPOGRAPHY AS A RELATIONAL AND CORPUS-BASED APPROACH TO EARLY ISLAMIC HISTORY

GEORG LEUBE[1]

## Introduction: Early Islam as a Prosopographical Problem?

The vast corpus of early and classical Arabic-Islamic historiography[2] narrating the history of the first three generations of Islam makes this period one of the most documented periods of pre-modern human culture. In large parts of this corpus, the 'atomist' mode of Arabic-Islamic scholarly discourses deploys multiple individual narrations or *akhbār* paratactically, frequently together with their respective chain of transmission or *isnād*.[3] The eponymous

[1] The author would like to thank the anonymous reviewers and colleagues who have contributed to shaping this methodological reflection on deploying prosopography to early and classical Arabic-Islamic compilations. Where not otherwise indicated, all translations are by the author.

[2] For the purpose of this chapter, I envision historiography as an entangled deployment of a referential dimension (referring to events claimed to be 'factual history') and a narrative dimension (the dynamics and logics of language- and discourse-bound narrative). Accordingly, any piece of historiographical writing can be approached both as a claim for 'historical' truth and a continuation of discursive dynamics. The entanglement of both dimensions somewhat pre-empts the all to common question of modern history asking for 'fact or fiction'.

[3] For the 'aural' culture of Muslim scholarly traditions as the foundation of this structure, see the collected studies of Gregor Schoeler, *The Oral and the Written in Early Islam* (London: Routledge, 2006).

compilers of the extant collections, however, only very rarely offer explicit commentary or validation on the frequently contradictory information given in the narrations.[4] Therefore, very little of the information concerning the genesis of Islam and the Muslim community is uncontested in this corpus.

As the formative period of Islam continues to be deployed as the most important cultural memory of Muslim societies,[5] this multiplicity of contradictory information should be interpreted as reflecting a multitude of competing normativities that intersect in the corpus of early and classical Arabic-Islamic historiography.[6] As will be shown below, this contestedness of early Islamic memory is not restricted to the emblematic episodes of political succession that are particularly contested between the 'master narratives' of

[4] See the programmatic suggestion of al-Ṭabarī of 'transmitting what has been transmitted' as 'only the eye-witness may know which information is true', al-Ṭabarī, *Taʾrīkh*, ed. Muṣṭafā al-Sayyid and Ṭāriq Sālim (Cairo: al-Maktaba al-Tawfīqiyya, n.d.), 1, 11. The inherent multiplicity of Muslim cultures has been underlined as an integral part of Islam in recent years, see Thomas Bauer, *Die Kultur der Ambiguität. Eine andere Geschichte des Islams* (Berlin: Verlag der Weltreligionen, 2011); Shahab Ahmad, *What is Islam? The Importance of Being Islamic* (Princeton, NJ: Princeton University Press, 2016).

[5] The concept of cultural memories was pioneered by Maurice Halbwachs, *Les cadres sociaux de la mémoire* (Paris: Éditions Albin Michel, 1994) and *La topographie légendaire des évangiles en Terre sainte* (Paris: Presses Universitaires de France, 2008). Subsequently, it was most influentially developed by Pierre Nora (ed.), *Les Lieux de Mémoire I. La République* (Paris: Gallimard, 1984); and Jan Assmann, *Das kulturelle Gedächtnis. Schrift, Erinnerung und politische Identität in frühen Hochkulturen* (Munich: Beck, 1992). For a nuanced and up-to-date discussion of more recent developments in memory studies, see also Aaltje Hidding, *The Era of the Martyrs: Remembering the Great Persecution in Late Antique Egypt* (Berlin: De Gruyter, 2020).

[6] See for the constructivist criticism of substantialised narratives of memory and tradition as frequently counterfactual constructs rooted in specific social and institutional configurations the magisterial work of Eugen Weber, *Peasants into Frenchmen: The Modernization of Rural France 1870–1914* (Stanford: Stanford University Press, 1976), and the provocative deconstruction of Scottish 'national' traditions by Hugh Trevor-Roper, 'The Invention of Tradition: The Highland Tradition of Scotland', in Eric Hobsbawm and Terence Ranger (eds), *The Invention of Tradition* (Cambridge: Cambridge University Press, 1983). See for subsequent influential elaborations of this criticism Benedict Anderson, *Imagined Communities: Reflections on the Origin and Spread of Nationalism* (London: Verso, 2006); and Louis Althusser, *Sur la reproduction* (Paris: Presses Universitaires de France, 2011).

contemporary and historical Islamic traditions.[7] Instead, the internal contradictions attesting to the contestedness of early Islamic memory constitute a pervasive feature in early and classical Arabic-Islamic historiography.

The multiplicity of Muslim cultural memories of the formative period of Islam is especially significant due to the frequently over-confident and substantialising engagement with this literature conducted both in nationalist–Islamist and colonialist–Orientalist epistemological frameworks.[8] This substantialising and unsystematic engagement with early and classical Arabic-Islamic historiography has been critiqued by John Wansbrough, Patricia Crone and others since the 1970s.[9] Nonetheless, the alternative frameworks proposed by these authors are frequently not based on less controversial methodologies than those interpretations they critique.[10] The methodical 'step outside' in engaging

[7] See for the most coherent reconstruction of a 'factionalist-*shīʿī*' master-narrative of the first three generations of Islam Wilferd Madelung, *The Succession to Muḥammad* (Cambridge: Cambridge University Press, 1997). Significantly, Madelung concludes his reconstruction of this particular perspective on the formative period of Islam with Giordano Bruno's proverbial dictum 'se non è vero, è ben trovato', which can be translated as 'even if it is not true, it's well invented' (Madelung, *Succession*, 355). See for an overview over the competing master-narratives also the overview given by Gernot Rotter, *Die Umayyaden und der Zweite Bürgerkrieg, 680–692* (Wiesbaden: Steiner, 1982).

[8] The critique of orientalist scholarship as rooted in frequently colonialist configurations of exploitation was pioneered by Edward W. Said, *Orientalism* (London: Routledge, 1978). A comprehensive overview over the fascinating interplay of multiple intellectual traditions engaging with early Islamic history from within the epistemological and institutional frameworks of Islam and the political Geography of the Islamic World during the long twentieth century remains to be written.

[9] See for the initial impetus of 'revisionist' engagements with Muslim cultural memories John Wansbrough, *Quranic Studies: Sources and Methods of Scriptural Interpretation* (Oxford: Oxford University Press, 1977); and Patricia Crone and Michael Cook, *Hagarism: The Making of the Islamic World* (Cambridge: Cambridge University Press, 1977).

[10] The methodological discussion on engaging with early Islamic history was recently continued by Robert G. Hoyland, *In God's Path: The Arab Conquests and the Creation of an Islamic Empire* (Oxford: Oxford University Press, 2015), which should be read together with the reviews by Fred M. Donner, *al-ʿUṣūr al-Wusṭā* 23 (2015): 134–40, and Jens J. Scheiner, *Bustan* 7(1) (2016): 19–32, as well as the ensuing response to the reviews by Robert G. Hoyland, 'Reflections on the Identity of the Arabian Conquerors of the Seventh-Century Middle East', *Al-ʿUṣūr al-Wusṭā* 25 (2017): 113–40. See also the evaluation of the debate in the review by Georg Leube, *Plekos* 20 (2018): 327–34.

with the formative period of Islam proposed so compellingly by Patricia Crone and Michael Cook therefore remains more of a *desideratum* than an accepted standard.[11] Nonetheless, I believe a scholarly consensus could be postulated concerning the following three methodological challenges that should be met by engagements with early Islamic history and cultural memory that aim to contribute to the deconstruction of substantialising narratives:

1. The description of early Muslim and Islamicate societies should proceed within a relational framework that grounds analytical categories in the sources pertaining to this period.[12]
2. Scholarly engagement with Muslim social history should aim to be precise in the localisation and description of agency. Specifically, agency should be localised exclusively in individual actors acting from within specific configurations.[13]

[11] See for the suggestion of a methodological 'step outside' Crone and Cook, *Hagarism*, 3, as well as Patricia Crone, *Slaves on Horses: The Evolution of the Islamic Polity* (Cambridge: Cambridge University Press, 1980), 15.

[12] Influential reconceptualisations of Islam in relational categories frequently depart from the description of Islam as a discoursive tradition suggested by Talal Asad, *The Idea of an Anthropology of Islam* (Washington DC: Center for Contemporary Arab Studies, Georgetown University, 1986); and the adaptation of Pierre Bourdieu's theories on habitus and capital proposed by Bradford Verter, 'Spiritual Capital: Theorizing Religion with Bourdieu against Bourdieu', *Sociological Theory* 21(2) (2003): 150–74. See for two recent contributions that apply this theoretical background to Islamic intellectual landscapes Paula Schrode, 'The Dynamics of Orthodoxy and Heterodoxy in Uyghur Religious Practice', *Die Welt des Islams* 48 (2008): 394–433; and Rüdiger Seesemann, 'Epistemology or Ideology? Toward a Relational Perspective on Islamic Knowledge in Africa', *Journal of Africana Religions* 6(2) (2018): 232–68.

[13] The importance of localising agency within specific actors for interpretations of early Islamic history will be discussed in one of the two case studies below. The suggestion that agency should be localised exclusively within specific actors as opposed to within institutions or other supra-personal entities was systematically proposed as an axiom of 'methodological individualism' by Joseph Schumpeter, *Das Wesen und der Hauptinhalt der theoretischen Nationalökonomie* (Berlin: Duncker & Humblot, 1970), 88–98. For the field of Islamic social history, the paramount importance of interpersonal ties of loyalty and patronage was demonstrated by Roy Mottahedeh, *Loyalty and Leadership in an Early Islamic Society* (London: I. B. Tauris, 2001), as well as by Jürgen Paul, *Herrscher, Gemeinwesen, Vermittler. Ostiran und Transoxanien in vormongolischer Zeit* (Stuttgart: Franz Steiner, 1996). For a

3. In order to preclude the *a priori* determination of results by an unsystematic (and thereby unfalsifiable selection) of data, scholarly engagement with early Islamic history should proceed from the systematical analysis[14] of clearly circumscript bodies of sources. In addition to the discourses of Arabic-Islamic scholarly traditions that constitute the resonating body and cultural memory of Muslim societies, these sources should also include the plentiful administrative and epigraphic documentation that continues to become available, as well as the narrative traditions and non-narrative sources of non-Muslim traditions.[15]

The present contribution proposes that prosopography, or *the systematical study of a group of individuals sharing a common identifiable marker*, is a method that is particularly suited to be applied in accordance with these three methodological challenges. Prosopography constitutes a well-established method that has been fruitfully deployed to various areas of pre-modern history.[16] One of the areas that has profited most from prosopographic research is the history of the western Greek world during the so-called 'middle Byzantine' period. In his methodological reflection on prosopographical approaches to this field, Paul Magdalino suggested the following principles as constitutive for prosopographic research:

theory of a 'derived' agency exerted by material artefacts, see Alfred Gell, *Art and Agency: An Anthropological Theory* (Oxford: Clarendon Press, 1998). For the sake of clarity, I will in this contribution implicitly treat non-material artefacts such as traditions and memories as imbued with a 'derived' agency similiar to that proposed by Gell for material artefacts.

[14] I use the term 'systematical analysis' to indicate a methodical engagement with a clearly demarcated and internally coherent body of sources. This does not depart from a claim that the 'system' takes precedence over individual utterances ('systemic analysis'), nor does it see the methodology of approach as sufficient for meaningful engagement with any (possibly ill-defined or *hétéroclite*) body of sources ('methodical analysis').

[15] Possible guidelines for the establishment of a systematically compiled corpus of sources will be suggested below.

[16] See in addition to the eponymous journal *Medieval Prosopography* (Western Michigan University), which published in its 35th issue in 2020, and scholarly series such as *Prosopographica et Genealogica* (Oxford) in particular the methodological reflections contained in Averil Cameron (ed.), *Fifty Years of Prosopography: The Later Roman Empire, Byzantium and Beyond* (Oxford: Oxford University Press, 2003).

> that every piece of historical data should, as far as possible, be related to an identifiable person, that multiple identities should not be confused, single identities should not be multiplied and collective identities should always be defined in terms of connections between individuals.[17]

As will be shown below, these principles resonate closely with the emic epistemological structures of pre-modern Arabic-Islamic scholarly traditions.[18] In addition, prosopographical approaches specifically answer to the methodological challenges raised above as follows:

1. Prosopography as the study of 'the connections between individuals in a group'[19] develops analytical concepts and categories inductively from the sources within a relational framework.
2. Prosopography departs from a clearly demarcated group of individuals to analyse their respective agency within its specific context.
3. Prosopography constitutes a method that is exceptionally well suited for the integration of 'atomist' evidence, such as the multitude of narrations in Arabic-Islamic scholarly traditions and the frequently fragmentary administrative and epigraphic sources.

Nonetheless, the application of prosopography to the multiple narrative paradigms of Arabic-Islamic scholarly traditions also constitutes some degree of a change in direction compared with prosopographic approaches that have been established for other contexts. In the contribution cited above, Magdalino suggested that

> prosopography is most useful in the study of societies where the number of recorded individuals is relatively modest, and where the records do not lend themselves to the construction of major biographies, or yield enough new information to make the rewriting of biographies a major imperative.[20]

[17] Paul Magdalino, 'Prosopography and Byzantine Identity', in Averil Cameron (ed.), *Fifty Years of Prosopography*.(Oxford: Oxford University Press, 2003), 56.

[18] See below.

[19] Magdalino, 'Prosopography', 43.

[20] Magdalino, 'Prosopography', 42.

Following this rationale, Vera von Falkenhausen has scrutinised the highly complex and fragmentary documentary and narrative sources on pre-modern southern Italy and Sicily to establish a prosopographical database of functionaries mentioned in Greek along with Arabic and Latin sources that allows the nuanced reconstruction of a cultural history of the administrative practices in these regions from Byzantine to Angevine rule.[21] In contrast, I suggest the deployment of prosopographical approaches to early Islamic history not as a response to a dearth of sources or a lack of 'master narratives'. Instead, I argue that prosopography establishes a methodicologically sound foundation for a systematic (and to some degree falsifiable) quest for specificity. This quest for specificity is especially important to a field such as early Islamic history, which is, as argued above, described in a vast corpus of internally contradictory narrative and administrative-epigraphic sources. Prosopographical engagement with the first three generations of Islamic history thereby presents an alternative to the frequently Orientalist and alterising frameworks based on selective and unsystematic engagements with the internally contested cultural memories of Muslim societies that continue to structure the academic field of early Islamic history.

## Literature

Due to the pragmatic (if potentially deceptive) straightforwardness of prosopography as a method, I will not offer an abstract discussion of prosopography from a methodological perspective. Instead, I will ground this section of my contribution in three dimensions: (1) prosopography as an emic epistemological paradigm in Arabic-Islamic scholarly traditions; (2) prosopographical approaches to early Islamic history in modern scholarship; and (3) some very pragmatic lessons learned during a prosopographical study of the Arab 'tribe' (*qabīla*) of Kinda during the first three generations of Islamic history.

[21] See the culmination of almost fifty years of prosopographical research presented by Vera von Falkenhausen, 'I funzionari greci nel regno normanno', in Maria Re and Cristina Rognoni (eds), *Giorgio di Antiochia. L'arte della politica in Sicilia nel XII secolo tra Bisanzio e l'Islam* (Palermo: Istituto Siciliano di studi Bizantini e Neoellenici 'Bruno Lavagnini', 2009), 165–202.

### *Prosopography as an Emic Epistemological Paradigm in Arabic-Islamic Scholarly Traditions*

It is difficult to overstate the importance of prosopography in the sense of 'a means of profiling any group of recorded persons linked by any common factor'[22] as one of the dominant epistemological paradigms of Arabic-Islamic scholarly traditions.[23] Apart from the genre of biographies dedicated to specific functional groups within the early Islamic empire,[24] this epistemological paradigm attained its most elaborate refinement in the study of transmitters of hadith or *muḥaddithūn*, which was crucial to the critical study of Muslim traditions. The scope of information that had to be established for each individual who was alleged to have participated in the transmission of hadith is succinctly indicated in the *Muqaddima* of Ibn al-Ṣalāḥ (d. 643/1245 CE), arguably the most influential handbook of hadith studies.

> All of the leading scholars of *ḥadīth* and Islamic normative traditions (*a'immat al-ḥadīth wa-l-fiqh*) agree that anybody who is quoted as a transmitter must be honest and precise in his narration. In particular, he[25] must be a Muslim adult of sound mind, free of any type of vice or blemish on his virtue (*murū'a*), alert and not simple-minded, of excellent memory, if he transmits from memory, and precise in his writing, if he transmits from writing.[26]

[22] Magdalino, 'Prosopography', 44.

[23] See the path-breaking reflection on the epistemology that subsequently gave rise to the genre of biographical dictionaries, Wadad al-Qadi, 'Biographical Dictionaries as the Scholars' Alternative History of the Muslim Community', in Gerhard Endress (ed.), *Organizing Knowledge: Encyclopaedic Activities in the Pre-Eighteenth Century Islamic World* (Leiden: Brill, 2006), 23–75.

[24] See, for instance, the collection of biographies of governors and judges of Egypt compiled by al-Kindī, *Kitāb al-Wulāt wa-l-Quḍāt*, ed. Rhuvon Guest (Cairo: Dār al-Kitāb al-Islāmī, n.d.), or the biographies of ministers and secretaries in al-Jahshiyārī, *Kitāb al-Wuzarā' wa-l-Kuttāb*, facsimile ed. Hans von Mžik (Leipzig: Harrassowitz, 1926). The influence of this genre is also visible within Arabic-Islamic historiography, see, for instance, the lists of incumbent functionaries given in particular detail by Khalīfa b. Khayyāṭ, *Ta'rīkh*, ed. Muṣṭafā Najīb Fawwāz and Ḥikmat Kashlī Fawwāz (Beirut: Dār al-Kutub al-ʿIlmiyya, 1995).

[25] The male gender of the transmitter follows the Arabic, which reflects the greater credibility attributed to male witnesses in Islamic normative discourses.

[26] Ibn al-Ṣalāḥ, *Muqaddima fī ʿUlūm al-Ḥadīth*, ed. Ismāʿīl Zarmān (Damascus: Mu'assasat al-Risāla, 2013), 68. Cf. the extensive literature on the assessment of these qualities produced within the discursive tradition of 'Islamic law' (*fiqh*).

Specific categories of biographical data necessary for this critical assessment of transmitters of any given hadith include the intricate science of multi-component Arabic-Islamic names,[27] the lifespan of the transmitters,[28] as well as the countries of origin and residence of the transmitters,[29] and such specific information as transmitters whose memory deteriorated during the end of their life.[30] This wide range of information crucial for the critical evaluation of the soundness of Islamic tradition is reflected in the flourishing genre of biographical dictionaries or *Ṭabaqāt*, which arranged brief biographical sketches of thousands of individuals according to generation, place of residence, and genealogical affiliation.[31] The geographical–genealogical framework that structured the genre of *Ṭabaqāt* also manifested itself in the central and provincial administration of the *dīwān* or army registers,[32] which supposedly regulated the interpersonal networks of patronage and military mobilisation in early Muslim society. This epistemic paradigm also gave rise to the impressive synthetic scholarly productions of *Ansāb* or genealogical compilations structured according to descent[33] and dictated the regular inclusion of the *nasab* or patrilineal line of descent and a *nisba* or 'tribal' affiliation as two of the standard components of names recorded for

[27] Ibn al-Ṣalāḥ, *Muqaddima*, 195–231.

[28] Ibn al-Ṣalāḥ, *Muqaddima*, 232–5.

[29] Ibn al-Ṣalāḥ, *Muqaddima*, 245–7.

[30] Ibn al-Ṣalāḥ, *Muqaddima*, 238–40.

[31] The most influential early exponent of this genre is the biographical dictionary of Ibn Saʿd, *Kitāb al-Ṭabaqāt al-Kubrā*, ed. Muḥammad ʿAbdalqādir ʿAṭā (Beirut: Dār al-Kutub al-ʿIlmiyya, 2012). See also the more succinct early biographical dictionary of Khalīfa b. Khayyāṭ, *Kitāb al-Ṭabaqāt*, ed. Suhayl Zakkār (Beirut: Dār al-Fikr, 1993).

[32] See the classical study by Gerd-Rüdiger Puin, *Der Dīwān von ʿUmar ibn al-Ḫaṭṭāb. Ein Beitrag zur frühislamischen Verwaltungsgeschichte* (Bonn: Dissertationsschrift, 1970).

[33] Likely the most influential synthetic formulation of the genealogies of the Arabs is the monumental *Jamharat al-Nasab* of Ibn al-Kalbī, which is conveniently accessible in Werner Caskel and Gert Strenziok, *Ǧamharat al-Nasab. Das genealogische Werk des Hišām Ibn Muḥammad al-Kalbī* (Leiden: Brill, 1966). See also the even more comprehensive, if unfinished, presentation of (Islamic) history according to a genealogical framework al-Balādhurī, *Ansāb al-ʿArab*, ed. Muḥammad Muḥammad Tāmir (Beirut: Dār al-Kutub al-ʿIlmiyya, 2011).

individuals during the early Islamic period.[34] Due to the pervasive influence of these traditionarian and genealogical frameworks across a multitude of literary genres, prosopography should be understood as one of the dominant epistemological paradigms within Arabic-Islamic scholarly traditions.

### *A Brief Survey of Prosopographical Approaches to Early Islamic History in Modern Scholarship*

Due to the importance of emic prosopographical epistemological frameworks in Arabic-Islamic scholarly traditions, some sort of prosopographic or group-related categories arguably can be found in most modern scholarly approaches to early Islamic (social) history. Accordingly, I will focus this survey around a limited number of contributions that exemplify some of the most influential modes in which prosopographical approaches have been deployed in the reconstruction and interpretation of the formative period of Islam.

As the first mode of prosopographical engagement with early Islamic history prominently represented in modern scholarship, the synthetic analysis of the involvement of different 'tribally' formulated interpersonal networks in the early Islamic conquests,[35] as well as in the post-conquest Arab settlement in specific regions should be noted.[36] Although most of these studies are focused on a regional basis, Fred M. Donner in particular suggested a 'global' reconstruction of the early Islamic conquests by means of prosopographic study of the different regional scenes.[37] The second mode of prosopographical

[34] The importance of the *nisba*s affiliated to the tribal framework of the Arab 'tribe' of Kinda for the prosopographical examples presented in this chapter will be discussed below. The best introduction to the structure and realisation of Islamic onomastics is Annemarie Schimmel, *Islamic Names* (Edinburgh: Edinburgh University Press, 1989).

[35] This line of research was pioneered by Fred M. Donner, 'The Arab Tribes in the Muslim Conquest of Iraq', unpublished dissertation, Ann Arbor, 1975.

[36] See for Egypt the study of ʿAbdallah Khurshīd al-Barrī, *al-Qabāʾil al-ʿArabiyya fī Miṣr fī l-Qurūn al-Thalātha al-Ūlā li-l-Hijra* (Cairo: al-Hayʾa al-Miṣriyya al-ʿĀmma li-l-Kitāb, 1992), and for the post-conquest settlement in northern Syria Claus-Peter Haase, *Untersuchungen zur Landschaftsgeschichte Nordsyriens in der Umayyadenzeit* (Hamburg: Dissertationsschrift, 1972).

[37] Fred M. Donner, *The Early Islamic Conquests* (Princeton, NJ: Princeton University Press, 1981). It should be noted that this global reconstruction is methodologically less ambitious compared with his earlier work on the Muslim conquest of Iraq.

engagement with early Islamic history is represented in the exemplary study of individual 'tribal' networks (*qabīla*) within early Arabic-Islamic society. Likely the most ambitious project within this mode is represented by Michael Lecker's work on the Banū Sulaym.[38] A methodologically somewhat less rigorous reconstruction of the interpersonal networks of Azd across a longer historical period has recently been put forward by Brian Ulrich.[39] The study by the present author that will be discussed in greater detail below also represents a contribution to this mode of prosopographical work.[40]

The two other modes of prosopographical engagement with early Islamic history in modern scholarship are somewhat less rigorous in their geographic or 'tribal' focus. First is the study of early Muslim society within a social framework revolving around 'classes' in a loosely Marxist sense. A prosopographical underpinning to the study of the 'ruling classes' was pioneered by Patricia Crone, who suggested the social category of *ashrāf* or notables as a functional emic counterpart.[41] A number of studies have taken up this approach to focus more closely on individual lineages that were transgenerationally influential during the formative period of Islam.[42] Finally, prosopographical approaches have also been deployed to reconstruct the mechanisms of social dependency

[38] Michael Lecker, *The Banū Sulaym: A Contribution to the Study of Early Islam* (Jerusalem: Hebrew University Press, 1989). See also his subsequent work on various networks and individuals situated within the genealogically formulated structure of early Islamic society.

[39] Brian Ulrich, *Arabs in the Early Islamic Empire: Exploring al-Azd Tribal Identity* (Edinburgh: Edinburgh University Press, 2019). See the review of this work by Georg Leube, *Der Islam* 97(1) (2019): 292–6.

[40] Georg Leube, *Kinda in der frühislamischen Geschichte. Eine prosopographische Studie auf Basis der frühen und klassischen arabisch-islamischen Geschichtsschreibung* (Baden-Baden: Ergon, 2017).

[41] See in particular the monumental appendices in Crone, *Slaves*, 93–200.

[42] To quote but some recent examples of this important line of research, see Asad Q. Ahmed, *The Religious Elite of the Early Islamic Ḥijāz: Five Prosopographical Case Studies* (Oxford: Prosopographica et Genealogica, 2011); Teresa Bernheimer, *The 'Alids: The First Family of Islam, 750–1200* (Edinburgh: Edinburgh University Press, 2013); as well as Harry Munt, 'Caliphal Imperialism and Ḥijāzī Elites in the Second/Eighth century', *al-Masāq* 28 (2016): 6–21.

and administration in the early Islamic empire, as exemplified in the magisterial study of Eva Orthmann.[43]

*Some Pragmatic 'Lessons Learned'*

Before proceeding with the discussion of two examples of how methodologically grounded prosopography can contribute to the development of alternative frameworks for early Islamic history, I now list a number of 'lessons learned' while systematically reading some 20,000 pages of early and classical Arabic-Islamic historiography and noting every individual and group affiliated to the Arab 'tribe' (*qabīla*) of Kinda. This prosopographical database was then supplemented by the review of the remaining Arabic-Islamic historiographical and history-related literature pertaining to events of the first three generations of Islamic history, including all sources composed by eponymous scholars who died earlier than around the year 350 AH. While the format of succinct 'lessons learned' may be somewhat uncommon,[44] I hope the following suggestions will facilitate prosopographical work by future scholars.

Establishing a Corpus of Sources

The delimitation and establishment of a corpus of sources that is systematically reviewed has a significant influence on the result of prosopographical engagement with early Islamic history. Therefore, the definition of the corpus from which examples are systematically drawn should be transparent and unambiguous.

1. To establish a corpus of Arabic narrative sources, Carl Brockelmann, *Geschichte der arabischen Literatur*,[45] Fuat Sezgin, *Geschichte des ara-*

[43] Eva Orthmann, *Stamm und Macht: Die arabischen Stämme im 2. und 3. Jahrhundert der Hiǧra* (Wiesbaden: Reichert, 2002). See also the careful reconstruction of social mechanisms of dependency and administration within the province of Egypt by Kosei Morimoto, 'The Dīwāns as Registers of the Arab Stipendiaries in Early Islamic Egypt', in R.Curiel and R. Gyselen (eds), *Itinéraires d'Orient: Hommages à Claude Cahen* (Bures-sur-Yvette: Peeters, 1994), 353–65.

[44] But see the influential and – at least to the present author – extremely helpful 'practical' guidelines for scholarly engagement with Islamic history suggested by R. Stephen Humphreys, *Islamic History: A Framework for Inquiry* (London: I. B. Tauris, 1995).

[45] Carl Brockelmann, *Geschichte der arabischen Literatur* (Leiden: Brill, 1937–49).

*bischen Schrifttums*,[46] and Georg Graf, *Geschichte der christlichen arabischen Literatur*[47] present a suitable (if somewhat dated) overview over extant works sorted according to their respective authors or compilers.

2. The information contained in later compilations may differ substantially from the content of early and classical Arabic-Islamic historiography.[48] Accordingly, the corpora chosen for prosopographical research should include multiple sources compiled during any given period to allow for a meaningful contextualisation of reports within their contemporary intertextual context.

3. A cursory presentation of non-Arabic narrative sources on early Islamic history is presented by Robert G. Hoyland, *Seeing Islam as Others Saw It*.[49] Nonetheless, the omission of detail (including the majority of names) in Hoyland's paraphrasis means that the originals must always be consulted.

4. The most accessible corpus of diplomatic sources is the Arabic Papyrology Online Database at LMU, Munich.[50] A comprehensive introduction to this material is given by Lennart Sundelin.[51]

5. An evolving online database of Islamic epigraphy is the *Thesaurus d'Epigraphie Islamique* of the Fondation Max van Berchem.[52] Numerous additional *graffitti* and *dipinti*, particularly from the Arabian Peninsula, are currently being edited by scholars such as Ilkka Lindstedt.

46 Fuat Sezgin, *Geschichte des arabischen Schrifttums* (Leiden: Brill, 1967–2015).

47 Georg Graf, *Geschichte der christlichen arabischen Literatur* (Rome: Biblioteca Apostolica Vaticana, 1947–66).

48 See, for instance, the presentation of al-Ashʿath b. Qays in the twelfth-century CE compilation of Ibn ʿAsākir, *Taʾrīkh Madīnat Dimashq*, ed. Muḥibb al-Dīn Abū Saʿīd ʿUmar b. Gharāma al-ʿAmrawī (Beirut: Dār al-Fikr, 1995), 9, 116–45. The occasions when particular Qurʾānic verses were revealed (*asbāb al-nuzūl*) that constitute one of the main topics of Ibn ʿAsākir's compilation of biographical information for al-Ashʿath b. Qays in particular do not (to the best of my knowledge) have a parallel in early and classical Arabic-Islamic historiography whose eponymous compilators died before 350 AH.

49 Robert G. Hoyland, *Seeing Islam as Others Saw It* (Princeton, NJ: Darwin Press, 1997).

50 See at: http://www.apd.gwi.uni-muenchen.de:8080/apd/project.jsp. I am indebted to Dr Daniel Potthast for bringing this database to my attention.

51 Lennart Sundelin, 'Introduction: Papyrology and the Study of Early Islamic Egypt', in Petra M. Sijpesteijn and Lennart Sundelin (eds), *Papyrology and the History of Early Islamic Egypt* (Leiden, Brill, 2004), 1–19.

52 See at: http://www.epigraphie-islamique.uliege.be/thesaurus.

6. The numismatic evidence most conducive to prosopographic analysis is represented by Arabic and Pahlawī legends on so-called Arabo-Sasanian coinage. Although this material continues to be debated, a readily accessible overview is given by Heinz Gaube.[53]

## Identifying Names and Variants

As prosopography commonly departs from the names of individuals and groups, an awareness of (a typology of) variants both in editions and manuscripts is crucial.

1. The affiliation to an Arabic 'tribe' (*qabīla*) expressed in the onomastic element indicating 'tribal' affiliation or *nisba* constitutes a relatively stable and unambiguous criterion for the systematic establishment of a prosopographic database.[54]

2. The diacritical dots (*nuqaṭ*) tend to be more susceptible to variation compared with the undotted shapes of the letters (*rasm*).[55]

3. Uncommon *nisba*s are frequently misread.[56]

4. Depending on the positionality of the author/compilator, the *nisba*s used to identify individuals and groups may pertain to more inclusive or more specific levels of 'tribal' affiliation.[57]

[53] Heinz Gaube, *Arabosasanidische Numismatik* (Braunschweig: Klinkhardt und Biermann, 1973).

[54] See Leube, *Kinda*, 177–89, and the succinct review of the topic in Georg Leube, 'Insult the Caliph, Marry al-Ḥasan, and Redeem Your Kingdom: Freiheitsgrade of Kindī Elites During the 7th to 9th Century', in Hannah-Lena Hagemann and Stefan Heidemann (eds), *Transregional and Regional Elites – Connecting the Early Islamic Empire, Vol. 1: The Early Islamic Empire at Work* (Berlin: De Gruyter, 2020), 49–51.

[55] Cf. the consistent spelling of Muʿāwiya b. Ḥudayj as Muʿāwiya b. Khudayj in al-Masʿūdī, *Murūj al-Dhahab*, ed. Mufīd Muḥammad Qamīḥa (Beirut, Dār al-Kutub al-ʿIlmiyya, 1985), e.g., 2, 454, as well as in al-Kindī, *Kitāb al-Quḍāt*, ed. Richard J. H. Gottheil (Paris: Geuthner, 1908), e.g., 21.

[56] Cf. the consistent (mis)rendering of the (not so uncommon) *nisba* al-Ḥasanī for the descendants of Shuraḥbīl b. Ḥasana as al-Ḥusaynī in al-Kindī, *Quḍāt*, ed. Gottheil, e.g., 23.

[57] Cf. the recurring identification of individuals commonly affiliated to the overarching level of Kinda by the *nisba* al-Kindī in historiographical compilations of 'global' Islamic history as compared with their more specific affiliation to the Kindī 'sub-tribe' of Tujīb with the *nisba* al-Tujībī, for instance, in the compilation of the Egyptian scholar Ibn ʿAbdalḥakam, *Futūḥ Miṣr wa-l-Maghrib*, ed. ʿAlī Muḥammad ʿUmar (Cairo: Maktabat al-Thaqāfa al-Dīniyya, 2004). This likely reflects the prominence of Tujīb in early Islamic Egypt, cf. the general discussion of this phenomenon of greater or lesser specificity of *nisba*s in Richard W. Bulliett, *Conversion to Islam in the Medieval Period: An Essay in Quantitative History* (Cambridge, MA: Harvard University Press, 1979), 12.

5. Idiosyncratic or uncommon forms are frequently normalised.[58]

6. The widespread editorial practice of collating the manuscripts with quotations of the text contained in other works may normalise the names of individuals given in the resulting edition.[59]

## Interpreting Data

1. Notwithstanding the pervasive influence of particular genealogical systematisations and paradigms, alternative genealogical frameworks may be attested.[60]

2. Due to the encyclopaedic learning of Arabic-Islamic scholars, the fullest versions of information quoted more elliptically in historiographical works may frequently be found in compilations pertaining to other literary genres.[61]

[58] Cf. the 'normalized' spelling of the toponym *Dūmat al-Jandal* in the edited text of al-Wāqidī, *Kitāb al-Maghāzī*, ed. Muḥammad ʿAbdalqādir Aḥmad ʿAṭā (Beirut: Dār al-Kutub al-ʿIlmiyya, 2004), 2, 405, *pace* the indication of Yāqūt, *Muʿjam al-Buldān*, ed. Muḥammad ʿAbdarraḥmān al-Marʿashlī (Beirut: Dār Iḥyāʾ al-Turāth al-ʿArabī, 2008), 3/4, 325, that al-Wāqidī had transmitted *Dūmāʾ al-Jandal* as the correct form.

[59] Cf. the naming of a traitor affiliated to Kinda in Abū Mikhnaf, *Maqtal al-Imām al-Ḥusayn b. ʿAlī*, ed. Kāmil Salmān al-Jabūrī (Beirut: Dār al-Majalla al-Bayḍāʾ, 2000), 73, compared with the omission of the name in the translation based on a manuscript, Ferdinand Wüstenfeld, *Der Tod des Ḥusein ben ʾAlí und die Rache* (Göttingen: Dieterich, 1883), 38–40. The likely source in this case is the quotation attributed to Abū Mikhnaf in al-Iṣfahānī, *Maqātil al-Ṭālibiyyīn*, ed. Al-Sayyid Aḥmad Ṣaqr (Cairo: Dār Iḥyāʾ al-Kutub al-ʿArabiyya, n.d.), 103–5; cf. the programmatic argument for editorial collation made by the editor in his preface, Abū Mikhnaf, *Maqtal*, ed. al-Jabūrī, 35.

[60] See, for instance, the incompatibility of the genealogical framing of the offspring of a pre-Islamic Meccan *ḥalīf* or client of Quraysh known collectively as the Banū l-Ḥaḍramī suggested in al-Hamdānī, *Kitāb al-Iklīl*, ed. Muḥammad b. ʿAlī b. al-Ḥusayn al-Akwaʿ al-Ḥawālī (Beirut: Manshūrāt al-Madīna, 1986), 2, 54–61, as compared with the dominant genealogical paradigm upheld by the 'mainstream' tradition clustered around Ibn al-Kalbī, see Leube, *Kinda*, 38.

[61] See, for instance, the most extensive version of the different paradigms of *Herrschaftswissen* cited by Ibn al-Ashʿath, which is contained in the zoographical anthology al-Jāḥiẓ, *Kitāb al-Ḥayawān*, ed. Muḥammad Bāsil ʿUyūn al-Sūd (Beirut: Dār al-Kutub al-ʿIlmiyya, 2011), 5/6, 108.

3. Within extended families, the affiliation to the most prominent 'genealogical point of reference' is more important than the exact degree of kinship.[62]

4. Outside of prominent genealogical lineages, the affiliation of individuals to multiple genealogically formulated networks may be disputed. This is particularly true for those framed as 'villains' within the cultural memory of Muslim societies.[63] Pragmatically, it may be advisable to include doubtful cases in prosopographical analysis.

5. Similarly, the inclusion of larger genealogically formulated entities as 'sub-tribes' in one of the overarching 'tribal' formations may be disputed.[64] For these cases, a consistent and pragmatic in- or exclusion should be maintained in establishing prosopographical databases.

Cutting a Corner

1. A useful and accessible prosopographical database firmly rooted within Arabic-Islamic scholarly traditions is presented in the alphabetically organised second volume of the monumental reshuffling of Ibn al-Kalbī's *Jamharat al-Nasab* by Werner Caskel and Gert Strenziok.[65]

## Discussion

In this section of the present chapter, I will illustrate the possible impact of systematic prosopographical inquiry to overarching questions concerning the

[62] See the alternating affiliation of ʿUfayyif as an uncle or cousin to the prominent Kindī notable and 'genealogical point of reference' al-Ashʿath b. Qays, Leube, *Kinda*, 37–8. Cf. the perceptive remarks on the epistemological function of the eponymous founder of dynastic dispensations, John E. Woods, *The Aqquyunlu: Clan, Confederation, Empire* (Salt Lake City: University of Utah Press, 1999), 20–3.

[63] See the detailed reconstruction of the multiple affiliations proposed for those killers of the caliphs ʿUthmān and ʿAlī whose proposed affiliation includes some suggestion of having been affiliated to Kinda, Leube, 'Freiheitsgrade', 49–51, cf. Leube, *Kinda*, 180–5.

[64] See, for instance, the debated inclusion of al-Ṣadif within Kinda, Leube, *Kinda*, 186–9.

[65] Caskel and Strenziok, *Ǧamharat*, vol. 2.

history and memory of the formative period of Islam with two examples. As the impact of the sources outside the narrative texts of Arabic-Islamic scholarly traditions within the prosopographical database of Kinda during the first three generations of Islam is limited,[66] both examples use prosopography to propose innovative interpretations of the corpus of Arabic-Islamic narrative sources. Arguably, the primary impact of systematic analysis of the entire corpus of references to a specific 'tribal' entity such as Kinda lies in the relational reconstruction of the structure and function of this type of social affiliation.[67] This enables the systematic revision of the positivist suggestions of Arabic-Islamic scholars concerning Arab 'tribes', as well as the concepts used in modern scholarship, which are commonly based on a combination of contemporary anthropology with the emic views of 'tribal' affiliation in Arabic-Islamic scholarly traditions.

Nonetheless, the two examples chosen for this chapter transcend the question of reconstructing the shape and function of an Arab 'tribe' in early Islamic history. Instead, I follow the adaptation of the hermeneutics of Paul Ricoeur to early and classical Arabic-Islamic historiography proposed by Matthias Vogt to present one prosopographically grounded case study that analyses historiography in its 'referential' function of describing the history of events during the formative period of Islam.[68] In this example, I critically review the degree of centralisation during the early Islamic conquests based on the systematically established prosopographical database of Kinda. My second example demonstrates the possible impact of prosopographically grounded inquiry on the reconstruction and conceptualisation of the 'narrative' (or, in Vogt's terminology, 'fictional') dimension of historiography as a *mise en intrigue* of communal

[66] The notable exception is the independent corroboration of the apocalyptic iconography of the revolt of Ibn al-Ashʿath, for example, in al-Maqdisī, *Kitāb al-Badʾ wa-l-Taʾrīkh*, no editor given (Cairo: Maktabat al-Thaqāfa al-Dīniyya, n.d.), 2, 183–4, and 5, 35; as well as in al-Masʿūdī, *Kitāb al-Tanbīh*, ed. Michael J. de Goeje (Leiden: Brill, 1894), 314, in the numismatic legends on coins minted during his revolt. See Gaube, *Numismatik*, 32, 36 and 52, cf. Leube, *Kinda*, 211–20.

[67] The results of this systematic review of the prosopography of Kinda are presented in Leube, *Kinda*, 177–96.

[68] See Matthias Vogt, *Figures de califes entre histoire et fiction: al-Walīd b. Yazīd et al-Amīn dans la représentation de l'historiographie arabe de l'époque abbaside* (Würzburg: Ergon, 2006), 30.

memory. Thereby, I argue that systematic prosopographical inquiry suggests an alternative model for the processes of transmission that shaped the extant (narrative) sources, highlighting discursive practices that may have involved multiple groups within Muslim society that are systematically marginalised by the normativities underpinning the established modelling of the process of transmission as *isnād-cum-matn*. I conclude both examples with a brief reflection on the function and impact of prosopographical method on the respective case study from an epistemological perspective.

### *Kinda and the Centralisation of the Early Islamic Conquests*

It is difficult to overstate the significance of the degree of central leadership and authority during the initial conquests to the general framing of Islam. For the sake of brevity, I focus the following argument around an influential article by Fred M. Donner, which includes a succinct review over the debate.[69] Building on this review of the scholarly literature, Donner posits an exemplary typology of possible degrees of centralisation, which ranges from 'I. No centralisation is found on the conceptual, strategic, or tactical levels,' to 'IV. Centralization is found on all levels – conceptual, strategic, and tactical.'[70] Within this spectrum, one of the possible interpretations would see the conquests motivated by Islam and centrally coordinated by a Ḥijāzī Muslim elite personally bound to Muḥammad.[71] The personal talent and internal loyalty of this Ḥijāzī Muslim elite was in this view decisive in facilitating the political expansion of the Islamic realms. This interpretation also resonates well

[69] Fred M. Donner, 'Centralized Authority and Military Autonomy in the Early Islamic Conquests', in Averil Cameron (ed.), *The Byzantine and Early Islamic Near East III: States, Resources and Armies* (Princeton, NJ: Darwin Press, 1995), 340–6. The importance of this article is underlined by its inclusion in Donner's own selection of canonical contributions engaging with the history of the early Islamic conquests, Fred M. Donner (ed.), *The Expansion of the Early Islamic State* (Aldershot: Ashgate Variorum, 2008), 263–86.

[70] Donner, 'Centralized Authority', 340. Note Donner's caveat that these typologies should be seen as designating different points on a continuous 'broad spectrum of degrees of centralization', Donner, 'Centralized Authority', 338.

[71] Donner, 'Centralized Authority', 358–9. Note that much of the highly influential work of Fred M. Donner ultimately turns on similar arguments, see, for instance, Donner, *Tribes*, *passim*, and Donner, *Conquests*, *passim*.

with the 'salvational' interpretation of the early Islamic conquests in Muslim cultural memory, which sees the success of the military campaigns as a preordained divine miracle attesting to the truth of Islam.[72]

The extreme formulation of an opposing position would by contrast suggest that the weakness of the Byzantine and Sassanian empires enabled autonomous takings of power by Arab groups in various regions. These were then consolidated over the course of the seventh century CE by Islam as an ideology of Arabness whose origin was counterfactually retrojected to a period preceding the expansion of the sphere of Arab dominance.[73] This interpretation accordingly limits the significance of Islam as a 'centralising' force during the conquests. Building on a discussion of what he terms 'Problems of Strategic and Operational Centralization',[74] Donner concludes his article with the suggestion that 'the traditional view that the conquests displayed both conceptual and strategic–operational centralization or unity retains an explanatory power superior to revisionist alternatives'.[75]

Approaching Donner's argument from a prosopographical perspective, one should first note the suggestion that 'the conquests' in their entirety were more or less centrally directed as problematic. If we follow the methodological suggestion made in the introduction to this chapter that agency should be localised exclusively in individual actors acting from within specific configurations, we should instead proceed from a framework that allows for the intersecting agency of multiple individual actors who may have been motivated by differing degrees of loyalty to the early Islamic centre of Medina. Before following this conceptual critique of the interpretative

[72] See, for instance, the succinct prophecy attributed to Muḥammad during the battle of the Trench (*waqʿat al-khandaq*), which predicted the expansion of the Islamic realms across much of the Near and Middle East, for instance in al-Wāqidī, *al-Maghāzī*, 1, 385–6. A similar prophecy to the delegation of Kinda to Muḥammad is mentioned by al-Hamdānī, *al-Iklīl*, 1, 66.

[73] Donner, 'Centralized Authority', 344–5. See the provocative exploration of this line of interpretation by Moshe Sharon, 'The Birth of Islam in the Holy Land', in Moshe Sharon (ed.), *The Holy Land in History and Thought* (Leiden: Brill, 1988), 225–35.

[74] Donner, 'Centralized Authority', 346–59.

[75] Donner, 'Centralized Authority', 359.

framework of the conquests suggested by Donner, however, we will first check his argument as it is presented against the prosopographical database of Kinda.

In his discussion of the 'centralising bias' in Arabic-Islamic cultural memory of the conquests, Donner underlines the importance of the singularity of the independent agency defying caliphal authority attributed in some reports to ʿAmr b. al-ʿĀṣ during the conquest of Egypt as follows:

> Is it not misleading to generalize from this one example of military autonomy – assuming that it is an example? For we find reports of such independence or defiance of Caliphal authority for no other commander of the early conquest period on any other front – and there were many of them.[76]

Contrary to Donner's suggestion that ʿAmr represents a singular case, however, a parallel example is indeed contained in the prosopographical database that systematically compiles all mentions of individuals and groups affiliated to Kinda during the first three generations of Islamic history. This is the case of al-ʿAlāʾ b. al-Ḥaḍramī, the son of a pre-Islamic south Arabian client of Quraysh,[77] who is described as having defied ʿUmar's orders in embarking upon independent military expeditions:

> [The first caliph] Abū Bakr had appointed him [al-ʿAlāʾ b. al-Ḥaḍramī], authorizing him to fight the apostates (*ahl al-ridda*). [The second caliph] ʿUmar also appointed him, but forbade him from engaging in any naval expeditions (*nahāhu mina l-baḥr*). [. . . Nonetheless, al-ʿAlāʾ mobilized troops to raid the region of Fāris[78] in southern Iran]. Thus, he [al-ʿAlāʾ] sent them out over sea to Fāris without ʿUmar's permission, as ʿUmar had never allowed anybody to raid over sea. For ʿUmar disliked the risk to his army [posed by embarking on ships], following the example of the prophet, God bless him and grant him peace!, and Abū Bakr. For neither the prophet, God bless him and grant

[76] Donner, 'Centralized Authority', 348.

[77] See the discussion of the different genealogical affiliations proposed for this family in Leube, *Kinda*, 182–3.

[78] I vocalise according to Yāqūb, *Muʿjam*, 5/6, 407, *pace* the current vocalisation as Fārs in modern Persian.

him peace!, nor Abū Bakr had raided over sea. [The naval expedition ends in disaster and causes ʿUmar to relieve al-ʿAlāʾ from his post.][79]

As a first result of this deployment of the prosopographical database of Kinda to check the validity of Donner's argument, one should accordingly resume the systematic evaluation of the extensive corpus of early and classical Arabic-Islamic scholarly compilations to search for further instances where explicit orders of the caliph(s) are claimed to have been disobeyed.[80]

On a more fundamental level, however, the systematically compiled prosopographical database of Kinda enables the exemplary review of the different positionalities and 'degrees of centralisation' exhibited by the (limited) group of notables affiliated to Kinda. This in turn allows the suggestion of an exemplary typology of how different individual (Kindī) actors involved in the early Islamic conquests may have related to the Islamic 'centre' of Medina.

When evaluated systematically, the prosopographical database of individuals and groups affiliated to Kinda suggests a consistent correlation between an 'Islamic' legitimation of individual notables (early conversion to Islam and close ties to Muḥammad and the Ḥijāzī elites) and leadership over troops that are not mobilised according to interpersonal networks formulated in a terminology of shared 'tribal' descent (i.e., troops presumably mobilised along a shared affiliation to Islam and the Islamic centre). This first type of Kinda-affiliated leaders during the early Islamic conquests legitimated predominantly due to their supra-'tribal' affiliation to the Islamic centre includes the descendants of pre-Islamic clients of Quraysh, such

[79] al-Ṭabarī, *Taʾrīkh*, 2, 581. Al-ʿAlāʾ's engagement in raiding over sea is also mentioned in al-Balādhurī, *Futūḥ al-Buldān*, ed. Ayman Muḥammad ʿArafa (Cairo: Al-Maktaba al-Tawfīqiyya, n.d.), 428; and Ibn Saʿd, *Ṭabaqāt*, 4, 267. It should be noted, however, that ʿUmar's explicit interdiction is not mentioned in either of these compilations. By contrast, the disastrous end of al-ʿAlāʾ's naval expedition is referenced in a different context by al-Ṭabarī, *Taʾrīkh*, 2, 605, 638 and 691.

[80] A comparable example may be constituted by the naval raiding on Cyprus ascribed to the future caliph Muʿāwiya b. Abī Sufyān, however. I have not systematically noted all mentions of this expedition in the sources due to the systematic focus of my prosopographical work around individuals and groups affiliated to Kinda.

as the already-mentioned al-ʿAlāʾ b. al-Ḥaḍramī, Shuraḥbīl b. Ḥasana, or al-Miqdād b. ʿAmr/al-Aswad.[81]

By contrast, a second type of Kindī mobilisers during the early Islamic conquests is not described as being particularly close to Muḥammad (some were even prominently involved in the anti-Islamic wars of the *ridda*).[82] By contrast, these individuals are usually described as leading troops that are presented as having been mobilised predominantly due to a shared 'Kindī' affiliation. This type of Kindī notables includes figures such as al-Ashʿath b. Qays and Ḥujr b. ʿAdī during the conquest of ʿIrāq, Muʿāwiya b. Ḥudayj during the conquest of Egypt, and al-Simṭ b. al-Aswad during the conquest of Syria. The extent of independent agency displayed by these 'less centrally legitimated' mobilisers is exemplified in one of the accounts of post-conquest settlement in the Syrian town of Ḥimṣ/Emesa transmitted by al-Balādhurī:

> Some traditionaries suggest that al-Simṭ b. al-Aswad al-Kindī granted a treaty to the inhabitants of Ḥimṣ. When [the 'centrally' appointed leader of the conquests in Syria] Abū ʿUbayda arrived, he affirmed this treaty. They further suggest that al-Simṭ distributed the quarters of Ḥimṣ between the Muslims, so they might settle there. He settled them in every abandoned house, whose inhabitants had fled, as well as in empty lots.[83]

Significantly, al-Simṭ b. al-Aswad is not mentioned to have derived his authority from an appointment by one of the Muslim caliphs or another member of the 'centrally legitimated' Ḥijāzī elites. Within the systematically evaluated corpus of sources, there also exists no indication that al-Simṭ's presence in Syria was influenced by any type of 'central' strategic coordination of the conquests. Although this certainly represents an *argumentum ex negativo*, the parallel cases of Muʿāwiya b. Ḥudayj and Ḥujr b. ʿAdī, who similarly

[81] See for al-ʿAlāʾ b. al-Ḥaḍramī and his relatives Leube, *Kinda*, 38–40, for Shuraḥbīl b. Ḥasana Leube, *Kinda*, 40–1, and for al-Miqdād Leube, *Kinda*, 182–3.

[82] See for the narrative-dogmatic repercussions of the prominent involvement of al-Ashʿath b. Qays in the *ridda* Georg Leube, 'Obliterating Leadership? The Contested Excommunication of al-Ashʿath b. Qays in Early and Classical Arabic-Islamic Historiography', SI *al-Masaq*, 'Acts of Excommunication in the Late Antique and Early Islamic Middle East', ed. Ed Hayes, forthcoming.

[83] al-Balādhurī, *Futūḥ*, 170. Cf. the parallel account al-Balādhurī, *Futūḥ*, 177.

show up in Egypt and ʿIrāq, respectively, without any suggestion of having been sent there by central Islamic authorities, suggest the existence a second and 'less centrally motivated' type of Kindī mobilisers that were involved in the early Islamic conquests. As exemplified by the trajectories of the families of Shuraḥbīl b. Ḥasana and Muʿāwiya b. Ḥudayj in Egypt, this typological opposition converged in subsequent generations.[84]

Building on the suggestion of localising agency exclusively in individual actors rooted in specific configurations, the systematically compiled prosopographical database of Kinda accordingly suggests that Donner's modelling of the early Islamic conquests should be nuanced by the inclusion of at least two different types of mobilisers. The first type drew on an 'Islamic' legitimacy to lead troops not primarily mobilised due to an affiliation to Kinda shared by the troops and their leader. This group of Kindī notables presumably would have been integrated more closely with the Ḥijāzī elites focused on the early Islamic political centre of Medina during the strategic–operational centralisation of the conquests postulated by Donner. By contrast, the second type of Kindī notables were not remembered as having been particularly close to Muḥammad (or, for that matter, as particularly exemplary Muslims),[85] and mobilised significant bodies of troops that are described as affiliated to Kinda. The degree to which this second group was integrated in a centrally coordinated direction of the conquests would by contrast have to be discussed for each case individually.[86]

This second result derived from checking Donner's evaluation of the centralisation of the early Islamic conquests against the prosopographical database of Kinda suggests a conceptual elaboration of Donner's model. As in the preceding case of al-ʿAlāʾ's alleged disobedience of caliphal orders, this

[84] See Leube, 'Freiheitsgrade', 54–8.

[85] See, for instance, the allegation that horses and camels were sacrificed during the burial of al-Ashʿath b. Qays, al-Thaʿālibī, *Laṭāʾif al-Maʿārif*, eds Ibrāhīm al-Abyārī and Ḥasan Kāmil al-Ṣayrafī (Cairo: ʿĪsā al-Bābī al-Ḥalabī, 1960), 17.

[86] See for the dynamic processes of negotiation structuring the integration of transregionally mobile groups in centrally directed Islamic state-formations in later periods the study by Kurt Franz, *Vom Beutezug zur Territorialherrschaft. Das lange Jahrhundert des Aufstiegs von Nomaden zur Vormacht in Syrien und Mesopotamien 286 bis 420/889 bis 1029* (Wiesbaden: Reichert, 2007).

hypothesis is grounded in the systematic review of all individuals and groups affiliated to Kinda during the early Islamic conquests in early and classical Arabic-Islamic historiography and, accordingly, will in turn have to be discussed for other systematically established sets of (prosopographical) data.

*Recurring Patterns in the Narrative Depiction of Kinda*

In the preceding passage, we have methodically evaluated the systematically compiled prosopographical database of Kinda for examples of disobedience to explicit caliphal orders and suggested that a typology of mobilisers during the early Islamic conquests may allow for individuals affiliated more or less closely to the Islamic 'centre' of Medina. In both cases, we have approached the sources of Arabic-Islamic scholarly traditions as referential texts describing purported events. Somewhat surprisingly, however, the importance of systematical, corpus-based prosopographical research to the 'narrativity' of early and classical Arabic-Islamic historiography of the formative period of Islam may be even greater than its impact on the reconstruction of a history of events.

As indicated above, the prosopographical database of individuals and groups affiliated to Kinda systematically compiles all mentions pertaining to the first three generations of Islamic history, which is roughly equivalent to the seventh century CE. Within this timeframe, the prosopographical database contains reports pertaining to a variety of different episodes and topics of Muslim cultural memory due to the involvement of at least one individual affiliated to Kinda in the episode in question. Accordingly, the systematically established prosopographical database of individuals and groups affiliated to Kinda represents a data sample that stretches the geographical and chronological scope of the first three generations of Islam, systematically involving the width of compilations and the multiple strands of Arabic-Islamic tradition. Therefore, this data sample enables the systematic analysis of narrative dynamics and their impact on the shape and content of the reports transmitted in Arabic-Islamic scholarly discourses. This systematic assessment of the influence of narrative dynamics on the reports during the process of transmission builds on theoretical approaches developed in the study of medieval German and Latin philology that questions the paradigmatic stability of the 'original' version (*Urtext*) of a text. Instead, texts are seen as fundamentally fluid (*unfest*) and open to variation and adaptation by individual scribes, while the stability of some texts is taken as an indication of specific normative prestige imbued in its unchanged form.[87] Due to the importance of 'aurality'[88] in Arabic-Islamic discursive traditions and the normative significance of the formative period of Islam that involved numerous individuals and groups in its negotiation and debate, this approach is particularly suited for an engagement with the great compilations of Arabic-Islamic scholarly traditions. Indeed, the fluidity of a text during the process of transmission appears to have been recognised in early and classical Arabic-Islamic scholarly discourses as demonstrated by the famous saying attributed to one of the founders of an emic tradition of Arabic grammar and lexicography, al-Khalīl b. Aḥmad, 'When a book has been copied three times without being compared to another copy, it turns into Persian.'[89] From this perspective, the prosopographical database

[87] See for this theoretical background Joachim Bumke, *Die vier Fassungen der 'Nibelungenklage'. Untersuchungen zur Überlieferungsgeschichte und Textkritik der höfischen Epik im 13. Jahrhundert* (Berlin: De Gruyter, 1996), 3–88; Joachim Bumke, 'Der Unfeste Text. Überlegungen zur Überlieferungsgeschichte und Textkritik der höfischen Epik im 13. Jahrhundert., in Jan-Dirk Müller (ed.), *'Aufführung' und 'Schrift' in Mittelalter und Früher Neuzeit* (Stuttgart: Metzler, 1996); Rüdiger Schnell, 'Konstanz und Metamorphosen eines Textes. Eine überlieferungs- und geschlechtergeschichtliche Studie zur volkssprachlichen Rezeption von Jacobus' de Voragine Ehepredigten', *Frühmittelalterliche Studien* 33(1) (1999): 319–95; and Bernard Cerquiglini, *Éloge de la variante. Histoire critique de la philologie* (Paris: Éditions du Seuil, 1989). I thank my esteemed teacher Dr Lenka Jiroušková for shaping my understanding of this philological tradition. Similar suggestions concerning the interferences between text and society during the process of transmission have been made independently for Syriac manuscripts by Michael Philip Penn, 'Monks, Manuscripts, and Muslims: Syriac Textual Changes in Reaction to the Rise of Islam', *Hugoye* 12(2) (2009): 235–57; see also Philip Bockholt, *Weltgeschichtsschreibung zwischen Schia und Sunna. Ḫvāndamīrs Ḥabīb as-siyar im Handschriftenzeitalter* (Leiden: Brill, 2021).

[88] See Schoeler, *The Oral and the Written*, *passim*.

[89] *idhā nusikha l-kitābu thalātha marrātin wa-lam yuʿāraḍ taḥawwala bi-l-fārisiyya*, quoted after al-Sakhāwī, *Fatḥ al-Mughīth bi-Sharḥ Alfiyyat al-Ḥadīth*, ed. ʿAbdalkarīm b. ʿAbdallāh b. ʿAbdalraḥmān al-Khuḍayr and Muḥammad b. ʿAbdallāh b. Fahyad Āl Fahyad (al-Riyāḍ: Maktabat Dār al-Minhāj, 1426/2005–6), 3, 55. This saying was first brough to my attention by the editor Salmān al-Jabūrī in his preface to Abū Mikhnaf, *Maqtal*, ed. al-Jabūrī, 35. Cf. for another instance of al-Khalīl b. Aḥmad as a *locus adscriptionis* by Manfred Ullmann, *Zur Geschichte des Wortes* barīd *'Post'* (Munich: Beck, 1997), 10–11.

of Kinda serves not only as the systematic (and falsifiable) criterion for the selection of individual narrations, but also as an implicit 'common denominator' that may have influenced the depiction of Kindī actors and groups over the course of narrative transmission and debate.

As demonstrated by a close-reading of the narrative depiction of Kindīs across the timeframe under study, the 'image' of Kinda is shaped by pervasive narrative patterns that intertextually link multiple contexts and sources.[90] The close-reading of three emblematic episodes of early Islamic salvation history that involve Kindī protagonists demonstrates that the different versions are intertextually linked in a contested debate turning on the 'moral' assessment of the Kindī and non-Kindī actors involved.[91] Significantly, this intertextuality also connects individual narrations (*akhbār*) that do not feature common traditionaries in their respective chain of transmission (*isnād*). This intertextual connectedness of different versions of emblematic episodes involving Kindī actors also informs the depiction of Kindī individuals and groups in general, indicating that the 'general image' of Kinda influenced the material transmitted during the process of transmission.[92] Thereby, the common revilement of Kindīs as 'weavers' is intertextually linked to the frequent depiction of Kindīs wearing costly garments, and the general trend of blaming villains affiliated to Kinda for 'negative' episodes of early Islamic history may have contributed to the 'polarising sanctification' of Kindī 'heroes' such as Ḥujr b. ʿAdī.[93]

The influence of this type of narrative dynamics on the content of early and classical Arabic-Islamic scholarly discourses has commonly been discounted as 'counterfactual *topoi*', which should be 'weeded out' to arrive at a 'reliable'

[90] A similar point concerning the imprint left by narrative dynamics on Arabic-Islamic scholarly traditions is made by Robert G. Hoyland, 'History, Fiction and Authorship in the First Centuries of Islam', in Julia Bray (ed.), *Writing and Representation in Medieval Islam: Muslim horizons* (London: Routledge, 2006), 32: 'The most noticeable products of this process are . . . the recurrence of motifs . . . and . . . characterization.'

[91] See Leube, *Kinda*, 52–75.

[92] Leube, *Kinda*, 75–134.

[93] Leube, *Kinda*, 123–31.

corpus of information.[94] By contrast, a production-oriented interpretation of recurring narrative patterns or *topoi* as a link between the expectations of the audience and the productive agency of the author or transmitter has been suggested for Byzantine hagiography.[95] The importance of recurring narrative patterns in the depiction of the early Islamic conquests as the cultural memory of Muslim societies was also convincingly argued in a recent contribution by Boaz Shoshan.[96]

Nonetheless, these pervasive intertextual dynamics shaping the material of Arabic-Islamic scholarly discourses during the process of transmission sharply contradict the prevailing scholarly approach of *isnād-cum-matn*. This approach applies the method of textual criticism to multiple reports or *akhbār* describing the same episode, aiming for the establishment of a *stemma* of variants. This *stemma* of variants in the reports is then compared with the chains of transmission or *isnād*s, which are similarly arranged in a *stemma*. Wherever both *stemmata* match, the proponents of *isnād-cum-matn* suggest that the report should be seen as 'authentic' in the sense of having indeed been transmitted along the chains of transmission indicated in the *isnād*s.[97]

[94] See the pioneering work of Albrecht Noth, 'Iṣfahān – Nihāwand. Eine quellenkritische Studie zur frühislamischen Historiographie', *Zeitschrift der Deutschen Morgenländischen Gesellschaft* 118 (1968): 274–96; Albrecht Noth, 'Der Charakter der ersten großen Sammlungen von Nachrichten zur frühen Kalifenzeit'" *Der Islam* 47 (1971): 168–99; and the monograph Albrecht Noth, *Quellenkritische Studien zu Themen, Formen und Tendenzen frühislamischer Geschichtsüberlieferung* (Bonn: Selbstverlag des Orientalischen Seminars der Universität Bonn, 1973).

[95] Thomas Pratsch, *Der hagiographische Topos. Griechische Heiligenviten in mittelbyzantinischer Zeit* (Berlin: De Gruyter, 2005).

[96] Boaz Shoshan, *The Arabic Historical Tradition and the Early Islamic Conquests: Folklore, Tribal Lore, Holy War* (London: Routledge, 2016). The somewhat unsystematic methodology of this nonetheless very important contribution is discussed in the review article by Georg Leube, *Plekos* 19 (2017): 449–63.

[97] See the comprehensive review article by A. Kevin Reinhart, 'Juynbolliana, Gradualism, the Big Bang, and Hadith Study in the Twenty-First Century', *Journal of the American Oriental Society* 130(3) (2010): 413–44, as well as the exemplary deployment of *isnād-cum-matn* to the Arabic-Islamic historiography of the conquest of Damascus, Jens J. Scheiner, *Die Eroberung von Damaskus. Quellenkritische Untersuchung zur Historiographie in klassisch-islamischer Zeit* (Leiden: Brill, 2010).

The fundamental problem with this application of textual criticism to the wealth of individual reports transmitted in Arabic-Islamic scholarly compilations lies in its neglect to consider the question of intertextuality or, in philological terms, contamination. As Paul Maas suggested in his magisterial *Textkritik*:

> When texts are frequently read, however, contamination regularly takes place. In the context of contamination, the systematic establishment of a *stemma* must fail (*versagt die strenge Stemmatik*) . . . The *stemma* determines the mutual interdependency (*Abhängigkeitsverhältnis*) of the textual witnesses for every passage of the text, just as a chemical formula determines the arrangement of the atoms of every molecule of a compound. However, this is true only where the transmission is indeed entirely free from intertextual interpolation. Nothing helps against contamination (*Gegen die Kontamination ist kein Kraut gewachsen*).[98]

As demonstrated by the density of intertextual references and debates that structure the narrative depiction of even such a comparatively marginal subject as (the image of) Kinda, the process of transmission shaping the material contained in the extant compilations can impossibly be modelled as a separate transmission of individual reports by the traditionaries mentioned in the *isnād*. This in turn undermines the application of textual criticism to early and classical Arabic-Islamic historiography according to the method of *isnād-cum-matn*, as it is impossible to apply textual criticism to material shaped by pervasive intertextuality.[99]

By contrast, engagement with Arabic-Islamic scholarly traditions describing the formative period of Islam should depart from an interpretation of the *isnāds* not as *chains of transmission*, but as *chains of authorisation* established *ex post*. Contrary to the predominance of transgenerational ties explicitly mentioned

[98] Paul Maas, *Textkritik* (Leipzig: Teubner, 1957), 31.

[99] In characteristic honesty, this problem is indicated in the monumental study by Scheiner, *Damaskus*, 389, where Scheiner admits that 'the *isnāds* do not indicate the actual way of transmission'. Nonetheless, Scheiner does not build on this observation to question the epistemological assumptions of *isnād-cum-matn* in general.

in the *isnāds*,[100] the pervasive intertextuality shaping the transmitted material attests to dynamic intertextual debates that are not indicated in the *isnāds*.[101] These debates must have been motivated by the importance of early Islamic history as the formative period and salvation history of Muslim communities, which continues to be debated and contested until today.

The following two axioms encapsule this reinterpretation necessary to explain the pervasive intertextuality structuring the corpus of Arabic-Islamic historical memory:

a. Every transmitter was aware of more reports than she is cited with in the *isnāds*.
b. Every report was known to more transmitters than are mentioned in its *isnād*.

This reinterpretation in turn enables the re-inscription of individuals belonging to groups that are marginalised in the *isnāds* into the Muslim narrative and discursive community. While the *isnāds* predominantly indicate long-living, free, male Muslims who are seen as trustworthy according to the normative paradigms of Arabic-Islamic scholarly traditions, the pervasive intertextuality indicated by a close-reading of the systematically established prosopographical database of Kinda likely is the result of much more inclusive debates. Although the search for specific female or prematurely deceased participants in Arabic-Islamic discursive traditions is frequently impossible,[102] modelling the process of transmission on a more inclusive and less personalised basis represents an

[100] See the pioneering article by Richard W. Bulliet, 'The Age Structure of Medieval Islamic Education', *Studia Islamica* 57 (1983): 105–17; as well as the sociological study by Recep Senturk (Şentürk), *Narrative Social Structure: Anatomy of the Hadith Transmission Network, 610–1505* (Stanford: Stanford University Press, 2005).

[101] *Pace* Senturk, Narrative Social Structure, 39: '[The companions of Muḥammad] occupied themselves primarily with teaching hadith to the younger generations, called Successors (layers 2–4). Among themselves, however, there was very little narrative exchange.'

[102] See, for instance, the tantalising reference to two female scholars in *isnāds* cited by the travelling scholar Ibn Baṭṭūṭa, *Riḥla*, ed. Darwīsh al-Juwaydī (Beirut: al-Maktaba al-ʿAṣriyya, 2010), 1, 191 and 201.

important step towards recognising the importance of individuals 'read' as pertaining to marginalised groups for Muslim cultural memory.

## Conclusion

This contribution argues that systematical and corpus-based prosopographical research may be decisive in challenging and elaborating essentialising models and assumptions that continue to structure the academic field of early Islamic history. In systematically establishing a prosopographical database of individuals and groups affiliated to the Arab 'tribe' of Kinda, I followed the suggestion of molecular biology that the multiple and dynamic processes within a cell are best followed by 'marking' individual molecules and using them to 'trace' their involvement in wider processes. Similarly, I attempted a reconstruction of the wider historical and narrative processes shaping the Arabic-Islamic scholarly discourses on the first three generations of Islam by 'tracing' the systematically established prosopography of Kinda across multiple contexts and episodes.

As suggested above, this prosopographical case study suggested on a 'referential' dimension of historiography that interpretation of the early Islamic conquests should depart from an interpretative framework that differentiates between different degrees of 'central' affiliation for different individual actors. This in turn allows the development of an actor-based framework for the history of the formative period of Islam that re-establishes the intersecting positionalities and agencies of multiple actors in the processes leading to the political formation of the Marwānid caliphate.

On the 'narrative' dimension of historiography, the same case study indicated a pervasive intertextuality shaping the depiction of Kindī individuals and groups both within particular episodes and across the entire corpus of Arabic-Islamic scholarly traditions. As this pervasive intertextually is impossible to reconcile with the dominant paradigm of *isnād-cum-matn*, I have suggested that the application of the method of textual criticism by *isnād-cum-matn* depends on a misinterpretation of the process of transmission. Instead of interpreting the *isnād*s of individual reports as chains of transmission describing the factual ways in which individual reports were transmitted, I suggest that the *isnād*s should be seen as chains of authorisation that serve to legitimise material that was transmitted and negotiated in a much broader process of transmission that involved large parts of Muslim society. Accordingly, this alternative modelling of the process of transmission allows for the re-inscription of individuals 'read' as belonging to groups marginalised by the normative paradigms of Arabic-Islamic scholarly traditions into the communal history of Islamic memory.

Provocative as these suggestions may be, however, the primary importance of the prosopographical case study of Kinda during the first three generations of Islamic history lies in its methodical and thereby falsifiable selection of individual reports for interpretation. Overcoming frequently colonialist and Orientalist assumptions and frameworks of interpretation is predicated on the methodologically reflected systematisation of the selection of individual reports from the vast corpus of Arabic-Islamic scholarly traditions. I sincerely hope the prosopographical case study of Kinda presented in this chapter will encourage further innovative engagements along these lines.

## Bibliography

Abū Mikhnaf, *Maqtal al-Imām al-Ḥusayn b. ʿAlī*, ed. Kāmil Salmān al-Jabūrī. Beirut: Dār al-Majalla al-Bayḍāʾ, 2000.

Ahmad, Shahab, *What is Islam? The Importance of Being Islamic*. Princeton, NJ: Princeton University Press, 2016.

Ahmed, Asad Q., *The Religious Elite of the Early Islamic Ḥijāz: Five Prosopographical Case Studies*, Prosopographica et Genealogica 14. Oxford: Prosopographica et Genealogica, 2011.

Althusser, Louis, *Sur la reproduction*. Paris: Presses Universitaires de France, 2011.

Anderson, Benedict, *Imagined Communities: Reflections on the Origin and Spread of Nationalism*. London: Verso, 2006.

Asad, Talal, *The Idea of an Anthropology of Islam*. Washington DC: Center for Contemporary Arab Studies, Georgetown University, 1986.

Assmann, Jan, *Das kulturelle Gedächtnis. Schrift, Erinnerung und politische Identität in frühen Hochkulturen*. Munich: Beck, 1992.

al-Balādhurī, *Ansāb al-ʿArab*, ed. Muḥammad Muḥammad Tāmir, 8 vols. Beirut: Dār al-Kutub al-ʿIlmiyya, 2011.

al-Balādhurī, *Futūḥ al-Buldān*, ed. Ayman Muḥammad ʿArafa. Cairo: Al-Maktaba al-Tawfīqiyya, n.d..

al-Barrī, ʿAbdallah Khurshīd, *al-Qabāʾil al-ʿArabiyya fī Miṣr fī l-Qurūn al-Thalātha al-Ūlā li-l-Hijra*. Cairo: al-Hayʾa al-Miṣriyya al-ʿĀmma li-l-Kitāb, 1992.

Bauer, Thomas, *Die Kultur der Ambiguität. Eine andere Geschichte des Islams*. Berlin: Verlag der Weltreligionen, 2011.

Bernheimer, Teresa, *The 'Alids: The First Family of Islam, 750–1200*. Edinburgh: Edinburgh University Press, 2013.

Bockholt, Philip, *Weltgeschichtsschreibung zwischen Schia und Sunna. Ḫvāndamīrs Ḥabīb as-siyar im Handschriftenzeitalter*, Iran Studies 20. Leiden: Brill, 2021.

Brockelmann, Carl, *Geschichte der arabischen Literatur*, 5 vols. Leiden: Brill, 1937–49.

Bulliett, Richard W., *Conversion to Islam in the Medieval Period: An Essay in Quantitative History*. Cambridge, MA: Harvard University Press, 1979.

Bulliett, Richard W., 'The Age Structure of Medieval Islamic Education', *Studia Islamica* 57 (1983): 105–17.

Bumke, Joachim, *Die vier Fassungen der 'Nibelungenklage'. Untersuchungen zur Überlieferungsgeschichte und Textkritik der höfischen Epik im 13. Jahrhundert*, Quellen und Forschungen zur Literatur- und Kulturgeschichte 8. Berlin: De Gruyter, 1996.

Bumke, Joachim, 'Der Unfeste Text. Überlegungen zur Überlieferungsgeschichte und Textkritik der höfischen Epik im 13. Jahrhundert', in Jan-Dirk Müller (ed.), *'Aufführung' und 'Schrift' in Mittelalter und Früher Neuzeit*, Germanistische Symposien-Berichtsbände 17. Stuttgart: Metzler, 1996.

Cameron, Averil (ed.), *Fifty Years of Prosopography: The Later Roman Empire, Byzantium and Beyond*, Proceedings of the British Academy 118. Oxford: Oxford University Press, 2003.

Caskel, Werner and Gert Strenziok, *Ǧamharat al-Nasab. Das genealogische Werk des Hišām Ibn Muḥammad al-Kalbī*, 2 vols. Leiden: Brill, 1966.

Cerquiglini, Bernard, *Éloge de la variante. Histoire critique de la philologie*, Des travaux 8. Paris: Éditions du Seuil, 1989.

Crone, Patricia, *Slaves on Horses: The Evolution of the Islamic Polity*. Cambridge: Cambridge University Press, 1980.

Crone, Patricia and Michael Cook, *Hagarism: The Making of the Islamic World*. Cambridge: Cambridge University Press, 1977.

Donner, Fred M., 'The Arab Tribes in the Muslim Conquest of Iraq', unpublished dissertation, Ann Arbor, 1975.

Donner, Fred M., *The Early Islamic Conquests*, Princeton Studies on the Near East. Princeton, NJ: Princeton University Press, 1981.

Donner, Fred M., 'Centralized Authority and Military Autonomy in the Early Islamic Conquests', in Averil Cameron (ed.), *The Byzantine and Early Islamic Near East III: States, Resources and Armies*, Studies in Late Antiquity and Early Islam 1. Princeton, NJ: Darwin Press, 1995, 337–60.

Donner, Fred M. (ed.), *The Expansion of the Early Islamic State*, The Formation of the Classical Islamic World 5. Aldershot: Ashgate Variorum, 2008.

Donner, Fred M., 'Review of Hoyland', *Path. Al-ʿUṣūr al-Wusṭā* 23 (2015): 134–40.

Falkenhausen, Vera von, 'I funzionari greci nel regno normanno', in Maria Re and Cristina Rognoni (eds), *Giorgio di Antiochia. L'arte della politica in Sicilia nel XII secolo tra Bisanzio e l'Islam*, Quaderni 17, Byzantino-Sicula V. Palermo: Istituto Siciliano di studi Bizantini e Neoellenici 'Bruno Lavagnini', 2009, 165–202.

Franz, Kurt, *Vom Beutezug zur Territorialherrschaft. Das lange Jahrhundert des Aufstiegs von Nomaden zur Vormacht in Syrien und Mesopotamien 286 bis 420/889 bis 1029*, Nomaden und Sesshafte 5, 1. Wiesbaden: Reichert, 2007.

Gaube, Heinz, *Arabosasanidische Numismatik*. Braunschweig: Klinkhardt und Biermann, 1973.

Gell, Alfred, *Art and Agency: An Anthropological Theory*. Oxford: Clarendon Press, 1998.

Graf, Georg, *Geschichte der christlichen arabischen Literatur*, 5 vols, Studi e Testi. Rome: Biblioteca Apostolica Vaticana, 1947–66.

Haase, Claus-Peter, *Untersuchungen zur Landschaftsgeschichte Nordsyriens in der Umayyadenzeit*. Hamburg: Dissertationsschrift, 1972.

Halbwachs, Maurice, *Les cadres sociaux de la mémoire*. Paris: Éditions Albin Michel, 1994.

Halbwachs, Maurice, *La topographie légendaire des évangiles en Terre sainte*. Paris: Presses Universitaires de France, 2008.

al-Hamdānī, *Kitāb al-Iklīl*, ed. Muḥammad b. ʿAlī b. al-Ḥusayn al-Akwaʿ al-Ḥawālī, 10 vols. Beirut: Manshūrāt al-Madīna, 1986.

Hidding, Aaltje, *The Era of the Martyrs: Remembering the Great Persecution in Late Antique Egypt*, Millenium Studies 87. Berlin: De Gruyter, 2020.

Hoyland, Robert G., *Seeing Islam as Others Saw It*. Princeton, NJ, Darwin Press, 1997.

Hoyland, Robert G., 'History, Fiction and Authorship in the First Centuries of Islam', in Julia Bray (ed.), *Writing and Representation in Medieval Islam: Muslim Horizons*, Routledge Studies in Middle Eastern Literatures 11. London: Routledge, 2006, 16–46.

Hoyland, Robert G., *In God's Path: The Arab Conquests and the Creation of an Islamic Empire*, Ancient Warfare and Civilization 4. Oxford: Oxford University Press, 2015.

Hoyland, Robert G.. 'Reflections on the Identity of the Arabian Conquerors of the Seventh-Century Middle East', *Al-ʿUṣūr al-Wusṭā* 25 (2017): 113–40.

Humphreys, R. Stephen, *Islamic History: A Framework for Inquiry*. London: I. B. Tauris, 1995.

Ibn ʿAbdalḥakam, *Futūḥ Miṣr wa-l-Maghrib*, ed. ʿAlī Muḥammad ʿUmar. Cairo: Maktabat al-Thaqāfa al-Dīniyya, 2004.

Ibn ʿAsākir, *Taʾrīkh Madīnat Dimashq*, ed. Muḥibb al-Dīn Abū Saʿīd ʿUmar b. Gharāma al-ʿAmrawī, 80 vols. Beirut: Dār al-Fikr, 1995.

Ibn Baṭṭūṭa. *Riḥla*, ed. Darwīsh al-Juwaydī, 2 vols. Beirut: al-Maktaba al-ʿAṣriyya, 2010.

Ibn Saʿd, *Kitāb al-Ṭabaqāt al-Kubrā*, ed. Muḥammad ʿAbdalqādir ʿAṭā, 9 vols. Beirut: Dār al-Kutub al-ʿIlmiyya, 2012.

Ibn al-Ṣalāḥ, *Muqaddima fī ʿUlūm al-Ḥadīth*, ed. Ismāʿīl Zarmān. Damascus: Muʾassasat al-Risāla, 2013.

al-Iṣfahānī, *Maqātil al-Ṭālibiyyīn*, ed. al-Sayyid Aḥmad Ṣaqr. Cairo: Dār Iḥyāʾ al-Kutub al-ʿArabiyya, n.d.

al-Jāḥiẓ, *Kitāb al-Ḥayawān*, ed. Muḥammad Bāsil ʿUyūn al-Sūd, 7 vols. Beirut: Dār al-Kutub al-ʿIlmiyya, 2011.

al-Jahshiyārī, *Kitāb al-Wuzarāʾ wa-l-Kuttāb*, facsimile ed. Hans von Mžik, Bibliothek arabischer Historiker und Geographen 1. Leipzig: Harrassowitz, 1926.

Khalīfa b. Khayyāṭ, *Kitāb al-Ṭabaqāt*, ed. Suhayl Zakkār. Beirut: Dār al-Fikr, 1993.

Khalīfa b. Khayyāṭ, *Taʾrīkh*, ed. Muṣṭafā Najīb Fawwāz and Ḥikmat Kashlī Fawwāz. Beirut: Dār al-Kutub al-ʿIlmiyya, 1995.

al-Kindī, *Kitāb al-Quḍāt*, ed. Richard J. H. Gottheil. Paris: Geuthner, 1908.

al-Kindī, *Kitāb al-Wulāt wa-l-Quḍāt*, ed. Rhuvon Guest. Cairo: Dār al-Kitāb al-Islāmī, n.d.; reprint of original edition Leiden 1912.

Lecker, Michael, *The Banū Sulaym: A Contribution to the Study of Early Islam*, Max Schloessinger Memorial Series 4. Jerusalem: Hebrew University Press, 1989.

Leube, Georg, *Kinda in der frühislamischen Geschichte. Eine prosopographische Studie auf Basis der frühen und klassischen arabisch-islamischen Geschichtsschreibung*, Materialien zur Sozial- und Kulturgeschichte der islamischen Welt 41. Baden-Baden: Ergon, 2017.

Leube, Georg, 'Review Article of Shoshan, *Historical Tradition*,' *Plekos* 19 (2017): 449–63.

Leube, Georg, 'Review of Hoyland, *Path*', *Plekos* 20 (2018): 327–34.

Leube, Georg, 'Review of Ulrich, *al-Azd*', *Der Islam* 97(1) (2019): 292–6.

Leube, Georg, 'Insult the Caliph, Marry al-Ḥasan, and Redeem Your Kingdom: Freiheitsgrade of Kindī Elites During the 7th to 9th Century', in Hannah-Lena Hagemann and Stefan Heidemann (eds), *Transregional and Regional Elites – Connecting the Early Islamic Empire, Vol. 1: The Early Islamic Empire at Work Volume 1*, Studies in the History and Culture of the Middle East 36. Berlin: De Gruyter, 2020, 47–68.

Leube, Georg, 'Obliterating Leadership? The Contested Excommunication of al-Ashʿath b. Qays in Early and Classical Arabic-Islamic Historiography', *al-Masaq*, SI 'Acts of Excommunication in the Late Antique and Early Islamic Middle East', ed. Ed Hayes, forthcoming.

Maas, Paul, *Textkritik*. Leipzig: Teubner, 1957.

Madelung, Wilferd, *The Succession to Muḥammad*. Cambridge: Cambridge University Press, 1997.

Magdalino, Paul, 'Prosopography and Byzantine Identity', in Averil Cameron (ed.), *Fifty Years of Prosopography: The Later Roman Empire, Byzantium and Beyond*. Oxford: Oxford University Press, 2003, 41–56.

al-Maqdisī, *Kitāb al-Badʾ wa-l-Taʾrīkh*, no ed. given (Clément Huart?), 6 vols. Cairo: Maktabat al-Thaqāfa al-Dīniyya, n.d.

al-Masʿūdī, *Kitāb al-Tanbīh*, ed. Michael J. de Goeje. Leiden: Brill, 1894.

al-Masʿūdī, *Murūj al-Dhahab*, ed. Mufīd Muḥammad Qamīḥa, 4 vols. Beirut, Dār al-Kutub al-ʿIlmiyya, 1985.

Morimoto, Kosei, 'The Dīwāns as Registers of the Arab Stipendiaries in Early Islamic Egypt,' in R.Curiel and R. Gyselen (eds), *Itinéraires d'Orient: Hommages à Claude Cahen*, Res Orientales 6. Bures-sur-Yvette: Peeters, 1994, 353–65.

Mottahedeh, Roy, *Loyalty and Leadership in an early Islamic Society*. London: I. B. Tauris, 2001.

Munt, Harry, 'Caliphal Imperialism and Ḥijāzī Elites in the Second/Eighth Century,' *al-Masāq* 28 (2016): 6–21.

Nora, Pierre (ed.), *Les Lieux de Mémoire I. La République*. Paris: Gallimard, 1984.

Noth, Albrecht, 'Iṣfahān – Nihāwand. Eine quellenkritische Studie zur frühislamischen Historiographie', *Zeitschrift der Deutschen Morgenländischen Gesellschaft* 118 (1968): 274–96.

Noth, Albrecht, 'Der Charakter der ersten großen Sammlungen von Nachrichten zur frühen Kalifenzeit', *Der Islam* 47 (1971): 168–99.

Noth, Albrecht, *Quellenkritische Studien zu Themen, Formen und Tendenzen frühislamischer Geschichtsüberlieferung*, Bonner orientalistische Studien 25. Bonn: Selbstverlag des Orientalischen Seminars der Universität Bonn, 1973.

Orthmann, Eva, *Stamm und Macht: Die arabischen Stämme im 2. und 3. Jahrhundert der Hiǧra*, Nomaden und Sesshafte 1. Wiesbaden: Reichert, 2002.

Paul, Jürgen, *Herrscher, Gemeinwesen, Vermittler. Ostiran und Transoxanien in vormongolischer Zeit*, Beiruter Texte und Studien 59. Stuttgart: Franz Steiner, 1996.

Penn, Michael Philip, 'Monks, Manuscripts, and Muslims: Syriac Textual Changes in Reaction to the Rise of Islam', *Hugoye* 12(2) (2009): 235–57.

Pratsch, Thomas, *Der hagiographische Topos. Griechische Heiligenviten in mittelbyzantinischer Zeit*, Millenium-Studien 6. Berlin: De Gruyter, 2005.

Puin, Gerd-Rüdiger, *Der Dīwān von ʿUmar ibn al-Ḫaṭṭāb. Ein Beitrag zur frühislamischen Verwaltungsgeschichte*. Bonn: Dissertationsschrift, 1970.

al-Qadi, Wadad, 'Biographical Dictionaries as the Scholars' Alternative History of the Muslim Community', in Gerhard Endress (ed.), *Organizing Knowledge: Encyclopaedic Activities in the Pre-Eighteenth Century Islamic World*. Leiden: Brill, 2006, 23–75.

Reinhart, A. Kevin, 'Juynbolliana, Gradualism, the Big Bang, and Hadith Study in the Twenty-First Century', *Journal of the American Oriental Society* 130(3) (2010): 413–44.

Rotter, Gernot, *Die Umayyaden und der Zweite Bürgerkrieg, 680–692*. Wiesbaden: Steiner, 1982.

Said, Edward W., *Orientalism*. London: Routledge, 1978.

al-Sakhāwī, *Fatḥ al-Mughīth bi-Sharḥ Alfiyyat al-Ḥadīth*, ed. ʿAbdalkarīm b. ʿAbdallāh b. ʿAbdalraḥmān al-Khuḍayr and Muḥammad b. ʿAbdallāh b. Fahyad Āl Fahyad. al-Riyāḍ: Maktabat Dār al-Minhāj, 1426/2005–6.

Scheiner, Jens J., *Die Eroberung von Damaskus. Quellenkritische Untersuchung zur Historiographie in klassisch-islamischer Zeit*, Islamic History and Civilization 76. Leiden: Brill, 2010.

Scheiner, Jens J., 'Review of Hoyland, *Path*', *Bustan* 7(1) (2016): 19–32.

Schimmel, Annemarie, *Islamic Names*, Islamic Surveys. Edinburgh: Edinburgh University Press, 1989.

Schnell, Rüdiger, 'Konstanz und Metamorphosen eines Textes. Eine überlieferungs- und geschlechtergeschichtliche Studie zur volkssprachlichen Rezeption von Jacobus' de Voragine Ehepredigten', *Frühmittelalterliche Studien* 33(1) (1999): 319–95.

Schoeler, Gregor, *The Oral and the Written in Warly Islam*. London: Routledge, 2006.

Schrode, Paula, 'The Dynamics of Orthodoxy and Heterodoxy in Uyghur Religious Practice', *Die Welt des Islams* 48 (2008): 394–433.

Schumpeter, Joseph, *Das Wesen und der Hauptinhalt der theoretischen Nationalökonomie*. Berlin: Duncker & Humblot, 1970.

Seesemann, Rüdiger, 'Epistemology or Ideology? Toward a Relational Perspective on Islamic Knowledge in Africa', *Journal of Africana Religions* 6(2) (2018): 232–68.

Senturk (Şentürk), Recep, *Narrative Social Structure: Anatomy of the Hadith Transmission Network, 610–1505*. Stanford: Stanford University Press, 2005.

Sezgin, Fuat, *Geschichte des arabischen Schrifttums*, 17 vols. Leiden: Brill, 1967–2015.

Sharon, Moshe, 'The Birth of Islam in the Holy Land', in Moshe Sharon (ed.), *The Holy Land in History and Thought*, Publications of the Eric Samson Chair in Jewish civilization 1. Leiden: Brill, 1988, 225–35.

Shoshan, Boaz, *The Arabic Historical Tradition and the Early Islamic Conquests: Folklore, Tribal Lore, Holy War*, Routledge Studies in Classical Islam 4. London: Routledge, 2016.

Sundelin, Lennart, 'Introduction: Papyrology and the Study of Early Islamic Egypt', in Petra M. Sijpesteijn and Lennart Sundelin (eds), *Papyrology and the History of Early Islamic Egypt*, Islamic History and Civilization 55. Leiden: Brill, 2004, 1–19.

al-Ṭabarī, *Taʾrīkh*, ed. Muṣṭafā al-Sayyid and Ṭāriq Sālim, 6 vols. Cairo: al-Maktaba al-Tawfīqiyya, n.d.

al-Thaʿālibī, *Laṭāʾif al-Maʿārif*, ed. Ibrāhīm al-Abyārī and Ḥasan Kāmil al-Ṣayrafī. Cairo: ʿĪsā al-Bābī al-Ḥalabī, 1960.

Trevor-Roper, Hugh, 'The Invention of Tradition: The Highland Tradition of Scotland', in Eric Hobsbawm and Terence Ranger (eds), *The Invention of Tradition*. Cambridge: Cambridge University Press, 1983.

Ullmann, Manfred, *Zur Geschichte des Wortes* barīd *'Post'*. Munich: Beck, 1997 (Bayerische Akademie der Wissenschaften, Philosophisch-Historische Klasse, Sitzungsberichte, Jahrgang 1997, Heft 1).

Ulrich, Brian, *Arabs in the Early Islamic Empire: Exploring al-Azd Tribal Identity*. Edinburgh: Edinburgh University Press, 2019.

Verter, Bradford, 'Spiritual Capital: Theorizing Religion with Bourdieu against Bourdieu', *Sociological Theory* 21(2) (2003): 150–74.

Vogt, Matthias, *Figures de califes entre histoire et fiction: al-Walīd b. Yazīd et al-Amīn dans la représentation de l'historiographie arabe de l'époque abbaside*, Beiruter Texte und Studien 106. Würzburg: Ergon, 2006.

Wansbrough, John, *Quranic Studies: Sources and Methods of Scriptural Interpretation*, London Oriental Series 31. Oxford: Oxford University Press, 1977.

al-Wāqidī, *Kitāb al-Maghāzī*, ed. Muḥammad ʿAbdalqādir Aḥmad ʿAṭā, 2 vols. Beirut: Dār al-Kutub al-ʿIlmiyya, 2004.

Weber, Eugen, *Peasants into Frenchmen: The Modernization of Rural France 1870–1914*. Stanford: Stanford University Press, 1976.

Woods, John E., *The Aqquyunlu: Clan, Confederation, Empire*. Salt Lake City: University of Utah Press, 1999.

Wüstenfeld, Ferdinand, *Der Tod des Ḥusein ben ʾAlí und die Rache*. Göttingen: Dieterich, 1883.

Yāqūt, *Muʿjam al-Buldān*, ed. Muḥammad ʿAbdarraḥmān al-Marʿashlī, 8 vols. Beirut, Dār Iḥyāʾ al-Turāth al-ʿArabī, 2008.

# 5

# JUXTAPOSITION, TENSION, PLAY: THE DEVELOPMENT OF ISLAMIC LAW AND LEGAL THEORY

ATEEB GUL[1]

> [T]he test of a first-rate intelligence is the ability to hold two opposed ideas in the mind at the same time, and still retain the ability to function.[2]

## Juxtaposition, Tension, Play

It is difficult to ascertain whether the concepts of 'juxtaposition', 'tension' and 'play' have occupied a crucial place in the study of religion or if they have been at the periphery struggling to find their way to the centre. The very exercise of determining an accurate response to this conundrum would assume that there is indeed a core and a periphery to the academic study of religion. However, what can be said with confidence is that many scholars of religion, or theorists in other fields whose work has been directly relevant to the study of religion, have adumbrated on these categories and processes and have made a strong case for the relevance of these ideas for a better understanding of the

[1] I would like to express my gratitude to Margarita Guillory for her comments on the first draft of this chapter, and to Adnan Zulfiqar, Roshan Iqbal, Zubair Abbasi, and the editors of this volume Abbas Aghdassi and Aaron Hughes for their feedback on the revised version.

[2] F. Scott Fitzgerald, 'The Crack-Up', *Esquire*, 7 March 2017 (originally published in 1936), available at: https://www.esquire.com/lifestyle/a4310/the-crack-up, last accessed 20 July 2021.

minutiae of religious experiences and hermeneutics. Be it the many writings of J. Z. Smith in which he talks about informed comparisons in order to develop a richer understanding of different religious (sub-)traditions,[3] or D. W. Winnicott's category of the 'personal intermediate area' or the 'potential space',[4] or Ronald Grimes' discussion of the 'spaces *between* boundaries',[5] or Jeffrey Kripal's 'space' that enables a meeting of two phenomena 'beyond' their respective boundaries,[6] or Sam Gill's brilliant essay on the importance of 'play' in the study of religions[7] – all these point to a particular meta-approach employed to understand issues in religious studies.

How does this meta-approach work? To begin with, it comes into play (pardon the pun!) when we, in our quest to understand a specific aspect of a particular religion, come face to face with two different, opposing or mutually exclusive categories. For J. Z. Smith,[8] the mutual exclusivity between

[3] J. Z. Smith, 'Adde parvum parvo magnus acervus erit', *History of Religions* 11(1) (1971): 67–90.

[4] 'If . . . the adult can manage to enjoy the personal intermediate area without making claims, then we can acknowledge our own corresponding intermediate areas, and are pleased to find a degree of overlapping, that is to say, common experience between members of a group in art or religion or philosophy.' D. W. Winnicott, *Playing and Reality* (London: Tavistock, 1971), 10.

[5] Ronald L. Grimes, 'Defining Nascent Ritual', *Journal of the American Academy of Religion* 50(4) (1982): 539–55.

[6] 'As a humble way of beginning, we might say that the psychical and the paranormal appear in that space where the humanities and the sciences meet beyond both, where mind and matter, subjectivity and objectivity merge in ways that can only violate and offend our present order of knowledge and possibility.' Jeffrey Kripal, *Authors of the Impossible: The Paranormal and the Sacred* (Chicago: University of Chicago Press, 2010), 24.

[7] Sam Gill, 'Play', in Willi Braun and Russell T. McCutcheon (eds), *Guide to the Study of Religion* (London: Continuum, 2000).

[8] Jonathan Z. Smith (d. 2017) was an expert in the study of religion and is credited as one of the field's most accomplished and prolific theorists. He was especially interested in questions of definitions, classifications and categories. He was Robert O. Anderson Distinguished Professor of the Humanities at the University of Chicago. Russell T. McCutcheon, another giant in the field, called Smith 'arguably the world's most influential scholar of religion over the past fifty years'. For a brief summary of his scholarly life and accomplishments, see Russell T. McCutcheon, 'In Memoriam: Jonathan Z. Smith (1938–2017)', *Religious Studies News*, 5 January 2018, available at: https://rsn.aarweb.org/articles/memoriam-jonathan-z-smith-1938%E2%80%932017, last accessed 2 October 2021.

categories could be found in almost anything related to the study of religions – it could be between two texts, between two methods of approaching a text or between two different parts of the same text. Smith highlights the importance of constantly struggling with two opposing viewpoints in order to create an interplay between them so that the potential for a creative resolution emerges that takes our understanding of a phenomenon forward, not necessarily by resolving the opposition but through the joy of continued engagement with it. I call this the 'potential perpetuality of play'. Sam Gill[9] summarised Smith's theory of 'juxtaposition' (which involves both tension and play) efficiently: 'An effective juxtaposition engages a tension among the items juxtaposed, a tension that raises questions not easily answered.'[10] Gill informs us that Smith's method entails three parts: comparison between two items (juxtaposition); the illumination of the differences between them (tension); and reflection that does not necessarily lead to a neat resolution (play).

Gill himself has elaborated on the importance of play in the academic study of religion. For Gill, the ability to attempt to make sense of contradictory data defines the best feature of the human race – the ability to play. When applied to the study of religion, it has the ability not only to raise crucial questions and possibilities, but also give rise to intellectual 'pleasure'. Gill writes:

> Our challenge is to find a meaningful way to hold together at once two or more irreconcilable positions and to do so without smoke and mirrors and without forced or too easy difference-denying solutions. Our ability to do this is among the crowning human capabilities. That this ability, which may be called 'play', is a common one at the root of so much human pleasure and so many aspects of human culture.[11]

[9] Sam Gill is Professor Emeritus of Religious Studies at the University of Colorado at Boulder. He has written on a wide variety of topics such as religion and religious theory, dance, ritual and movement. His most recent publication is actually a book that engages with and builds upon the contributions of J. Z. Smith: Sam Gill, *The Proper Study of Religion: Building on Jonathan Z. Smith* (Oxford: Oxford University Press, 2020).

[10] Sam Gill, 'No Place to Stand: Jonathan Z. Smith as *Homo Ludens*, The Academic Study of Religion *Sub Specie Ludi*', *Journal of the American Academy of Religion* 66(2) (1998): 283–312, 284. Gill highlights the importance of this discourse once again in his latest book on J. Z. Smith: Gill, *Proper Study of Religion*.

[11] Gill, 'Play', 451–2.

I would also like to address another question at the outset – the question about how appropriate this approach is to the study of Islam. I refer to Gill who summarises Smith's position:

> Smith does not limit this dynamic process to the technical academic methods of a student of religion and culture. He recognizes that they are present as well in the structures of religious experience. His analyses tend to move easily between the study of some aspect of a specific religious tradition and the study of religion itself and, even more broadly, the whole educational process.[12]

In other words, these categories of juxtaposition, tension and play have wide-ranging applications. Not only do these shed light on particular problems within a specific religious tradition, they also have the capacity to throw light on the comparison between different religious traditions, and may perhaps have applications beyond the field of religious studies itself. If Smith himself has applied his method of juxtaposition to learn about the study of religions, then it seems apt, even if only as an experiment, to apply this method to the history of a particular religion in order to see if it adds something to our understanding of it.

After all, if the categories are broad enough to deal with tensions between text and interpretation as a whole (as in the case of Smith), or between the Christianity-centric history of the academic study of religion and the contemporary necessity of 'accepting diverse worldviews' (as in the case of Gill), then we can and must broaden its scope and apply it to specific religious traditions to see if this method can illuminate those traditions for us in new ways. This is precisely what this chapter will attempt to do with the history of the Islamic legal enterprise. In the subsequent sections, I will apply this method[13] of juxtaposition, tension, and play to explain three crucial developments in the history of Islamic law and legal theory.

[12] Gill, 'No Place to Stand', 284.

[13] While literature in the academic study of religion usually differentiates between the terms 'method', 'approach',' 'theory' and 'categories', it is not always the case. Also, whenever such attempts have been made, they have had their own share of problems. Much like the debates and discourses in the Islamic legal tradition, the exact definitions of these terms have always been a work in progress. See Patrick Hart, 'Theory, Method, and Madness in Religious Studies', *Method and Theory in the Study of Religion* 28(1) (2016): 3–25.

## The Development of Islamic Legal Theory and Practice

### *Tension between Qur'ān and Sunna*

I postulate that the entire discipline of Islamic legal theory (*uṣūl al-fiqh*) arose out of a central tension between the Qur'ānic text and the reported sayings of the Prophet Muḥammad (which were later compiled as Ḥadīth literature).[14] This tension between the two primary sources of Islamic law, and in some cases between verses of the Qur'ān itself, has informed Muslim societies' beliefs, cultures and actions for centuries. In fact, one of the earliest Islamic legal treatises, produced by Muḥammad ibn Idrīs al-Shāfiʿī (d. 820 CE) *c.* 805 CE, revolves around this tension, namely, how to extrapolate laws when there is an apparent contradiction between the Qur'ānic text and the Prophetic sayings. This treatise, titled *al-Risāla*, set up the enterprise of Islamic legal theory for centuries to come, thereby elevating the Qur'ān–ḥadīth tension and ways to resolve it at the very core of Islamic law. As a result, then, the entire field of Islamic legal theory can trace back its origins to the tension between Qur'ān and ḥadīth and the 'playfulness' on the part of the eighth–ninth-century figure al-Shāfiʿī who strived to 'raise critical questions and possibilities' (in Gill's terms) and play with that tension by being creative.[15] (We must remember that being creative is essential to the method of juxtaposition.[16])

Al-Shāfiʿī was born in Gaza (modern-day Palestine) and died in Fusṭāṭ (modern-day Egypt). He lived and studied in several other cities in the region. While his most voluminous extant book remains *Kitāb al-Umm* (*The Exemplar*), he is best known for his short treatise called *Kitāb al-Risāla fī Uṣūl al-Fiqh* (*The Epistle on Legal Theory*), known simply as *al-Risāla* or *Risāla* (*Epistle*). Joseph Lowry has called it 'the foundational document of Islamic legal theory'.[17] The reason that it enjoys this praise is because it was one of

[14] Ḥadīth literature refers to the sayings of the Prophet Muḥammad as they were passed through one generation to the next, many of which are now considered to be 'authentic' after several centuries of sifting through and eliminating 'fabricated' reports.

[15] Kecia Ali, 'Foreword', in Joseph Lowry, *The Epistle on Legal Theory: A Translation of al-Shafi'i's* Risalah (New York: New York University Press, 2015), xiii.

[16] Gill, 'Play', 455.

[17] Joseph Lowry, *The Epistle on Legal Theory: A Translation of al-Shafi'i's* Risalah (New York: New York University Press, 2015), cover.

the first extant attempts at acknowledging the tension between the religious edicts of the Qurʾān and the religious instructions from Prophetic sayings. At the time when al-Shāfiʿī began to write the *Risāla*, the compilation of Prophetic hadith reports had started to present a problem: the reports had begun to contradict the Qurʾān in places and had begun to present a 'conflicting collection of legal precedents'.[18] As a result, al-Shāfiʿī made his 'concern with apparent contradictions among revealed texts and with the use of *Hadiths* for legal analysis . . . [the] primary focal points of the *Risāla*'.[19] Joseph Lowry, John Burton and Kecia Ali would agree that 'Shāfiʿī's legal reasoning is overwhelmingly concerned with harmonizing apparent contradictions in the legal source texts, that is, in the Qurʾān and the Sunna'.[20]

But how exactly did al-Shāfiʿī harmonise these apparent contradictions – or attempted the playful resolution of these apparent tensions – between the two sources? There could only be three primary possibilities. One, that the Qurʾān were to be declared the only source of Islamic law. Two, that the Prophetic reports were to be considered enough to construct positive Islamic law. And, three, that the contradictions between them were not to be considered real or so hermetically sealed from each other that there was not even a possibility of a shared space where they could be brought into a mutual conversation. Since these contradictions (or tensions) were seen as apparent, or resolvable, they allowed al-Shāfiʿī to be creative with his methods in an attempt to find a way forward. (It must also be noted that nowhere in the literature by Smith and Gill did I find a conceptual distinction between *real* opposites and *apparent* opposites; if that is indeed the case, al-Shāfiʿī can be credited with being a step ahead of both theorists of religion in that he gave us a further conceptual category with which to work.)

Once al-Shāfiʿī had claimed that these tensions were apparent and could be played with, he came up with several ways to do it. One of the ways included the creation of a distinction between unrestrictive (*ʿāmm*) and restrictive (*khāṣṣ*) commands. This method works when there is a command

[18] Lowry, *Epistle*, xix–xx.

[19] Joseph Lowry, *Early Islamic Legal Theory: The Risala of Muhammad ibn Idris al-Shafiʿi* (Leiden: Brill, 2007), 8.

[20] Lowry, *Early Islamic Legal Theory*, 16.

in the Qurʾān that appears to be for all believing Muslims for all times to come, while at the same time there is an instruction in the Prophetic sayings that says the opposite. By using the unrestrictive–restrictive distinction, the Shāfiʿī-an method would allow for the Qurʾānic command to reign supreme for all believing Muslims for eternity, while a small exception would have been made for a time- and space-specific context for some Muslims through a reading of the Prophetic sayings. The Qurʾānic command is not rejected. The Prophetic instruction is not rejected. And the apparent tension between the two is dealt with in a manner creative enough for the element of play to continue with every new case that requires the unrestrictive/restrictive distinction.

This further allows al-Shāfiʿī to ensure that Islamic legal theory distanced itself as much as possible from the possibility of one source abrogating the other. Abrogation (*naskh*) is a method in Islamic legal theory that allows a later commandment to repeal a previous commandment, thereby rendering its legal content inoperative. However, al-Shāfiʿī feared that if inter-source abrogation between the Qurʾān and ḥadīth were to be allowed unchecked, the Qurʾān would 'overwhelm the Sunna in all cases of asserted conflict between the two'.[21] Unlike inter-source abrogation, the unrestrictive–restrictive distinction allows a jurist to work with both sources at the same time, not necessarily elevating one over the other. This shows that for al-Shāfiʿī the entire exercise of Islamic legal theory rests upon the necessity of tension between two apparently contradictory sources. Without this tension, there would be no Islamic legal theory as we know it today.

Al-Shāfiʿī was dealing with a profound problem: on the one hand, he had to maintain the supremacy of the Qurʾān as a source of law since the Qurʾānic text was, in terms of the theory of *tawātur*, certain.[22] On the other hand, he could not dismiss the *sunna* of the Prophet in its entirety either. He had to maintain the supremacy of the Qurʾān while simultaneously making sure

[21] Lowry, *Early Islamic Legal Theory*, 91.

[22] For a detailed study of what *tawātur* means and how central it is for understanding the Islamic textual and epistemological traditions, see Suheil Laher, 'Twisted Threads: Genesis, Development and Application of the Term and Concept of Tawatur in Islamic Thought', PhD dissertation, Harvard University, 2014.

that the status of the Prophetic sayings was not diminished. It is precisely by acknowledging the tension between the two sources that al-Shāfiʿī laid the foundations of Islamic legal theory, since it was in an attempt to find a creative resolution to that tension that he came up with several methods that to this day form the substratum of Islamic legal interpretation.[23]

### *Tension between* Fiqh *and* Siyāsa

Another crucial development in Islamic law that ended up expanding the meaning and function of *fiqh* (or *sharīʿa*, although there is a difference between the two)[24] concerns the tension between those who practiced *fiqh* and those who ruled over Muslim lands and localities through their political power and discretion – between jurists who had the authority to define the boundaries of normative law (*fiqh*, or *sharīʿa*) and political rulers who had to govern their populations administratively (*siyāsa*). Scholars of Islamic law define the amalgamation of the two as *siyāsa-sharʿiyya*, a legal framework that brings political and administrative law-making within the fold of the normative boundaries of Islamic law. According to Sadiq Reza, this doctrine of *siyāsa-sharʿiyya* 'cedes daily governance to political authorities *as a matter of* the *sharia*',[25] meaning that political authority is effectively brought under

[23] This tendency to attempt to create some functional resolution to a set of contradictions was continued by later jurists as well, including those who appeared immediately after al-Shāfiʿī. For instance, here is Ahmed El Shamsy writing about al-Athram (d. 886 CE): 'it is clear that several traditionalists in this period adopted al-Shāfiʿī's methods of legal reasoning and used his hermeneutic tools in their own work . . . The staunch traditionalist Abū Bakr al-Athram employed al-Shāfiʿī's hermeneutic concepts, such as *bayān* and the general/specific (*ʿāmm/khāṣṣ*) dichotomy, in his work. His adoption of al-Shāfiʿī's legal theory in order to reconcile conflicting textual sources stands in marked contrast to the approach of the previous generation of traditionalists: these presented seemingly contradictory reports without seeking to reconcile their contents, merely noting the relative strength of the chain of transmission for each report.' Ahmed El Shamsy, *The Canonization of Islamic Law: A Social and Intellectual History* (Cambridge: Cambridge University Press, 2013), 199.

[24] In simplest terms, if *sharīʿa* is defined as the totality of divine law, then *fiqh* is the human interpretation and understanding of it.

[25] Sadiq Reza, 'Islam's Fourth Amendment: Search and Seizure in Islamic Doctrine and Muslim Practice', *Georgetown Journal of International Law* 40(3) (2009): 715.

the banner of the *sharīʿa*. Mohammad Fadel too has argued that *fiqh* (normative aspect of the law) subsumes within it the *siyāsa* (administrative lawmaking).[26] Asifa Quraishi-Landes puts forward a similar definition, one that I particularly admire for its mathematical clarity – according to her, the very concept of *sharīʿa* includes '*fiqh* rules extrapolated from scripture by religious legal scholars articulating right conduct for Muslims, and . . . *siyasa* laws created by temporal rulers, legitimated on service of the public good'.[27] In other words, for Quraishi-Landes, *sharīʿa* = *fiqh* + *siyāsa*. Effectively, *siyāsa-sharʿiyya* is the same as *fiqh-siyāsa*; it is just that Quraishi-Landes' formulation of the concept avoids the confusion and makes it clear that what we call *sharīʿa* was a combination of *fiqh* (Islamic normative law produced by *fiqh* specialists) and *siyāsa* (administrative law as a product of political rule and will).

Ovamir Anjum, in his encyclopaedia entry on 'al-Siyāsa al-Sharʿiyya', points out:

> the term *Sharīʿah* be understood not as a body of law derivable by jurists strictly through disciplined scriptural hermeneutics, but more generally as 'Islamic normativity', which may also include the discretionary policies of a legitimate Islamic government.[28]

But in his discussion of the concept, Anjum goes a step further. He acknowledges that there was indeed tension between the rulers' decisions (based on their authoritative discretion) and the normative *fiqh* of the jurists, thereby implying that the two were, or at least could be conceived of as, separate, and therefore in opposition to each other, and that the act of merging one into the other was a conscious exercise on the part of jurists. Anjum writes:

> Ibn Taymīyah's *Sharīʿah*-based politics . . . constituted the contention that the *Sharīʿah*, understood as the ideals contained in the Qurʾān and

[26] Mohammad Fadel, 'Islam, Constitutionalism and Democratic Self-government', in Khaled Abou El Fadl, Ahmad Atif Ahmad, and Said Fares Hassan (eds), *Routledge Handbook of Islamic Law* (New York: Routledge, 2019), 419.

[27] Asifa Quraishi-Landes, 'The Sharia Problem with Sharia Legislation', *Ohio Northern University Law Review* 41 (2015): 546.

[28] See Ovamir Anjum, 'al-Siyasa al-Sharʿiyya', *Oxford Islamic Studies Online*, available at: http://www.oxfordislamicstudies.com/article/opr/t349/e0077, last accessed 7 May 2020.

the sunnah, encompassed Islamic law as well as political ethics . . . In the domain of Islamic politics, the notion of *maṣlaḥah* (welfare; interest) thus replaces textual indications as the central concern. Although maṣlaḥah was classically understood as the 'interests' already inherent in divine injunctions or sometimes as a small realm for juristic discretion where the texts were silent, Ibn Taymīyah and his followers used a broader conception of *maṣlaḥah* to argue against those who wished to limit Islamic politics to the explicit statements of the sacred texts. *Maṣlaḥah* could legitimately encompass all acts, norms, and arrangements that are demanded by justice and public welfare, although they cannot contradict explicit and agreed-upon rules of the *Sharīʿah*.

What Anjum seems to be highlighting is the historical claim that since it was Ibn Taymiyya who was the first jurist to title his book *al-Siyāsa al-Sharʿiyya*, and that he and his school expanded the meaning of *maṣlaḥa* (interest, or public good) in order to bring public-interest administrative law-making within the ambit of normative Islamic law, it shows that some serious theoretical work indeed had to be undertaken to make sure that the *siyāsa* portion of the framework could supplement the normativity of the *fiqh*. It took playing around with abstract ideas and categories (like *maṣlaḥa*) and creative ingenuity on the part of Ibn Taymiyya and his disciples that led to the concept of *siyāsa-sharʿiyya*, as we know it today. Anjum began his article with these words:

In Islamic tradition, given the obvious potential *tension* between the ruler's discretion . . . and other articulations of the Shariʿah, the concept of Shariʿah-based politics has had a complex and contested history . . . politics, understood as redistribution of resources among various competing interest groups, cannot be conceptualized without the notion of a territorially bounded community. The very idea of Islamic rule and politics necessitates that the ruler now rule over a community and not a mere territory, and this leads to a potential mismatch between the community and the territory: a community of Muslims may be dispersed in various lands as well as interspersed with non-Muslim subjects. Muslim thought responded to this predicament by *minimizing the mismatch* between territory and the community.[29]

[29] Anjum, 'al-Siyasa al-Sharʿiyya' (added italics).

Not only does Anjum use the word 'tension' to describe the intellectual conflict, his articulation of the resolution in terms of 'minimizing the mismatch' beautifully captures the gist of creativity required in the process of play. I would repeat that for both Smith and Gill, resolving the conflict neatly and completely is not *necessarily* the goal. Gill writes: 'Smith's is a comparative method framed by juxtaposition and fueled by difference directed less toward final resolution than toward raising questions and revealing insights . . . Smith's method is akin to play.'[30] A neat and complete resolution of competing concerns would spell the end of play since it would eliminate tension from the equation.

The reason why I categorise the Qurʾān–ḥadīth and *siyāsa–sharīʿa* dichotomies in terms of Smith and Gill's tension and play is because the dichotomies never *really* dissolve into each other;[31] they maintain their independent existence and stature but find their resolution by creating a third space, which is a safe space for them to collide, harmonise and evolve – the same space that would enable Gill's play.

### *Tension between Tradition and Modernity*

With the arrival of colonialism in South Asia also came what we generally refer to as 'modernity'. From matters of governance to record-keeping to the system of education and the role of religion in public spheres, to the arbitrary breaking up of countries into modern nation-states, the forces of colonial modernity ruptured the very existence of South Asia (as they did elsewhere as well). While different groups and communities in the region had different reactions and responses to these forces, what bound most of them together was the contradictory desires to both push back against as well as to learn to live with the new reality. What resulted was the creation of a multitude of layers

[30] Gill, 'Play', 455.

[31] As Anjum points out in the same entry, even when Ibn Taymiyya and his disciples expanded the scope of *maṣlaḥa*, they still had to impose the restriction that *maṣlaḥa*, however expansive and necessary, 'cannot contradict explicit and agreed-upon rules of the *Sharīʿah*'. This demonstrates that even though, theoretically, the category of *siyāsa* is fully immersed within the framework of *sharīʿa*, the tool that makes it happen is itself in constant need of definition, namely, where does *maṣlaḥa* begin to encroach upon explicit Islamic rules? Hence, at some level the tension survives and is not fully resolved.

of tension – between the old ways and the new world, between the desire to rebel and the aspiration for some kind of a status quo, and, after the creation of Pakistan in 1947, between the *ʿulamāʾ*'s desire to create a truly Islamic state and to preserve a separate space and authority for themselves in that new state. It is these tensions, among others, that I will now explore, with the intent to analyse the *ʿulamāʾ*'s responses to them. In this section, I will primarily rely upon Muhammad Qasim Zaman's *The Ulama in Contemporary Islam*, while also incorporating more recent findings into the discussion.[32]

Since pre-modern times, the main vehicle of both religious and rationalist knowledge in the Islamic world has been commentaries (*shurūḥ*, sing. *sharḥ*) and glosses (*ḥāshiya*, pl. *ḥawāshī*; or marginalia). Through these commentaries and glosses, the *ʿulamāʾ* elaborated upon, critiqued and added to already-existing texts. This palimpsestic textual tradition allowed for several layers of meaning-making within the confines of a particular discipline and sometimes within the boundaries of a specific discourse within a particular discipline. To begin with, this commentarial tradition in itself seemed perfectly customised to facilitate the existence of different (sometimes contradictory) opinions within the same religious disciplines.[33] Citing Baber Johansen's work on *fiqh*,

[32] Mashal Saif's work on the tensions between *ʿulamāʾ* and the nation-state of Pakistan raises several fascinating points. In the process, she also builds upon Zaman's work. She writes: 'In assessing the relationship between the Pakistani 'ulama' and their nation-state, I assert that the 'ulama's engagements with the state are best understood as a dexterous navigation between affirmation, critique, contestation and cultivation. In proposing this manner of thinking about the Pakistani 'ulama's engagements with their state, I provide a more detailed and nuanced view of the 'ulama'-state relationship compared to earlier commentaries and other works. For example, Qasim Zaman uses the terms "ambiguity" and "ambivalence" to describe the Pakistani 'ulama's views on, and engagement with, their state. While acknowledging the significance of Zaman's views as a vital conversation starter, this dissertation provides more clarity on the issue by examining it in detail and moving the discussion beyond "ambiguity and "ambivalence."' Mashal Saif, 'The 'Ulamā' and the State: Negotiating Tradition, Authority and Sovereignty in Contemporary Pakistan', PhD dissertation, Duke University, 2014, 26.

[33] Lit defines these commentaries as 'structural textual correspondence', implying that it is not as if the medium allows for any and all opinions to be expressed with an equal air of validity; rather, these opinions address specific and narrow intellectual discourses and problems, thereby making the possibility of contradictory opinions less likely and more meaningful. L.W.C. van Lit, 'Commentary and Commentary Tradition: The Basic Terms for Understanding Islamic Intellectual History', *Mélanges de l'Institut dominicain d'études orientales* 32 (2017): 3–26.

Zaman states that these different, potentially contradictory, opinions existed simultaneously within the textual tradition, 'not necessarily in complete harmony with one another'.[34] This is a crucial observation since it demonstrates the tendency within the *ʿulamāʾ* of the pre-modern as well as modern times (especially in South Asia) to stay away from the either/or dilemma when it came to hermeneutical approaches: that is, either staying completely within the fold of traditional textual authority and discourses, or rejecting them *in toto* in the interest of something new, thereby having no connection at all with the past. Instead, the medium of the commentarial tradition allowed the *ʿulamāʾ* to 'retain earlier, authoritative school doctrines *while also* modifying those doctrines in practice'.[35] The phrase 'while also' serves as a fortunate call-back to the necessity of two contradictory ideas for the element of 'play' to come into effect, play that does not seek to resolve the contradiction but only to provide a third space where something creative transpires.

But if this commentarial tradition was so central to Arabo-Islamic epistemology (since it allowed for continuous debate and discussion), why is it that the *ʿulamāʾ* in the early years of the creation of Pakistan developed a sudden obsession with codification, something that is the polar opposite of a lively, discursive tradition?

Zaman has a three-pronged response to this question. He argues, first, that the *ʿulamāʾ* of South Asia overwhelmingly hailed from the Ḥanafī School which insisted on assigning great weight to authoritative opinions already decided upon by the traditionalist authorities (although this does *not* imply

[34] M. Qasim Zaman, *The Ulama in Contemporary Islam: Custodians of Change* (Princeton: Princeton, NJ University Press, 2002), 38.

[35] Zaman, *The Ulama in Contemporary Islam*, 38 (added italics). It is also important to mention here that this commentarial tradition suffered a blow with the arrival of the printing press in South Asia. However, displaying the same tendency to make the best out of an unavoidable situation, the *ʿulamāʾ* in South Asia accepted the printing press while also continuing with the production of commentaries and glosses. This period of parallel construction of discourse through the two different mediums of the press and the commentaries continued albeit briefly. Zaman writes: 'That this age-old and elitist medium has continued to exist in a democratizing age of print and other media is a point worth underscoring', Zaman, *The Ulama in Contemporary Islam*, 55.

that they were wary of *ijtihād*, since they were not). As a result of this prior tendency to acquiesce, to a sufficient degree, to authoritative, written-down rulings, the *ʿulamāʾ* were in a sense predisposed to accept the need for codification in principle.[36] Secondly, historically, the *ʿulamāʾ* had seen many of the laws already codified during the British occupation of India. As a result, their own worldview became more accepting of the idea of 'discrete' law-making, the result of which can then be implemented on the population. Zaman is quick to note that this tendency does prove a changed conception of *sharīʿa* in the community of the *ʿulamāʾ* – they began to see 'the shariʿa as content rather than process'.[37]

Third, and most importantly for our purposes, the *ʿulamāʾ* began to approach the issue of the modern Islamic state as well as their authority and place in it in very pragmatic – and, for me, creative – terms. Zaman writes:

> codification is also a pragmatic way of implementing Islamic law. On the one hand . . . it can be argued that much of the law that already exists in a codified form will remain unaffected insofar as it is not repugnant to the shariʿa, so the legal system would not have to be dismantled and built afresh. On the other hand, ʿulama have also argued that the judges educated in the modern secular legal tradition can be retrained to implement shariʿa law in its codified form. The modernist judges need not fear, then, that they would necessarily be replaced once the shariʿa becomes the law of the land . . . *[This] argument is patently meant to assuage modernist fears.*[38]

Time has proven that judges in Pakistan have automatically assumed the role of Islamic legal practitioners in order to facilitate certain quarters of the population in light of their own non-specialist understanding of Islamic edicts and instructions. For instance, Zubair Abbasi has pointed out that judges in Pakistan have effectively 'reformed Islamic family law by extending women's right to no-fault based divorce (*khulʿ*)'.[39] Having said that, there is

[36] Zaman, *The Ulama in Contemporary Islam*, 97.

[37] Zaman, *The Ulama in Contemporary Islam*, 98.

[38] Zaman, *The Ulama in Contemporary Islam*, 98 (added italics).

[39] M. Zubair Abbasi, 'Judicial *Ijtihād* as a Tool for Legal Reform: Extending Women's Right to Divorce under Islamic Law in Pakistan', *Islamic Law & Society* 24(4) (2017): 384–411.

indeed a difference between Zaman's subject and the argument put forward by Abbasi. While Abbasi is talking about the judges breaking away from the shackles of obedience to traditionalist juridical authorities and their Islamic legal opinions (thereby exercising a form of *ijtihād*), Zaman is referring to the *ʿulamā*'s satisfaction at the prospect of judges learning to adhere to past *ʿulamā*'s authoritative legal opinions.

For our purposes, what this means is that the *ʿulamā*', yet again, created a meaningful and productive third space. On the one hand, they could have rejected the very idea of codification by labelling it antithetical to the centuries-old Islamic textual ethos of continuous discourse. On the other hand, they could have adopted the proposal for the codification of *sharīʿa* in Pakistan wholeheartedly, effectively breaking away from that centuries-old tradition. What they actually did was to create a third space where they accepted the merits of codification while at the same time tying it to the discourse-rich tradition in which they were heavily invested, to the extent that they did not even make mandatory the hiring of judges who would have had the proper credentials to undertake the implementation of the codified *sharīʿa*; instead, they proposed that the same judges who were part of the modern nation-state apparatus and trained in common or secular law be 'retrained' so that they could be retained. In an epistemological sense as well as a pragmatic sense, then, the *ʿulamā*' in the early decades of the creation of Pakistan continued the tradition of creating the potentialities of play when faced with two contradictory and mutually exclusive possibilities – and this epistemic act of playfulness was never meant to permanently resolve those contradictions; instead, in the appropriated words of F. Scott Fitzgerald quoted at the very beginning of this chapter, it was meant to allow for a way 'to hold two opposed ideas in the mind at the same time, and still retain the ability to function'.

## Conclusion

In this chapter, I have tried to study three crucial developments in Islamic history through the ideas of juxtaposition, tension, and play as put forward by J. Z. Smith and Sam Gill, theorists of religion who used these ideas to improve upon existing understandings of religion as well as the evolution of the academic study of religion. I have argued that taking these ideas and applying them to Islamic legal history, which I believe has hitherto not been done (at least not in any systematic way),[40] is not only valid; it is essential – it would make complete sense in the intellectual worldviews of Smith and Gill, and it has turned out to be immensely useful as it has allowed us to study the aforementioned developments in Islamic history in a new light. I must admit that the argument presented in this chapter could be seen as somewhat provocative. I maintain that it is valid as an historical argument rather than a normative one. In other words, I am not suggesting that this is how we *should* study Islamic legal history; only that we *can*, even if just to see what emerges out of this experiment. I do not wish at all to suggest that there is something essential or even unique about the legal and textual traditions of Islam.[41] Nor

[40] It is both serendipitous and fascinating to note that Roshan Iqbal's forthcoming book on *mutʿa* (temporary marriage in Islam) contains a section that summarises an important argument in it and bears remarkable similarity to the method discussed in this chapter. Writing about the tensions between traditionalist Islamic legal experts and the most current scientific findings in the field of sexuality, she writes: '*Juxtaposing* Muslim scholars' ideas about fe/male sexuality with current scientific research exposes the gaps and *contradictions* present in both. Exploring the *interplay* between sexuality and Islamic law is crucial to moving Islamic law forward in a just and equitable manner.' My italicisations in the quotation above by Iqbal make it abundantly clear that there is an awareness within Islamic scholarly circles, to whatever extent, of the way in which several issues in Islamic legal discourse get resolved by this method of juxtaposition, tension and play. See Iqbal's forthcoming book, titled *Rethinking Marital and Sexual Ethics in Islamic Law: The Case of Temporary Marriage*, based primarily on her dissertation – Roshan Iqbal, 'A Thousand and One Wives: Investigating the Intellectual History of the Exegesis of Verse 4:24', PhD dissertation, Georgetown University, 2016.

[41] Although, when a similar problem presented itself to European scholars who studied Buddhism, a problem of two different kinds of sources from which to extrapolate Buddhist theology (textual sources and archaeological evidence), several key scholars in the field decided to elevate the status of textual sources and ended up ignoring the epistemological value of archaeological evidence. Rather than acknowledge any tension – or even possible complementarity – between the two sources and working with both in order to create a playful third space, several key scholars of the time decided to work only with one of those sources and virtually reject the other. This is, of course, not a commentary on Buddhists writing about their own tradition since it was the Europeans who were making these source selections for their own academic purposes and in light of their own 'Protestant presuppositions'. Still, it shows that there are instances in the context of the study of other world religions where the contradiction in choices was not allowed the creative third space; rather, the potential tension arising out of the contradiction was permanently removed by elevating one possibility to the total exclusion of the other. See Gregory Schopen, 'Archaeology and Protestant Presuppositions in the Study of Indian Buddhism', *History of Religions* 31(1) (1991): 1–4.

do I argue that the three case studies discussed in this chapter constitute the entirety of the *summum bonum* of Islamic legal history; there could very well be important exceptions. I simply wish to point out that the categories of juxtaposition, tension and play – categories that admittedly were formed in disciplines other than the academic study of Islam – do illuminate some crucial episodes in the development of Islamic legal history in ways that enrich our understanding of it. This method provides us with a new way, or at the very least a new terminology, with which to study the development of the Islamic legal enterprise; may be even Islamic intellectual and textual history in general.[42]

[42] In addition to Islamic legal theory, the history of Islamic philosophy and science too provides evidence in support of our thesis that juxtaposition, tension and play seemed to be a preferential method of argumentation in Arabo-Islamic textual discourses. Among the most important concepts to come out of the Islamic intellectual tradition was the idea of 'secondary causality', especially as argued by Abū Ḥāmid al-Ghazālī (d. 1111 CE) in this eleventh-century work titled *Tahāfut al-Falāsifa* (*The Incoherence of the Philosophers*). Al-Ghazālī rejected the traditional idea of natural causality because accepting it at its face value would have meant that there would be no room for prophetic miracles in the natural world. This tension between natural causality and the possibility of miracles in many ways defined the medieval period of Islamic philosophy. Al-Ghazālī was associated with the school of theology that advocated for occasionalism and argued that what we consider causality – for example, a match burning a cotton ball – is actually God's decree. That it is only by God's will that the cotton ball catches fire every time the match touches it. Effectively, al-Ghazālī dislocates causality from the domain of the natural universe and places it in the realm of theology, whereby it is not a natural law that leads to a match combusting a cotton ball every time; it is God's will that always enables it. And since the essence of the idea of causality is regularity and predictability – that A will lead to B every single time – Muslim occasionalists were able to provide an equally valid epistemological foundation for the community of scholars who were practicing rationalist sciences such as astronomy, medicine, surgery, etc. By recognising this critical tension between natural causality and divine will, and not dismissing one possibility in favour of the other, the medieval Islamic intellectual discourse was able to create a third category – one of secondary causality – which made the epistemological foundations of science possible without removing God's will from the equation. The juxtaposition was recognised; the tension was acknowledged; and the creative play 'minimized the mismatch' between the two approaches. See 'al-Ghazali', *Stanford Encyclopedia of Philosophy*, 14 August 2007, revised 8 May 2020, available at: https://plato.stanford.edu/entries/al-ghazali, last accessed 2 October 2021.

## Bibliography

Abbasi, M. Zubair, 'Judicial *Ijtihād* as a Tool for Legal Reform: Extending Women's Right to Divorce under Islamic Law in Pakistan', *Islamic Law & Society* 24(4) (2017): 384–411.

Ali, Kecia, 'Foreword', in Joseph Lowry, *The Epistle on Legal Theory: A Translation of al-Shafiʿi's* Risalah. New York: New York University Press, 2015.

Anjum, Ovamir, 'al-Siyasa al-Sharʿiyya', *Oxford Islamic Studies Online*, available at: http://www.oxfordislamicstudies.com/article/opr/t349/e0077, last accessed 7 May 2020.

El Shamsy, Ahmed, *The Canonization of Islamic Law: A Social and Intellectual History* Cambridge: Cambridge University Press, 2013.

Fadel, Mohammad, 'Islam, Constitutionalism and Democratic Self-government', in Khaled Abou El Fadl, Ahmad Atif Ahmad, and Said Fares Hassan (eds), *Routledge Handbook of Islamic Law* (New York: Routledge, 2019), 415–27.

Fitzgerald, F. Scott, 'The Crack-Up', *Esquire*. 7 March 2017 (originally published in 1936), available at: https://www.esquire.com/lifestyle/a4310/the-crack-up, last accessed 20 July 2021.

'al-Ghazali', *Stanford Encyclopedia of Philosophy*, 14 August 2007, revised 8 May 2020, available at: https://plato.stanford.edu/entries/al-ghazali, last accessed 2 October 2021.

Gill, Sam, 'No Place to Stand: Jonathan Z. Smith as *Homo Ludens*, The Academic Study of Religion *Sub Specie Ludi*', *Journal of the American Academy of Religion* 66(2) (1998): 283–312.

Gill, Sam, 'Play', in Willi Braun and Russell T. McCutcheon (eds), *Guide to the Study of Religion*. London: Continuum, 2000.

Gill, Sam, *The Proper Study of Religion: Building on Jonathan Z. Smith*. Oxford: Oxford University Press, 2020.

Grimes, Ronald L., 'Defining Nascent Ritual', *Journal of the American Academy of Religion* 50(4) (1982): 539–55.

Hart, Patrick, 'Theory, Method, and Madness in Religious Studies', *Method and Theory in the Study of Religion* 28(1) (2016): 3–25.

Iqbal, Roshan, 'A Thousand and One Wives: Investigating the Intellectual History of the Exegesis of Verse 4:24', PhD dissertation, Georgetown University, 2016.

Iqbal, Roshan, *Rethinking Marital and Sexual Ethics in Islamic Law: The Case of Temporary Marriage*. Lanham, MD: Rowman & Littlefield, forthcoming 2022.

Kripal, Jeffrey, *Authors of the Impossible: The Paranormal and the Sacred*. Chicago: University of Chicago Press, 2010.

Laher, Suheil, 'Twisted Threads: Genesis, Development and Application of the Term and Concept of Tawatur in Islamic Thought', PhD dissertation, Harvard University, 2014.

Lit, L. W. C. van, 'Commentary and Commentary Tradition: The Basic Terms for Understanding Islamic Intellectual History', *Mélanges de l'Institut dominicain d'études orientales* 32 (2017): 3–26.

Lowry, Joseph, *Early Islamic Legal Theory: The Risala of Muhammad ibn Idris al-Shafi'i*. Leiden: Brill, 2007.

Lowry, Joseph, *The Epistle on Legal Theory: A Translation of al-Shafi'i's* Risalah. New York: New York University Press, 2015.

Quraishi-Landes, Asifa, 'The Sharia Problem with Sharia Legislation', *Ohio Northern University Law Review* 41 (2015): 545–66.

Reza, Sadiq, 'Islam's Fourth Amendment: Search and Seizure in Islamic Doctrine and Muslim Practice', *Georgetown Journal of International Law* 40(3) (2009): 703–806.

Saif, Mashal, 'The 'Ulamā' and the State: Negotiating Tradition, Authority and Sovereignty in Contemporary Pakistan', PhD dissertation, Duke University, 2014.

Schopen, Gregory, 'Archaeology and Protestant Presuppositions in the Study of Indian Buddhism', *History of Religions* 31(1) (1991): 1–4.

Smith, J. Z., 'Adde parvum parvo magnus acervus erit.', *History of Religions* 11(1) (1971): 67–90.

Winnicott, D. W., *Playing and Reality*. London: Tavistock, 1971.

Zaman, M. Qasim, *The Ulama in Contemporary Islam: Custodians of Change*. Princeton: Princeton University Press, 2002.

# 6

# NEW THEORETICAL APPROACHES TO THE QUR'ĀN AND QUR'ĀNIC STUDIES: AN ANALYSIS OF THE QUR'ĀNIC (DISABLED) BODY IN LIGHT OF CONCEPTUAL METAPHOR AND CONCEPTUAL BLENDING THEORY

JOHANNE LOUISE CHRISTIANSEN

## Theory, the Qur'ān and Qur'ānic Studies

The field of western Qur'ānic Studies has never been as vibrant as it is today. More people, more departments, more funding and, as a result, more well-grounded research into this religious text is seeing the light of day. In line with the overall aim of this volume, however, we still only find a few theoretically based approaches to the Qur'ān within this field. Perhaps Qur'ānic Studies can be considered somewhat 'traditional' in this regard, focused on the classical textual methods of study.[1] There are many reasons for this state of affairs. First, although western Qur'ānic Studies have existed since the nineteenth century (originally breaking out from the historical–critical study of the Bible), the comparison between this field and Biblical Studies is unfair. Considering the difference in (again) numbers of people, departments and funding, Qur'ānic Studies remains and will probably continue to remain

[1] Thomas Hoffmann, 'The Moving Qur'ān: A Cognitive Poetics Approach to the Qur'ān', in Mohammed Nekrouni and Jan Meise (eds), *Modern Controversies in Qur'ānic Studies* (Hamburg-Schenefeld: EB-Verlag, 2009), 141–52 at 142.

a much smaller field. As such, there is still a vast amount of primary research to be done compared with studies of the Bible. Other reasons perhaps include a lack of access to the rich and massive traditional Islamic literature, as well as a general (and sometimes reasonable) concern about using this material. There is no doubt that a confessional outlook prevails in the majority of works studying the Qurʾān from within this tradition. But we could also ask, as many others have done before me: where would studies of Christianity be if Christian sources on the earliest days of the religion were completely disregarded?[2] The Muslim exegetical literature is an immense source of philological and literary insights that will not be ignored in this study. A third reason may relate to the approach to theory and applying theoretical frameworks in general. Here, I call for an understanding of theory not as something necessarily resulting in facts or truths, but rather as a way of offering hypotheses that can and should be repeatedly evaluated based on their probability and consistency.

In this chapter, I will not demonstrate a non-textual approach or method. Rather, I advocate for a close, synchronic reading of the Qurʾānic text, albeit a reading supplemented by a theoretical perspective. In this way, the chapter complies with the textual focus of current Qurʾānic Studies, seeing as the synchronic part of the study may stand alone. The theorical framework – the Conceptual Metaphor Theory (CMT) and the Conceptual Blending[3] Theory (CBT) – taken in this study originated in the field of Cognitive Linguistics. Besides my own work on conceptual metaphors of darkness in the Qurʾān, to which I return below, especially Thomas Hoffmann has advocated for the consideration of cognitive theories as a fruitful research endeavour within Qurʾānic Studies.[4] For example, taking his point of departure in the Force Dynamics theory by Leonard Talmy, Hoffmann shows that the Qurʾān is a highly 'forceful'

[2] See, for example, Devin Stewart, 'Reflections on the State of the Art in Western Qurʾanic Studies', in Carol Bakhos and Michael Cook (eds), *Islam and Its Past: Jahiliyya, Late Antiquity, and the Qurʾan* (Oxford: Oxford University Press, 2017), 4–68; Patricia Crone, 'What Do We Actually Know about Mohammad?' available at: https://www.opendemocracy.net/faith-europe_islam/mohammed_3866.jsp, 2008.

[3] Also sometimes called Conceptual Integration.

[4] Thomas Hoffmann, 'Force Dynamics and the Qurʾân: An Essay in Cognitive Qurʾânic Poetics', in Roberta Sterman Sabbath (ed.), *Sacred Tropes: Tanakh, New Testament, and Qurʾan as Literature and Culture*. Leiden: Brill, 2009; Hoffmann, 'The Moving Qurʾān';

text, not only in its employment of certain Arabic grammatical constructions like the second stem verb, signifying 'that an act is done with *great force*', but also in the description of its god using highly causative terms.[5] Hoffmann has also applied the theoretical frame of CMT to the Qurʾān. In another study, he discusses various alimentary metaphors, including those specifying reward but especially those evoking punishment (e.g., Q 3:106; 44:43–49; 73:12–13).[6] In accordance with Hoffmann's work, this chapter calls for the academic field's consideration of such cognitive approaches to the Qurʾānic text.

The chapter consists of two parts: first, an introduction to the two theories, CMT and CBT; and secondly, an overview of (disabled) bodily metaphors in the Qurʾān, followed by an analysis of what I term the Qurʾān's metaphorical 'disability clusters' (Q 2:18, 171; 5:71; 6:39; 8:22; 10:42–43; 11:24; 17:97; 25:73; 27:80–81; 30:52–53; 41:44; 43:40; 47:43), addressed in the light of these theoretical frameworks.

## Conceptual Metaphor and Conceptual Blending Theory

As noted above, CMT and CBT are rooted in the academic field of Cognitive Linguistics.[7] Indeed, here, they are as it were 'old news', having been

Thomas Hoffmann, 'Notes on Qurʾānic Wilderness – and Its Absence', in Laura Feldt (ed.), *Wilderness in Mythology and Religion*. Berlin: De Gruyter, 2012, 157–82; Thomas Hoffmann, '*Taste My Punishment and My Warnings* (Q. 54:39): On the Torments of Tantalus and Other Painful Metaphors of Taste in the Qur'an', *Journal of Qur'anic Studies* 21(1) (2019): 1–20. Cognitive theories have to some extent been considered in relation to the Qurʾān within applied linguistics. See, for example, Khan Sardaraz and Roslan Ali, 'A Cognitive–Semantic Study of the Spatial Preposition *Fī* (فِي) in the Quran', *KEMANUSIAAN: Asian Journal of Humanities* 24(2) (2017): 89–122; Khan Sardaraz and Roslan Ali, 'A Cognitive–Semantic Approach to the Interpretation of Death Metaphor Themes in the Quran', *Journal of Nusantara Studies (JONUS)* 4(2) (2019): 219–46; Amani M. Alhusban and Mohammad Alkhawaldah, 'Meaning Construction of Selected Quranic Metaphors', *International Journal of Linguistics* 10(6) (2018): 134–48.

[5] Hoffmann, 'Force Dynamics and the Qur'ân', 73–6; Leonard Talmy, *Toward a Cognitive Semantics, Volume I: Concept Structuring Systems* (Cambridge, MA: MIT Press, 2000); Leonard Talmy, 'Force Dynamics in Language and Cognition', *Cognitive Science* 12(1) (1988): 49–100.

[6] Hoffmann, '*Taste My Punishment*'.

[7] For an introduction to this field, see Dirk Geeraerts and Hubert Cuyckens (eds), *The Oxford Handbook of Cognitive Linguistics* (Oxford: Oxford University Press, 2007).

originally formulated and later developed through the 1980s and 1990s.[8] Whereas CMT – as indicated in the name – deals only with metaphorical language, CBT is much broader, incorporating interaction between mental spaces in all aspects of human language.[9] Through this broad perspective, CBT nuances a cognitive approach to metaphors, and it is in this form that the theory will be used here.[10]

Valid for both theories is a break with the (Aristotelian) notion that metaphors are only imaginative, ornamental devices of grammar and rhetoric.[11] Instead, metaphorical language is grounded in human cognition: humans think, reason and understand metaphorically.[12] By exploring a particular text with a particular worldview (such as the Qurʾān) from this theoretical perspective, it is possible to discern non-linguistic backgrounds for the text's metaphorisations, its conceptualisation and its comprehension of the world.[13] While some metaphors might be termed 'transcultural', others are bound to a certain cultural context, potentially indicating an underlying mental representation of a specific social reality.[14]

[8] Gilles Fauconnier and Mark Turner, *The Way We Think: Conceptual Blending and the Mind's Hidden Complexities* (New York: Basic Books, 2003); Mark Turner and Gilles Fauconnier, 'Conceptual Integration and Formal Expression', *Metaphor and Symbolic Activity* 10(3) (1995): 183–204; George Lakoff and Mark Turner, *More than Cool Reason: A Field Guide to Poetic Metaphor* (Chicago: University of Chicago Press, 1989); George Lakoff, *Women, Fire, and Dangerous Things: What Categories Reveal about the Mind* (Chicago: University of Chicago Press, 1987); George Lakoff and Mark Johnson, *Metaphors We Live By* (Chicago: University of Chicago Press, 1980).

[9] Fauconnier and Turner, *The Way We Think*, 6.

[10] Gilles Fauconnier and Mark Turner, 'Conceptual Integration Networks', *Cognitive Science* 22(2) (1998): 135.

[11] See, for example, Aristotle, *Poetics*, ed. W. William Fyfe (London: Heinemann, 1965), 1457b; Samuel R. Levin, 'Aristotle's Theory of Metaphor', *Philosophy & Rhetoric* 15(1) (1982): 24–46. For another, albeit related approach to metaphors and reality, the so-called 'interaction model', see Paul Ricoeur, *The Rule of Metaphor: The Creation of Meaning in Language*, trans. Robert Czerny (London: Routledge, [1975] 2004).

[12] Lakoff and Johnson, *Metaphors We Live By*, 4–5.

[13] Hoffmann, 'The Moving Qurʾān', 146–7; Hoffmann, 'Qurʾānic Wilderness', 172.

[14] Antje Labahn, 'Heart as a Conceptual Metaphor in Chronicles. Metaphors as Representations of Concepts of Reality: Conceptual Metaphors – a New Paradigm in Metaphor Research', in Antje Labahn (ed.), *Conceptual Metaphors in Poetic Texts* (Piscataway, NJ:

Let us begin with CMT. In the works of George Lakoff, Mark Johnson and Mark Turner, particularly *Metaphors We Live By* (1980) and *More than Cool Reason: A Field Guide to Poetic Metaphor* (1989), a cognitive theory of metaphors is presented. According to the theory, metaphors are grounded in human experiences and everyday language, and especially their 'embodiment' considered capable of explaining abstract concepts.[15] Thus, how humans experience the body, movement and objects – basically, the physical and sociocultural world in which we live and by which we are surrounded – plays a dominant part in the ways our minds work and communicate. According to CMT, a metaphor emerges in a so-called 'metaphorical mapping' between two conceptual domains, a process by which certain structures from 'the source domain' are transferred to 'the target domain'.[16] The target domain is often something abstract, constituting what is to be explained by the metaphorical construction. In the Qurʾān, for example, the heart frequently figures in such metaphorical mappings.[17] As a source domain, several heart metaphors relate to ideas of human understanding and faith, all deriving from the basic conceptual metaphor, A PLACE OF UNDERSTANDING IS THE HEART:[18]

Gorgias Press, 2013), 7–12; Matthias Becker et al., 'Metaphor', in Eric Ziolkowski et al. (eds), *Encyclopedia of the Bible and Its Reception*, vol. 18 (Berlin: De Gruyter, 2010), 972.

[15] Lakoff and Johnson, *Metaphors We Live By*; Mark Johnson, *The Body in the Mind: The Bodily Basis of Meaning, Imagination, and Reason* (Chicago: University of Chicago Press, 1987); Lakoff and Turner, *More than Cool Reason*. Among other things, CMT has been criticised for not offering a clear definition of nor distinction between what is metaphorical and what is literal. For Lakoff's response to this criticism, see his 'The Meanings of Literal', *Metaphor and Symbolic Activity* 1(4) (1986): 291–6. In Gary Alan Long, 'Dead or Alive? Literality and God-Metaphors in the Hebrew Bible', *Journal of the American Academy of Religion* 62(2) (1994): 509–19, a useful overview of this debate is provided.

[16] Lakoff and Turner, *More than Cool Reason*, 59, 63–5.

[17] For scholarly works on the heart in the Qurʾān and the Bible, see, for example, Jane D. McAuliffe, 'Heart', *Encyclopaedia of the Qurʾān (EQ)* (online), 2001–; Heikki Räisänen, *The Idea of Divine Hardening: A Comparative Study of the Notion of Divine Hardening, Leading Astray and Inciting to Evil in the Bible and the Qurʾān* (Helsinki: Publications of the Finnish Exegetical Society, 1976), 13–95; Labahn, 'Heart as a Conceptual Metaphor in Chronicles', 13–28.

[18] The denotation for a cognitive metaphor is TARGET DOMAIN IS SOURCE DOMAIN.

> We have created many *jinn* and men for *Jahannam* (*wa-la-qad dhara'nā li-jahannama kathīran mina l-jinni wa-l-insi*). They have hearts, with which they do not understand (*lahum qulūbun lā yafqahūna bihā*); they have eyes, with which they do not see (*wa-lahum a'yunun lā yubṣirūna bihā*); they have ears, with which they do not hear (*wa-lahum ādhānun lā yasma'ūna bihā*). These are like animals (*ulā'ika ka-l-an'āmi*) – no, they are further astray (*bal hum aḍallu*). These are the heedless (*ulā'ika humu l-ghāfilūn*). (Q 7:179)[19]

In this verse, the Qur'ān identifies the heart as a cognitive organ, a place of understanding. This is also why the heart can be 'sealed' (from *kh-t-m*; e.g., Q 2:7), 'veiled' (from *k-n-n*; e.g., Q 18:57) and 'hardened (from *q-s-w*; e.g., Q 6:43), specifically via the submetaphor LACK OF UNDERSTANDING IS A CLOSED HEART. Both metaphors attempt to explain the abstract notion of (lack of) understanding through a prototypical human conceptualisation of what the heart does.[20] But the heart can also be a target domain itself. Exemplified in the cognitive metaphor THE HEART IS A CONTAINER, this organ is able to have 'sickness' (*maraḍ*; e.g., Q 9:125), 'fear' (*wajila*; e.g., Q 23:60) and 'hypocrisy' (*nifāq*; Q 9:77) *in* it.[21] The container metaphor is a so-called 'image-schema', a construct, often spatial and three-dimensional, giving structure to several different cognitive domains.[22] The verse Q 7:179 contains more than these two metaphors. Not only does it present additional related submetaphors, namely, LACK OF UNDERSTANDING IS NOT SEEING/BLINDNESS and LACK OF UNDERSTANDING IS NOT HEARING/DEAFNESS, which I return to in the next section, but also the metaphor THE UNBELIEVERS ARE (MORE ASTRAY THAN) ANIMALS, which I revisit below.

Another example is found in my article, 'The Dark Koran: A Semantic Analysis of the Koranic Darknesses (*ẓulumāt*) and their Metaphorical Usage',

[19] In translations of the Qur'ān, I follow Alan Jones, trans., *The Qur'ān* (Cambridge: Gibb Memorial Trust, 2007).

[20] Following this theoretical framework, such a conceptualisation of the heart is, of course, also metaphorical.

[21] See here Sardaraz and Ali, 'A Cognitive–Semantic Study of the Spatial Preposition *Fī* (فِي)', 106–9.

[22] Lakoff and Johnson, *Metaphors We Live By*, 29–30; Johnson, *The Body in the Mind*, 19–40; Zoltán Kövecses, *Emotion Concepts* (New York: Springer, 1990), 144–59; Hoffmann, 'The Moving Qur'ān', 146.

in which I examine darkness (*ẓulumāt*) as a literary image in the Qur'ān from the theoretical basis of Lakoff, Johnson and Turner.[23] The article shows that even though *ẓulumāt* is not a central word in the Qur'ānic vocabulary, the term continuously connects to some of the text's most important topics, including the relationship between God and man, human understanding and salvation. In joining CMT with the Qur'ānic material, I demonstrate that darkness is often explained through two different conceptual metaphors, A MENTAL STATE IS DARKNESS and PROTECTION IS DARKNESS. Whereas the former is employed in the Qur'ān to illustrate the imperative difference between belief–light and unbelief–darkness (based on human experiences such as not being able to see, being confused or being confined), the latter elucidates the protection (of divine knowledge) and omniscience of the Qur'ānic god. While darkness is generally applied in a negative sense in the Qur'ān, this is not the whole picture. The metaphorical nature of darkness also provides positive images of protection or even of a hiding place for crucial information (e.g., Q 6:59).

As for CBT, the two-domain model of CMT is turned into a '*many-space* model'.[24] In the early 1990s, Turner, now joined by Gilles Faucounnier, argued that a simple mapping between two domains was not always able to explain all aspects of a metaphorical construction.[25] They therefore added two 'spaces',[26] the first being 'the generic space', a space containing 'skeletal structure that

[23] Johanne Louise Christiansen, 'The Dark Koran: A Semantic Analysis of the Koranic Darknesses (*ẓulumāt*) and Their Metaphorical Usage', *Arabica* 62(2/3) (2015): 185–233.

[24] Turner and Fauconnier, 'Conceptual Integration and Formal Expression', 184.

[25] Fauconnier and Turner, 'Conceptual Integration Networks', 135.

[26] According to Fauconnier and Turner, a mental space is not the same as a conceptual domain. A conceptual domain is defined as 'a vast organization of knowledge such as our knowledge of journey or dreaming or education', having 'a basic structure of entities and relations at a high level of generality – for example, the conceptual domain for journey has roles for traveler, path, origin, destination, and so on'. Mental spaces, on the other hand, are 'conceptual packets' that are repeatedly constructed when humans think and communicate, for example, from the same or different conceptual domains. Such spaces give cognitive structure to our memory and experiences, humans being able to connect different mental spaces not necessarily related to each other (Turner and Fauconnier, 'Conceptual Integration and Formal Expression', 183–4; Turner and Fauconnier, *The Way We Think*, 40). This human ability seems to be at the very centre of CBT.

applies to both input spaces [corresponding roughly to the CMT source and target domains]'.[27] The second additional space was dubbed 'the blended space', a space 'integrating, in a partial fashion, specific structure from both of the input spaces'. Regarding the latter, they continued: 'The blended space often includes structure *not* projected to it from either input space.'[28] In other words, the generic space encompasses those concepts which the target and the source have in common, and the blended space those conceptual aspects and relations that become mixed to create something new and possibly distinct from both the target and the source. This is what Faucounnier and Turner call 'emergent structures', which denote the unfolding of meaning and implications not directly originating in either of the input spaces.[29] The last element of their theory entails that such (new) meaning does not remain strictly within the blend. Often, it is projected back to the input spaces, which in turn are affected by and reinterpreted in light of the metaphorical blend.[30] Returning to the Qurʾānic verse Q 7:179, specifically to the conceptual metaphor THE UNBELIEVERS ARE (MORE ASTRAY THAN) ANIMALS, such a blend seems to appear:

> These are like animals (*ulāʾika ka-l-anʿāmi*) – no, they are further astray (*bal hum aḍallu*). These are the heedless (*ulāʾika humu l-ghāfilūn*).

The metaphor follows a bipartite composition, initially as THE UNBELIEVERS ARE ANIMALS, then as THE UNBELIEVERS ARE MORE ASTRAY THAN ANIMALS. However, for either part of the metaphorical composition to make sense, the translation[31] needs to be nuanced. Regarding the Arabic term *anʿām* (pl. from *n-ʿ-m*), Arne A. Ambros and Stephan Procházka translate it as '"livestock"

[27] The idea of a generic space is not new. In classical rhetoric, this is often termed *tertium comparationis* or 'the third [element] of the comparison'. See Pierre van Hecke, 'Conceptual Blending: A Recent Approach to Metaphors. Illustrated with the Pastoral Metaphor in Hos 4,16', in Pierre van Hecke (ed.), *Metaphor in the Hebrew Bible* (Leuven: Leuven University Press, 2005), 220.

[28] Turner and Fauconnier, 'Conceptual Integration and Formal Expression', 184 (added emphasis).

[29] Fauconnier and Turner, *The Way We Think*, 42–4.

[30] Fauconnier and Turner, *The Way We Think*, 44.

[31] Here Jones, *The Qurʾān*, 166.

([Q] 5/95) . . . (defined as comprising *ḍaʾn* "sheep", *maʿz* "goats", *ʾibil* "camels" and *baqar* "cattle"',[32] and Hans Wehr as 'grazing livestock (sheep, camels, cattle, goats)'.[33] Many translators, evidently not including Alan Jones, therefore specify *anʿām* in Q 7:179 as 'cattle'.[34] In this way, the conceptual metaphor is more likely to be either THE UNBELIEVERS ARE (GRAZING) LIVESTOCK or THE UNBELIEVERS ARE CATTLE.[35] Secondly, the metaphor should be seen in context with the preceding sentences – *these* being evoked by *ulāʾika* and *hum* and refer back to humans (and *jinn*) whom God has created to dwell in Hell, without understanding – as well as the preceding verses, Q 7:177–178:[36]

> 177)Evil as an example are those who have denied the truth of Our signs (*sāʾa mathalan l-qawmu lladhīna kadhdhabū bi-āyātinā*) and who used to wrong themselves (*wa-anfusahum kānū yaẓlimūn*).
>
> 178)Those whom God guides are rightly guided (*man yahdi llāhu fa-huwa l-muhtadī*). Those whom He leads astray (*wa-man yuḍlil*) – they are the losers (*fa-ūlāʾika humu l-khāsirūn*).

32 Arne A. Ambros and Stephan Procházka, *A Concise Dictionary of Koranic Arabic* (Wiesbaden: Reichert Verlag, 2004), 271.

33 Hans Wehr, *A Dictionary of Modern Written Arabic*, ed. J. Milton Cowan, 3rd edn (Ithaca, NY: Spoken Languages Services, 1976), 1150.

34 Muhammad Abdel Haleem, *The Qur'an: A New Translation by M.A.S. Abdel Haleem* (Oxford: Oxford University Press, 2004), 107; Abdullah Yusuf Ali, *The Meaning of the Holy Qur'an* (Markfield: Islamic Foundation, [1934–8] 2003), 397; Arthur J. Arberry, *The Koran Interpreted: A Translation by A.J. Arberry* (Oxford: Oxford University Press, [1955] 1983), 165.

35 See also the much-related Q 25:44: 'Or do you reckon that most of them hear or understand (*am taḥsabu annā aktharahum yasmaʿūna aw yaʿqilūna*)? They are only like beasts (*in hum illā ka-l-anʿāmi*) – No! They are further from the way (*bal hum aḍallu sabīlā*).' Once again, Jones does not translate *anʿām* as 'cattle', but instead as 'beasts', thereby, as we shall see, missing the point of the metaphorical mapping (Jones, *The Qur'ān*, 584). A verse that actually contains the Qur'ānic term for 'beasts' in relation to disabilities is Q 8:22: 'The worst of beasts in God's view are the deaf and mute who do not understand (*inna sharra l-dawābbi ʿinda llāhi l-ṣummu l-bukmu lladhīna lā yaʿqilūn*).'

36 Q 7:177–179 occurs within a larger section, Q 7:175–186, that I – in line with Angelika Neuwirth – call polemics of revelation. Neuwirth further terms the passage Q 7:178–179 'Rechtleitung / Irreleitung, Beschreibung der Verstockten' (Angelika Neuwirth, *Studien zur Komposition der mekkanischen Suren* (Berlin: Walter de Gruyter, 1981), 293).

Thus, the designation 'the unbelievers' as a generic group may be deduced from such previous characteristics: they are to be located in a future Hell (v. 179), they are 'losers' (*khāsirūn*; v. 178), they deny the truth of 'God's signs' (*āyāt Allāh*) and they have 'wronged themselves' (*ẓulm al-nafs*; v. 178).[37]

As for the first part of the metaphorical passage, THE UNBELIEVERS ARE CATTLE, the two input spaces, target and source, comprise the relation between unbelievers and their lack of understanding, corresponding to cattle and their lesser cognitive abilities in comparison with humans. The generic space, then, is the implicit background knowledge required to make this metaphorical mapping. In the case of THE UNBELIEVERS ARE CATTLE, such an overall frame includes an idea of what understanding entails, that there is something to be understood (God's *āyāt*),[38] and some level of knowledge about cattle and their

[37] For a few studies on what such 'self-wronging' (*ẓulm al-nafs*) in the Qur'ān may entail, see Johanne Louise Christiansen, 'A Woman's "Self-Wronging": A Gender Subtheme in the Qur'anic Encounter between Solomon and the Queen of Sheba', *Literature and Theology* 32(4) (2018): 397–422; Kenneth Cragg, 'The Meaning of Zulm in the Qur'ān', *Muslim World* 49(3) (1959): 196–212; George F. Hourani, '"Injuring Oneself" in the Qur'ān, in the Light of Aristotle', in *Reason and Tradition in Islamic Ethics* (Cambridge: Cambridge University Press, 1985), 49–56.

[38] One of the major themes in the Qur'ān is the relation between God sending something down and human reactions to such communication (Toshihiko Izutsu, *God and Man in the Qur'an: Semantics of the Qur'anic Weltanschauung* (Kuala Lumpur: Islamic Book Trust, [1959] 2002); Toshihiko Izutsu, *Ethico-Religious Concepts in the Qur'ān* (Montreal: McGill-Queens University Press, [1964] 2002)). For a verse on this theme that uses a bodily metaphor, see Q 39:23: 'God has sent down the fairest discourse (*allāhu nazzala aḥsana l-ḥadīthi*), a consistent scripture, oft-repeated (*kitāban mutashābihan mathāniya*), at which the skins of those who fear their Lord creep (*taqsha'irru minhu julūdu lladhīna yakhshawna rabbahum*); but then their skins and their hearts soften to remembrance of God (*thumma talīnu julūduhum wa-qulūbuhum ilā dhikri llāhi*). That is God's guidance, by which He guides those whom He wishes (*dhālika hudā llāhi yahdī bihi man yashā'u*); and those whom God leads astray have no guide (*wa-man yuḍlili llāhu fa-mā lahu min hād*) . . .'. In the verse, the skins (*julūd*) of the believers both 'creep' and 'soften' as a result of God's communication. In this metaphorical transfer, skins are aligned with hearts, exemplifying again that such bodily features have cognitive value according to the Qur'ān. Moreover, the meaning of the term *mathānī* – 'oft-repeated', 'tales, stories' or 'recounted, recited' – is much debated. See, for example, Ambros and Procházka, *Concise Dictionary*, 54; James A. Bellamy, 'Some Proposed Emendations to

cognitive abilities. Turning to the second part of the metaphorical passage, THE UNBELIEVERS ARE MORE ASTRAY THAN CATTLE, the transferred relation is now between the unbelievers and their lack of understanding in relation to cattle and being astray (since unbelievers apparently can be *more astray* than cattle; cf. Q 25:44). The background appears to entail more than simply the knowledge of cattle's cognition: cattle may go astray if they are not driven. However, another more implicit level of the input spaces also emerges in the second part of the metaphor. Especially from Q 7:178 and the beginning of Q 7:179, we learn that the metaphor has something to do with the relationship between God and man: God is the agent of both guiding and leading astray.[39] In the source space, this association parallels that between a driver and his or her cattle. As for the blend, there are a few things that are not immediately explained by the three spaces treated so far, namely, that seeing and hearing also means understanding (the expression being based on the three preceding metaphors – LACK OF UNDERSTANDING IS A CLOSED HEART, LACK OF UNDERSTANDING IS NOT SEEING/BLINDNESS and LACK OF UNDERSTANDING IS NOT HEARING/DEAFNESS). How else can we read the linking of cattle with not being able to see or hear? Another blended aspect occurs in the connection between the two parts of the metaphorical composition. Considering the necessary background knowledge of cattle-driving, including the driver–cattle relation, one could argue that the equation between cattle and being astray does not really make sense: not all cattle are astray, especially not if the driver is doing his or her job. Here, we must include v. 178, in which the Qurʾān expresses that God, perhaps already metaphorically evoked as a cattle-driver, is someone who both guides and leads astray. Finally, the second part does not end in the notion of being astray (*ḍ-l-l*). The unbelievers are, as we have seen, *more* astray than cattle, subsequently defined as being 'heedless'

the Text of the Koran', *Journal of the American Oriental Society* 113(4) (1992): 567–68; Abū Jaʿfar Muḥammad ibn Jarīr al-Ṭabarī (d. 310/923), *Tafsīr al-Ṭabarī: Jāmiʿ al-Bayān ʿan Taʾwīl Āy al-Qurʾān*, ed. ʿAbd Allāh ibn ʿAbd al-Muḥsin Turkī (Cairo: Dār Har, 2001), 20, 190–4; Seyyed Hossein Nasr et al., *The Study Quran: A New Translation and Commentary* (New York: Harper One, 2015), 1124.

39 For the theological implications of this argument, see W. Montgomery Watt, *Free Will and Predestination in Early Islam* (London: Luzac, 1948), and the next section.

or *ghāfilūn*. Ambros translates *ghāfilūn* in its verbal basis as 'to neglect something, to leave something unattended' and the active participle as 'paying no attention to something, neglecting something, heedless of something'.[40] Following the complex metaphorical composition argued for Q 7:179, the term concurs well with a metaphorical source of cattle and cattle-driving. The unbelievers are not just astray, they are *ghāfilūn*, 'inattentive' (or even perhaps 'left unattended'?). The metaphorical process of Q 7:179 may be schematised as in Figure 6.1.

| **Generic** | **Input spaces** | | **Blend** |
|---|---|---|---|
| | **Part 1/Source 1** | **Part 1/Target 1** | |
| Cattle, their cognition → | Cattle | Unbelievers | *LACK OF UNDERSTANDING IS A CLOSED HEART-NOT SEEING/ BLINDNESS- NOT HEARING/ DEAFNESS |
| | (Lack of) cognitive abilities | Lack of understanding | |
| *Understanding<br>*God's *āyāt* | **Part 2/Source 2** | **Part 2/Target 2** | *Cattle can both see and hear |
| Cattle-driving Superior/agent → | Cattle | Unbelievers | *Not all cattle are astray |
| | Being astray | Lack of understanding | *God decides who is guided and who is astray |
| | Driver | God | **more* astray than cattle = *ghāfilūn*, 'inattentive' ('left unattended'?) |

Figure 6.1 Conceptual Blending in Q 7:179

In the schema, I have specified two sources and two targets for the bipartite metaphor of Q 7:179. This is done for overview since the metaphor shares and contributes to several but *not all* aspects in both the generic space and the blended space.

To my knowledge, CBT has not yet been applied to the Qur'ān within western Qur'ānic Studies.[41] However, both CMT and CBT have been

[40] Ambros and Procházka, *Concise Dictionary*, 202.

[41] CBT has sporadically been considered outside this field. See, for example, Cobra Rastgoo, 'Cognitive Study of Anthropomorphic Metaphors in Qur'anic Discourse Based on Conceptual Theory', *Language Related Research* 11(6) (2021): 167–200; Cobra Rastgoo and Seyede Fatemeh Salimi, 'The Intellectual Metonymy; Metonymy or Reality through the Conceptual Blending Approach in the Quranic Discourse', *Journal of Arabic Language & Literature* 11(1) (2019): 25–55 (both in Farsi).

widely accepted and used within Biblical Studies.[42] Considering the amount of research joining these theories with the Biblical material, it is beyond the scope of this chapter to provide an overview of this strand of Biblical research.[43] Here, I only account for one such study, a study much-related to the Qur'ānic metaphor of THE UNBELIEVERS ARE (MORE ASTRAY THAN) CATTLE in Q 7:179. Pierre van Hecke, in his article 'Conceptual Blending: A Recent Approach to Metaphor', discusses the interpretation of a metaphorical passage from Hosea, utilising CBT.[44] The passage, Hos 4:16, is as follows:

> Truly, like a balking heifer, Israel is balking (כי כפרה סררה סרר ישראל)
> and now the Lord shall shepherd them as sheep in a wide area (עתה ירעם יהוה ככבש במרחב).[45]

As van Hecke presents, Biblical scholars vary on how to interpret the passage. While the first sentence is clearly polemical, the second seems to bode well for Israel's prospects of salvation. A promise of salvation, however, is not evident from the context of the passage, which is devoted to the prophet Hosea's general criticism of Israel's wrongful behaviour.[46] Taking

42 For example M. B. Szlos, 'Body Parts as Metaphor and the Value of a Cognitive Approach', in Pierre van Hecke (ed.), *Metaphor in the Hebrew Bible* (Leuven: Leuven University Press, 2005), 185–96; Kurt Feyaerts (ed.), *The Bible through Metaphor and Translation: A Cognitive Semantic Perspective* (Bern: Peter Lang, 2003); David H. Aaron, *Biblical Ambiguities: Metaphor, Semantics and Divine Imagery* (Leiden: Brill, 2001); Lieven Boeve and Kurt Feyaerts (eds), *Metaphor and God-Talk* (Bern: Peter Lang, 1999); Long, 'Literality and God-Metaphors in the Hebrew Bible'; van Hecke, 'Conceptual Blending: A Recent Approach to Metaphors'; Labahn, 'Heart as a Conceptual Metaphor in Chronicles'.

43 For a brief survey of this research strand as well as the general tendencies in the scientific approach to metaphors, see Labahn, 'Heart as a Conceptual Metaphor in Chronicles', 3–12. See also the whole volume in which several relevant contributions are collected; Antje Labahn (ed.), *Conceptual Metaphors in Poetic Texts* (Piscataway, NJ: Gorgias Press, 2013).

44 Van Hecke, 'Conceptual Blending: A Recent Approach to Metaphors'.

45 Van Hecke's own translation (p. 216). The translation in the New King James version is: 'For Israel is stubborn. Like a stubborn calf; Now the Lord will let them forage. Like a lamb in open country.' As we shall see, this translation accords better with van Hecke's analysis.

46 Van Hecke, 'Conceptual Blending: A Recent Approach to Metaphors', 216–17; Francis I. Andersen and David Noel Freedman, *Hosea: A New Translation with Introduction and Commentary* (New York: Doubleday, 1980), 342–79, esp. 372–8.

CBT into account, van Hecke argues that the two sentences are based on two different sources, cattle-driving and pastoralism. In the first sentence, Israel is juxtaposed with a balking or stubborn cow, but that stubbornness can be fully understood only in relation to an owner or a driver (in the target, God). Furthermore, the stubbornness seems to refer specifically to an idea of 'straying from the path', a conceptualisation much like the one we have seen as valid for Q 7:179.[47] The source space for the first sentence is thus the relation balking cow–driver–path, demanding (again) some background knowledge of cattle-driving (the generic space). The second sentence, however, is based on another source, namely, pastoralism or shepherding. Here we find the relation sheep–shepherd–wide area which necessitates, among other things, a familiarity with what it means to shepherd in a 'wide area'. According to van Hecke, because shepherds drive their flocks from behind, the flocks have (restricted) freedom to roam around in the open space before them.[48] To the connection between the two sentences of Hos 4:16, van Hecke concludes:

> The opposition with the first colon now becomes clear: if Israel behaves like a cow straying from the path its driver has set out before it, how will the Lord ever drive them as sheep in the freedom of the open field?[49]

In sum, the passage in Hos 4:16 applies an intricate metaphor grounded in two sources. These two sources, however, share a generic space, contributing different elements to the blend. In the blend, God is perceived as not guiding Israel because it is a stubborn cow, and such divine guidance or shepherding should not be taken for granted. The emergent structure of the blend, that is, the new meaning not entirely present in either of the input spaces, becomes that: 'God will force his people back into following the right course of life, without leaving them any freedom. The leisure of being able to roam around like sheep tended in a wide space will not be granted to them any

[47] For his argument based on the correlation between the Hebrew verb סָרַר (*sārar*), 'to be stubborn' and the root סור (*s-w-r*), 'to stray', see van Hecke, 'Conceptual Blending: A Recent Approach to Metaphors', 224.

[48] Van Hecke, 'Conceptual Blending: A Recent Approach to Metaphors', 225.

[49] Van Hecke, 'Conceptual Blending: A Recent Approach to Metaphors', 225.

longer.'[50] The blended conceptual metaphor of Hos 4:16 may be presented in the schema in Figure 6.2.[51]

| **Generic** | **Input spaces** | | **Blend** |
|---|---|---|---|
| | **Source 1** | **Target** | |
| | Balking cow | Israel | *Israel = balking cow |
| Cattle-driving → | Driver | God | *God is *not* tending to Israel as His sheep [emergent structure] |
| Agent/superior/task or purpose | Path | 'Correct' life | *'Israel should not expect to behave like a balking cow and, at the same time, be shepherded by God' (p. 228) |
| | **Source 2** | – | |
| | Sheep | Israel | |
| Pastoralism → | Shepherd | God | |
| | Open space | 'Correct' life | |

Figure 6.2 Conceptual Blending in Hos 4:16

Having laid out the overall theoretical frame of both CMT and CBT, I now consider the Qurʾān and its metaphorical language in general, and in particular its use of various body-related conceptual metaphors.

## The Qurʾān and its (Bodily) Metaphors

The Qurʾān is a metaphorical text. It speaks in metaphors, similes, parables, allegories, metonymies and many other forms of figurative language.[52] Despite this, the Qurʾān's use of diverse metaphorical language continues to be a source of novel research. Many of the text's metaphorical features, their interrelation, their structural significance and their socio-cultural relevance remain as yet unexplored. Of course, some scholarly work does exist on this

[50] Van Hecke, 'Conceptual Blending: A Recent Approach to Metaphors', 226.

[51] Van Hecke's own illustration follows the visual model of Fauconnier and Turner more directly (van Hecke, 'Conceptual Blending: A Recent Approach to Metaphors', 227).

[52] The different forms of figurative language is not the focus of this study and will not be further treated. Here, the reader is referred to David Punter, *Metaphor* (London: Routledge, 2007) or for the Qurʾān and Bible specifically, Peter Heath, 'Metaphor', *EQ* (online), 2001–; A. H. Mathias Zahniser, 'Parable', *EQ* (online), 2001–; Frederick S. Colby, 'Symbolic Imagery', *EQ* (online), 2001–; Becker et al., 'Metaphor'; Aryeh Amihay et al., 'Image, Imagery', in Constance M. Furey et al. (eds), *Encyclopedia of the Bible and Its Reception*, vol. 12 (Berlin: De Gruyter, 2010), 913–49.

subject, both within Qurʾānic Studies[53] and the Muslim tradition itself.[54] Also worthy of mention regarding bodily metaphors in the Qurʾān is the chapter titled 'The Face, Divine and Human, in the Qurʾān', in Muhammad Abdel Haleem's *Understanding the Qur'an*, as well as the entries 'Anatomy', 'Face', 'Hand(s)', 'Feet', 'Eyes' and 'Ears' in the *Encyclopaedia of the Qurʾān*.[55]

[53] For example, Charles C. Torrey, *The Commercial Theological Terms in the Koran* (Leyden: Brill, 1892); Moses Sister, *Metaphern und Vergleiche im Koran: Inaugural-Dissertation* (Berlin: Friedrich-Wilhelms-Universität, 1931); Toufic Sabbagh, *La Métaphore dans le Coran* (Paris: Université de Paris, 1943); Angelika Neuwirth, 'Images and Metaphors in the Introductory Sections of the *Makkan Sūras*', in G. R. Hawting and Abdul-Kader A. Shareef (eds), *Approaches to the Qur'ān* (London: Routledge, 1993), 3–36; Andrew Rippin, 'Metaphor and the Authority of the Qur'ān', in Khaleel Mohammad and Andrew Rippin (eds), *Coming to Terms with the Qur'an: A Volume in Honor of Professor Issa Boullata* (North Haledon: Islamic Publications International, 2008), 47–62; Christiansen, 'The Dark Koran'.

[54] For example, Abū ʿUbayda (d. 209/824–5), *Majāz al-Qur'ān*, ed. Fuat Sezgin, 2 vols (Cairo: Khānjī, 1955); Muḥammad b. al-Ḥusayn al-Sharīf al-Raḍī (d. 406/1016), *Talkhīṣ al-Bayān fī Majāzāt al-Qur'ān*, ed. Muḥammad ʿAbd al-Ghanī Ḥasan, 5 vols (Cairo: Dār Iḥyāʾ al-Kutub al-ʿArabīyah, 1955); ʿAbd al-Qāhir al-Jurjānī (d. 471/1078), *Asrār al-Balāgha*, ed. Helmut Ritter (Istanbul: Government Press, 1954); ʿAbd al-Qāhir al-Jurjānī, *Dalā'il al-Iʿjāz*, ed. Muḥammad Rashīd Riḍā, 3rd edn (Dār al-Manār: Cairo, 1946). See also Kamal Abu Deeb, 'Studies in the *Majāz* and Metaphorical Language of the Qur'ān: Abū ʿUbayda and al-Sharīf al-Raḍī', in Issa J. Boulatta (ed.), *Literary Structures of Religious Meaning in the Qur'ān* (New York: Routledge, 2000), 310–53; Kamal Abu Deeb, *Al-Jurjānī's Theory of Poetic Imagery* (Warminster: Aris & Phillips, 1979); Kamal Abu Deeb, 'Al-Jurjānī's Classification of *Istiʿāra* with Special Reference to Aristotle's Classification of Metaphor', *Journal of Arabic Literature* 2(1) (1971): 48–75; John Wansbrough, '*Majāz al-Qur'ān*: Periphrastic Exegesis', *Bulletin of the School of Oriental and African Studies* 33(2) (1970): 247–66.

[55] Muhammad Abdel Haleem, *Understanding the Qur'an: Themes and Styles* (London: I. B. Tauris, 1999), 107–22; Qamar-ul Huda, 'Anatomy', *EQ* (online), 2001–; Frederick Mathewson Denny, 'Face', *EQ* (online), 2001–; Frederick Mathewson Denny, 'Hand(s)', *EQ* (online), 2001–; Frederick Mathewson Denny, 'Feet', *EQ* (online), 2001–; Frederick Mathewson Denny, 'Eyes', *EQ* (online), 2001–; Frederick Mathewson Denny, 'Ears', *EQ* (online), 2001–. See again Hoffmann, '*Taste My Punishment*', in which he comments on several bodily senses in Qurʾānic metaphors. Also Toufic Sabbagh and Moses Sister's works contain material on the metaphorical body in the Qurʾān. For the former, the chapter 'L'Homme: les parties du corps humain' (Sabbagh, *La Métaphore*, 112–38), for the latter, the section 'Die Körperteile' in the chapter 'Der Mensch und sein Leben' (Sister, *Metaphern*, 27–35). Both are useful for overview but remain introductory.

In its metaphorical repertoire, the Qur'ān frequently evokes the simile and the parable, in Arabic called *mathal* (pl. *amthāl*). Such metaphorical forms are presented by the use of this particular word, as well as through the simple comparative preposition *ka-*.[56] We have already seen the former in use: 'Evil as an example (*mathalan*) are those who have denied the truth of Our signs' (Q 7:177); as well as the latter: 'These are like animals (*ka-l-anʿāmi*).' What follows is another example, utilising a number of body parts and movements:

> The call that is true is made to Him alone (*lahu daʿwatu l-ḥaqqi*). Those on whom they call, apart from Him, make no response to them (*wa-lladhīna yadʿūna min dūnihi lā yastajībūna lahum bi-shay'in*), except as one who stretches out his hands to water, that it may reach his mouth, and it does not do so (*illā ka-bāsiṭi kaffayhi ilā l-mā'i li-yablugha fāhu wa-mā huwa bi-bālighihi*). The prayer of the unbelievers only goes astray (*wa-mā duʿā'u l-kāfirīna illā fī ḍalāl*). (Q 13:14)[57]

In this verse, a comparison is made between those who pray to gods other than the Qur'ānic god and to a person who vainly attempts to quench his thirst by reaching his hands out for water. The result of the first is that such prayer will not receive any response, corresponding in the metaphor to not getting any water. The overall conclusion is that God alone constitutes the source of water (see also Q 6:99). This simile certainly illustrates the utility of bodily experiences as a way of understanding abstract notions.

As we have seen with both Q 7:179 and Q 13:14 cited above, the Qur'ān is filled with bodily metaphors. Indeed, metaphorical usages of the body, its parts and its possible defects are much more common in the Qur'ān than actual physical ones. These, however, are on occasion mentioned. In legal verses, such as those regarding ritual cleansing, believers are before prayer admonished to wash their faces, hands and arms, heads and feet (e.g., Q 5:6). Also indicated by the context of Q 7:179, references to body parts – physical or metaphorical – can have major theological implications, many of which

[56] Wolfdietrich Fischer, *A Grammar of Classical Arabic*, 3rd edn (New Haven, CT: Yale University Press, 2002), §297.

[57] For Hoffmann's treatment of this verse as a reference to Tantalus' torments, see his '*Taste My Punishment*', 2–3, 7–9.

have been discussed extensively within post-Qurʾānic traditions.[58] Here, I am referring explicitly to the issue of anthropomorphism, the tension between an idea of the Qurʾānic god as, on the one hand, absolutely transcendent, apart from anything else, and, on the other, the same god being described in human – and often bodily – terms.[59] An example of such an anthropomorphic description appears in Q 28:88:

> And do not call on another god together with God (*wa-lā tadʿu maʿa llāhi ilāhan ākhara*). There is no god except Him (*lā ilāha illā huwa*). Everything will perish except His face (*kullu shayʾin hālikun illā wajhahu*). To Him belongs the Judgement and you will be returned to Him (*lahu l-ḥukmu wa-ilayhi turjaʿūn*).[60]

While Jones[61] directly uses the word 'face' (*wajh*), other translators insert a metaphorical understanding in the translation. For example, Marmaduke W. Pickthall writes: 'Everything will perish save His countenance.'[62]

[58] See, for example, Sabine Schmidtke, 'Introduction', in Sabine Schmidtke (ed.), *The Oxford Handbook of Islamic Theology* (Oxford: Oxford University Press, 2016), 1–23; A. J. Wensinck, *The Muslim Creed: Its Genesis and Historical Development* (London: Cambridge University Press, 1932), 58–82; Josef van Ess, 'Tas̲h̲bīh wa-Tanzīh', in *Encyclopaedia of Islam2* (*EI²*) (online), 1960–; Watt, *Free Will and Predestination*; Abū al-Ḥasan ʿAlī ibn Ismāʿīl al-Ashʿarī (d. 324/936), *Kitāb Maqālāt al-Islāmiyyīn wa-Ikhtilāf al-Muṣallīn (Die Dogmatischen Lehren der Anhänger des Islam)*, ed. Hellmut Ritter, 2nd edn (Wiesbaden: Franz Steiner:, 1963), 182–90; David Bennett, 'The Muʿtazilite Movement (II): The Early Muʿtazilites', in Sabine Schmidtke (ed.), *The Oxford Handbook of Islamic Theology* (Oxford: Oxford University Press, 2016), 142–58.

[59] Anthropomorphic statements about the divine are not unique to the Qurʾān. In the Hebrew Bible, God is also depicted as having a face (Gen 27:7), hands (Isa 41:13) and feet (Zech 14:4), as well as being in absolute distance from that which is human (e.g., Isa 40:25, 46:5; Ps 89:7). A comparative study on anthropomorphism in these traditions can be found in Wesley Williams, 'A Body Unlike Bodies: Transcendent Anthropomorphism in Ancient Semitic Tradition and Early Islam', *Journal of the American Oriental Society* 129(1) (2009): 19–44.

[60] See also Q 2:255; 3:73; 11:37; 42:11; and Haleem, *Understanding the Qur'an*, 107–22.

[61] Jones, *The Qurʾān*, 362.

[62] Marmaduke W. Pickthall, *The Meaning of the Glorious Koran: An Explanatory Translation* (London: A. A. Knopf, 1930), 403.

Considering the many Qurʾānic terms relating to the body (e.g., face (*wajh*), occurring 72 times; hands (*yad*), as well as right hand (*yamīn*) and left hand (*shimāl*), 178 times; head (*raʾs*), 18 times; heart (*qalb*, *albāb*, *fuʾād*), 164 times; eye (*ʿayn*), 39 times; ear (*udhun*), 18 times; mouths (*afwāh*), 12 times; and so on),[63] it is beyond the chapter's scope to provide an exhaustive survey of bodily metaphors in the Qurʾān.[64] Here, I only remark on a few of the major, recurring Qurʾānic metaphors involving the body before turning to the text's application of bodily disabilities and defects.

Metaphorical understandings of the body and its parts occur frequently within the overall topic of eschatology. Especially in Qurʾānic descriptions of a future Judgement Day, the body plays a role in the division of humans into those deserving of either Paradise or Hell. Among the metaphorical expressions used, we find that the two groups' faces are either white or black (e.g., Q 3:106–107; 75:22–25), that their hands will have 'forwarded' deeds and misdeeds to this day for which they will be judged (*bi-mā qaddamat aydīhim* in Q 2:95; see also, e.g., Q 8:51; 42:48) and that their body will testify against them:

> [20)]Then, when they reach it (*ḥatta idhā mā jāʾūhā*), their hearing and their sight and their skins bear witness against them about what they had been doing (*shahida ʿalayhim samʿuhum wa-abṣāruhum wa-julūduhum bi-mā kānū yaʿmalūn*).
>
> [21)]And they say to their skins (*wa-qālū li-julūdihim*), 'Why do you testify against us?' (*li-ma shahidttum ʿalaynā*); they say (*qālū*), 'We have been given speech by God, who can give speech to everything (*anṭaqanā llāhu lladhī anṭaqa kulla shayʾin*) and who created you the first time (*wa-huwa khalaqakum awwala marratin*) and to whom you will be returned (*wa-ilayhi turjaʿūn*). (Q 41:20–21)[65]

Among other body parts that take on this function of witnessing are tongues (*lisān*, pl. *alsina*), hands and feet (*rijl*, pl. *arjul*; e.g., Q 24:24; 36:65). Additionally, the experience of different bodily actions and movements seems to

[63] For additional roots and terms, see Arne A. Ambros, *The Nouns of Koranic Arabic Arranged by Topics* (Wiesbaden: Reichert Verlag, 2006), 44–9, and below.

[64] To my knowledge, such a survey does not exist in the field of Qurʾānic Studies.

[65] See also Q 39:23 cited in n. 38.

be a sign of the Judgement. For example, a leg will be 'entangled with leg (*wa-l-taffati l-sāqu bi-l-sāqi*)' (Q 75:29) or 'be bared (*yukshafu ʿan sāqin*)' (Q 68:42); eyes will stare (*sh-kh-ṣ*), 'their gaze not returning (*lā yartaddu . . . ṭarfuhum*)' (Q 14:42–43), and be obliterated (from *ṭ-m-s*; Q 36:66); and hands will be bitten (from *ʿ-ḍ-ḍ*; Q 25:27; cf. Q 3:119).

As we have already seen, the relationship between God and man is regularly depicted through bodily metaphors. On the one hand, a positive and intimate connection between the two is established through phrases like '. . . We are nearer to him [man] than his jugular vein (*wa-naḥnu aqrabu ilayhi min ḥabli l-warīdi*)' (Q 50:16) and 'know [believers] that God is between a man and his own heart (*wa-ʿlamū annā llāha yaḥūlu bayna l-marʾi wa-qalbihi*)' (Q 8:24); on the other hand, God sometimes punishes humans through their body:

> 44)If he [a noble messenger (*rasūl karīm*), see v. 40] had invented any sayings against Us (*wa-law taqawwala ʿalaynā baʿḍa l-aqāwīl*),
> 45)We would have seized him by the right hand (*la-akhadhnā minhu bi-l-yamīn*),
> 46)Then We would have severed his aorta (*thumma la-qaṭaʿnā minhu l-watīn*). (Q 69:44–46)

In this passage, it is presumably the Prophet Muḥammad himself and his body that is being threatened by God – lest he lie about the Qurʾānic message (see also Q 6:93).[66]

## Qurʾānic Disabilities and Defects

As is evident from the above, the Qurʾān is permeated by references to the body. While some descriptions of the physical body occur, it is also one of the main bases for the Qurʾān's application of figurative language. In the remaining part of this chapter, I analyse one particular aspect of the body

[66] This study follows the general consensus within Qurʾānic Studies that Muḥammad is often thought of as the 'implied second-person singular addressee' in the Qurʾān. See Neal Robinson, *Discovering the Qur'an: A Contemporary Approach to a Veiled Text* (Washington, DC: Georgetown University Press, 2003), 240–4; Alford T. Welch, 'Al-Ḳurʾān', in *EI*[2] (online), 1960–; Nicolai Sinai, *The Qur'an: A Historical-Critical Introduction* (Edinburgh: Edinburgh University Press, 2017), 12–14.

(and bodily metaphors) in the Qurʾān, namely, when it is disabled or characterised by defects. Disability is a contested and politicised term with various meanings.[67] Here, I apply the basic and simple definition of disability as:

> the [permanent or temporary] effects of a [physical or mental] impairment which limit a person's ability to complete valued tasks and roles.[68]

Similar to the Hebrew Bible and the New Testament, the Qurʾān contains a vocabulary for such impairments.[69] In this vocabular, Arabic roots denote 'blindness' (*ʿ-m-y* occurring thirty-three times; *k-m-h*, two times), 'deafness' (*ṣ-m-m*, fifteen times; and *w-q-r*, lit. 'hardness of hearing' or 'heaviness in the ears', six relevant times),[70] and 'muteness' (*b-k-m*, six times) in particular, but also 'leprosy' (*b-r-ṣ*, two times),[71] 'lameness' (*ʿ-r-j*, two relevant times), 'weakness' (*ḍ-ʿ-f*, thirty-two relevant times), 'sickness' (often from *m-r-ḍ*,

[67] For a survey of the field of Disability Studies and this field in relation to studies of the Bible, see Jeremy Schipper, *Disability Studies and the Hebrew Bible: Figuring Mephibosheth in the David Story* (New York: Bloomsbury T. & T. Clark, 2006), 7–9, 15–24. See also Judith Z. Abrams et al., 'Disability, Disabilities', in Constance M. Furey et al. (eds), *Encyclopedia of the Bible and Its Reception*, vol. 6 (Berlin: De Gruyter, 2013), 864–86; Jeremy Schipper and Candida R. Moss, *Disability Studies and Biblical Literature* (New York: Palgrave Macmillan, 2011); Jeremy Schipper, *Disability and Isaiah's Suffering Servant* (Oxford: Oxford University Press, 2011); Deborah Beth Creamer, *Disability and Christian Theology: Embodied Limits and Constructive Possibilities* (Oxford: Oxford University Press, 2009); Saul M. Olyan, *Disability in the Hebrew Bible: Interpreting Mental and Physical Differences* (Cambridge: Cambridge University Press, 2008); Rebecca Raphael, *Biblical Corpora: Representations of Disability in Hebrew Biblical Literature* (New York: T. & T. Clark, 2008); Hector Avalos et al., *This Abled Body: Rethinking Disabilities in Biblical Studies* (Atlanta, GA: Society of Biblical Literature, 2007); Edward Hersh and Rosemarie Scotti Hughes, 'The Role of Suffering and Disability: Evidence from Scripture', *Journal of Religion, Disability & Health* 9(3) (2006): 85–92. So far, the insights from Disability Studies have not been considered within Qurʾānic Studies.

[68] Abrams et al., 'Disability, Disabilities', 866.

[69] Among the many examples of disabilities mentioned in the Bible are Exod 4:11; Deut 28:28–29; Isa 29:18; Mark 2:1–12; and John 9:39–41. For additional examples, see Abrams et al., 'Disability, Disabilities'.

[70] Ambros and Procházka, *Concise Dictionary*, 294.

[71] Leprosy only occurs in a literal sense and in relation to the Qurʾānic Jesus (Q 3:49; 5:110).

twenty-four times, but also, e.g., *ʾ-dh-y* 'harm, injury, ailment'),[72] and perhaps likewise ideas of 'mental illness' (through *s-f-h*, 'a fool' or 'stupid, foolish'),[73] or 'madness/insanity' (often depicted as 'demonic possession', *j-n-n*, eleven relevant times; *f-t-n*, potentially 'afflicted by madness' in Q 68:6, one time; the combination of *kh-b-ṭ* (V) and 'Satan's touch (*al-shayṭānu mina l-massi*)' in Q 2:275, one time; and, finally, *s-ʿ-r*, two relevant times).[74] All of the preceding may be included within the category of disabilities.[75] As for mental disabilities, it may be additionally argued that the Qurʾān features a notion of depression. In Q 18:5–6, for example, the Prophet Muḥammad appears to be close to such a state, as he is once again rejected by his contemporaries (cf. Q 26:3):

> [5)]They [probably Christians, vv. 4–5] have no knowledge of it, nor did their forefathers (*mā lahum bihi min ʿilmin wa-lā li-ābāʾihim*). It is a monstrous word that comes from their mouths (*kaburat kalimatan takhruju min afwāhihim*). They speak nothing but a lie (*in yaqūlūna illā kadhibā*).

[72] Ambros and Procházka, *Concise Dictionary*, 23.

[73] Ambros and Procházka, *Concise Dictionary*, 135.

[74] For a useful overview of how madness and insanity occur in the Qurʾān, see Thomas Bauer, 'Insanity', *EQ* (online), 2001–. For mental disabilities in general and in the Bible, see Olyan, *Disability in the Hebrew Bible*, 62–77.

[75] References to disabled functions can also emerge from the negation of a bodily function; that is, for example, 'not seeing' (e.g., negated *b-ṣ-r*), 'not hearing' (e.g., negated *s-m-ʿ*) and 'not speaking' (e.g., negated *q-w-l* or *k-l-m*; see Q 7:179 and Q 19:26). Other impairments described in the Qurʾān could be included. See, for instance, Q 22:5, which portrays the possible frailty of old age: 'O people, if you are in doubt about the raising (*yā-ayyuhā l-nāsu in kuntum fī raybin mina l-baʿthi*) – We have created you from dust (*fa-innā khalaqnākum min turābin*), then from a drop (*thumma min nuṭfatin*), then from a clot (*thumma min ʿalaqatin*), then from a lump (*thumma min muḍghatin*), formed or unformed, that We may make [things] clear to you (*mukhallaqatin wa-ghayri mukhallaqatin li-nubayyina lakum*). We settle what We wish in the wombs to a stated term (*wa-nuqirru fī l-arḥāmi mā nashāʾu ilā ajalin musamman*), then We bring you forth as infants (*thumma nukhrijukum ṭiflan*). Then [We nurture you] that you may reach maturity (*thumma li-tablughū ashuddakum*). Among you are those who die [young] (*wa-minkum man yutawaffā*), and among you are some who are returned to the most abject state of life, so that he knows nothing after having had knowledge (*wa-minkum man yuraddu ila ardhali l-ʿumuri li-kaylā yaʿlama min baʿdi ʿilmin shayʾan*) . . .' (Q 22:5).

> [6)]Perhaps you will exhaust yourself following them up (*fa-laʿallaka bākhiʿun nafsaka ʿala āthārihim*), if they do not believe in this discourse (*in lam yuʾminū bi-hādhā l-ḥadīthi*), with grief (*asafā*).

The sentence *fa-laʿallaka bākhiʿun nafsaka . . . asafan* is also sometimes translated as 'but are you going to worry yourself to death' or even 'then perhaps you would kill yourself through grief'.[76]

The Qurʾānic references to disabilities may be divided into three overall categories. First, in a few instances, the Qurʾān refers to people with actual physical disabilities, which may indicate that its historical community and milieu did have experiences with such a social group (cf. e.g., Jer 31:8; Mark 7:31–37). Secondly, and more commonly, however, are diverse metaphors referencing disabilities to such notions as the unbelievers' lack of understanding. Thirdly, and finally, some passages involving features associated with disabilities are difficult to classify in a clear-cut dichotomy between the literal and the metaphorical. In the following, I present examples of the first and third category, before focusing the remaining part of this chapter on the second.

An example from the Qurʾān describing actual disabled people can be found in Q 24:61:

> There is no blame for the blind (*laysa ʿalā l-aʿmā ḥarajun*), no blame for the lame (*wa-lā ʿalā l-aʿraji ḥarajun*), and no blame for the sick (*wa-lā ʿalā l-marīḍi ḥarajun*), or for yourselves (*wa-lā ʿalā anfusikum*) to eat in your houses (*an taʾkulū min buyūtikum*), or the houses of your fathers (*aw buyūti ābāʾikum*) [list of permitted owners]. It is no fault for you to eat together or in separate groups (*laysa ʿalaykum junāḥun an taʾkulū jamīʿan aw ashtātan*) . . . Thus, God makes the signs clear for you (*kadhālika yubayyinu llāhu lakumu l-āyāti*), so perhaps you will understand (*laʿallakum taʿqilūn*).

Also in Q 48:17, these same people are described as having similar 'religious conditions' as the rest of the Qurʾānic community: either they obey God and Muḥammad and are getting rewarded in Paradise, or they turn away and are punished. While the exception from blame in Q 24:61 relates specifically to the issue of eating in other peoples' houses, Q 48:17 classifies the blind with

[76] Haleem, *The Qur'an: A New Translation*, 183; Ṣaḥīḥ International 1997, 391.

the lame and the sick, being included in an overall blameless category.[77] Also in Q 2:282 and Q 4:5, the 'fool' (*al-safīh*) is exempted from specific tasks (i.e., functioning as a scribe in loan agreements) and is to be treated in a certain way (i.e., the provision of money, clothes and respectful behaviour from others). And finally, in Q 80:1–10, the Qur'ān presents an episode involving Muḥammad and 'the blind man' (*al-aʿmā*), the latter apparently ignored by the Prophet, something for which Muḥammad is subsequently admonished. By emphasising that the disabled are not to blame (*ḥaraj*; both in a legal sense and what seems to be in general terms), these passages show some knowledge of people with disabilities and a generally tolerant treatment towards them.[78]

There are, however, other Qur'ānic passages describing disabilities that may be discussed further. One example is Q 16:76, in which a man is by simile compared with a mute servant.

> God has coined a comparison (*wa-ḍaraba llāhu mathalan*): two men, one of them mute (*rajulayni aḥaduhumā abkamu*), who has control of nothing (*lā yaqdiru ʿalā shay'in*), a burden on his owner (*wa-huwa kallun ʿalā mawlāhu*) – wherever he sends him he brings back no good (*aynamā yūajjihhu lā ya'ti bi-khayrin*). Is he equal to one who enjoins justice and is on a straight path (*hal yastawī huwa wa-man ya'muru bi-l-ʿadli wa-huwa ʿalā ṣirāṭin mustaqīm*)?

In the context of this *mathal* (vv. 73–74), the Qur'ān gives different polemical examples of how having gods other than God is problematic. Contrary to Q 2:282, 4:5, 24:61, 48:17 and 80:1–10, the verse portrays the mute servant in negative terms: he is not in 'control', he is a burden (*kall*) and he brings 'no good'. These characteristics are then compared with those of the other man, who is 'just' (from *ʿ-d-l*) and 'on a straight path' (*ʿalā ṣirāṭin mustaqīm*).[79] Considering such an evocation of 'justice' and a 'straight path', two highly

[77] For Jeremy Schipper's similar argument, valid for the Hebrew Bible, see Schipper, *Disability Studies and the Hebrew Bible*, 66–7.

[78] For the legal sense of *ḥaraj*, see Johanne Louise Christiansen, *The Exceptional Qur'ān: Flexible and Exceptive Rhetoric in Islam's Holy Book* (Piscataway, NJ: Gorgias Press, 2021), 105–17; Joseph E. Lowry, 'Exculpatory Language in the Qur'an: A Survey of Terms, Themes, and Theologies', *Mélanges de l'Université Saint-Joseph* LXVI (2015–16): 100–3.

[79] See also the simile in Q 16:75, in which a slave is similarly depicted.

ethico-religious terms in the Qurʾān, it is not completely clear whether muteness in this particular context should be understood figuratively.[80] Related to this question of disability and blame is the origin of human disability. Are disabilities a result of sin? Not surprisingly, the Qurʾān describes its god as one who can give and take away sight, hearing and speech (see again Q 7:178 and Q 41:21). In Q 47:22–23, this divine ability correlates with disability being a result of sin:

> [22)]If you turn away, are you likely to wreak corruption in the land (*fa-hal ʿasaytum in tawallaytum an tufsidū fī l-arḍi*) and sever the ties of kinship (*wa-tuqaṭṭiʿū arḥāmakum*)?
>
> [23)]Those are the ones whom God has cursed (*ulāʾika lladhīna laʿanahumu llāhu*) and has made them deaf and blinded their sight (*fa-aṣammahum wa-aʿmā abṣārahum*). (see also Q 2:17–20; cf. e.g., John 9:1–4)

In the Qurʾānic version about Zechariah (*Zakariyyā*), however, his temporary muteness is – contrary to that of the Bible – not a punishment for unbelief, but rather a sign from God (Q 3:37–44; 19:2–15; 21:89–90, specifically Q 19:10–11; cf. e.g., Luke 1:20, 64).

As for the Qurʾān's metaphorical use of disabilities, some overall observations can also be made: disabilities as spiritual lackings are mainly evoked in the Qurʾān through the mention of blindness, deafness and muteness. These three are also my main concern here. Moreover, similar to Q 24:61 and Q 48:17, spiritual blindness, deafness and muteness often occur in clusters.[81] In the Qurʾān, the combination of 'deaf, mute and blind (*ṣumm bukm ʿumy*)' appears in Q 2:18, 171 and Q 17:97; 'deaf and mute (*ṣumm wa-bukm*)' in Q 6:39 and Q 8:22; and 'blind and deaf' (from *ʿ-m-y* and *ṣ-m-m* or from *ʿ-m-y* and *w-q-r*) in Q 5:71, 10:42–43, 11:24, 25:73, 27:80–81, 30:52–53, 41:44, 43:40 and 47:23.[82] While 'muteness' (*b-k-m*) and 'deafness' (in the form of *ṣ-m-m*) only appear once each outside these clusters (the former in the aforementioned

[80] Izutsu, *Concepts*, 203–40. For a metaphorical interpretation of this verse within the Muslim tradition, see al-Ṭabarī, *Jāmiʿ*, 14, 309–13.

[81] See again Schipper, *Disability Studies and the Hebrew Bible*, 66–7.

[82] Again, the impairments may also appear together when the particular bodily function, for example, hearing, is negated. See n. 75.

Q 16:76; the latter in Q 21:45, polemically terming the deaf as those who 'do not hear the call (*wa-lā yasmaʿu l-ṣummu l-duʿāʾa*)'), the other spiritual disabilities also occur separately. For example, spiritual blindness is evoked in repeated Qurʾānic phrases such as the following rhetorical question (perhaps connected to Q 16:76): 'Are the man who is blind and the man who sees equal (*hal yastawī l-aʿmā wa-l-baṣīru*)?' (Q 6:50; 13:16; see also Q 35:19; 40:58).[83] Furthermore, as we have seen in Q 7:179, many of the spiritual disabilities are frequently combined with mention of the heart. In Q 6:25, another repeated Qurʾānic phrase seems to refer to the Prophet's adversaries, portrayed in such figurative language (cf. Q 17:46; 18:57):

> Among them are those who listen to you[s], but over whose hearts We have placed veils, so that they do not understand it (*wa-minhum man yastamiʿu ilayka wa-jaʿalnā ʿalā qulūbihim akinnatan an yafqahūhu*), and heaviness in their ears (*wa-fī ādhānihim waqran*). If they see a sign, they do not believe in it (*wa-in yaraw kulla āyatin lā yuʾminū bihā*) . . .

As is also clear from Q 6:25, the main metaphorical transfer relating to the Qurʾān's usage of blindness, deafness and muteness is as a lack of understanding. Many of the passages involving spiritual disability refer directly to understanding or its lack in the immediate context. Another example may be found in Q 22:46:

> Have they not travelled in the land, so that they have hearts with which they can understand and ears with which they can hear (*a-fa-lam yasīrū fī l-arḍi fa-takūna lahum qulūbun yaʿqilūna bihā aw ādhānun yasmaʿūna bihā*)? It is not the eyes that go blind, but the hearts, which are in their breasts (*fa-innahā lā taʿma l-abṣāru wa-lākin taʿma l-qulūbu llatī fī l-ṣudūr*).

Sometimes, following the Lakoff/Johnson/Turner/Fauconnier paradigm, the metaphorical mapping is to a certain extent depicted within the context of the metaphor. This is the case in Q 2:171:

[83] Rhetorical questions such as those cited are quite common in the Qurʾān, occurring frequently in passages dealing with disabilities, physical or metaphorical (e.g., Q 7:195; 11:24; 28:71; 32:26).

> The comparison of those who do not believe is like the one who shouts out to what can hear nothing but a call and a cry (*wa-mathalu lladhīna kafarū ka-mathali lladhī yanʿiqu bi-mā lā yasmaʿu illā duʿāʾan wa-nidāʾan*): deaf, mute and blind (*ṣummun bukmun ʿumun*), they have no understanding (*fa-hum lā yaʿqilūn*).

At least for the notion of deafness, this verse entails references to 'shouting' (from *n-ʿ-q*), 'hearing' (*s-m-ʿ*), a 'call' (from *d-ʿ-w*) and a 'cry' (from *n-d-w*) – all audible phenomena. At other times, however, the relation between the two sources or domains in the metaphorical mapping seems completely detached (see also Q 17:97):

> 70)In times past We took a covenant from the Children of Israel (*la-qad akhadhnā mīthāqa banī isrāʾīla*) and We sent messengers to them (*wa-arsalnā ilayhim rusulan*). Whenever a messenger came to them with what their souls did not desire (*kullamā jāʾahum rasūlun bi-mā lā tahwā anfusuhum*), a number they denied (*farīqan kadhdhabū*), a number they killed (*wa-farīqan yaqtulūn*).
> 71) They thought that there would be no trial (*wa-ḥasibū allā takūna fitnatun*), and so they were blind and deaf (*fa-ʿamū wa-ṣammū*). Then God relented towards them (*thumma tāba llāhu ʿalayhim*), but [yet again] many of them were blind and deaf (*thumma ʿamū wa-ṣammū kathīrun minhum*). But God is observer of what they do (*wa-llāhu baṣīrun bi-mā yaʿmalūn*). (Q 5:70–71)

In this passage, the children of Israel, *Banū Isrāʾīl*, are 're-disabled' by God after first having denied the 'trial' (*fitna*), next having been forgiven, and then finally having been made blind and deaf once again. Nothing in the passage gives any indication of the metaphorical link between such disabilities and their original physical features.

Taking these metaphorical 'disability clusters' in the Qurʾān as my textual basis, I conclude this chapter by explicitly inserting them into the theoretical frame of CMT and CBT. Valid for all of them is that at least one of the disabilities mentioned is *not* explained by a simple metaphorical mapping between two domains. For example, the context of the verse Q 8:22 – 'The worst of beasts in God's view are the deaf and mute who do not understand (*inna sharra l-dawābbi ʿinda llāhi l-ṣummu l-bukmu lladhīna lā yaʿqilūna*)' – clearly emphasises hearing as the human faculty necessary for understanding

God's communication, the root *s-m-ʿ* occurring five times in the short passage of Q 8:20–24.[84] While the metaphorical evocation of deafness makes sense, it remains unclear how the notion of muteness is added to the mix. The same appears to be applicable for Q 6:39:

> Those who deny the truth of Our signs are deaf and mute, in darkness (*wa-lladhīna kadhdhabū bi-āyātinā ṣummun wa-bukmun fī l-ẓulumāti*). God sends astray those whom He wishes, and He places on a straight path those whom He wishes (*man yashaʾi llāhu yuḍlilhu wa-man yashaʾ yajʿalhu ʿalā ṣirāṭin mustaqīm*).

Once again, the verse concerns Qurʾānic communication: among other things, God communicates his signs (*āyāt*), to which humans react positively or negatively (see n. 38). In Q 6:39, a negative reaction is specified, with the comparison of 'those who deny the truth of God's signs', according to Jones' translation,[85] to those who are deaf and mute, as well as those in darkness (cf. Q 7:177; 18:6 cited above). The verse is part of a longer passage on polemics and confirmations of the revelation (vv. 4–73), occurring in a smaller section containing polemical questions and their answers (vv. 37–39).[86] In this immediate context, there is no mention of the ability to speak nor of how darkness as a source for the metaphor is to be understood.[87] In v. 36, however, the Qurʾān presents the following statement: 'Only those who hear can respond (*innamā yastajību lladhīna yasmaʿūna*) . . .', providing some contrast to the notion of deafness.

Thus, the target of the metaphor – 'those who deny the truth of God's signs' – is based on three different sources: deafness, muteness and darkness. The implicit background knowledge for inducing these sources – that is, the generic space – seems to be disability as an overall category. The basic feature brought from this category into the metaphor is the limitation of a disability – any disability – on 'a person's ability to complete valued tasks

[84] See again n. 35.

[85] Jones, *The Qurʾān*, 233.

[86] Neuwirth, *Studien*, 290.

[87] Arthur A. Arberry continuously translates *kh-dh-b* (II) as 'to *cry* lies', which provides some context for the contrast between 'speaking' and 'muteness' (for Q 6:39, see Arberry, *The Koran Interpreted*, 125).

and roles'.[88] For this particular target, the limitation acts on the ability to properly understand and react to God's communication. However, the specific disabilities mentioned also demand additional information, namely, what it means not to hear or speak. Regarding the third source (darkness), the appertaining generic space also entails a level of bodily experience of being in darkness: inability to see, being confined or lost.[89]

Several elements from the spaces treated thus far are entered into the blend, while others are completely disregarded. Among the new structures to emerge are the use of already established metaphorical mappings, including a LACK OF UNDERSTANDING IS DEAFNESS/MUTENESS/DARKNESS. Moreover, being *in* darkness (*fī l-ẓulumāti*) does not at first sight seem to have anything to do with being either deaf or mute (though it probably relates to blindness, cf. Q 2:17–18). The logical link between darkness and the specific disability of blindness is not present, but only the conceptualisation that darkness can have disabling effects. Finally, darkness is explained as a target itself by utilising the aforementioned image-schema of a container: DARKNESS IS A CONTAINER because the liars are perceived as being *in* it. Figure 6.3 shows the schema for the blended conceptual metaphor of Q 6:39.

| **Generic** | **Input spaces** | | **Blend** |
|---|---|---|---|
| | **Source 1** | **Target** | |
| Disabilities<br>-(not) to hear /speak<br>Communication<br><br>Body in darkness | Deaf<br>**Source 2**<br>Mute<br>**Source 3**<br>In darkness | Those who deny the truth of God's signs | *LACK OF UNDERSTANDING IS DEAFNESS/MUTENESS/DARKNESS<br>*The deaf and mute can still see in darkness?<br>* DARKNESS IS A CONTAINER<br>**Blindness=Deafness=Muteness=Darkness |

Figure 6.3 Conceptual Blending in Q 6:39

From this theoretical reading, I argue that in all the metaphorical disability clusters used in the Qurʾān, central features of a distinct disability mentioned are often excluded, thus equating and blending blindness with

[88] See again Abrams et al., 'Disability, Disabilities', 866.

[89] Christiansen, 'The Dark Koran'.

deafness, deafness with muteness, and so on. Not being able to understand the Qurʾānic god's message is a disability without its specific characteristics.

## Concluding Remarks

Through an introduction to the two cognitive theories, CMT and CBT, and the application of these to the Qurʾān, particularly Q 7:179 and the metaphorical 'disability clusters' occurring in such verses as Q 6:39 and Q 8:22, this chapter has demonstrated how new theoretical approaches to the Qurʾānic texts can supplement classical textual methods of study. By focusing on the cognitive aspect of metaphors, CMT and CBT considers underlying, non-linguistic, human conceptualisations of the world which are reflected in the use of figurative language. For the textual examples treated here, it seems that we are dealing with a common Semitic (and possibly broader) metaphorical repertoire, the Hebrew Bible, the New Testament and the Qurʾān, evoking many of the same images to be used in different contexts (e.g., cattle-driving, pastoralism, body, disability as metaphorical sources). Among other things, analyses into such conceptual metaphors within these texts have consequences for their translation, as exemplified in the discussion of the Arabic term *anʿām* above.

As do the Hebrew Bible and the New Testament, the Qurʾān employs a vocabulary of the body and its possible disabilities.[90] As for the latter, which have comprised the focus of this chapter, the Qurʾān presents very different approaches to the disabled. Disabled persons are not to blame, presumably existing as an actual social group in the original milieux of these texts, including the Qurʾān. However, spiritual disablement – equated to not understanding the point of God's communication or even forthright rejection of it – demands another approach according to the Qurʾānic worldview. In such metaphorical evocations, disability becomes an overall conceptual category in which distinct features of a disability, for example, blindness, disappear. The disabilities are clustered without many of their fundamental features. The verse Q 16:76, however, disturbs this overall dichotomy. Containing an unusually

[90] With some differences, of course. Leprosy, for example, is not a disease that seems relevant to the Qurʾān, the two examples occurring in the text being used in relation to Jesus. See again n. 71.

negative reference to and treatment of the mute servant, this Qurʾānic simile may have been affected by the metaphorical use of the very same disability in other Qurʾānic texts. Again following Fauconnier and Turner, it is possible that blended meaning can be projected back to the input spaces, causing a reinterpretation of either the target or the source of the original metaphor.[91] To move beyond such a tentative hypothesis regarding Q 16:76, future studies might consider exploring the (hypothetical) chronological occurrences of Qurʾānic disabilities and their possible metaphorical interrelations.

## Bibliography

Aaron, David H., *Biblical Ambiguities: Metaphor, Semantics and Divine Imagery*. Leiden: Brill, 2001.

Abrams, Judith Z., George D. Chryssides, Sandie Gravett, William Loader, Katherine Marsengill, Rebecca Raphael and Jeremy Schipper, 'Disability, Disabilities', in Constance M. Furey, Joel Marcus LeMon, Brian Matz, Thomas Chr. Römer, Jens Schröter, Barry Dov Walfish, and Eric Ziolkowski (eds), *Encyclopedia of the Bible and Its Reception*. Berlin: De Gruyter, 2013, 6:864–86.

Abu Deeb, Kamal, 'Al-Jurjānī's Classification of *Istiʿāra* with Special Reference to Aristotle's Classification of Metaphor', *Journal of Arabic Literature* 2(1) (1971): 48–75.

Abu Deeb, Kamal, *Al-Jurjānī's Theory of Poetic Imagery*. Warminster: Aris & Phillips, 1979.

Abu Deeb, Kamal, 'Studies in the *Majāz* and Metaphorical Language of the Qur'ān: Abū ʿUbayda and al-Sharīf al-Raḍī', in Issa J. Boulatta (ed.), *Literary Structures of Religious Meaning in the Qur'ān*. New York: Routledge, 2000, 310–53.

Alhusban, Amani M. and Mohammad Alkhawaldah, 'Meaning Construction of Selected Quranic Metaphors', *International Journal of Linguistics* 10(6) (2018): 134–48.

Ambros, Arne A., *The Nouns of Koranic Arabic Arranged by Topics*. Wiesbaden: Reichert Verlag, 2006.

Ambros, Arne A. and Stephan Procházka, *A Concise Dictionary of Koranic Arabic*. Wiesbaden: Reichert Verlag, 2004.

Amihay, Aryeh, Francis Borchardt, Rhonda Burnette-Bletsch, Susanne Gillmayr-Bucher, Sven Rune Havsteen, Rainer Hirsch-Luipold, Dorothy A. Lee et al., 'Image, Imagery', in Constance M. Furey, Joel Marcus LeMon, Brian Matz,

[91] Fauconnier and Turner, *The Way We Think*, 44.

Thomas Chr. Römer, Jens Schröter, Barry Dov Walfish, and Eric Ziolkowski (eds), *Encyclopedia of the Bible and Its Reception*. Berlin: De Gruyter, 2010, 12:913–49.

Andersen, Francis I. and David Noel Freedman, *Hosea: A New Translation with Introduction and Commentary*. New York: Doubleday, 1980.

Arberry, Arthur J., *The Koran Interpreted: A Translation by A.J. Arberry*. Oxford: Oxford University Press, [1955] 1983.

Aristotle (d. 322 BC), *Poetics*, ed. W. William Fyfe. London: Heinemann, 1965.

Abū al-Ḥasan ʿAlī ibn Ismāʿīl al-Ashʿarī (d. 324/936), *Kitāb Maqālāt al-Islāmiyyīn wa-Ikhtilāf al-Muṣallīn (Die Dogmatischen Lehren der Anhänger des Islam)*, ed. Hellmut Ritter, 2nd edn. Wiesbaden: Franz Steiner, 1963.

Avalos, Hector, Sarah J. Melcher and Jeremy Schipper (eds), *This Abled Body: Rethinking Disabilities in Biblical Studies*. Atlanta, GA: Society of Biblical Literature, 2007.

Bauer, Thomas, 'Insanity', *EQ* (online), 2001–.

Becker, Matthias, Joshua Canzona, Mordechai Z. Cohen, Susanne Gillmayr-Bucher, Ulrike Kaiser, Todd Lawson, Stewart Moore et al., 'Metaphor', in Eric Ziolkowski, Barry Dov Walfish, Jens Schröter, Thomas Chr. Römer, Brian Matz, Joel Marcus LeMon and Constance M. Furey (eds), *Encyclopedia of the Bible and Its Reception*. Berlin: De Gruyter, 2010, 18:969–1008.

Bellamy, James A., 'Some Proposed Emendations to the Text of the Koran', *Journal of the American Oriental Society* 113(4) (1992): 562–73.

Bennett, David, 'The Muʿtazilite Movement (II): The Early Muʿtazilites', in Sabine Schmidtke (ed.), *The Oxford Handbook of Islamic Theology*. Oxford: Oxford University Press, 2016, 142–58.

Boeve, Lieven and Kurt Feyaerts (eds), *Metaphor and God-Talk*. Bern: Peter Lang, 1999.

Christiansen, Johanne Louise, 'The Dark Koran: A Semantic Analysis of the Koranic Darknesses (*ẓulumāt*) and Their Metaphorical Usage', *Arabica* 62(2/3) (2015): 185–233.

Christiansen, Johanne Louise, 'A Woman's "Self-Wronging": A Gender Subtheme in the Qur'anic Encounter between Solomon and the Queen of Sheba', *Literature and Theology* 32(4) (2018): 397–422.

Christiansen, Johanne Louise, *The Exceptional Qur'ān: Flexible and Exceptive Rhetoric in Islam's Holy Book*, Islamic History and Thought. Piscataway, NJ: Gorgias Press, 2021.

Colby, Frederick S., 'Symbolic Imagery', *EQ* (online), 2001–.

Cragg, Kenneth, 'The Meaning of Zulm in the Qur'ān', *Muslim World* 49(3) (1959): 196–212.

Creamer, Deborah Beth, *Disability and Christian Theology: Embodied Limits and Constructive Possibilities*. Oxford: Oxford University Press, 2009.

Crone, Patricia, 'What Do We Actually Know about Mohammad?' available at: https://www.opendemocracy.net/faith-europe_islam/mohammed_3866.jsp, 2008.

Denny, Frederick Mathewson, 'Ears', *EQ* (online), 2001–.

Denny, Frederick Mathewson, 'Eyes', *EQ* (online), 2001–

Denny, Frederick Mathewson, 'Face', *EQ* (online), 2001–.

Denny, Frederick Mathewson, 'Feet', *EQ* (online), 2001–.

Denny, Frederick Mathewson, 'Hand(s)', *EQ* (online), 2001–.

Ess, Josef van, 'Tas͟hbīh wa-Tanzīh', in *EI²* (online), 1960–.

Fauconnier, Gilles and Mark Turner, 'Conceptual Integration Networks', *Cognitive Science* 22(2) (1998): 133–87.

Fauconnier, Gilles and Mark Turner, *The Way We Think: Conceptual Blending and the Mind's Hidden Complexities*. New York: Basic Books, 2003.

Feyaerts, Kurt (ed.), *The Bible through Metaphor and Translation: A Cognitive Semantic Perspective*. Bern: Peter Lang, 2003.

Fischer, Wolfdietrich, *A Grammar of Classical Arabic*, 3rd edn. New Haven, CT: Yale University Press, 2002.

Geeraerts, Dirk and Hubert Cuyckens (eds), *The Oxford Handbook of Cognitive Linguistics*. Oxford: Oxford University Press, 2007.

Haleem, Muhammad Abdel, *Understanding the Qur'an: Themes and Styles*. London: I. B. Tauris, 1999.

Haleem, Muhammad Abdel, *The Qur'an: A New Translation by M.A.S. Abdel Haleem*. Oxford: Oxford University Press, 2004.

Heath, Peter, 'Metaphor', *EQ* (online), 2001–.

Hecke, Pierre van, 'Conceptual Blending: A Recent Approach to Metaphors. Illustrated with the Pastoral Metaphor in Hos 4,16', in Pierre van Hecke (ed.), *Metaphor in the Hebrew Bible*. Leuven: Leuven University Press, 2005, 215–31.

Hersh, Edward and Rosemarie Scotti Hughes, 'The Role of Suffering and Disability: Evidence from Scripture', *Journal of Religion, Disability & Health* 9(3) (2006): 85–92.

Hoffmann, Thomas, 'Force Dynamics and the Qur'ân: An Essay in Cognitive Qur'ânic Poetics', in Roberta Sterman Sabbath (ed.), *Sacred Tropes: Tanakh, New Testament, and Qur'an as Literature and Culture*. Leiden: Brill, 2009, 65–76.

Hoffmann, Thomas, 'The Moving Qur'ān: A Cognitive Poetics Approach to the Qur'ān', in Mohammed Nekrouni and Jan Meise (eds), *Modern Controversies in Qur'ānic Studies*. Hamburg-Schenefeld: EB-Verlag, 2009, 141–52.

Hoffmann, Thomas, 'Notes on Qur'ānic Wilderness – and Its Absence', in Laura Feldt (ed.), *Wilderness in Mythology and Religion*. Berlin: De Gruyter, 2012, 157–82.

Hoffmann, Thomas, '*Taste My Punishment and My Warnings* (Q. 54:39): On the Torments of Tantalus and Other Painful Metaphors of Taste in the Qur'an', *Journal of Qur'anic Studies* 21(1) (2019): 1–20.

Hourani, George F., '"Injuring Oneself" in the Qur'ān, in the Light of Aristotle', in *Reason and Tradition in Islamic Ethics*. Cambridge: Cambridge University Press, 1985, 49–56.

Huda, Qamar-ul, 'Anatomy', *EQ* (online), 2001–.

Izutsu, Toshihiko, *Ethico-Religious Concepts in the Qur'ān*. Montreal: McGill-Queens University Press, [1959] 2002.

Izutsu, Toshihiko, *God and Man in the Qur'an: Semantics of the Qur'anic Weltanschauung*. Kuala Lumpur: Islamic Book Trust, [1964] 2002.

Johnson, Mark, *The Body in the Mind: The Bodily Basis of Meaning, Imagination, and Reason*. Chicago: University of Chicago Press, 1987.

Jones, Alan, trans., *The Qur'ān*. Cambridge: Gibb Memorial Trust, 2007.

ʿAbd al-Qāhir al-Jurjānī (d. 471/1078), *Asrār al-Balāgha*, ed. Helmut Ritter. Istanbul: Government Press, 1954.

ʿAbd al-Qāhir al-Jurjānī (d. 471/1078), *Dalāʾil al-Iʿjāz*, ed. Muḥammad Rashīd Riḍā, 3rd edn. Dār al-Manār: Cairo, 1946.

Kövecses, Zoltán, *Emotion Concepts*. New York: Springer, 1990.

Labahn, Antje (ed.), *Conceptual Metaphors in Poetic Texts*. Piscataway, NJ: Gorgias Press, 2013.

Labahn, Antje, 'Heart as a Conceptual Metaphor in Chronicles: Metaphors as Representations of Concepts of Reality: Conceptual Metaphors – a New Paradigm in Metaphor Research', in Antje Labahn (ed.), *Conceptual Metaphors in Poetic Texts*. Piscataway, NJ: Gorgias Press, 2013, 3–29.

Lakoff, George, 'The Meanings of Literal', *Metaphor and Symbolic Activity* 1(4) (1986): 291–6.

Lakoff, George, *Women, Fire, and Dangerous Things: What Categories Reveal about the Mind*. Chicago: University of Chicago Press, 1987.

Lakoff, George and Mark Johnson, *Metaphors We Live By*. Chicago: University of Chicago Press, 1980.

Lakoff, George and Mark Turner, *More than Cool Reason: A Field Guide to Poetic Metaphor*. Chicago: University of Chicago Press, 1989.

Levin, Samuel R., 'Aristotle's Theory of Metaphor', *Philosophy & Rhetoric* 15(1) (1982): 24–46.

Long, Gary Alan, 'Dead or Alive? Literality and God-Metaphors in the Hebrew Bible', *Journal of the American Academy of Religion* 62(2) (1994): 509–37.

Lowry, Joseph E., 'Exculpatory Language in the Qur'an: A Survey of Terms, Themes, and Theologies', *Mélanges de l'Université Saint-Joseph* LXVI (2016–15): 97–120.

McAuliffe, Jane D., 'Heart', *EQ* (online), 2001–.

Nasr, Seyyed Hossein, Caner K. Dagli, Maria Massi Dakake, Joseph E. B. Lumbard and Mohammad Rustom, *The Study Quran: A New Translation and Commentary*. New York: Harper One, 2015.

Neuwirth, Angelika, 'Images and Metaphors in the Introductory Sections of the *Makkan Sūras*', in G. R. Hawting and Abdul-Kader A. Shareef (eds), *Approaches to the Qur'ān*. London: Routledge, 1993, 3–36.

Neuwirth, Angelika, *Studien zur Komposition der mekkanischen Suren*. Berlin: Walter de Gruyter, 1981.

Olyan, Saul M., *Disability in the Hebrew Bible: Interpreting Mental and Physical Differences*. Cambridge: Cambridge University Press, 2008.

Pickthall, Marmaduke W., *The Meaning of the Glorious Koran: An Explanatory Translation*. London: A. A. Knopf, 1930.

Punter, David, *Metaphor*. London: Routledge, 2007.

Muḥammad b. al-Ḥusayn al-Sharīf al-Raḍī (d. 406/1016), *Talkhīṣ al-Bayān fī Majāzāt al-Qur'ān*, ed. Muḥammad ʿAbd al-Ghanī Ḥasan, 5 vols. Cairo: Dār Iḥyāʾ al-Kutub al-ʿArabīyah, 1955.

Räisänen, Heikki, *The Idea of Divine Hardening: A Comparative Study of the Notion of Divine Hardening, Leading Astray and Inciting to Evil in the Bible and the Qur'ān*. Helsinki: Publications of the Finnish Exegetical Society, 1976.

Raphael, Rebecca, *Biblical Corpora: Representations of Disability in Hebrew Biblical Literature*. New York: T. & T. Clark, 2008.

Rastgoo, Cobra, 'Cognitive Study of Anthropomorphic Metaphors in Qur'anic Discourse Based on Conceptual Theory', *Language Related Research* 11(6) (2021): 167–200.

Rastgoo, Cobra and Seyede Fatemeh Salimi, 'The Intellectual Metonymy; Metonymy or Reality through the Conceptual Blending Approach in the Quranic Discourse', *Journal of Arabic Language & Literature* 11(1) (2019): 25–55.

Ricoeur, Paul, *The Rule of Metaphor: The Creation of Meaning in Language*, trans. Robert Czerny. London: Routledge, 2004.

Rippin, Andrew, 'Metaphor and the Authority of the Qur'ān', in Khaleel Mohammad and Andrew Rippin (eds), *Coming to Terms with the Qur'an : A Volume in Honor of Professor Issa Boullata*. North Haledon: Islamic Publications International, 2008, 47–62.

Robinson, Neal, *Discovering the Qur'an: A Contemporary Approach to a Veiled Text*. Washington, DC: Georgetown University Press, 2003.

Sabbagh, Toufic, *La Métaphore dans le Coran*. Paris: Université de Paris, 1943.

Ṣaḥīḥ International, *The Qur'ān*. London: Abulqasim Publishing, 1997.

Sardaraz, Khan and Roslan Ali, 'A Cognitive–Semantic Study of the Spatial Preposition *Fī* (في) in the Quran', *KEMANUSIAAN: Asian Journal of Humanities* 24(2) (2017): 89–122.

Sardaraz, Khan and Roslan Ali, 'A Cognitive–Semantic Approach to the Interpretation of Death Metaphor Themes in the Quran', *Journal of Nusantara Studies (JONUS)* 4(2) (2019): 219–46.

Schipper, Jeremy, *Disability and Isaiah's Suffering Servant*. Oxford: Oxford University Press, 2011.

Schipper, Jeremy, *Disability Studies and the Hebrew Bible: Figuring Mephibosheth in the David Story*. New York: Bloomsbury T. & T. Clark, 2006.

Schipper, Jeremy and Candida R. Moss, *Disability Studies and Biblical Literature*. New York: Palgrave Macmillan, 2011.

Schmidtke, Sabine, 'Introduction', in Sabine Schmidtke (ed.), *The Oxford Handbook of Islamic Theology*. Oxford: Oxford University Press, 2016, 12–23.

Sinai, Nicolai, *The Qur'an: A Historical-Critical Introduction*. Edinburgh: Edinburgh University Press, 2017.

Sister, Moses, *Metaphern und Vergleiche im Koran: Inaugural-Dissertation*. Berlin: Friedrich-Wilhelms-Universität, 1931.

Stewart, Devin, 'Reflections on the State of the Art in Western Qur'anic Studies', in Carol Bakhos and Michael Cook (eds), *Islam and Its Past: Jahiliyya, Late Antiquity, and the Qur'an*. Oxford: Oxford University Press, 2017, 4–68.

Szlos, M. B., 'Body Parts as Metaphor and the Value of a Cognitive Approach', in Pierre van Hecke (ed.), *Metaphor in the Hebrew Bible*. Leuven: Leuven University Press, 2005, 185–96.

Abū Jaʿfar Muḥammad ibn Jarīr al-Ṭabarī (d. 310/923), *Tafsīr al-Ṭabarī: Jāmiʿ al-Bayān ʿan Taʾwīl Āy al-Qurʾān*, ed. ʿAbd Allāh ibn ʿAbd al-Muḥsin Turkī, 26 vols. Cairo: Dār Har, 2001.

Talmy, Leonard, 'Force Dynamics in Language and Cognition', *Cognitive Science* 12(1) (1988): 49–100.

Talmy, Leonard, *Toward a Cognitive Semantics, Volume I: Concept Structuring Systems*. Cambridge, MA: MIT Press, 2000.

Torrey, Charles C., *The Commercial Theological Terms in the Koran*. Leiden: Brill, 1892.

Turner, Mark and Gilles Fauconnier, 'Conceptual Integration and Formal Expression', *Metaphor and Symbolic Activity* 10(3) (1995): 183–204.

Abū ʿUbayda (d. 209/824–5), *Majāz al-Qurʾān*, ed. Fuat Sezgin, 2 vols. Cairo: Khānjī, 1955.

Wansbrough, John, '*Majāz al-Qurʾān*: Periphrastic Exegesis', *Bulletin of the School of Oriental and African Studies* 33(2) (1970): 247–66.

Watt, W. Montgomery, *Free Will and Predestination in Early Islam*. London: Luzac, 1948.

Wehr, Hans, *A Dictionary of Modern Written Arabic*, ed. J. Milton Cowan, 3rd edn. Ithaca, NY: Spoken Languages Services, 1976.

Welch, Alford T., 'Al-Ḳurʾān', *EI*$^2$ (online), 1960–.

Wensinck, A. J., *The Muslim Creed: Its Genesis and Historical Development*. London: Cambridge University Press, 1932.

Williams, Wesley, 'A Body Unlike Bodies: Transcendent Anthropomorphism in Ancient Semitic Tradition and Early Islam', *Journal of the American Oriental Society* 129(1) (2009): 19–44.

Yusuf Ali, Abdullah, *The Meaning of the Holy Qurʾan*. Markfield: Islamic Foundation, [1934–8] 2003.

Zahniser, A. H. Mathias, 'Parable', *EQ* (online), 2001–.

# Part III

## ISLAM AND/AS CRITIQUE

# 7

# ON THE RELATIONSHIP BETWEEN CULTURE/RELIGION AND POLITICS: A CRITIQUE OF THE CULTURALIST APPROACH TO ISLAM

HOUSAMEDDEN DARWISH

## Introduction

The (causal) relationship between culture and politics, and their mutual influence, is one of the most controversial topics in the philosophy of social sciences.[1] Despite the problematic character of this relationship and the difficulty in understanding its complexities, dimensions and its many and varied historical manifestations, it is noticeable that people tend to have opinions or take positions on this topic, varying from implicit and indirect to explicit and direct, from epistemically justified and constructed argumentation to merely intuitive, without any solid or clear basis. Sometimes these opinions or stances take the form of deep wisdom and aphorism, showing alleged depth, for example, by stating that the fruit (politics or the system of government) cannot be improved, reformed or even altered without changing the soil (religion, culture or society) that nourishes it. Such sayings clearly point to a causal relationship between culture and politics. This relationship

[1] For more details on the complexity of the relationship between culture and politics, see Sonia E. Alvarez, Evelina Dagnino and Arturo Escobar, 'Introduction: The Cultural and the Political in Latin American Social Movements', in Sonia E. Alvarez et al. (eds), *Cultures of Politics, Politics of Cultures: Re-visioning Latin American Social Movements* (New York: Routledge, 1998), 1–29.

or mutual influence can be addressed from different perspectives, which we can categorise in two main directions: reductionist and dialectical.

The *reductionist tendency* seeks to reduce politics to culture or vice versa. Reduction in this context means that one concept can be almost completely explained by the other. Some believe that politics is the result of culture (culturalism),[2] while others reduce culture to politics and believe that the former can be totally and exclusively understood through the latter (politicism).

In contrast, the *dialectical view* emphasises the mutual influence between politics and culture, and stresses the impossibility of reducing one to the other. Within this dialectical view, a distinction can be made between blurred or fluid dialectics and flexible dialectics. *Blurred and fluid dialectics* refers to the existence of mutual influence between culture and politics, without detailing the disparity and difference in the degree of influence, its conditions, dimensions and consequences, in different contexts in general, as well as in specific historical contexts.[3]

[2] The works of Samuel Huntington are exemplary of the culturalist approach in general and of what we call 'compound reductionism', that is, the reduction of politics to culture and the reduction of culture to religion, in particular. Huntington famously divided the post-Cold War world into civilisation blocs, considering religions as essential determinant of these blocs. He wrote: 'World politics is entering a new phase in which the great divisions among humankind and the dominating source of conflict will be cultural. Civilizations, the highest cultural groupings of people, are differentiated from each other by religion, history, language, and tradition.' Samuel P. Huntington, 'The Clash of Civilizations?' *Foreign Affairs* 72(3) (1993): 22. See also, Samuel P. Huntington, *The Third Wave: Democratization in the Late Twentieth Century* (Norman, OK: University of Oklahoma Press, 1991); Jonathan Fox, *Religion, Civilization and Civil War: 1945 through the New Millennium* (Lanham, MD: Lexington Books, 2004).

[3] We find an example of such dialectics in the following text: '[N]ot only do democracy and authoritarianism induce different value patterns, but the role of values in the constitution and stabilization of these two types of regimes differs, with likely consequences for responsiveness. For instance, in authoritarian regimes such as ideocracies and theocracies, problems that allow the regime to mobilize the masses in the name of its core ideological or religious values have an advantage. Conversely, the formulation in political terms of problems arising from values such as free speech or multiculturalism are likely to remain confined to small circles of opponents at the fringes of such authoritarian regimes, whose legitimacy is grounded in values of conformity and cultural homogeneity.' Damien Krichewsky, 'Political Responsiveness: The Identification and Processing of Problems in Modern Polities', in Anna L. Ahlers et al. (eds), *Democratic and Authoritarian Political Systems in 21st Century World Society, Vol. 1: Differentiation, Inclusion, Responsiveness* (Bielefeld: transcript Verlag, 2021), 137.

*Flexible dialectics* acknowledges the dialectical relationship between culture and politics, but underlines that mutual influence can vary, depending on the variables of historical context. According to flexible dialectics, the dialectical relationship between culture and politics in a democratic system differs greatly from that in a non-democratic system.[4] Within a flexible dialectic framework, it can be said that culture's influence on politics tends to be much greater in a democratic system than in an undemocratic system.

By using a flexible dialectical approach, this chapter aims to provide a critical overview of the reductionist perspective on politics, which reduces politics to culture. This is also known as culturalism, the culturalist approach, essentialism or cultural essentialism.[5] This approach is mainly discussed with reference to the situation in Arab and Islamicate countries, in particular Syria over the past five decades. The culturist point of view can be summarised as follows: authoritarian political systems are the product of the culture and the structure of a society. Furthermore, the factors and reasons behind the existence of an authoritarian political system can lie specifically in culture, which is also reduced to religion, rather than to politics,

[4] Pearl T. Robinson writes: 'In this regard, it is important to recall that a political regime is not a value neutral environment. Regimes are the formal rules that link the main political institutions of the state. They define the political nature of the ties between citizens and rulers . . . and over time shape the social construction of values. It is therefore reasonable to expect some degree of correlation between the ideational configuration of a culture of politics and the hegemonic ambitions of its regime. But the precise nature of that relationship is variable and should be treated as an empirical question.' Pearl T. Robinson, 'Democratization: Understanding the Relationship between Regime Change and the Culture of Politics', *African Studies Review* 37(1) (1994): 40.

[5] The terms culturalism, the culturalist approach, essentialism and cultural essentialism tend to be interchangeable and quasi-synonyms in the literature; see, for example, Karine Chemla and Evelyn Fox Keller, 'Introduction', Kenji Ito, 'Cultural Difference and Sameness: Historiographic Reflections on Histories of Physics in Modern Japan', and Evelyn Fox Keller, 'Worrying about Essentialism: From Feminist Theory to Epistemological Cultures', all in Karine Chemla and Evelyn Fox Keller (eds), *Cultures without Culturalism: The Making of Scientific Knowledge* (Durham, NC: Duke University Press, 2017), 3, 50, 101; Sep Neo Lim, 'Essentialising the Convenient Baba-Nyonyas of the Heritage City of Melaka (Malaysia)', in Fred Dervin and Regis Machart (eds), *Cultural Essentialism in Intercultural Relations* (Basingstoke: Palgrave Macmillan, 2015), 157.

or to other concepts.[6] Therefore any problem, including the existence of an authoritarian or undemocratic political system, indeed, the mother of all other problems, can be attributed to religion–culture, and here in the Arab and Islamicate countries, Islam–Islamicate culture.

This study is concerned with Islamicate culture and Islamic religion, and adopts the prevalent view that Islam is both religion and culture. However, it maintains a critical distance from the claim of Islamicate culture's uniqueness in this respect,[7] which is often used by culturalism to distinguish and create hierarchies between cultures, and to declare the existence of a peculiarity in Islamic religion–culture. This peculiarity is represented especially by the conflation of the spiritual and the temporal dimensions –preventing it from being compatible and in harmony with democracy, secularism and political modernity in general.[8] Instead, the chapter agrees with Gudrun Krämer that

[6] Francis Fukuyama is one of a number of culturalists who stress the important role of religions or religious cultures in the determination of modernity and democracy, considering it more compatible with Christianity than with other religion–religious cultures. On this supposed strong link between modernity, democracy and Christianity on the other he wrote: 'Modernity has a cultural basis. Liberal democracy and free markets do not work everywhere. They work best in societies with certain values whose origins may not be entirely rational. It is not an accident that modern liberal democracy emerged first in the Christian west, since the universalism of democratic rights can be seen as a secular form of Christian universalism.' Francis Fukuyama, 'The West Has Won: Radical Islam Can't Beat Democracy and Capitalism', *The Guardian*, 11 October 2010, available at: https://www.theguardian.com/world/2001/oct/11/afghanistan.terrorism30. For a more detailed and critical discussion of Fukuyama's culturalism, see Fares al-Braizat, 'Muslims and Democracy an Empirical Critique of Fukuyama's Culturalist Approach', *International Journal of Comparative Sociology* 43(269) (2002), 269–99.

[7] Louis Gardet, for instance, wrote: 'Islam is a religion. It is also, almost inseparably from this, a community, a civilization and a culture . . . The history of the Muslim peoples and countries is thus a unique example of a culture with a religious foundation, uniting the spiritual and the temporal . . .'. Louis Gardet, 'Religion and Culture', in Peter Holt, Ann K. S. Lambton and Bernard Lewis (eds), *The Cambridge History of Islam: Vol. 2B: Islamic Society and Civilization* (Cambridge: Cambridge University Press, 1970), 569.

[8] Lewis, Huntington and Fukuyama all argue that Islam is inherently different from other religions in general and from Christianity in particular, as it is more likely to adopt violence and less likely to be compatible and in harmony with modernity and democracy. See Bernard Lewis, 'The Roots of Muslim Rage', The Atlantic *Monthly* September 1990, available at: https://www.theatlantic.com/magazine/archive/1990/09/the-roots-of-muslim-rage/304643;

this combination is common and frequent in both monotheistic and non-monotheistic religions, and that Islamic religion–culture does NOT represent a unique case in this respect.[9]

Before embarking on a discussion of the main focus of this chapter – a critical analysis of the main characteristics of a culturalist approach to Islamicate culture – it is crucial to clarify the key terms 'culture' and 'politics', and the methodology of the study.

Samuel P. Huntington, *The Clash of Civilizations and the Remaking of World Order* (New York: Simon & Schuster, 1996); Fukuyama, 'The West has Won'. The existence of culturalist dimensions in the work of Fukuyama, Huntington and Lewis does not negate the many differences between them, nor deny the varying prevalence of culturalism. However, it is not infrequent for commonalities to be drawn out. Drucilla Cornell talks about 'the hierarchical models of history employed by the likes of Bernard Lewis, Frances Fukuyama, and Samuel Huntington – models that assert the superiority of Western civilization over and against the supposed darkness and evil of the Arab world.' Drucilla Cornell, *Defending Ideals: War, Democracy, and Political Struggles* (New York: Routledge, 2004), 35. In the same vein, Hamid Dabashi wrote: 'Manufacturing of colonial divides and civilizational boundaries (in turn corroborated and accented by a pervasive and paralyzing identitarian politics) are all predicated on assumptions of cultural authenticity and insurmountable differences, such as those suggested and sustained between "Islam and the West", "The West and The East", or even "The North and the South" or "The First and the Third Worlds". Bernard Lewis, Samuel Huntington and Francis Fukuyama are the principal ideologues of such binary oppositions.' Hamid Dabashi, *Post-Orientalism: Knowledge and Power in Time of Terror* (New Brunswick, NJ: Transaction Publishers, 2004), 194. As there are many differences between culturalists, there are various ways to classify culturalism. It can be secular or religious, left or right, liberal or conservative, etc. In this chapter I mainly elaborate on the perspective of secular culturalism versus Islamic–religious culturalism. On left- and right-wing culturalism, see Jens-Martin Eriksen and Frederik Stjernfelt, 'Culturalism: Culture as Political Ideology', *Eurozine*, 9 January 2009, available at: https://www.eurozine.com/culturalism-culture-as-political-ideology. Concerning liberal versus conservative culturalism, see Matthew Festenstein, 'The Limits of Liberal Culturalism', in *Negotiating Diversity: Culture, Deliberation, Trust* (Cambridge: Polity Press, 2005), 66–90; Aymeric Xu, *From Culturalist Nationalism to Conservatism: Origins and Diversification of Conservative Ideas in Republican China* (Berlin: De Gruyter Oldenbourg, 2021).

[9] Gudrun Krämer, 'Religion, Culture, and the Secular: The Case of Islam', *Working Paper Series of the CASHSS 'Multiple Secularities – Beyond the West, Beyond Modernities'* 23. Leipzig University, 2021. DOI: https://doi.org/10.36730/2020.1.msbwbm.23.

## Conceptual and Methodological Clarifications

Culture may generally refer to a system of values, ideas, beliefs, customs, traditions, symbols, rules and deeds that are widespread and prevalent in a given group or society.[10] This definition is general, non-normative and relative. Its generality is manifest in the fact that it does not establish a clear content of the values, ideas, etc. on which it is based, nor does it determine their relationships. Generality is also reflected by the possibility for it to include significantly different and distinct parties. Moreover, its non-normativity derives from the fact that it does not establish a hierarchy, nor contain an evaluative comparison between cultures, groups or individuals. This definition of culture is also relative because it may refer to humankind in general, so we can talk about human culture, or to a specific group or society, so we can talk, for instance, about Chinese culture or Buddhist culture.

Therefore, the concept of culture does not imply positive evaluation or praise of a specific group, community or culture. Culture is, in the non-normative sense,[11] a general human characteristic that applies to all human

[10] For a historical and conceptual discussion of the concept of culture, see, for example, Martyn Hammersley, *The Concept of Culture: A History and Reappraisal* (Cham: Palgrave Macmillan, 2019); Robert S. Wyer, Chi-yue Chiu and Ying-yi Hong, *Understanding Culture: Theory, Research, and Application* (New York: Psychology Press, 2009).

[11] Although I am talking about the non-normative sense of culture, I do not deny there are normative dimensions inherent in this and that there are ongoing normative uses of it. The concept of culture is a 'thick normative concept', that is, it is descriptive and evaluative at the same time. Krämer makes a distinction between several (normative) positions in the concept of culture: 'there are those who still work with the assumptions of the *Kulturkreis* school, which regarded cultures as closed, homogeneous, enduring, and static units . . . Then, there are those who reject the concept of culture as a product of othering, which, based on an essentialist construction of an "Other", first fixes its character, preferably with reference to a given textual tradition, to then use that Other as a negative foil for the superior "Self". Some want to abandon "culture" altogether, declaring the concept to be irredeemably tied to essentialist assumptions . . . A minority of critics go further, claiming that the term "culture" serves as a placeholder for "race", and that boundary drawing based on perceived or alleged cultural differences is, in essence, racist ("cultural racism", "racism without race").' Krämer, 'Religion, Culture', 8. This paper includes a critical presentation of some of the normative dimensions and uses of this concept in the culturalist approach. In order to show the normative dimension that is immanent to the concept of culture, we can

beings, to one degree or another, and in one way or another, and is shared by all, both intellectuals (with an elite culture) and common people (with a popular culture). Nevertheless, this does not deny the existence of differences in the contents of cultures of peoples, individuals and groups, this allowing for the establishment of differentiations and distinctions between them, without negating their overlapping and intertwining. Syrian culture, for example, is a human culture that partially and relatively belongs to the Arab and Islamicate culture, but is also distinct from it in consisting of a number of regional, class-based, ideological, religious, denominational or sectarian subcultures, etc.

Moving to politics, this means everything related directly to the ruling system of the state, the nature, ideas, values and practices inherent in this system, both in theory and in practice. In addition, the nature of a political system refers especially to its democratic, non-democratic or authoritarian characteristics.

In dealing with the problematic relationship between politics and culture, one can distinguish between three approaches or methods: (1) a theoretical, analytical and qualitative approach; (2) an empirical and quantitative approach; and (3) an ideological–critical approach. The theoretical–methodological distinction between these approaches does not negate the possibility of complementarity and synergy between them or the possibility of combining any number of them in one single, comprehensive approach. Such an approach may provide for analytical and qualitative thinking with an ideological–critical element or based on the available empirical and quantitative

adopt David L. McMahan's definition of what he called 'a culture's lived world': '[T]he daily repertory of practices, implicit ideas, and dispositions that structure perception and action, allowing people to engage in social intercourse, know what is appropriate and inappropriate, understand what to expect of each other, and discern power relations.' David L. McMahan, *The Making of Buddhist Modernism* (Oxford: Oxford University Press, 2008), 15. In the same vein, my understanding of culture is consistent with Krämer's definition: 'a web of interpretations and representations of the self and the world, or cosmos. The image of the web conveys a sense of coherence, stability, and continuity, and yet the web and its individual threads are constantly changing, conditioned by time, locale, and social context. The web is elastic but it cannot be stretched ad libitum, and the stretching is done by humans.' Krämer, 'Religion, Culture', 10.

information and data. This chapter adopts such a synergetic approach, with priority given to analytical, qualitative and ideological–critical elements.

## Presentation and Critique of the Basic Characteristics of the Culturalist Approach

In the following, the main characteristics of the culturalist approach to Islam, which is considered an ideal type,[12] are identified and critically analysed. It should be emphasised that these characteristics are incomplete and are not necessarily and/or not explicitly present in every culturalist approach. On the other hand, they are entangled and intertwined to the extent that none of them can be fully understood before or without knowing or understanding the content of the other characteristics.

### *Compound Reductionism*

Culturalism is not constrained to the reduction of politics or other spheres to culture, but rather reduces culture to religion or considers religion as its essence, before this religion is additionally reduced to the practices of a certain religious group or sect and/or to religious texts, for example, the Qurʾān, books of hadith or books of interpretation. In ideological and political conflict, secular culturalism is often associated with denominationalism or religious sectarianism due to its reduction of religion to a specific religious denomination or sect while ignoring the beliefs, practices and texts of other sects. Given the paradoxical characteristics of the 'sectarian secularism' phenomenon, it seems necessary to scrutinise the meaning of secularism and the motives behind its adoption, rather than simply denying the reality of such a paradox.

[12] In explaining ideal types, Max Weber wrote: 'It is obtained by means of a one-sided *accentuation* of one or a *number* of viewpoints and through the synthesis of a great many diffuse and discrete individual phenomena (more present in one place, fewer in another, and occasionally completely absent) which are in conformity with one-sided accentuated viewpoints into an internally consistent mental image. In its conceptual purity, this image cannot be found anywhere in reality. It is a utopia, and the task of the historian then becomes that of establishing, in each individual case, how close reality is to it, or how distant from, that ideal image . . .' Max Weber, 'Objectivity in Social Science and Social Policy', in *On The Methodology of the Social Sciences*, ed. Hans Henrik Brun and Sam Whimster, trans. Hans Henrik Brun (London: Routledge, 2012), 125.

Reducing culture to a given religion, and this religion to the practices or texts of a specific sect, can imply an ideological tendency in a negative sense, since this double reduction denies not only the relative distinction between culture and religion, but also the great and numerous diversities in understandings and interpretations of (sacred) texts, and in their direct and indirect impacts on the life and culture of society. Given the great and vast differences between cultures influenced by the same religion, as well as in a single (religious) culture through time, the difference between religion and culture is evident. Therefore, the identification of culture as religion destroys any possibility of understanding the countless differences between, for example, Pakistani culture (Islamic 'Sunni') and Syrian or Egyptian culture (Islamic 'Sunni'), or between contemporary Syrian culture and Syrian culture a hundred or a thousand years ago. It seems that ideological fanaticism or cognitive indiscretion is what often makes culturalism unable or unwilling to clearly distinguish between culture and religion, or between cultures with a similar strong ('Sunni') religious dimension. To deal with any differences between Islamicate cultures or differences between various historical stages in one Islamicate culture, requires a partial and relative distinction between religion and culture, and an understanding of their complex relationship and mutual influence in different historical contexts, and their political and economic dimensions in particular.

Culturalism often reduces culture to religion when seeking to diagnose the problems society and people suffer from, leading to two contradictory results. While Islamic culturalism (Islamism) raises the motto 'Islam is the solution',[13] secular culturalism embraces the slogan 'Islam is the problem'.[14]

[13] For an analysis of this slogan, see Kristen Stilt, '"Islam is the Solution": Constitutional Visions of the Egyptian Muslim Brotherhood', *Texas International Law Journal* 46 (2010): 73–108.

[14] Jean-Philippe Platteau offers an excellent explanation and critique of the view that 'Islam is the problem', in his book *Islam Instrumentalized: Religion and Politics in Historical Perspective* (Cambridge: Cambridge University Press, 2017). 'The Islam-is-the-problem view, which is widely diffused through the press and the media (see, e.g., *Economist*, 17–23 January 2015, 22), rests on the idea that Islam has historically determined features that have shaped the destiny and institutional trajectory of Muslim countries, even in the very long term. More specifically, the circumstances in which Islam was born and the ensuing fusion between the religious and the political spheres have prevented these countries from evolving toward democracy and from gradually developing civil societies able to confront autocratic rulers.' 15.

Between the alleged solution and the artificial or exaggerated problem, political, economic and social dimensions are often neglected or marginalized.[15] Consequently, one may argue that the double reduction of politics to culture and culture to religion is a symptom of the problem, rather than an aid in diagnosing it, let alone finding solutions to it.

*Flexibility and Diversity in the Employment of the Culturist Approach*

The culturalist approach has a flexible content that makes its employment attractive to different and even conflicting perspectives with different (ideological) goals or purposes. Those who embrace the culturist approach are extremely diverse, ranging from common people to elites, from European scholars to Arab scholars, from supporters of authoritarian regimes to their opponents, from the conservative right to the revolutionary left, and from anti-religion secularists to anti-secular religious people.

In the Syrian context, the culturalist approach is invoked by both supporters and opponents of the al-Assad authoritarian regime to provide arguments that defend their opinions. While many intellectual supporters of the regime adopt this approach to justify its existence, some revolutionary intellectuals use it in the search for the genuine and actual roots of authoritarianism; those who believe that there is no salvation from authoritarianism without it being preceded or accompanied, at least, by deliverance from the culture that produces it.[16] Under glorious titles, such as 'realism' and 'the necessity of self-criticism',[17] (common) culture is usually criticised and labelled 'backward' or 'degenerate' and charged with producing decadence. Furthermore, it is believed that contempt for the society and culture of these people comes in the name of love and with a desire to save them from the crisis in which they live. It is not uncommon for culturalist criticisms of common people

[15] For a critical discussion of both views, see, for example, Daniel Brumberg, 'Islam Is Not the Solution (or the Problem)', *Washington Quarterly* 29(1) (2005): 97–116.

[16] See, for example, Adonis, *Violence et Islam. Entretien avec Houria Abdelouahed* (Paris: Seuil, 2015); and for a critical view of Adonis' culturalism, see Yasin al-Haj Salih, *al-Thaqafa ka-Siyasa. Dawr al-Muthaqqafin wa-Mas'uliyyatuhum al-'Ijtima'iyya fi Zaman al-Ghilan* (Beirut: al-Muassasa al-ʿArabiyya li-l-Dirasat wa-l-Nashr, 2016), 42–51.

[17] See Sadiq J. al-ʿAzm, *al-Naqd al-Dhati ba'd al-Hazima* (*Self-Criticism After the Defeat*) (Damascus: Dar Mamduh ʿIdwan, 2007).

and their culture to demonstrate that an alleged or declared desire for the salvation or redemption of the people is in fact an unsuccessful sublimation of the desire for 'salvation' from this despised culture.

The flexibility of the culturalist approach is also evident in its evocation by two conflicting parties – secular and religious individuals and intellectuals – in agreeing where the problem lies in Arab and Islamicate societies, and that this problem is cultural–religious. They disagree, however, over other essential matters, including the nature of this problem, the type of solution required, and which culture should replace it. While secular culturalism believes that salvation necessarily requires an abandoning of Islamic–religious culture and embracing the culture of Western modernity,[18] religious culturalism calls for the abandonment of current degenerate culture in favour of a return to what they see as true or genuine religious–Islamicate culture.[19]

Even if one assumes that the culturalist description of reality and identification of problems in a given country or society is valid on a theoretical level, we believe we are obliged, in all cases, to be politicalists, not culturalists, on the practical level, should this country be ruled by a long-standing authoritarian political system. In most Arab and Islamicate countries, historical practice shows that there are no prospects for genuine revolutionary and positive cultural–religious changes without it being preceded or accompanied by genuine political reform. This political reform establishes a political system genuinely willing and interested in undertaking social and cultural reform aimed at addressing any related problems.

Starting from the culturalist perspective that culture produces politics, it is fair to say that any prospects for cultural–religious reform are diminished or faded in the absence of political reform. Given that cultural reform necessarily requires effective and strong intervention by the political authority in order to achieve it, the question to be asked here is: how can one expect that

[18] For more details, see Sadiq J. al-ʿAzm, *Critique of Religious Thought*, trans. George Stergios and Mansour Ajami (Berlin: Gerlach Press, 2015); Adonis, *Violence et Islam*, 71–2.

[19] See, for example, Muhammad Saʿid Ramadan al-Buti, *ʿala Tariq al-ʿAwda ila al-Islam. Rasm li-Minhaj wa-Hal li-Mushkilat* (Beirut: Muʾassasat al-Risala, 1981); Muhammad Saʿid Ramadan al-Buti, *al-Salafiyya: Marhala Zamaniyya Mubaraka la Madhhab Islami* (Damascus: Dar al-Fikr, 1988).

authoritarian power will carry out any intervention or reform that could lead to the disposal of the culture that produces it, and replace it with a different culture that rejects and opposes its authority? This question is meant to be rhetorical in the sense that it implies its own answer.

Moreover, even if we assume the possibility of the existence of a 'just, enlightened or benevolent despot',[20] this possibility seems slim and irrational given its theoretical self-contradiction,[21] the fact that it is nowhere to be seen in practice, and because of the existence of an inherent realistic harmony between authoritarianism and the corruption of religious and political culture in particular. Although the idea of the 'just despot' has been subjected to increasing criticism by other Arab and Islamic thinkers, one can agree with al-Jabri that 'the ideal rule, in the minds of those operating from a traditional point of reference, is that exercised by a "just despot".'[22]

[20] The idea of 'enlightened or benevolent despotism or absolutism' originally appeared in the description by German historians, politicians and intellectuals of those European rulers who were both despotic and trying to implement some of the ideas of the European Enlightenment at the same time, such as Peter the Great of Russia (r. 1682–1725), Frederick the Great of Prussia (r. 1740–86), Catherine the Great of Russia (r. 1762–96), Louis XVI of France (r. 1772–92). Cf. H. M. Scott (ed.), *Enlightened Absolutism: Reform and Reformers in Later Eighteenth-Century Europe* (London: Macmillan, 1990). This concept became popular and prominent in the work of some of the most important Arab or Islamic figures in the nineteenth century, such as Muhammad ʿAbdu and Jamal al-Din al-Afghani.

[21] See Kenneth Maxwell, 'Pombal: the Paradox of Enlightenment and Despotism', in H. M. Scott (ed.), *Enlightened Absolutism: Reform and Reformers in Later Eighteenth-Century Europe* (London: Macmillan, 1990), 75–118.

[22] Mohammed Abed al-Jabri, *Democracy, Human Rights and Law in Islamic Thought* (London: I. B. Tauris, 2009), 123. Since the prevailing understanding among Islamic (and non-Islamic) thinkers rightly indicates that the teachings of Islam include *al-shūrā*, which might be understood as 'anti-despotism', it is necessary to stress, once again, that *al-shūrā* 'in the Arab-Islamic tradition, is never an absolute substitute for despotism but only for the kind of despotism exercised by an unjust ruler, the kind of despotism predicated on injustice. The ruler can avoid oppression if he has the desire and is guided by God, so he adopts *al-shūrā*, as he resorts to the *fuqahāʾ* and the *ʿulamāʾ* of religion before making any decision. *Al-shūrā*, however, is not binding upon the ruler. He simply consults, but the final decision is his own. He may choose to follow the advice of the people whom he consulted or take another course.' al-Jabri, *Democracy*, 123–4.

*The Essentialist, Pastist and Non-historical View*

Culturalism adopts an essentialist view of religion, seeing it as a fixed core that has not undergone any real or substantial change, from its inception to the present time. Culturism also sees religion as a static essence without taking into account the multiple and varied forms and contents of religiosity.[23] Ideological blindness leads culturalists to ignore the distinctions between religion and religiosity, or between textual religion, belief or a founding historical moment, and religiosity as a historical religion – religion as reflected in the practices of religious people throughout history.

Culturalism treats religiosity theoretically from the essentialist view of religion, so it considers that genuine religiosity should be consistent with their unilateral view of the static essence of religion. The countless differences in religiosity or historical religion, are, from culturalism's point of view, deviations that do not represent the true religion, and are the result of ignorance or hypocrisy.

The characterisation of culturalism as essentialism turns it into a pastist and non-historical view, despite its frequent and recurring references to history. It is pastist, because it believes that the essence of culture–religion is linked to a historical moment at which this essence was born, crystallised, established and entrenched. The importance of this historical moment is stressed by religious culturalism, which sees necessity in stimulating it and working on reviving it, while overlooking the historical differences between the past and the present. From the perspective of religious–Islamic culturalism, history is not a field of succession, change and development, but rather a field of repetition of the embodiment of the founding essence, and any deviation from it should be corrected in order to repeat this essence.

Secular culturism agrees with religious–Islamic culturalism that the essence of culture, religion or Islam is rooted in a past historical moment, which is the basis of everything that has happened since, including all ideas

[23] In this regard, Andrea Teti and Andrea Mura wrote: 'One of the most common misunderstandings about Islam is that it contains some kind of essential "core" which dictates the fundamental nature of political movements adopting its banner.' Andrea Teti and Andrea Mura, 'Islam and Islamism', in Jeffrey Haynes (ed.), *Routledge Handbook of Religion and Politics* (London: Routledge, 2009), 92.

and values that make up Syrian, Arab and/or Islamicate culture. However, secular culturism disagrees with religious culturalism, considering this non-historical static essence inherent in a past moment as a negative core of culture so far, stressing the need to be rid of this non-historical essence while building a new culture that breaks completely from the past and develops a new history.

The pastist feature of religious culturalism makes it incapable of realising that reproducing the founding past is impossible due to the radical economic, social, political, cultural and institutional changes that have taken place at both local and global levels over the many centuries since that founding historical moment. It also seems that seeking to repeat, replicate and regain that moment is not only an impossible dream, but more a nightmare that alienates people from their current and actual time, reality and problems. Religious culturalism often deals with basic economic and political problems only in terms of celebrating the better reality of a glorious past that should be restored.

While Islamic culturalism protests against the lack of influence that the past has in the present, and seeks to increase this influence as much as possible, secular culturalism overstates it and considers the present situation as mainly and fundamentally an outcome of the past. Secular culturalism often adopts a naive view of the relationship between the past and the present: the existence of the past in the present is automatic and mechanical, rather than it being summoned and evoked by current and dominant powers, authorities and elites. In this respect, it is important to distinguish between heritage and tradition. Tradition is the living part of heritage that exists until now, whereas heritage refers to dead values, ideas and traditions, meaning they are not adopted, followed or extant in the prevailing culture of the present. The evocation of heritage and the consolidation of traditions is not an innocent act; it is often governed by current political powers, interests, institutions and directives.

In other words, the appearance of the past in the present is mostly due to evocation, permission or encouragement, for reasons related to this present and its dominant powers and forces. As such, it can be said that the influence of the present on the past is stronger than the influence of the past on the present, and this remains governed by present circumstances and dominant forces and their interests in invoking specific parts of the past.

### *Anti-hermeneutic Dogmatism*

Culturalism is also characterised by anti-hermeneutic dogmatism given its essentialist character and that religion, represented primarily by its founding texts, has only ONE true and genuine meaning.[24] While this unilateral meaning is normatively negative and rejected by secular culturalism, for religious culturalism it is a positive meaning that must be accepted and embraced by everyone. Adopting a unilateralist view, culturalism does not accept the possibility of multiple readings or the legitimacy of huge differences between understandings and interpretations of religion. Readings by culturalists are usually normative and loaded with one-sided evaluations. Therefore, the ideological and anti-hermeneutic features of culturalism lead to an understanding of religion as nothing but positive meanings, connotations and values for religious or Islamic culturalism, or negative meanings, connotations and values for secular culturalism.

There is a paradox in secular culturalism's reduction of religion to specific practices, beliefs and texts that carry only one meaning while disregarding all other contradictory practices and beliefs, and different understandings or interpretations of these texts by various religious people. This paradox lies in its adoption of what can be called a 'secular *takfir* mindset', which is similar to the mindset embraced by religious culturalism. Secular and religious culturalisms both reject multiple interpretations of religious texts and various understandings of religion, only accepting a single respective interpretation and understanding. From this *takfir* mindset, secular culturalism believes there is one truth that has no second, and excludes from its circles anyone who does not believe in its view of a 'genuine Islam'. It is therefore entirely non-hermeneutic. Speaking of a 'secular *takfir* mindset' means that secular culturalism: (1) reduces religion–Islam to a single and unilateral cognitive and normative vision; (2) rejects all other visions that differ from or contradict it, because those visions do not embrace ('genuine') Islam, nor do

[24] In their emphasis on the historicity of Islam and the hermeneutic or interpretative character of its texts, principles and teachings, Teti and Mura wrote: 'Beyond this [the 'Five Pillars'], however, Islam's principles have been interpreted in widely different ways, and the practices carried out by Muslims themselves have varied just as much as those of any other "world religion",' Teti and Mura, 'Islam and Islamism', 93.

they express its essence; and (3) accuses those who adopt a different view of illusion, hypocrisy or of committing an intentional, unintentional or involuntary error.

The unilateralism of the culturalist understanding of culture, religion or Islam is clearly reflected in the denial of the legitimacy of any alternative understanding or interpretation. One can observe the prevalence of a one-sided, unilateral and exclusive mentality in the discourses of culturalism around, for example, the phenomenon of ISIS and al-Qaeda. There are, on the one hand, those who say: 'ISIS (or al-Qaeda) does not represent Islam',[25] while others claim that 'ISIS is the (only authentic and true) representative of Islam, and every Muslim has, actually or eventually, the same fundamental and destructive Ideology as ISIS', 'ISIS is the (real) Islam, and every Muslim is, necessarily or by definition and essence, an ISIS by force or action'.[26]

When moving away from the 'mindset of *takfir*' and considering the richness of religious texts and the principled or actual possibility of difference in their understanding and interpretation, according to various perspectives and in different historical contexts, one can notice that the difference between Islamic religious interpretations is not one between Islam and infidelity, or Islam and non-Islam. It is rather a difference in and within Islam, between diverse interpretations, all of which are based on the same religious texts, but which cannot be understood in isolation without considering their direct or indirect relationship to the historical context and political conflicts that surround them, and in which they are, in one way or another, involved.

### *Mechanical and Non-dialectical*

Culturalism has a simple or simplistic mechanical view of the relationship between alleged cause (culture) and effect (politics). Generally speaking, culturalism considers that culture mainly produces or influences politics and not

[25] See generally, Chahinaz Seghiri, 'ISIS not Representative of Islamic Beliefs, Teaching', *The Lantern*, 4 September 2014, available at: https://www.thelantern.com/2014/09/opinion-isis-not-representative-of-islamic-beliefs-teachings; Sveinung Sandberg and Sarah Colvin, "ISIS is not Islam": Epistemic Injustice, Everyday Religion, and Young Muslims' Narrative Resistance', *British Journal of Criminology* 60(6) (2020): 1585–605.

[26] See generally, Glenn Beck, *It IS About Islam: Exposing the Truth About ISIS, Al Qaeda, Iran, and the Caliphate* (New York: Threshold Editions, 2015).

the other way around, and this is always the case in every time and place. This is what is said about the European Renaissance and Enlightenment: these changes and all related modern developments would not have taken place without an intellectual revolution, which broke from the backward culture, leading to a new and progressive culture underpinning political, legal, economic and social modernity. Secular culturalism thus believes that the Arab-Islamicate worlds are in need of a similar cultural revolution. This revolution would establish an Arab and Islamic Renaissance or Enlightenment, and lead to a new culture on which political, economic, social, intellectual and ethical modernity in the Arab-Islamicate worlds would be based.

In contrast to the reductionist and culturalist view, and unlike blurred and fluid dialectics that advocate a mutual influence between culture and politics, without recognising its diversity from one temporal context to another, it is necessary to emphasise the flexibility of the dialectical relationship between cause and effect, between culture and politics. Flexible dialectics refers to the following two points: (1) the constant possibility of cause turning into effect and vice versa; and (2) the inability of establishing a general and fixed rule for the causal relationship between culture and politics. This is because the mutual influence between culture and politics can change and vary according to the conditions of various historical contexts and situations.

When considering the difference between a democratic system and an authoritarian system, one can note that the influence of culture on politics is much greater in a democratic system than in an authoritarian system.[27] Moreover, it seems that the influence of politics on culture increases in authoritarian systems.[28] This is often directly proportional to the duration of rule and the intensity of dominance and control over the state and society. While this thesis needs to be proven empirically and in detailed research beyond

[27] See, for example, Jonida Mehmetaj, 'The Impact of the Political Culture in Political System and Rule of Law: Albania Case', *European Scientific Journal* 1 (2014): 487–9. Here Mehmetaj compares the political culture in Albania during the authoritarian communist era and the post-communist democratic era, and its impact on the political system.

[28] See Franz Neumann, 'Notes on the Theory of Dictatorship', in Herbert Marcuse (ed.), *The Democratic and the Authoritarian State: Essays in Political and Legal Theory* (London: Free Press of Glencoe, 1964), 243–7; Krichewsky, 'Political Responsiveness', 136–7.

the scope of this chapter, it would seem plausible merely by referring to the nature of democratic and authoritarian regimes.

A democratic system is, by definition, the rule of the people over themselves, whereby citizens enjoy equal rights and duties, including the right and duty to choose who governs them, or rather who governs in their name and on their behalf.[29] Assuming that political choices and orientations are usually influenced by culture, in one way or another and to varying degrees, it seems plausible to suggest culture meaningfully influences politics in the democratic system. This allows us, partly and relatively, to say, in this context: rulers reflect the nature of the people they govern. On the contrary, an authoritarian regime is based on suppressing freedoms and imposing its preferences and agenda on the people, society and the state that they rule.[30] Against this background, and with the continuity of a long-standing authoritarian political system, the influence of politics on culture gradually increases while virtually eliminating the possibility of culture influencing politics,

[29] 'The 1955 (fifteenth) edition of the Encyclopaedia Britannica defined "democracy" as "a form of government based upon self-rule of the people and in modern times upon freely elected representative institutions and an executive responsible to the people, and a way of life based upon the fundamental assumption of the equality of all individuals and of their equal right of life, liberty (including liberty of thought and expression) and the pursuit of happiness.' Adam Przeworski, *Democracy and the Limits of Self-Government* (Cambridge: Cambridge University Press, 2010), 5.

[30] In this chapter, I talk about democracy and authoritarianism as opposite and contradictory political systems or states, adopting the distinction made by Alatas. 'The democratic state is defined as one in which (1) the posts of the executive are elective, (2) political parties are prominent and their members can be elected to representative bodies such as parliament,(3) there is genuine competition among opposing political parties for votes, (4) elections are honestly conducted, (5) it is civilians which are prominent in the political process, and (6) there is a separation of powers such that the executive of the state is itself subject to the law. In a democratic state, it should be possible for the majority of the people to change their government through the electoral system should they so desire. The authoritarian state is defined, first negatively, as one in which the above traits of democracy are absent, or if they are present, are shams. In the modern world there are several types of authoritarian states that include fascist, totalitarian, and military states and dictatorships.' Syed Farid Alatas, *Democracy and Authoritarianism in Indonesia and Malaysia: The Rise of the Post-Colonial State* (London: Palgrave Macmillan, 1997), 1–2.

allowing us to say in this context: 'the people are the mirror of their ruler'.[31] This consequently leads to the justification of despotism by the culture that becomes at the same time a cause for the continuation of authoritarianism, and an outcome or consequence of its existence.

The reciprocal influence or dialectical relationship between culture and politics should not be transformed into a vicious circle from which it is impossible to escape. If one takes into account the unlikelihood that a 'just despot' will seek democratisation, the only way out of the dialectical relationship between political despotism and a culture backing such despotism would be to change the political system. This change should entail the potential to build a democratic system that opens the way for the disposal of values and ideas that justify and support authoritarianism.

Given the hegemony of authoritarian regimes in the Arab and Islamicate world in general and in Syria in particular, political change would be the relative and perhaps absolute priority over cultural change. Even if one assumes that culturalism is right, and thus that culture–religion is the founder and producer of politics, changing culture–religious thought necessarily requires the support of the state and its institutions. Without this, reform will remain a myth that only produces illusions, since the authoritarian regime controls the likelihood its success or failure. Furthermore, such regimes are always keen to preserve society and the state of a culture that justifies and promotes authoritarianism and consecrates its existence and continuation.

### *It is Immorality, Even When it is Based on Moral Grounds*

Culturalism represents a common and powerful trend that holds victims responsible for the crimes committed against them, to one degree or another, thus depicting and evaluating them as criminals against themselves due to

[31] In response to Huntington's argument in *The Clash of Civilizations* that 'Islam in its "essence" constitutes a "civilization" inherently different from, and more violent than, any other,' Teti and Mura wrote: 'This argument, however tempting such simple answers might be, ignores the causes of the emergence of radical ideologies and violent practices and the relationship between political oppression and radical politics generally (not just religious radicalism). In the Middle East, it is clear that what has radicalized the opposition is the inability and/ or unwillingness of local regimes and their international counterparts to accept the consequences of genuine pluralism.' Teti and Mura, 'Islam and Islamism', 101–2.

their behaviour, thought or belief. The culturalist perspective has an immoral dimension: transforming the criminal or victimiser into a victim and the victim into a criminal or victimiser, or in equating them, at best, with responsibility for existing crimes, disadvantages or negatives. Those who adopt this perspective look down on ordinary people, their cultures and beliefs, and hold them primarily responsible for what has happened to them. There are also many victims who embrace such a view of themselves, which we can call 'self-contempt'. The intended subject here is not the individual self, but the collective self: that is, the whole of society in general.

Take, for example, the Assad regime in Syria, which has ruled the country for the past five decades with an iron hand, committing gross atrocities, especially since the break up of the uprising in March 2011. Basic human morality calls for condemnation of grave crimes and their perpetrators, and shows sympathy with the victim. Instead of expressing such sympathy, culturalism will often state that political and non-political authoritarianism is inherent or immanent in Syrian (or Arab-Islamicate) culture–religion, and is a natural product of this culture. Moreover, according to culturalism, no benefit can be sought from changing the ruler or the authoritarian regime without changing the prevailing culture, because this culture can only produce an authoritarian regime, which is likely to be worse than the present one. Therefore, culturalism argues that it is better to not seek a change to the authoritarian political system or ruler, but rather, first and foremost, to work to change the (religious) culture–thought and discourse that establishes this authoritarianism.[32]

As explained before, in order for any religious–cultural change to truly materialise, radical political change must, by necessity, precede or, at least accompany it. Approaching the Syrian situation from the perspective of culturalism leads regrettably to transforming the authoritarian political authority (the victimiser) into a victim of the religion, culture or society on which it is based. In doing so, one partly and relatively justifies crimes committed by

[32] This is why confrontation with, or opposition to, authoritarian regimes in the Arab and Islamicate context is sometimes accompanied, or should be, by a critique of culturalism. Yasin al-Haj Salih, for example, one of the most prominent Syrian opponents of the Assad regime, wrote one of the most important Arabic critiques of culturalism: al-Haj Salih, *al-Thaqafa ka-Siyasa*.

this authority and diminishes one's moral responsibility for hideous atrocities. From the point of view of culturalism (especially secular culturalism), political authoritarian power is an inevitable outcome of the religion, culture or society and of the decadence and authoritarianism inherent in their essence, and therefore is a victim. Immorality becomes more pronounced when culturalists consider that the problem lies mainly in the culture of the masses, rather than in the culture of the elite, and that these masses bear responsibility for, and deserve, the practices of the authoritarian elites against them. Culturalism (especially secular culturalism) strongly criticises common people and their popular culture, including its roots, contents, values and backward ideas, as well as its echo in elitist culture, and warns of the risk of allowing this culture to express itself freely in the political sphere.

It may seem repulsive to make moral or normative judgements in cognitive and academic research, as it can be seen as a reprehensible and disapproved confusion between two disparate fields, that of cognitive facts and their description, on one side, and of moral values and evaluation, on the other. As such, it is possible to argue against the moral judgement made of culturalism and its adopters in this chapter. In response, it should be emphasised that the culturalist vision engages in a number of concepts that do not belong to the realm of pure description nor to the realm of pure evaluation, but are in fact what are called 'thick normative concepts' – simultaneously including, by their very nature, description and non-descriptive evaluation.[33] Concepts such as cause, responsibility, victim, democracy, authoritarianism, etc. are thick normative concepts par excellence, because their primary and secondary connotations include description and evaluation. For example, when one says culture explains how politics works, and the backwardness of society is responsible for the nature of the authoritarian regime and practices, one is not only in the realm of description and analysis, but also indulges in judgement with clear evaluative or ethical dimensions, regardless of one's intention. On this basis, it seems impertinent to believe in the logic of the total and absolute rejection of the existence of normative judgements and ethical evaluations in the cognitive and academic field, as these judgements

[33] See Simon Kirchin (ed.), *Thick Concepts* (Oxford: Oxford University Press, 2013); Simon Kirchin, *Thick Evaluation* (Oxford: Oxford University Press, 2017).

are inherent to that field, to its topics and vocabulary or terminology at the same time.

*Culturalism between Culture and Politics*

Proponents of culturalism sometimes claim that its thought revolves around culture, and should be understood from this perspective rather than from the perspective of politics. While it is necessary to distinguish between culture and politics, or between the intellectual and the politician, it seems that the culturalist perspective has a clear political position despite its desire to deny it. This political position is evident in culturalism's direct or indirect justification of authoritarianism in Arab and Islamicate countries, by saying that the prevailing culture in these countries does not allow for the establishment of democracy. Therefore, it is common for Arab intellectuals to say: Arab and Islamicate societies are not ready for democracy, and therefore only have a limited range of options, between religious and non-religious authoritarianism.[34]

Culturalism has an ideological tendency, and thus it necessarily includes a political dimension. Works by culturalists also assume a political point of view even when refraining from declaring their positions. Moreover, the lack of an explicit political view among culturalists can be read, in many cases, as an implicit political stance at least. By placing themselves in the realm of culture rather than politics, culturalists may wish to avoid confronting any authoritarian regime, seeking to devote their efforts to what they see as the mother of all battles: against Islamism or political Islam. As Islam, Islamic religiosity and Islamicate culture are the main targets, it seems that culturalists are almost prepared to sacrifice democracy, and endorse or tolerate authoritarianism, and thus prioritise secularism over democracy despite claiming to support it.

[34] For example, Adonis said: 'There can be no democratic regimes under the current Arab circumstances. That's impossible,' 'Syrian Poet Adonis: There Can Be No Democracy in the Arab World under Present Circumstances', *Memri*, 11 August 2017, available at: https://www.memri.org/tv/syrian-poet-adonis-no-democracy-in-arab-world-people-undergoing-extinction; see also, Adonis, *Violence et Islam*; George Tarabishi, ''Ishkaliyyat al-Dimuqratiyya fi al-ʿAlam al'-ʿArabi', in *Hartaqat ʿan al-Dimuqratiyya wa-al-ʿAlmaniyya wa-l-Hadatha wa-l-Momanaʿa al-ʿArabiyya* (Beirut: Dar al-Saqi, 2006), 9–18.

Secular culturalists seem to slip easily into direct or indirect support for authoritarianism due to their justified or unjustified fear of religious culture that, from their point of view, cannot produce anything other than (religious–Islamic) authoritarianism on the political level, when it has an opportunity to express itself freely. Secular culturalism's opposition to political Islam is therefore greater than its belief in democracy.

The culturalist understanding of secularism seems to play an important role in further shifting their stance on democracy to that of antagonism. In the Arab and Islamicate contexts, Arab secularists do not understand secularism as merely a separation between religion and state, but rather as a complete separation, expunging religion from the public sphere, and restricting it to the private sphere of individuals, with the aim of establishing a non-religious culture along the lines of western modernity, according to the common image of the contemporary West, which is often delusional. Arab secular culturalism can also be linked to Ataturk Turkish secularism, and to a lesser extent French secularism, in that it calls for the state to act as anti-religious rather than as neutral.[35] There is thus a clear contrast which stems from secular culturalism's advocacy of a modern and secular culture while still willing to sacrifice democracy in favour of secularism.

Culturalism's extremist understanding of secularism can also be perceived as biased and short-sighted. Regardless of the fact that secularism is a separation of religion from the state or from politics, secular culturalism mainly criticises the employment of religion–Islam by religious people in politics, without paying attention to, or being much concerned with, the instrumentalisation of religion by politicians in order to justify and consolidate their authoritarian policies. Secular authoritarianism's use of religion to extend its suppressive rule does not pose a threat to the beloved secularism of secular culturalists. However, the use of politics by clergy and Islamic–religious actors, and their control of political power in the state is a major danger that should be excluded at any price.

Secular culturalism could be considered apolitical in a specific sense, which is reflected by its rejection of any possibility of reconciliation with religious culture in the public sphere in general, and in the field of politics

[35] See al-ʿAzm, *Critique of Religious Thought*, 7–75.

in particular. If we agree on the existence of a distinction between war and politics, as the former is the field of mutual violence and exclusion, and the latter is the field of negotiation, settlement and mutual concession, it can be said that culturalism is apolitical, since it is an ideology of war in politics. Secular culturalism does not accept the possibility of coexistence with its enemies, even if these enemies consent to this possibility, which is necessary and beneficial for all. Secular culturalism is therefore in a state of perpetual war, not against authoritarianism for the sake of democracy, but against religious culture for the sake of secularism.

Regardless of the political or non-political aspect of culturalism, the culturalist discourse often intersects with the discourse of authoritarian regimes in the Arab and Islamicate worlds.[36] This intersection is common, because the great majority of sheikhs, clerics and religious intellectuals are affiliated with the institutions of authoritarian regimes and are willing to obey their instructions. The fear of backward Islamicate culture and its religious representatives is also a main driver of secular culturalism's intellectual and political, ideological or normative position, which consciously or unconsciously becomes cultural introspection of oppressive political power. It seems logical that the suppressed realm of politics is not a potential arena for public criticism under an authoritarian regime, unlike the realm of culture and religion, where an extreme critical debate against Islamicate culture can be conducted by secular culturalists without any problem, as the authoritarian regime may profit from it.

Given that democracy should not be undermined by prioritising secularism over democratic values, the hostility of secular culturalism towards religious culture could be considered as an intentional or unintentional complicity with authoritarian regimes to divert people's thirst away from democratic demands by creating cultural fears and aversion against a particular religious group of people, thus tearing society apart in favour of authoritarianism. In this sense, culturalism appears to be a symptom of the greater

[36] For example, Adonis ('Ali Ahmad Sa'id), one of the most well-known culturalists in the Arab and Islamicate context. Although he is opposed to the authoritarian regime in Syria, he nevertheless seems to be in alliance with it due to his culturalist stance. See, for example, Adonis, *Violence et Islam*; al-Haj Salih, *al-Thaqafa ka-Siyasa*.

problem in the Arab and Islamicate worlds – authoritarianism – enhancing and reinforcing its existence, rather than a theoretical approach for diagnosing and dealing with this problem, as it claims.

## Concluding Remarks

In order to eliminate any misunderstanding, it is important to emphasise that the criticisms of the culturalism approach to religious culture mentioned above do not diminish or deny the importance, necessity and legitimacy of conducting a critical analysis of culture, including Arab and Islamicate culture. The critique and criticism of contents of culture is, in principle, a right and duty as well as a necessity in the current Arab-Islamicate contexts. However, the critical approach of culturalism, as explained above, is neither necessary nor useful – there are many other forms of criticism that differ from, and even contrast to culturalism. These other forms of cultural criticism can be identified more easily when carried out in the context of self-criticism or when distanced from 'reproaching' and 'blaming' the 'common people' for what is happening at the political level, for the type of political system and other negatives in society and its culture. A critique of culture can also seek to understand cultural and social problems and flaws, search for the root causes in society and identify their objective reasons, including political and economic elements, with a view to dealing with these problems. Any criticism of contemporary Arab and Islamicate societies and cultures that omits, minimises or marginalises the political and economic dimensions of the problem is twisted or straightforward culturalist criticism.

Although the main critique in this chapter is directed at both secular and religious versions of culturalism, the critical overview focuses more on secular culturalism. This focus should not give the impression that religious–Islamic culturalism is a better, or rather less bad, form of culturalism. On the contrary, secular and religious culturalism appear to be largely 'in the same boat' in terms of their relationship to authoritarianism, its justification and reinforcement. On the other hand, when considering secular culturalist claims about democracy and freedoms, it seems necessary to draw more attention to its willingness to abandon the demand for democracy and the commitment to human rights in the midst of confrontation with their enemies: Islamist or even Islamic ideologies.

Holding the victims responsible for the crimes committed against them may, in some cases, stem from a desire for positive mobilisation, agitation, stimulation and the pursuit of necessary self-criticism. Having said that, this desire and good intentions do not prevent culturalism from often turning into a reproach that insults and humiliates society and culture, and even denies the possibility of any change or reform. This is due to the belief that Islamicate society and culture are backward by virtue of their original or acquired nature. Therefore, instead of searching for the roots of the problem and discussing its plausible dimensions, possible solutions and future prospects, culturalism intends to use the mechanisms of slapping, scolding and whining.

The critiques of culturalism made by another approach, which sees the problem lying more with politics than with culture, are often inherently paradoxical. When focusing on a criticism of culturalism and holding it responsible, to a great extent, for the negative cultural, social and political reality it condemns, such approaches contain what is called 'performative contradiction' – it attaches great importance to culture, which it simultaneously considers to be of no great importance, except for politics. In other words, if critics of culturalism hold that cultural thought is a product of the political and economic reality, and not vice versa, and that culture has no major role in creating this reality, the question is: why do they engage so much, or even at all, in criticising cultural thought when dealing with reality. Critics of culturalism sometimes slide to the implicit adoption of some of the most important foundations of the culturalism they seek to criticise.

This paradox relates to the culture of the elite and to any intellectual view that reduces the importance of thought and culture, and exalts the influence of material, economic and political forces. Against this background, the question to be asked is: why do we write, if we believe that writing, as an expression of thought, a description of reality and thought, and a critiquing of it, has no significant or tangible effect in producing or changing material and intellectual reality? In the face of such a paradox, thought must regain some self-confidence and realise that it is part of the actual struggle in reality, and not just an external observer. In this actual struggle, a speech can be an effective action and an active voice, and not just a psychological expression of emotions, which has no physical echo or practical benefit. Based on this, it is possible to agree with culturalism on the importance of culture and thought in general, and its great impact on politics, but also to disagree with it by stressing that culture is also an effect and not just a cause, and that in some cases it may be more of a result than a cause. This has been the case in the Syrian (Arab-Islamicate) cultures over recent decades, living under the shadow of Assad's authoritarianism.

## Bibliography

### Arabic Sources

al-ʿAzm, Sadiq J., *al-Naqd al-Dhati baʿd al-Hazima*. Damascus: Dar Mamduh ʿIdwan, 2007.

al-Buti, Muhammad Saʿid Ramadan, *al-Salafiyya. Marhala Zamaniyya Mubaraka la Madhhab Islami*. Damascus: Dar al-Fikr, 1988.

al-Buti, Muhammad Saʿid Ramadan, *ʿala Tariq al-ʿAwda ila al-Islam. Rasm li-Minhaj wa-Hal li-Mushkilat*. Beirut: Muʾassasat al-Risala, 1981.

al-Haj Salih, Yasin, *al-Thaqafa ka-Siyasa. Dawr al-Muthaqafin wa-Masʾuliyyatuhum al-ʾIjtimaʿiyya fi Zaman al-Ghilan*. Beirut: al-Muʾassasa al-ʿArabiyya li-l-Dirasat wa-l-Nashr, 2016.

Tarabishi, George, *Hartaqat ʿan al-Dimuqratiyya wa-l-ʿAlmaniyya wa-l-Hadatha wa-l-Momanaʿa al-ʿArabiyya*. Beirut: Dar al-Saqi, 2006.

### English and French Sources

Adonis, 'Syrian Poet Adonis: There Can Be No Democracy in the Arab World under Present Circumstances', *Memri*, 11 August 2017, available at: https://www.memri.org/tv/syrian-poet-adonis-no-democracy-in-arab-world-people-undergoing-extinction.

Adonis, *Violence et Islam. Entretien avec Houria Abdelouahed*. Paris: Seuil, 2015.

Alatas, Syed Farid, *Democracy and Authoritarianism in Indonesia and Malaysia: The Rise of the Post-Colonial State*. London: Palgrave Macmillan, 1997.

al-ʿAzm, Sadiq J., *Critique of Religious Thought*, trans. George Stergios and Mansour Ajami. Berlin: Gerlach Press, 2015.

al-Braizat, Fares, 'Muslims and Democracy an Empirical Critique of Fukuyama's Culturalist Approach', *International Journal of Comparative Sociology* 43(269) (2002): 269–99.

al-Jabri, Mohammed Abed, *Democracy, Human Rights and Law in Islamic Thought*. London: I. B. Tauris, 2009.

Alvarez, Sonia E., Evelina Dagnino and Arturo Escobar, 'Introduction: The Cultural and the Political in Latin American Social Movements', in Sonia E. Alvarez et al.

(eds), *Cultures of Politics, Politics of Cultures Re-visioning Latin American Social Movements*. New York: Routledge, 1998, 1–29.

Beck, Glenn, *It IS About Islam: Exposing the Truth About ISIS, Al Qaeda, Iran, and the Caliphate*. New York: Threshold Editions, 2015.

Brumberg, Daniel, 'Islam Is Not the Solution (or the Problem)', *Washington Quarterly* 29(1) (2005): 97–116.

Chemla, Karine and Evelyn Fox Keller, 'Introduction', in Karine Chemla and Evelyn Fox Keller (eds), *Cultures without Culturalism: The Making of Scientific Knowledge*. Durham, NC: Duke University Press, 2017, 1–25.

Cornell, Drucilla, *Defending Ideals: War, Democracy, and Political Struggles*. New York: Routledge, 2004.

Dabashi, Hamid, *Post-Orientalism: Knowledge and Power in Time of Terror*. New Brunswick, NJ: Transaction Publishers, 2004.

Eriksen Jens-Martin and Frederik Stjernfelt, 'Culturalism: Culture as Political Ideology', *Eurozine*, 9 January 2009, available at: https://www.eurozine.com/culturalism-culture-as-political-ideology.

Festenstein, Matthew, 'The Limits of Liberal Culturalism', in *Negotiating Diversity: Culture, Deliberation, Trust*. Cambridge: Polity Press, 2005, 66–90.

Fox, Jonathan, *Religion, Civilization and Civil War: 1945 through the New Millennium*. Lanham, MD: Lexington Books, 2004.

Fukuyama, Francis, 'The West Has Won: Radical Islam Can't Beat Democracy and Capitalism', *The Guardian*, 11 October 2010, available at: https://www.theguardian.com/world/2001/oct/11/afghanistan.terrorism30.

Gardet, Louis, 'Religion and Culture', in Peter Holt, Ann K. S. Lambton and Bernard Lewis (eds), *The Cambridge History of Islam, Vol. 2B: Islamic Society and Civilization*. Cambridge: Cambridge University Press, 1970, 569–603.

Huntington, Samuel P., *The Third Wave: Democratization in the Late Twentieth Century*. Norman, OK: University of Oklahoma Press, 1991.

Huntington, Samuel P., 'The Clash of Civilizations?' *Foreign Affairs* 72(3) (1993): 22–49.

Huntington, Samuel P., *The Clash of Civilizations and the Remaking of World Order*. New York: Simon & Schuster, 1996.

Hammersley, Martyn, *The Concept of Culture: A History and Reappraisal*. Cham: Palgrave Macmillan, 2019.

Ito, Kenji, 'Cultural Difference and Sameness. Historiographic Reflections on Histories of Physics in Modern Japan', in Karine Chemla and Evelyn Fox Keller (eds), *Cultures without Culturalism: The Making of Scientific Knowledge*. Durham, NC: Duke University Press, 2017, 49–68.

Keller, Evelyn Fox, 'Worrying about Essentialism: From Feminist Theory to Epistemological Cultures', in Karine Chemla and Evelyn Fox Keller (eds), *Cultures without Culturalism: The Making of Scientific Knowledge*. Durham, NC: Duke University Press, 2017, 99–114.

Kirchin, Simon (ed.), *Thick Concepts*. Oxford: Oxford University Press, 2013.

Kirchin, Simon, *Thick Evaluation*. Oxford: Oxford University Press, 2017.

Krämer, Gudrun, 'Religion, Culture, and the Secular: The Case of Islam', *Working Paper Series of the CASHSS 'Multiple Secularities – Beyond the West, Beyond Modernities'* 23. Leipzig University, 2021. DOI: https://doi.org/10.36730/2020.1.msbwbm.23.

Krichewsky, Damien, 'Political Responsiveness: The Identification and Processing of Problems in Modern Polities', in Anna L. Ahlers et al. (eds), *Democratic and Authoritarian Political Systems in 21st Century World Society, Vol. 1: Differentiation, Inclusion, Responsiveness*. Bielefeld: transcript Verlag, 2021, 121–47.

Lewis, Bernard, 'The Roots of Muslim Rage', *The Atlantic Monthly*, September 1990, available at: https://www.theatlantic.com/magazine/archive/1990/09/the-roots-of-muslim-rage/304643.

Lim, Sep Neo, 'Essentialising the Convenient Baba-Nyonyas of the Heritage City of Melaka (Malaysia)', in Fred Dervin and Regis Machart (eds), *Cultural Essentialism in Intercultural Relations*. Basingstoke: Palgrave Macmillan, 2015, 153–77.

Maxwell, Kenneth, 'Pombal: the Paradox of Enlightenment and Despotism', in H. M. Scott (ed.), *Enlightened Absolutism: Reform and Reformers in Later Eighteenth-Century Europe*. London: Macmillan, 1990, 75–118.

McMahan, David L., *The Making of Buddhist Modernism*. Oxford: Oxford University Press, 2008.

Mehmetaj, Jonida, 'The Impact of the Political Culture in Political System and Rule of Law: Albania Case', *European Scientific Journal* 1 (2014): 483–90.

Neumann, Franz, 'Notes on the Theory of Dictatorship', in Herbert Marcuse (ed.), *The Democratic and the Authoritarian State: Essays in Political and Legal Theory*. London: Free Press of Glencoe, 1964, 233–256.

Platteau, Jean-Philippe, *Islam Instrumentalized: Religion and Politics in Historical Perspective*. Cambridge: Cambridge University Press, 2017.

Przeworski, Adam, *Democracy and the Limits of Self-Government*. Cambridge: Cambridge University Press, 2010.

Robinson, Pearl T., 'Democratization: Understanding the Relationship between Regime Change and the Culture of Politics', *African Studies Review* 37(1) (1994): 39–67.

Sandberg, Sveinung and Sarah Colvin, '"ISIS is not Islam": Epistemic Injustice, Everyday Religion, and Young Muslims' Narrative Resistance', *British Journal of Criminology* 60 (6) (2020): 1585–605.

Scott, H. M., ed. *Enlightened Absolutism: Reform and Reformers in Later Eighteenth-Century Europe*. London: Macmillan, 1990.

Seghiri, Chahinaz, 'ISIS not Representative of Islamic Beliefs, Teaching', *The Lantern*, 4 September 2014, available at: https://www.thelantern.com/2014/09/opinion-isis-not-representative-of-islamic-beliefs-teachings.

Stilt, Kristen, '"Islam is the Solution": Constitutional Visions of the Egyptian Muslim Brotherhood', *Texas International Law Journal* 46 (2010): 73–108.

Teti, Andrea and Andrea Mura, 'Islam and Islamism', in Jeffrey Haynes (rd.), *Routledge Handbook of Religion and Politics*. London: Routledge, 2009, 92–110.

Weber, Max, 'Objectivity in Social Science and Social Policy', in *On The Methodology of the Social Sciences*, ed. Hans Henrik Brun and Sam Whimster, trans. Hans Henrik Brun. London: Routledge, 2012, 100–38.

Wyer, Robert S., Chi-yue Chiu and Ying-yi Hong, *Understanding Culture: Theory, Research, and Application*. New York: Psychology Press, 2009.

Xu, Aymeric, *From Culturalist Nationalism to Conservatism: Origins and Diversification of Conservative Ideas in Republican China*. Berlin: De Gruyter Oldenbourg, 2021.

# Part IV

## NEW COMPARISONS

# 8

# CAN COMPARATIVE THEOLOGY HELP MUSLIMS TO A BETTER UNDERSTANDING OF RELIGIOUS DIVERSITY?

ESRA AKAY DAĞ

## Introduction

Religions have always been in relation to each other, so the believers of diverse religions somehow related their faith in a broader diverse religious context. But since the nineteenth century, there has been ongoing interest in studying diverse world religions in the western academic world. This has been sharpened more as the coexistence of diverse religions has become a norm in western societies. Thus, Christian academics have developed two forms of theologies, namely, theology of religions and comparative theology, to respond to religious diversity. While the former sought to respond to diversity from inside a specific religion by focusing on the problem of religious truth and salvation, the latter tried to understand their faith in the light of other traditions engaging deeply with religious others' texts, doctrines, etc. Although these two areas have been developed widely in the western Christian context, Muslims, especially those who are somehow connected with the western education system, have also contributed to the discussion of religious diversity. However, Muslims' engagement with religious others has been limited. While they have somehow offered various theologies of religions, their engagement with comparative theology has remained insufficient.

In this study, I will present comparative theology as a new way to embrace religious diversity. I will first provide an overview of comparative theology in the Christian tradition, then move on to offer an Islamic comparative theology. I will present methodological, practical and theological bases for comparative theology. I will present that theorising non-Islamic religions before engagement (theology of religions) may not be a helpful way to approach religious others. Thus, methodological deficiencies of Islamic theology of religions necessitate searching for a new way to respond to religious diversity. Then I will present three practices of comparative learning within Islamic tradition and argue that engaging with diverse worldviews helped Muslims to better understand themselves. Finally, I will provide a theological need for comparative theology by engaging with the Qurʾān. With all these, I will argue that the area of comparative theology seems to be promising for a better Islamic perspective of religious others. I will offer that by using the method of comparative theology, which necessitates deep learning from other religious traditions, Muslim theologians can obtain a more nuanced understanding of religious others. By comparative theology, the real engagement, a willingness to learn from others through their text and teachings, then to be challenged with the new learnings would provide Muslims with a better understanding of the religious others and their difference and themselves.

Before starting, I would like to remark in which context this study resided. Diverse theologies exist in a particular cultural context. The contemporary context of western academia in terms of interreligious learning promotes hospitality and openness. Thus, the Muslim writings on the Islamic perception of other religions are not exempt from this context. The questions Christians ask for their beliefs, the literature on interreligious relations, the language that speaks about it, and the environment where Muslims meet with religious others in the western world naturally affect Muslim academics. Thus, the context of comparative theology I am offering is based on a western context. I have a western academic background though I am of Turkish origin, and I am now working at a Turkish university. Within the universities in Turkey, academics study non-Islamic religions in the history of religions departments. But for most Turkish academics, 'religious others' is an abstract notion as almost 99 per cent of the population is Muslim. I have encountered diverse religious worldviews not only within academic circles but through my friends, neighbours and colleagues. This experience has taught me that interreligious learning is possible and enriching for a better understanding of myself and diversity among and within religions.

## Comparative Theology in Christian Theology

Comparative theology as a discipline is not a new area within Christian theology.[1] But it has been offered as a Christian response to religious diversity in the late twentieth and early twenty-first century. In the twentieth century, Christian theologians developed a number of methods to respond to religious diversity: interreligious dialogue, intercultural theology and theology of religions. All these have tried to relate the largely Christian West to the contemporary situation of religious diversity. The theology of religions, however, has become the dominant area, especially in the light of Alan Race's threefold typology of exclusivism, inclusivism and pluralism.[2] Not only have some Christians made contributions to the theology of religions,[3]

[1] The term was in use in the nineteenth century when Christians started scientifically to study non-Christian religions. Since the early representatives of comparative theology generally concluded their theology by affirming the superiority of Christian faiths, the term was not used in the academic study of religions until the late twentieth century. See Hugh Nicholson, *Comparative Theology and the Problem of Religious Rivalry* (Oxford: Oxford University Press, 2011), 22–6.

[2] Alan Race, *Christians and Religious Pluralism: Patterns in the Christian Theology of Religions* (London: SCM Press, [1983] 1993). Race presents exclusivism as a view 'as the revelation in Jesus Christ as the sole criterion by which all religions, including Christianity, can be understood and evaluated' (Race, *Christians and Religious Pluralism,*11). He then states that inclusivism is shaped by two equally binding convictions: 'universal will of God to save, and the uniqueness of the revelation in Christ' (54). The second part is shared by exclusivism, whereas the first part with pluralistic theology. Finally, Race explains pluralism with a connection to tolerance. By tolerance, he does not include only moral imperative as he thinks even exclusivist theologians would agree, but he also stresses a Christian theological necessity. Thus, he explains pluralism as that 'knowledge of God is partial in all faiths, including Christian faith. Religions must acknowledge their need of each other if the full truth about God is to be available to all mankind' (72). Since he presented his threefold typology, each category has been described by diverse theologians with different nuances.

[3] See, for example, Gavin D'Costa, *Christianity and World Religions: Disputed Questions in the Theology of Religions* (Chichester: Wiley-Blackwell, 2009); Gavin D'Costa, *Theology and Religious Pluralism: The Challenge of Other Religions* (Oxford: Blackwell, 1986); Paul F. Knitter, *Introducing Theologies of Religions* (Maryknoll: Orbis Books, 2002); Paul Hedges, *Controversies in Interreligious Dialogue and the Theology of Religions* (London: SCM Press, 2010).

some non-Christian thinkers[4] have also taken the fundamental questions (the question of truth and the possibility of salvation of other religions) raised in the theology of religions to religious diversity in their own communities. However, in 1995 Francis Clooney published a review of recent books on comparative theology and described comparative theology as an 'exciting and quickly developing field, and a relatively uncharted one'.[5] In the same vein, James Fredericks has offered comparative theology as an alternative to the theology of religions.[6] Since then, on the one hand, some theologians have been writing on comparative theology; on the other hand, they have been discussing whether theology of religions is at an impasse or whether comparative theology should replace the theology of religions.

Francis Clooney, along with Robert Neville and Keith Ward, are among the foundational figures of the comparative theology of the late twentieth century.[7] Though they employ comparative theology, their visions for this differ in many ways. While Neville and Ward make a more general comparison between diverse world religions for the sake of finding commonalities/similarities,[8] Clooney's comparative project focuses on a more specific

[4] See Perry Schmidt-Leukel, *Religious Pluralism and Interreligious Theology: The Gifford Lectures – An Extended Edition* (Maryknoll, NY: Orbis Books, 2017). Schmidt-Leukel, here, particularly engages with non-Christian theologians' pluralist theologies.

[5] Francis X. Clooney, 'Current Theology, Comparative Theology: A Review of Recent Books', *Theological Studies* 56 (1995): 521.

[6] James L. Fredericks, 'A Universal Religious Experience? Comparative Theology as an Alternative to a Theology of Religions', *Horizons* 22(1) (1995): 67–87.

[7] Paul Hedges, *Comparative Theology: A Critical and Methodological Perspective* (Leiden: Brill, 2017), 7, 10.

[8] See, for example, Neville and Ward's book series in which they evaluate diverse religions' perspectives on certain themes. Robert Neville (ed.), *The Human Condition: A Volume in the Comparative Religious Ideas Project* (Albany, NY: State University of New York Press, 2001); Robert Neville (ed.), *Religious Truth: The Cross Cultural Comparative Religious Ideas Project* (Albany, NY: State University of New York Press, 2001); Robert Neville (ed.), *Ultimate Realities: A Volume in the Comparative Religious Ideas Project* (Albany, NY: State University of New York Press, 2001); Keith Ward, *Religion and Revelation: A Theology of Revelation in the World's Religions* (Oxford: Clarendon Press, 1994); Keith Ward, *Religion and Creation* (Oxford: Clarendon Press, 1996); Keith Ward, *Religion and Human Nature* (Oxford: Clarendon Press, 1999); Keith Ward, *Religion and Community* (Oxford: Clarendon Press, 2000).

comparison between two faiths. Additionally, Ward and Neville's comparative theology has a lineage to liberal theology, which Ward explicitly locates in the work of Friedrich Schleiermacher,[9] whilst Clooney's theology takes its roots from Catholicism, especially from the Second Vatican Council. However, Clooney's comparative project has become much more influential shaping comparative theology among the Catholic theologians, such as James Fredericks, Michelle Voss Roberts, Klaus von Stosch, Marianne Moyaert and Ulrich Winkler.

Comparative theology is a hermeneutical enterprise that aims to understand 'the otherness of the religious other'.[10] It requires *deep learning* from other religious traditions. It compromises two notions: comparison and theology. Taking interreligious learning as something valuable, it seeks to study other religion(s) while being committed its their own tradition (Christianity in this case). It engages with other religions with '*a benevolence, a willingness to learn,* and *critical appreciation*'.[11] Clooney defines comparative theology as:

> [A theological practice which] marks acts of faith seeking understanding which are rooted in a particular faith tradition but which, from that foundation, venture into learning from one or more other faith traditions. This learning is sought for the sake of fresh theological insights that are indebted to the newly encountered tradition/s as well as the home tradition.[12]

For Clooney, the comparison is not a simple evaluation of two kinds, but rather it requires both intuitive and rational insight, practical and theological engagement. Thus, it is a theological and spiritual exercise in which 'we see the other in light of our own, and our own in light of the other'.[13] Looking upon the truths of other faith 'as resources for understanding their own

[9] Ward, *Religion and Revelation*, 46.

[10] Marianne Moyaert, 'Comparative Theology in Search of a Hermeneutical Framework', in David Cheetham et al. (eds), *Interreligious Hermeneutics in Pluralistic Europe Between Texts and People* (Leiden: Brill, 2011), 169.

[11] Ulrich Winkler, 'What is Comparative Theology?' in David Cheetham et al. (eds), *Interreligious Hermeneutics in Pluralistic Europe Between Texts and People* (Leiden: Brill, 2011), 241.

[12] Francis X. Clooney, *Comparative Theology: Deep Learning Across Religious Borders* (Malden, NY: Wiley-Blackwell, 2010), 10.

[13] Clooney, *Comparative Theology*, 10–11.

faith'[14] is what comparative theology is about. Producing new insights in the light of engagement with other theology/ies is the primary objective of comparative theology. It can be seen that comparative theology requires three steps; studying and being committed to one's own tradition, then deeply engaging with one or more tradition(s), before returning to home with the new insights, and thus reinterpreting the home tradition is a natural consequence of this process.

Comparative theologians not only study non-Christian traditions deeply for the sake of learning from them, but they also take non-Christians' theologies seriously in their desire to seek a fuller knowledge of God. The theological base for comparative theologians is 'to know God more fully'.[15] The teachings of the Catholic Church after the Second Vatican Council and the council documents are the primary sources for Clooney[16] and other Catholic comparative theologians'[17] comparative agenda. In other words, they engage in comparative theology from a confessional perspective.[18] Thus, their theology of religions is in line with the inclusivist teaching of the Catholic Church, though each of the comparative theologians' theologies may have different nuance. However, comparative theologians offer their theologies as an alternative to theology of religions,[19] so they want to shift the fundamental questions (the question of truth and salvation in theology of religions) to make

[14] James L. Fredericks, *Faith among Faiths: Christian Theology and Non-Christian Religions* (Mahwah, NJ: Paulist Press, 1999), 140.

[15] Francis X. Clooney, *Hindu God, Christian God: How Reason Helps Break Down the Boundaries between Religions* (Oxford: Oxford University Press, 2001), 177.

[16] Clooney, *Comparative Theology*, 115.

[17] For example, in her review of 'Theology Today: Comparative Theology as a Catholic Theological Approach', *Theological Studies* 76(1) (2015): 43–64, Marianne Moyaert shows how comparative theology is shaped by the Catholic teachings.

[18] Clooney, *Hindu God, Christian God*, 26; Moyaert, 'Theology Today', 44; Winkler, 'What is Comparative Theology?' 241; Klaus von Stosch, 'Comparative Theology as Liberal and Confessional Theology', *Religions* 3(4) (2012): 983–92. It should also be noted that Ward's comparative theology is situated against denominational–confessional theologies (Ward, *Religion and Revelation*, 36–42).

[19] Klaus von Stosch, 'Comparative Theology as a Challenge for the Theology of the 21st Century', *Religious Inquiries* 1(2) (2012): 8; Fredericks, 'A Universal Religious Experience?'; Fredericks, *Faith among Faiths*, 6–8, 169.

interreligious learning possible. While the former prioritises interreligious learning from other religions' texts, beliefs and teachings themselves, theorising other religions is embedded in the latter. Dealing with different questions does not mean that the former does not make use of the latter. Clooney himself states that his comparative theology is in harmony with other inclusivist theologies offered by Karl Rahner and Jacques Dupuis.[20] Moreover, Hedges,[21] Kiblinger[22] and Schmidt-Leukel[23] argue that in order to engage in comparative theology, an inclusivist theory is needed. I am not going to discuss further the relationship between comparative theology and theology of religions as it is beyond this study to do so, but my emphasis is that Catholic teachings have been theorised as an inclusivist approach are primary sources for contemporary (Catholic) comparative theologians.

## Comparative Theology in Islam

Comparative theology is a novel approach in Islamic tradition. Though there has been comparative learning throughout history, there have been a restricted number of studies that methodologically apply the tools of comparative theology. Recently, some promising works have been published by young Muslim scholars. Mohammed Gamal Abdelnour, in his *A Comparative History of Catholic and Aš'arī Theologies of Truth and Salvation*, makes use of comparative theology together with theology of religions' methodology. He states that his comparative approach is a synthesis of Ward, Neville and Clooney's approaches.[24] Throughout his book, he analytically and critically looks at the historical development of exclusivism and inclusivism–majoritarianism and minoritarianism in Christianity and Islam, respectively, by focusing on prominent figures within Catholic and Ashʿari theologies. What

[20] Clooney, *Comparative Theology*, 16.

[21] Hedges, *Controversies*, 52–4; Hedges, *Comparative Theology*, 16.

[22] Kristin B Kiblinger, 'Relating Theology of Religions and Comparative Theology', in Francis X. Clooney (ed.), *The New Comparative Theology: Interreligious Insights from the Next Generation* (London: T. & T. Clark, 2010).

[23] Perry Schmidt-Leukel, *Transformation by Integration: How Inter-Faith Encounter Changes Christianity.* (London: SCM Press, 2009), 50–1.

[24] Mohammed Gamal Abdelnour, *A Comparative History of Catholic and Aš'arī Theologies of Truth and Salvation: Inclusive Minorities, Exclusive Majorities* (Leiden: Brill, 2021), 10.

makes it interesting is that he not only provides the historical and theological developments of a particular theology but also demonstrates major theologians with the parallels, connections, correlations, differences and similarities within their theological views. By doing so, he manages to show the particular understanding of central concepts, that is, revelation (Jesus Christ/Qur'ān), scripture (the Bible/Qur'ān), in both religions, which prevents juxtaposition of these concepts in either religion.

Betül Avci also employs comparative theology, though in a short article, to stress the asymmetry between Christianity and Islam. She particularly focuses on the concept of revelation and history in Catholicism and Sunni Islam. In her comparative reading of both traditions, she concludes that Christian understanding of revelation offers a progressivist view of history, the time period before Jesus Christ has been considered as the preparation for such a focal point. She claims that that view has been wrongly applied to Islam, which for her Islam offers a different view of history, degeneration versus regeneration. Her comparative agenda aims to emphasise 'the particularity, the uniqueness of a tradition',[25] but she claims that comparative theology provides her 'more nuanced understanding of her own tradition'.[26]

Lastly, Jerusha Lamptey engages with comparative theology in a more nuanced and sophisticated way. In *Divine Words, Female Voices: Muslima Explorations in Comparative Feminist Theology*, she applies feminist theological methods and concerns to her comparative reading of the divine words in the two traditions, the Qur'ān and Jesus, respectively. Her comparative theology is also in line with Clooney. She problematises a major theme within Islamic feminist theology at the beginning of each chapter; she then presents Christian feminist theologies with their own particularities without making critical judgements and analyses. She claims that this process 'is the act of learning, listening, and accurately representing'.[27] Finally, she returns to home tradition 'attempting to offer at least some small insights

[25] Betül Avci, 'Comparative Theology and Scriptural Reasoning: A Muslim's Approach to Interreligious Learning', *Religions* 9(10) (2018): 12.

[26] Avci, 'Comparative Theology and Scriptural Reasoning', 12.

[27] Jerusha Tanner Lamptey, *Divine Words, Female Voices: Muslima Explorations in Comparative Feminist Theology* (New York: Oxford University Press, 2018), 41.

into new trajectories, considerations, interpretative approaches, and pragmatic strategies in Muslima theology'.[28]

These are important works, which suggest that comparative theology has been employed beyond the Christian tradition. Both Abdelnour and Avci do not employ comparative theology with back-and-forth studying of two religions, but rather they look at a common theme in two religions by comparing symmetries–asymmetries. Their employment is helpful for understanding the distinct nature of theologies–religions but lacks, to some degree, a theological justification for engaging in comparative theology. Lamptey's comparative engagement, however, does provide, on the one hand, theological motivation and justification for doing comparative theology, which is in line with her Muslima theology of religions,[29] and, on the other hand, offers a practice of comparative theology–learning by using the feminist methodology simultaneously.

These are contemporary Muslim writings of comparative theology, yet this type of theology has been associated with Catholic theology even in the Christian circles. However, while Marianne Moyaert was discussing whether comparative theology is Catholic or not, she claims that it is not exclusively Catholic, and that it can be adopted outside the Christian tradition in case a particular confessional approach is developed.[30] I argued elsewhere that comparative theology could be a new way for Muslims' engagement with the believers of non-Islamic traditions.[31] Here, I propose reasons for making this kind of engagement possible. I propose that there are methodological, practical and theological necessities for constructing comparative theology.

### *Why the Need for a New Methodology?*

Given the important works on theology of religions by some Christian theologians and given increased initiatives of interreligious dialogue, some Muslim

[28] Lamptey, *Divine Words, Female Voices*, 41.

[29] Jerusha Tanner Lamptey, *Never Wholly Other: A Muslima Theology of Religious Pluralism* (New York: Oxford University Press, 2014).

[30] Moyaert, 'Theology Today', 44.

[31] Esra Akay Dağ, *Christian and Islamic Theology of Religions: A Critical Appraisal* (London: Routledge, 2017), 113.

scholars – particularly those connected to the western academy – have begun the task of relating Islam to other religions. Though not yet as systematic, these Muslim scholars are involved in the discussions within theology of religions and are trying to find answers to the fate of non-Muslims and whether Islam is the only true religion. Consequently, they have offered a pluralistic Islamic theology of other religions, which from many perspectives object to traditional Muslim understanding of religious others. Traditionally, Muslim theologians accepted the multiple divine revelations before the time of Prophet Muḥammad as stated in the Qurʾān,[32] but with the Prophet Muḥammad, who is also the seal of the prophets,[33] divine revelation has reached its zenith. The Qurʾānic revelation, thus, superseded/abrogated other revelations not because God contradicts himself, but rather, according to the Qurʾānic account, there has been corruption and distortion in previous revelations by people.[34] Consequently, the mainstream Islamic view, both Sunni and Shiite, has been that Islam is the only true religion in the sight of God, which is destined for all humanity.[35] Contemporary scholars' objections to this traditional account have shaped what is considered Islamic pluralism. Even though not all contemporary scholars define themselves or their theology as pluralist, their theology has been categorised within the pluralist discourse. Schmidt-Leukel, in his recent works,[36] while presenting Islamic pluralism, identifies Mahmut Aydin, Mahmoud Ayoub, Ashgar Ali Engineer, Hasan Askari, Abdulaziz Sachedina, Imtiyaz Yusuf, Jerusha Lamptey, Rifat Atay, Abdolkarim Soroush, Seyyed Hosain Nasr and Reza Shah-Kazemi as Muslim pluralist theologians.

[32] Qurʾān: 5:19, 48; 10:47; 13:7; 14:4; 35:24.

[33] Qurʾān: 33:40.

[34] Qurʾān: 4:46; 5:15.

[35] See, for example, Abdulaziz Sachedina, 'The Qur'ān and Other Religions', in Jane Dammen McAuliffe (ed.), *The Cambridge Companion to the Qur'ān* (New York: Cambridge University Press, 2007), 297–302. He elaborates how traditionally Muslim commentators present Islam as an exclusivist religion towards others.

[36] Perry Schmidt-Leukel, 'Pluralist Approaches in Some Major Non-Chritsitian Religions', in Elizabeth Harris, Paul Hedges, and Shanthikumar Hettiarachchi (eds), *Twenty-First Century Theologies of Religions: Retrospection and Future Prospects* (Leiden: Brill, 2016), 165–9; Schmidt-Leukel, *Religious Pluralism and Interreligious Theology*, 42–54.

Although each scholar has a different nuance within their theology, I will summarise the primary arguments offered by them in four points.

First, they redefine the term Islam by offering two distinct definitions: universal and historical. Islam as a universal religion is a divine ordination for all humanity, whereas historical Islam is formed by the Prophet Muḥammad. They emphasise an inclusivist vision of Islam, like submission and obedience to God, rather than an institutionalised religion in the seventh century. In this respect, they offer the view that the terms Muslim and Islam can be used beyond the Islamic religion for all those who submit their will to God.[37] The second point is that the divine promise for salvation is not only for those who define themselves as Muslims, but is also for those who are outside the Islamic religion. In this vein, the Qurʾānic verses 2:62 and 5:69 are used for justification of this claim. These two points offer something new in the Islamic tradition, and function as an internal discourse on the Islamic understanding of other religions, and not to impose Islamic terms on other religions. But they are problematic as extending the concept of Islam and Muslim to non-Muslims, on the one hand, does not help to appreciate the real otherness of other religions, and, on the other hand, it diminishes the meaning of what it means to be a Muslim. In this regard, one of the criticisms of pluralistic Christian theology can be extended to this. James L. Fredericks, for example, claims that pluralist theology suggests that pluralists know more about other religions than the believers know about themselves.[38] It, thus, prevents creative interreligious engagement with others. Pluralist theology, in general, has been connected with religious tolerance and openness.[39] However, the '[a]cceptance

[37] Farid Esack, *Qur'an, Liberation and Religious Pluralism: An Islamic Perspective of Interreligious Solidarity against Oppression* (Oxford: One World, 1997), 126–34; Mahmut Aydin, 'Religious Pluralism: A Challenge for Muslims – Theological Evaluation', *Journal of Ecumenical Studies* 38(2/3) (2001): 330–52; Hasan Askari, 'Within and Beyond Experience of Religious Diversity', in John Hick and Hasan Askari (eds), *The Experience of Religious Diversity* (Aldershot: Gower, 1985), 199; Reza Shah-Kazemi, *The Other in the Light of One: The Universality of the Qur'ān and Interfaith Dialogue* (Cambridge: Islamic Texts Society, 2006), 186.

[38] Fredericks, *Faith among Faiths*, 108.

[39] Race, while presenting his threefold typology, starts explaining pluralism with its connection to tolerance, *Christians and Religious Pluralism*, 72.

of all religions as equal' might seem to reflect tolerance and openness towards others, but the following phrase 'to the same Reality/Absolute Truth' in fact disregards religious difference. While the primary aim of pluralist theologians (both Christians and Muslims) is to show openness and tolerance to religious others, they often leave us with a problem that a single religious worldview imposes its own vision and terminology on others, which may not be as meaningful or important as they think.[40] Defining and including non-Muslims within the Islamic boundary, then, means that non-Muslims are no different from Muslims. From this point of view, engaging with comparative theology might give Muslims a better understanding of the believers of other faiths, as well as themselves, since it does not prioritise theorising the other before the engagement.

The third point is that Muslim pluralists consider religious diversity as a divine will. Taking verse 49:13 into account, Muslim pluralists have theoretically indicated the importance of religious diversity and why interreligious learning is possible and important. However, there has been little tendency to learn from others. In other words, they have theoretically appreciated religious diversity, but they have not shown an interest in learning the real difference of other faiths. The fourth and final point is that Christian theologians' pluralist ideas have had a considerable impact on Muslims' pluralist approaches. For example, we can read Hasan Askari's claim that diverse (referring to Abrahamic) faiths are a different and equal response to the 'Absolute Truth'[41] in line with Hick's famous claim that diverse religions 'constitute different ways of experiencing, conceiving, and living in relation to an ultimate divine Reality which transcends all our varied versions of it'.[42] There are more parallels like this in the writings of so-called Muslim pluralist theologians. This means that Muslim theologians somehow engage with Christian theologies and use them in an Islamic context. In other words, there has been back-and-forth studying

[40] Fredericks rightly states that 'pluralism should be taken as a practical suggestion, a working presupposition for dealing with religious diversity with tolerance and openness. The theory should not be taken as a simple assertion about all religions, but rather as an appropriate way to make sense out of the facts, better way than skepticism and dogmatism.' *Faith among Faiths*, 106,

[41] Askari, 'Within and Beyond Experience of Religious Diversity', 191.

[42] John Hick, *An Interpretation of Religion* (New Haven, CT: Yale University Press, 1989), 14.

of religious others – Islamic texts are in the centre whilst Christian pluralistic perspectives provide such insights for Muslim scholars to read their texts in another form and eventually present Muslim pluralist approaches. Certainly, there are some elements of comparative theology, but they have not employed it systematically.

As has been shown, there needs to be a new and fresh methodology to address religious diversity in the Islamic tradition. The discourse of theology of religions in Islam is not yet fully helpful for an actual engagement. While I do not want to diminish the role of a pluralistic theory in interreligious dialogue, many Muslim theologians pay too much attention to theorising other religions; indeed, even the concept of learning from others is theorised. Theorising other religions can only lead to a willingness to learn from others, but the act of theorising itself is not a learning process. This, however, can be achieved by the use of comparative theology. Here I am with comparative theologians like Fredericks and others who distinguish between theory and process–practice,[43] while in the first, other religions are in an abstract form which can be theorised, there is a learning process and practice in the second. In other words, one can employ theology of religions without having sufficient knowledge about other religions, whereas comparative theology requires deep knowledge about other religions.

### *Practical Bases*

The history of diverse religions can be described as 'a history of difference and interaction between religions and cultures'.[44] Thus, almost every religious community has experienced interreligious and comparative learning.[45] Since the emergence of Islam in the seventh century, Muslims have engaged with the believers of non-Islamic religions. Like the New Testament's reference to Jewish people and their beliefs, the Qurʾān as a primary Islamic source, speaks both positively and negatively of the other two Abrahamic faiths, *ahl al-kitāb* (People of the Book). It is a fact that the Islamic tradition did not develop in isolation from the practices and belief systems of other religions. The type

[43] Fredericks, *Faith among Faiths*, 9.

[44] Winkler, 'What is Comparative Theology?' 234.

[45] Clooney, *Comparative Theology*, 24.

of Muslim confrontation with other religions has always depended on the context. While there were certainly some cases in which what we now call an interreligious dialogue was in operation,[46] we must not forget that apologetic and polemical writings have constituted the great extent of Muslim study of other religions.

I will refer to three historical Muslim engagements with non-Islamic faiths and try to present why comparative learning is important.

The Qur'ān mentions the prophets before Muḥammad without chronology and complete details. These prophets are mainly Biblical figures such as Adam, Abraham, Joseph, Moses, Jesus and more. The fundamental object of Qur'ānic reference to the previous prophets is to give theological and moral lessons.[47] Yet, on the grounds that the Qur'ān only presents some parts of these prophets' life, from early on, Muslims took the Biblical narratives into account and used them in their works. Some successors' narrations of the Biblical narratives had been used as the source within *tafsīr* and history books such as Wahb Ibn Munabbih (d. 738) and Kaʿb al-Ahbār (d. 652). Many classical mufassirs, al-Tabarī (d. 923), al-Zamakhsharī (d. 1143), al-Rāzī (d. 1210), al-Qurtubī (d. 1273), Muqatīl Ibn Sulaymān (d. 767) and so on, did not find any problem with citing Biblical narratives as long as they did not contradict Islamic belief. Additionally, the genre of *qissas al-anbiyā* (the tales of the prophets) included Biblical narratives in order to present a fuller account of the prophets. This genre has also been used as a source in Islamic mysticism and poetry, and such tales have also played an important role in popular Islamic belief, movies, poems and history books. Biblical narratives, in other words, have helped Muslims to make a full account of the prophets, and early Muslims certainly engaged comparative, if largely selective, learning.

Islamic philosophy is another example of comparative learning. From the eighth to the tenth centuries, under the Abbasid Empire, Muslims were confronted with Greek philosophy during the translation movement. As a result, Muslim philosophers incorporated Greek philosophy into their reasoning, and

[46] Jacques Waardenburg, *Muslims and Others: Relations in Context* (Berlin: Walter de Gruyter, 2003), 110–21.

[47] Tamara Sonn, 'Introduction', in Andrew Rippin and Jawid Mojaddedi (eds), *The Wiley Blackwell Companion to the Qur'an* (Chichester: John Wiley, 2017), 12.

they introduced philosophy to the Islamic world.[48] Great Muslim philosophers such as al-Farabi (872–950) and Ibn al-Sina (980–1037) were also influential outside Islam. Muslim philosophers deeply engaged with Greek philosophy, and they took the knowledge and interpreted it in a new way, and they subsequently created what is known as Islamic philosophy. The reception of and reaction to Islamic philosophy, on the one hand, influenced *kalām* (Islamic theology) through al-Ghazālī's contribution,[49] and, on the other hand, Thomas Aquinas adopted Ibn Sina's reading of Aristotelian philosophy and provided a sophisticated Christian theology. Even though the whole process cannot be identified as comparative theology, there have been certain elements of comparative learning, which challenged Ghazālī and Aquinas, consequently, they provided a new way of thinking and reasoning about theology.

The third example is that in parallel with the translation period, between the eighth and fourteenth centuries, Muslims produced more works on other traditions than other civilisations at that time.[50] In this context, the great Muslim scholars, Ibn al-Nadim (d. 995), al-Bīrūnī (d. 1050) and al-Shahrastānī's (d. 1158) works were great examples of comparative learning. However, the tradition they started did not continue, and interest in studying other religions declined after the fourteenth century.[51]

When Muslims were more interested in learning about other cultures and civilisations, Islamic civilisation was a great power in the scientific, cultural and economic realms. Appreciation of diverse worldviews provides fresh insights not only in theology but also in other areas. Today's multi-religious environments should, ideally, lead us to learn about and from others, both for a better understanding of others and our own self-understanding. Comparative theology is, thus, one way to achieve this.

### *Theological Bases*

I have tried to demonstrate the deficiencies of contemporary pluralist discourse on learning from and about religious others. Practically, comparative

[48] Oliver Leaman, *Islamic Philosophy* (Cambridge: Polity, 2009), 20.

[49] Though he was critical of philosophers, which he presented in his critique of philosophers in *Tahāfut al-Falāsifa*, he is considered the one who put philosophy and *kalām* together.

[50] Waardenburg, *Muslims and Others*, 162.

[51] Waardenburg, *Muslims and Others*, 162.

learning helped Muslims to develop knowledge on both the theological and metaphysical levels. Here, I will argue how Qurʾānic teachings can be the basis for Muslims to employ comparative theology.

Justification of Muslim pluralists for both the existence and appreciation of diverse faiths can be used as a primary base for employing comparative theology,[52] and should function as the starting point for the perception of religious diversity[53] and engagement with comparative theology. Muslim scholars' primary inspiration for their pluralistic vision is the Qurʾānic verses, and the Qurʾān states that the purpose of diversity within humanity is for a better apprehension of mutual understanding and the achievement of righteousness. It states, for example, that 'O mankind! We created You from a single (pair) of a male and a female, and made you into nations and tribes, that You may know each other (Not that you may despise Each other). Verily The most honoured of you in the sight of God is (he who is) the most Righteous of you' (Q 49:13, see also Q 10:19). This verse proves that the diversity of human beings is divine will, and not a result of human corruption or historical accident. The Qurʾān not only accepts diverse traditions and cultures, but also includes the diversity of religions as part of divine will. It is stated 'To thee We sent the Scripture in truth confirming the scripture that came before it and guarding it in safety . . . To each among you have We prescribed a Law and an Open Way. If God had so willed He would have made you a single people but (His plan is) to test you in what He hath given you: so strive as in a race in all virtues' (Q 5:48).

Qurʾānic texts such as these supply a valid reason to embrace religious diversity. The Qurʾān acknowledges the diversity of the human race and ethnicity, including the multiplicity of scriptures and prophets.[54] This should

[52] I pointed this out in the third point while evaluating the pluralistic arguments of Muslims.

[53] Almost all Muslim pluralists use the Qurʾānic verses as the root of religious diversity. Just mention to a few, see Haifaa Jawad, 'A Muslim Response to the Christian Theology of Religions', in Elizabeth Harris, Paul Hedges, and Shanthikumar Hettiarachchi (eds), *Twenty-First Century Theologies of Religions: Retrospection and Future Prospects* (Leiden: Brill, 2006), 333–8; Esack, *Qur'an, Liberation and Religious Pluralism*, 155–61; Ali Engineer, 'Islam and Religious Pluralism', in Paul F. Knitter (ed.), *The Myth of Religious Superiority: A Multifaith Exploration* (Maryknoll, NY: Orbis Books, 2005), 212–14.

[54] Q 10:47; 4:78.

not necessarily lead us to impose these concepts on other religions, but, rather, the Qur'ānic verses cited above, in addition to others, offer a vision of the acceptance and appreciation of difference. By employing comparative theology, Muslims can learn about religious others and be challenged with the different worldviews. Today's multicultural and multi-religious environment pushes us to involve diverse kinds of engagement with others. Many Muslims have accepted the challenge, and many have been part of interreligious dialogue initiatives in western societies. To have a more fruitful dialogue (formal–informal, theological–social, and so on) with others, we need a better understanding of others. Catherine Cornille rightly states that 'dialogue presupposes some degree of humility about one's own conception of truth and a certain receptivity, even hospitality, to the truth of the other'.[55] Comparative theology can provide a new direction for Muslims for their interreligious theologies.

Despite accepting the usefulness and validity of the theology of religion, theorising others with Islamic concepts does not necessarily lead Muslims to apprehend the otherness of religious others. While pluralist theologies offered by Muslims, in spite of claiming to provide openness and tolerance, can be useful for the theorising and acceptance of the diversity of religions, they do not necessarily lead to a real embracement of others. In this respect, rather than employing the classification of theology of religions, I find Keith Ward's definition of open and closed theologies more useful. According to Ward, open theologies:

> seek a convergence of common core beliefs, clarifying the deep agreements which may underline diverse cultural traditions. It will seek to learn from complementary beliefs in other traditions, expecting that there are forms of revelation one's own tradition does not express. It will be prepared to reinterpret its beliefs in the light of new, well-established factual and moral beliefs. It will accept the full right of diverse belief systems to exist, as long as they do not cause avoidable injury or harm to innocent sentient beings. It will encourage a dialogue with conflicting and dissenting views, being prepared to confront its own tradition with critical questions arising out of such views.

[55] Catherine Cornille (ed.), *The Wiley-Blackwell Companion to Inter-Religious Dialogue* (Chichester: Wiley-Blackwell, 2013), xiii.

> And it will try to develop a sensitivity to the historical and cultural context of the formulation of its own beliefs, with preparedness to continue developing new insights in new cultural situations.[56]

Closed theology, in contrast;

> [will insist] on the total distinctiveness of its own beliefs, excluding others from any share in important truths. It rejects all contact with other systems of belief. It rejects any development of knowledge which would force a reinterpretation of its own tradition. It will, if possible, restrict or prevent the expression of criticism or dissent. It will seek to suppress other religions. It will insist that it possesses a complete or sufficient understanding of truth, which change could only impair or destroy.[57]

As long as Muslims are open to being challenged with diverse religious thoughts and are willing to study other religions, Muslim scholars can construct their own comparative theology based on their distinct beliefs and practices. Although comparative learning has been operated by Muslims, comparative theology is a new concept for them.

## Conclusion

Contemporary Islamic discourse on religious diversity urges us to develop a new methodology. The Islamic pluralistic discourse lacks nuances and fails to embrace religious diversity in its all forms. I believe that to engage a better and more useful comparative learning, there needs to be a theology in place that shows a willingness to learn from others. A willingness to learn can be done in two ways. Either one might engage with other beliefs to refute them, or one can encounter other religions to better understand one's own and other faiths. The pluralistic option shows this, but only in theory. Since comparative theology seeks to learn from other religious traditions on their own terms, this might offer a new method for an Islamic understanding of religious diversity.

The Qurʾānic vision of promotion of the acceptance of diversity is 'to know each other'. Even though traditionally, Muslims did not apply this concept to

[56] Ward, *Religion and Revelation*, 339–40.

[57] Ward, *Religion and Revelation*, 340.

seek knowledge of other religions, they have obtained some kind of comparative learning throughout history. Times have changed, however. We now live in a different phase in which religions are not abstract, but instead we are neighbours, friends, colleagues and, more importantly, we share the same world. Thus, our contemporary environment offers us an opportunity to develop a relationship that was not necessary in the past. Learning about diverse religions' beliefs and their main concerns can be helpful in two ways. First, we can correct our presuppositions and analogies about other religions' central themes, beliefs, motifs and practices. 'The combination of knowledge, attention to both continuities and discontinuities, and lack of assumptions of parity uniquely cultivates an ability to identify better starting points.'[58] Secondly, the insights we get from religious others can transform our own belief. Recent Muslim scholars' engagement with comparative theology promises that there are diverse areas that need to be addressed not just from the Christian perspectives but also from Islamic ones.

## Bibliography


Abdelnour, Mohammed Gamal, *A Comparative History of Catholic and Aš'arī Theologies of Truth and Salvation: Inclusive Minorities, Exclusive Majorities*. Leiden: Brill, 2021.

Askari, Hasan, 'Within and Beyond Experience of Religious Diversity', in John Hick and Hasan Askari (eds), *The Experience of Religious Diversity*. Aldershot: Gower Publishing, 1985, 191–218.

Avci, Betül, 'Comparative Theology and Scriptural Reasoning: A Muslim's Approach to Interreligious Learning', *Religions* 9(10) (2018): 1–14.

Aydin, Mahmut, 'Religious Pluralism: A Challenge for Muslims – A Theological Evaluation', *Journal of Ecumenical Studies* 38(2/3) (2001): 330–52.

Clooney, Francis X., 'Current Theology, Comparative Theology: A Review of Recent Books', *Theological Studies* 56 (1995): 521–50.

Clooney, Francis X., *Hindu God, Christian God: How Reason Helps Break Down the Boundaries between Religions*. Oxford: Oxford University Press, 2001.

Clooney, Francis X., *Comparative Theology: Deep Learning Across Religious Borders*. Malden, NY: Wiley-Blackwell, 2010.


[58] Lamptey, *Divine Words, Female Voices*, 36.

Cornille, Catherine (ed.), *The Wiley-Blackwell Companion to Inter-Religious Dialogue*. Chichester: Wiley-Blackwell, 2013.

Dağ, Esra Akay, *Christian and Islamic Theology of Religions: A Critical Appraisal*. London: Routledge, 2017.

D'Costa, Gavin, *Theology and Religious Pluralism: The Challenge of Other Religions*. Oxford: Blackwell, 1986.

D'Costa, Gavin, *Christianity and World Religions: Disputed Questions in the Theology of Religions*. Chichester: Wiley-Blackwell, 2009.

Engineer, Ali, 'Islam and Religious Pluralism', in Paul F. Knitter (ed.), *The Myth of Religious Superiority: A Multifaith Exploration*. Maryknoll, NY: Orbis Books, 2005, 211–19.

Esack, Farid, *Qur'an, Liberation and Religious Pluralism: An Islamic Perspective of Interreligious Solidarity against Oppression*. Oxford: One World, 1997.

Fredericks, James L., 'A Universal Religious Experience? Comparative Theology as an Alternative to a Theology of Religions', *Horizons* 22(1) (1995): 67–87.

Fredericks, James L., *Faith among Faiths: Christian Theology and Non-Christian Religions*. Mahwah, NJ: Paulist Press, 1999.

Hedges, Paul, *Controversies in Interreligious Dialogue and the Theology of Religions*. London: SCM Press, 2010.

Hedges, Paul, *Comparative Theology: A Critical and Methodological Perspective*. Leiden: Brill, 2017.

Hick, John, *An Interpretation of Religion*. New Haven, CT: Yale University Press, 1989.

Jawad, Haifaa, 'A Muslim Response to the Christian Theology of Religions', in Elizabeth Harris, Paul Hedges, and Shanthikumar Hettiarachchi (eds), *Twenty-First Century Theologies of Religions: Retrospection and Future Prospects*. Leiden: Brill, 2006, 328–58.

Kiblinger, Kristin B., 'Relating Theology of Religions and Comparative Theology', in Francis X. Clooney (ed.), *The New Comparative Theology: Interreligious Insights from the Next Generation*. London: T. & T. Clark, 2010, 21–42.

Knitter, Paul F., *Introducing Theologies of Religions*. Maryknoll, NY: Orbis Books, 2002.

Lamptey, Jerusha Tanner, *Never Wholly Other: A Muslima Theology of Religious Pluralism*. New York: Oxford University Press, 2014.

Lamptey, Jerusha Tanner, *Divine Words, Female Voices: Muslima Explorations in Comparative Feminist Theology*. New York: Oxford University Press, 2018.

Leaman, Oliver, *Islamic Philosophy*. Cambridge: Polity, 2009.

Moyaert, Marianne, 'Comparative Theology in Search of a Hermeneutical Framework', in David Cheetham, Ulrich Winkler, Oddbjørn Leirvik and Judith Gruber (eds),

*Interreligious Hermeneutics in Pluralistic Europe Between Texts and People*. Leiden: Brill, 2011, 161–85.

Moyaert, Marianne, 'Theology Today: Comparative Theology as a Catholic Theological Approach', *Theological Studies* 76(1) (2015): 43–64.

Neville, Robert (ed.), *Religious Truth: The Cross Cultural Comparative Religious Ideas Project*. Albany, NY: State University of New York Press, 2001.

Neville, Robert (ed.), *The Human Condition: A Volume in the Comparative Religious Ideas Project*. Albany, NY: State University of New York Press, 2001.

Neville, Robert (ed.), *Ultimate Realities: A Volume in the Comparative Religious Ideas Project*. Albany, NY: State University of New York Press, 2001.

Nicholson, Hugh, *Comparative Theology and the Problem of Religious Rivalry*. Oxford: Oxford University Press, 2011.

Race, Alan, *Christians and Religious Pluralism: Patterns in the Christian Theology of Religions*. London: SCM Press, [1983] 1993.

Sachedina, Abdulaziz, 'The Qur'ān and Other Religions', in Jane Dammen McAuliffe (ed.), *The Cambridge Companion to the Qur'ān*. New York: Cambridge University Press, 2007, 291–310.

Schmidt-Leukel, Perry, *Transformation by Integration: How Inter-Faith Encounter Changes Christianity*. London: SCM Press, 2009.

Schmidt-Leukel, Perry, 'Pluralist Approaches in Some Major Non-Christian Religions', in Elizabeth Harris, Paul Hedges, and Shanthikumar Hettiarachchi (eds), *Twenty-First Century Theologies of Religions: Retrospection and Future Prospects*. Leiden: Brill, 2016, 159–87.

Schmidt-Leukel, Perry, *Religious Pluralism and Interreligious Theology: The Gifford Lectures – An Extended Edition*. Maryknoll, NY: Orbis Books, 2017.

Shah-Kazemi, Reza, *The Other in the Light of One: The Universality of the Qur'ān and Interfaith Dialogue*. Cambridge: Islamic Texts Society, 2006.

Sonn, Tamara, 'Introduction', in Andrew Rippin and Jawid Mojaddedi (eds), *The Wiley Blackwell Companion to the Qur'an*. Chichester: John Wiley, 2017, 7–23.

Stosch, Klaus von, 'Comparative Theology as a Challenge for the Theology of the 21st Century', *Religious Inquiries* 1(2) (2012): 5–26.

Stosch, Klaus von, 'Comparative Theology as Liberal and Confessional Theology', *Religions* 3(4) (2012): 983–92.

Waardenburg, Jacques, *Muslims and Others: Relations in Context*. Berlin: Walter de Gruyter, 2003.

Ward, Keith, *Religion and Revelation: A Theology of Revelation in the World's Religions*. Oxford: Clarendon Press, 1994.

Ward, Keith, *Religion and Creation*. Oxford: Clarendon Press, 1996.

Ward, Keith, *Religion and Human Nature*. Oxford: Clarendon Press, 1999.
Ward, Keith, *Religion and Community*. Oxford: Clarendon Press, 2000.
Winkler, Ulrich, 'What is Comparative Theology?' in David Cheetham, Ulrich Winkler, Oddbjørn Leirvik, and Judith Gruber (eds), *Interreligious Hermeneutics in Pluralistic Europe Between Texts and People*. Leiden: Brill, 2011, 231–64.

# Part V

## LOCAL ISLAMS

# 9

# EASTERN OR WESTERN PARADIGM: THE STRUGGLE FOR METHODOLOGICAL DOMINANCE IN THE STUDY OF ISLAM IN UNIVERSITIES IN NORTHERN NIGERIA

DAUDA ABUBAKAR

> We would not allow someone who did not acquire all his/her BA, MA and PhD degrees in Islamic studies to teach Islam in this University. We will also not allow someone who has studied Islamic studies from a university in the western countries to teach in our university because he/she must have been indoctrinated with western thoughts and ideas that are probably detrimental to Islam.[1]

## Introduction

This chapter examines the dilemma and confusion that those studying Islamic studies in secular universities in northern Nigeria find themselves and the struggle for dominance among diverse interest groups within and without the system. The chapter problematises the complexity of situating Islamic studies in secular universities in northern Nigeria. The complexity of situating Islamic studies in secular universities in northern Nigeria started right from the British occupation of the region, which was established to model higher institutions in the secular West, to moderate the understanding of Islam.[2] Another reason for British establishment of western-style secular

[1] Statement by an interlocutor, university in northern Nigeria.

[2] Misbahu Na'iya Katsina, 'A Discourse on the Intellectual Legacies of Some Pre-Jihad Scholars of Katsina', in Isma'ila A. Tsiga and Abdalla U. Adamu (eds), *Islam and the History of Learning in Katsina* (Ibadan: Spectrum Books, 1997).

education in Nigeria was to achieve social change and as a means of ensuring political and economic independence of the citizens of the country. It is also a convenient way to produce citizens that will accept the British logic of a modern and plural state in Nigeria.[3] Nkulu Kiluba[4] emphasises that colonial administrative and political interest was also part of British interest in establishing tertiary education in Nigeria. The first tertiary institution established in Nigeria was the Yaba Higher College in 1932 (an upgraded version of the Kings College Lagos), and most of the graduates worked for the British as civil servants. On the other hand, the British are also accused of using tertiary education to achieve westernisation and other colonial interests. The new form of education was also accused of 'inculcating the attitude of the educated person as superior to the less educated'.[5] The first public research university established by the British in Nigeria was the University of Ibadan (UI) (now in Oyo State, a Yoruba-dominated area) in 1948 as a campus of the University of London, which became an independent university in 1963.[6] This was followed by the University of Nigeria, Nsukka (UNN) in Enugu State in 1960. It was initially started by Nnamdi Azikiwe in 1955 and officially opened in October 1960 after independence. This was followed by the Obafemi Awolowo University, Ile-Ife in Osun State in 1961; Ahmadu Bello University, Zaria in Kaduna State in 1962; and the University of Lagos in Lagos State in 1962. Today, there are more than 171 public science-oriented universities in Nigeria; forty-three owned by the federal government, forty-eight owned by different states, and eighty-one owned by private individuals and corporate bodies. Less than one-third of these universities are located in northern Nigeria and are mostly either federal or state; thirteen federal universities, eleven state universities, and less than ten are private.

Faculties and departments in these universities are science research-oriented, therefore, apart from teaching, every academic staff member is

[3] Sounaye Abdoulaye, 'Salafi Revolution in West Africa', Leibniz-Zentrum Moderner Orient Working Paper number 19, 2017), 9, https://www.ssoar.info/ssoar/handle/document/54611.

[4] Nkulu Kiluba, *Serving the Common Good: A Postcolonial African Perspective on Higher Education*, Series of Society and Politics in Africa 15 (New York: Peter Lang, 2005), 45.

[5] Nkulu, *Serving the Common Good*, 50.

[6] Nkulu, *Serving the Common Good*, 54.

expected to conduct research and publish the result in books, chapter contributions and journals, etc. Some of these publications remain in circulation among the local universities and academics while others go outside Nigeria as international. The popular aphorism 'publish or perish' applies so much in Nigerian universities among academics that publication has become a strong basis for academic promotion, a ladder to greater elevation. Therefore, academic staff are tenure-track and must maintain steady promotion via publication. The clamour for local promotion among the academics has reduced the enthusiasm for quality research, which further reduces the academic value of local publications in books and journals to mere avenues of 'promotion publications', not quality academic efforts to promote and exchange scientific knowledge. While, on the other hand, research is often seen as 'systematic investigation of issues with the sole aim of solving societal problems'.[7,8]

Departments of religious studies were also part of the departments established in some of the Nigerian secular universities with the aim of conducting scientific study of religion; a range of courses on religion are being studied: Islam, Christianity, Hinduism, Buddhism, etc. One of these courses, which is the focus of this study, is Islamic Studies. Some universities in northern and southwestern Nigeria, areas with majority Muslim populations, have established departments for the study of Islam in the secular universities in their areas, although northern Nigeria specifically is the focus of this research. The curriculum of Islamic studies, teaching, research and publication in these departments seem to present serious challenges for the university administrators, academics and students. Three different approaches were examined in this work: traditional local Islamic studies; theological study of Islam from the Arab world; and the western–scientific research approach to the study

[7] James Afebuameh Aiyebelehin, '"Add-my-name" as a Parody of Research Collaboration among Nigerian Researchers', *Journal of Accountability in Research* 1 (2021): 1–10, available at: https://www.tandfonline.com/loi/gacr20.

[8] The printing of local academic papers in the name of local journals have become a good business venture for some academics in Nigerian universities who charge money ranging from N20,000 to N30,000 (i.e., \$60–\$72) per paper and print it in book form without regard to any peer review process or quality. The more papers they produce in a volume the more income they make.

of Islam. This work argues that the study of Islam in secular universities in northern Nigeria has presented Muslims with much confusion. What method should these departments and academics adapt for teaching and research on Islam? Should the departments of Islamic Studies in universities in northern Nigeria promote theology or western scientific research? Who should teach Islamic studies, those locally trained, or those trained in the Arab world or those trained within the secular system?

I have throughout this work referred to the different methods (both the imitation of Saudi Arabian system and locally acquired) in the study of Islam in universities in northern Nigeria as traditional. By tradition, I do not mean a static and unchanged system, rather, I adopt the views of Frede Britta[9] that: 'a tradition is in an ongoing process of transmission'. This is despite the fact that traditional Islamic studies in northern Nigeria has been transmitted from past to the present through maintaining religious values and ideas.[10] Therefore, I have interchangeably used secular and western education to refer to western or modern education, which emphasise scientific inquiry and method of research. While traditional education refers to the informal Muslim educational system that still survives and is seen by traditional Muslim scholars in northern Nigeria as an authentic and genuine means of acquiring a sound Islamic education.

This work is embedded within the concept of knowledge production, which consists of three dimensions that determine the epistemology of knowledge processes that can differ from one place to the another due to economic, cultural diversity and authority in any given place and system. Thus, how is what is known and what is worth knowing developed and recognised within the context of the society? The local or global level of knowledge and avenue of disseminating it determines the interest it will likely generate; that is, which journal or publisher publish it? Actors in academia and industry build consensus over the meaning of concepts and theories, and this is usually done through epistemological and methodological means as well as by the

[9] Frede Bretta, 'What does Traditional Islamic Education Mean? Examples from Nouakchott's Contemporary Female Learning Circles', in Ousmane Oumar Kane (ed.), *Islamic Scholarship in Africa: New Directions and Global Contexts* (Woodbridge: Boydell & Brewer 2021), 306.

[10] Bretta, 'What does Traditional Islamic Education Mean?' 305.

exchange of ideas through different conferences and publications.[11] Lastly, the topic preference provides the topical structure of different disciplines. These are important processes of knowledge interaction among the agencies and actors involved. Research can be compared with market principles of supply and demand, which create academic markets for publications that can be either local or global.[12] Considering this assumption, the world can be divided into two: the 'world of ideas and concepts' that includes modern, strong economies and advanced societies that have achieved knowledge economies and development, and others outside this circle. In advanced societies, research and development is embedded into science and technology to advance knowledge on every aspect of life.[13]

In developed countries, science and knowledge are inseparable, a major reason why many fields of knowledge always cooperate with one another for greater benefit. Societies today are more and more questing for beneficial knowledge from research.[14] Hisham Ghassib stressed that 'the scientific revolution ultimately transformed knowledge production from a marginal craft into a major, if not the major industry in the world'.[15] In fact, Ghassib sees knowledge production as a great and autonomous factory that does not need religion or political authorities to survive due to its scientific base, otherwise it will be constrained.[16] The twenty-first century has witnessed an exponential growth of knowledge factories in the world that constantly interact and negotiate the process of knowledge production.[17]

[11] Konstantinos Zougris, 'Communities of Scholars: A Conceptual Scheme of Knowledge Production', *Societies* 8(4) (2018): 1–10; Helen M. Gunter, 'Knowledge Production and Theory Development: The Case of Educational Administration', paper presented to the Political Studies Association Conference, Cardiff, March 2013.

[12] Elias G. Carayannis et al., 'Mode 3 Knowledge Production: Systems and Systems Theory, Clusters and Networks', *Journal of Innovation and Entrepreneurship* 5(17) (2016): 1–24.

[13] Carayannis, 'Mode 3 Knowledge Production'.

[14] Michael Gibbons, *The New Production of Knowledge: The Dynamics of Science and Research in Contemporary Societies* (London: SAGE Publications, 2002).

[15] Hisham Ghassib, *A Theory of the Knowledge Production Industry*, 2011, available at: https://www.researchgate.net/publication/230750331_A_Theory_of_the_Knowledge_Industry.

[16] Ghassib, *A Theory of the Knowledge Production Industry.*

[17] Helge Kragh, *Quantum Generations: A History of Physics in the 20th Century*. Princeton, NJ: Princeton University Press 1999.

Today, scientific research has been identified as a means of knowledge production in secular universities especially in developed countries, which can hardly be defined through a single criterion applicable everywhere. The conditions and requirements keep changing and it is becoming more and more interwoven with society.[18] Actors within a substantial system often determine the direction of research within the context of defined methodology that differs across fields. Each researcher, therefore, see him/herself as an individual capable of understanding the society around him/her and the world at large.[19]

In conducting this research, I have used the qualitative method and conducted semi-structured interviews with twenty-two interlocutors, who were divided into four groups: academics teaching Islamic studies in the different universities in northern Nigeria; traditional Islamic sheikhs; graduates from Arab universities; and students either still studying or recently graduated from Islamic Studies in universities in northern Nigeria. The interview approach varied from one person to another, although sometimes phone interviews were conducted either due to distance or COVID-19 regulations. The chapter is divided into four sections: introduction, literature review, discussion of findings and conclusion.

## Traditional Muslim Education within the Context of Modern Education in Nigeria

Nigeria is the most populous country in Africa with a population of more than 206 million people, more than half whom are Muslims (sixth largest Muslim population in the world). The country is therefore faced with a crisis of internal and external struggle for influence between Muslim and western countries, what John Paden[20] refers to as 'forces at play'. For example, Arab countries such as Saudi Arabia are struggling to infuse and control young Muslim scholars, while western countries mostly neglect their role in constructive engagement with Muslims especially in the area of education

[18] Bjørn Gustavsen, 'New Forms of Knowledge Production and the Role of Action Research', *Action Research* 1(2), (2003): 153–64.

[19] Gustavsen, 'New Forms of Knowledge Production'.

[20] John N. Paden, *Muslim Civic Cultures and Conflict Resolution: The Challenge of Democratic Federalism in Nigeria* (Washington, DC: Brookings Institution Press, 2005), 2.

and scientific research. Despite the huge Muslim population in Nigeria, they have been historically disadvantaged in formal education right from the colonial period. During that period, Christian missionaries were the major providers of western education, and Muslims in the north refused to enrol their children in such schools for fear of them being converted to Christianity or forced to participate in Christian religious services. Another fear was that of western influence on the morality of Muslim children. This produced serious negative repercussions for Muslims since a western education was a requirement in the job market, especially in the secular state.[21] As a replacement, the Muslims mostly created self-sustained business ventures.

Nigeria is a diverse country consisting of more than 470 ethnic and linguistic groups, as well as different religions living side-by-side, citizens coexist in mix settings and relate with one another. The state that governs over these ethnic and religious groups is secular, which enables citizens to coexist on mutual grounds with equal rights and freedoms.[22] All federal institutions are established by the state in Nigeria and funded by public funds for the benefit of all citizens, therefore, universities are banned from aligning with any religion or ethnicity due to their notional public nature. But in northern Nigeria, out of the nineteen states in the region (excluding Abuja, also in the north), only three are dominated by Christians and even in those states, Muslims form between 30 and 40 per cent of the population; that is, Plateau, Benue and Taraba states.[23] Muslim and Christian groups are making desperate efforts to establish their own conventional universities in Nigeria, but it is not clear whether they will prefer a theological approach to studying religion in such universities.

Whereas, the major responsibilities of modern universities in the world are research and dissemination of knowledge generated from different fields

[21] Melina Platas Izama, 'Muslim Education in Sub-Saharan Africa', paper presented at the AALIMS Graduate Student Workshop, April 2013, 5, available at: https://aalims.org/uploads/Izama_AALIMS.pdf.

[22] Alemika E. O. Etanbi and Okoye Festus (eds), *Ethno-Religious Conflicts and Democracy in Nigeria: Challenges* (Kaduna: Human Rights Monitor), 1.

[23] Peter Bauna Tanko, 'Ethnicity, Religion and the Survival of Democracy in Nigeria', in Alemika E. O. Etanbi and Okoye Festus (eds), *Ethno-Religious Conflicts and Democracy in Nigeria: Challenges* (Kaduna: Human Rights Monitor, 2002), 201.

of studies. In Stephen Mutula's view,[24] universities are expected to produce research results either to enrich academic literature and initiate academic discourse, or its possible application in political, social and economic situations in society. The benefit of research in African universities is limited. For example, world university ranking shows that African universities (except, of course, South Africa) are performing poorly probably due to lack of professional academics, research facilities, and an information and communication technology (ICT) friendly environment. The university rankings also take into account the perceived research funding attracted by universities or individual researchers within the universities, quality of research and publications produced, etc.[25] These are seriously lacking especially in Nigerian universities. For example, the first five universities in Nigeria that appear in the January 2021 world universities ranking were between 1,219 and 1,894: University of Ibadan (1,219), Covenant University Ota (1,326), Obafemi Awolowo University, Ile-Ife (1,614), University of Nigeria, Nsukka (1,615) and University of Lagos (1,894). None of these universities is in northern Nigeria. Otherwise, the first five universities that appear in the world university ranking from northern Nigeria are Ahmadu Bello University, Zaria (2,305), Bayero University Kano (3,032), Federal University of Technology Minna (3,078), University of Ilorin (3,572), and University of Abuja (3,666). The National Universities Commission (NUC) in Nigeria expresses the government position and pointed out that the reasons for poor performance among universities in Nigeria include low impact local journals, lack of publications in international peer review journals and the absence of visibility of Nigerian universities on the internet.[26] While Sawyerr Akilagpa[27] challenged this assumption and stressed the failure of public policy in reinforcing and ensuring the importance and development of higher education in Nigeria.

[24] Stephen Mutula, 'Challenges of Doing Research in Sub-Saharan African Universities: Digital Scholarship Opportunities', *Inkanyisa Journal of Humanities and Social Sciences* 1(1) (2009): 1.

[25] Mutula, 'Challenges of doing Research', 2.

[26] Mutula, 'Challenges of doing Research', 3.

[27] Sawyerr Akilagba, 'Renewal of the African University', paper presented on the Development of African Universities, 20 May 2006, Association of African Universities, Accra, 2006, 43, available at: https://www.cedol.org/wp-content/uploads/2012/02/155-159-2007.pdf.

According to Mahmood Mamdani,[28] universities in Nigeria have witnessed two periods in their history: a period of academic boom from the 1960s to 1970s, when the state in Nigeria invest heavily in university education and research; and from the 1980s until today, when university funding declined continually, affecting its productivity. Today, the salaries of university staff in Nigeria remain low, there is lower research funding, a lack of adequate infrastructure, a lack of adequate funding to attend international conferences and interact with other scholars and international collaboration, and exchange is crippled due to the security situation in Nigeria. University staff are constantly uncertain of the future, which increases the brain drain.

However, despite this situation in Nigerian universities, the universities conduct some sort of research to study religion, while, as I stated earlier, the traditional method of studying Islam in northern Nigeria is embedded in theology, mainly towards the defence of the religion against non-Muslim criticism in Nigeria, and to especially defend it from what most local Muslim scholars believe is a western conspiracy against Islam. According to local understanding, those who engage in the traditional method of studying Islam in northern Nigeria must be believers who already hold the assertion of truth about Islam and will defend it against all odds. While contrary to this assumption, Islamic studies in secular universities is supposed to adopt the scientific approach, devoted to the scientific method of research into the effect of, for instance, the Muslim belief in individuals and groups of Muslims and their behaviours and institutions in the society. It studies Muslim societies and scientifically attempts to advance knowledge by advancing the understanding of Muslim cultures, religious motivation, etc. For example, what is the impact of Muslim distribution of *zakāt* in certain societies, or how do Muslim women understand, design and use *hijab* within certain social contexts. According to Rahina Muazu, on her Facebook site (2021), '*Musulunci* in Academia',[29] modern or academic studies of Islam utilise different

[28] Mahmood Mamdani, Keynote Address to the 16th Conference of Commonwealth Education Ministers: Access to Quality Education: For the Good of All', Report of the Canadian Delegation, Cape Town, 2006, 4, available at: https://www.cmec.ca/Publications/Lists/Publications/Attachments/96/16ccem.countryreport.en.pdf.

[29] Rahina Muazu, Musulunci in academia, *tattauna ilimi, musamman abinda ya shafi karatun Musulunci na zamani.*

methods to objectively study Islam and Muslim societies using anthropological, sociological, historical, gender studies, cultural studies, etc. approaches, which can be done even by a non-Muslim, a dominant culture in the West, for example, in especially Germany with which she is most familiar.

Some Muslims northern Nigeria have since discovered the necessity of a western education, especially for securing employment and achieving a meaningful livelihood after graduation without forgetting their Islamic education for the purpose of their private worship and practice of Islam. In order for children to achieve dual understanding of life, Muslims began to establish their own schools providing both western and Islamic education and the children can also go to university through such schools.[30] Combining the two systems in a person is central because as western education equips a Muslim with learning new social and economic skills, most Muslims believe that Islamic education, on the other hand, shapes their spiritual endeavour, belief and moral values in society.[31] But still, there are Muslims in northern Nigeria that view western education with dismay, as negative and evil, and, therefore, despised it. This group see western education as an attempt to impose western culture on Muslims in Nigeria, which must be resisted by all means possible.[32] This is because in their understanding of education in Islam, it must go hand in hand with morality, and teachers are expected to be important living examples to their students and should have a level of social control in society, which is missing in the study of Islam in secular universities since the assumption is that teachers could even be non-Muslims.[33] Also, universities in Nigeria comprise of mixed settings including Muslims, Christians and members of other religious groups.

[30] Izama, 'Muslim Education in Sub-Saharan Africa', 7.

[31] Abdulhamid Ozohu-Suleiman and Mohammed Enesi Etudaiy, 'Clash of Cultures: The Interface between Islam and the West', *Global Journal of Politics and Law Research* 1(2) (2013): 7–26 at 12.

[32] Abdoulaye, 'Salafi Revolution in West Africa', 9; Ozohu-Suleiman and Etudaiy, 'Clash of Cultures', 14.

[33] Samsoo Sa-u, Nik Abd Rahman, Nik Suryani and Nordin, Ahamad Sahari, 'Infusing Islamic Manners (*adāb*) in Secular Classroom: Its Relationship with Islamic Work Ethic and Organizational Commitment', paper presented at the International Conference on Teacher Education in Muslim World (ICTEM), Crown Princess Hotel, Kuala Lumpur, 2008, 19.

Uzma Anzar[34] emphasises that Islam recognises two types of knowledge: religious (from Qur'ān and hadith sources), and earthly (from human endeavour, i.e., science), and both are considered important for individual and societal development and each must compliment the other. For instance, early Muslim *madrasas* emphasised this dual knowledge, which produces scholars versed in both spiritual and mundane knowledge; mathematics, sciences, poetry, grammar, logic, philosophy and general knowledge.[35] In an effort to win the soul of Muslims in Africa, Saudi Arabia provides scholarships to young Muslims to study at the University of Madina, and are sent back to Nigeria after graduation as preachers and *du'at* (missionaries).[36] Some of these graduates find their way into the secular universities in Nigeria and emphasise theological study of Islam in the universities. Sounaye Abdoulaye[37] emphasises that the young African Salafi generation criticises the way and manner in which Islam is being taught and studied in tertiary institutions in Africa, especially in northern Nigeria and Niger. Abdoulaye concludes that: 'Against the Secular system, Salafi emerged as the guardians of an Islamic moral order for which the school system is not only a major symbol, but also the institution any [Islamic] reform agenda should target.'

## Islamic Studies in Secular Universities in Northern Nigeria

Part of the question I attempt to engage with in this section is who determines what should be taught in Islamic studies departments in secular universities in northern Nigeria? A too simplistic answer to this question is that the National Universities Commission (NUC) has the sole right to approve

[34] Uzma Anzar, 'Islamic Education: A Brief History of Madrassas with Comments on Curricula and Current Pedagogical Practices', (2003), 2, available at: https://www.academia.edu/3218472/Islamic_education_A_brief_history_of_madrassas_with_comments_on_curricula_and_current_pedagogical_practices.

[35] Anzar, 'Islamic Education', 4.

[36] On returning to Nigeria, most of the students become Salafi and promote the Saudi-type of Muslimness. Their missionary activities are mainly within Muslims trying to purify Islamic understanding and practice. They try to penetrate into the affairs of especially Islamic learning in northern Nigeria to reform it according to what they were taught, what Abdoulaye refers to as the 'Salafi Revolution in Africa'.

[37] Abdoulaye, 'Salafi Revolution in West Africa', 9.

what should be taught. But can the NUC as a body follow every lecturer to make sure that what it approves is what is being taught to students, and since social science and humanities is unlike mathematics, for instance, where 2 + 2 = 4, lecturers have the liberty to teach what they understand from the course. To analyse the situation with regard to Islamic Studies, there is a need to into understand the major challenges that Muslims face in northern Nigeria and elsewhere of the crisis of authority. Many Muslim groups as well as individual scholars and leaders of groups tend to speak for Islam and the Muslims in the north, with no consensus between them. Every Muslim scholar seems to be an independent authority on Islam. Muslim figures (both puritans and moderates) pretend to speak on Allah's behalf, which represents a chaotic situation for 'common Muslims' in northern Nigeria. I will explain the reason for that challenge shortly especially in regard to Islamic Studies in secular universities in northern Nigeria. For example, Khalid Abou El Fadl (2005) traces this Muslim confusion right from the colonial era especially after the 1950s.[38] Muslims in Nigeria do not speak with one voice on almost every issue, and each Muslim scholar contradicts the other whether on religious issues, social, political or economic issues. These Muslim scholars in northern Nigeria come from diverse educational backgrounds, some study in the traditional *zaure* (local study circle, under a specific scholar and following specific methodology) or *madrasa* systems (using certain curriculum in classes with numerous teachers). Others study in a more modern setting in universities either within Nigeria or abroad, such as the example of the University of Madina in Saudi Arabia. All these educational systems produce local theological scholars for the Muslim community in Nigeria. The opinion of these scholars carries 'persuasive authority' in their localities or within their different groups and circles, especially in northern Nigeria.

The traditional stages of education are a well-established system in northern Nigeria from childhood to adulthood. Children are initially sent to the *allo* school (slate schooling) at a tender age where they learn to read and write the Arabic script of the Qur'ān, though the vocabulary is foreign to them, but they then gradually learn to recite the Qur'ān text in Arabic and

[38] Abou El Fadl Khaled, *The Great Theft: Wrestling Islam from the Extremists* (San Francisco: HarperOne, 2005), 26.

in some instances even memorise a portion or the entire Qur'ān.[39] This type of Qur'ānic school is found in different localities in cities, towns and villages of northern Nigeria. In this type of Qur'ānic studies, a *malam* (Qur'ān teacher) within the neighbourhood teaches the children during the week for few hours of the day except for weekends (traditionally Thursday and Friday), five days a week (Saturday to Wednesday) and the *malam* is paid regularly by the parents on every Wednesday (*kudin laraba*).[40] Another type of Qur'ānic school similar to this is the *almājiri* school where little children are taken away from their locality to a different location under the leadership of a *malam* on the assumption that being away from home will force them to learn the Qur'ān, strict morals, and entire livelihood. Most children that participate in the *almājiri* traditional school system come from rural areas of northern Nigeria and mainly settle in urban cities.[41] In both approaches, pupils spend reasonable years under the tutorship of a *malam*. For example, in Katsina State, female and male children are sent to Qur'ān school at age four. Salihu Lawal[42] emphasises the stage as *Kotso* or *Kolo* (nursery pupil), and after that the pupils move to the elementary level (Hausa: *Titibiri, masomin gardi*) to start learning to read the Arabic alphabet and un-vowelled letters (Hausa: *babbaku*) and then Arabic words (Hausa: *farfaru*). Salihu analyses the intricacy of the system:

39 Salihu Lawal, 'Education and Change in Katsina Kingdom'. Islma'il A. Tsiga and Abdalla U. Adamu (eds), *Islam and the History of Learning in Katsina* (Ibadan: Spectrum Books, 1997), 68.

40 The *kudin labara* (weekly or Wednesday fees) forms a salary for the *malam*, therefore, the more children the *malam* has the more money he gets from the collection. Any child that cannot pay the Wednesday fee is punish and sometimes sent back home.

41 Presently, according to an interlocutor, Aliyu Ibrahim Yalwa, a renown *Islamiyya* teacher in Kano, because parents in rural areas have realised the importance of sending their children to cities, they therefore send the children hoping that they will find other opportunities in the cities in disguise of *almājirci* (i.e., *almājiri* schooling). Aliyu Ibrahim Yalwa, an interlocutor emphasised that 80 per cent of the *almājiri* children end up as drug addicts, apprentices to businesspersons, labourers, and sometimes even thieves and armed robbers, which indicates the decline of the *almājiri* system of education today.

42 Salihu Lawal, 'Innovative Approach to Qur'anic Education in Nigeria: Reflections on the Development of Qur'anic Education in Katsina from Nigerian Independence to the Present', *Al-Maher Journal for Qur'anic Studies* (2016): 47.

> The next stage is *tattashiya* and *hajartu* which mark the beginning of syllables identification and real reading. Later, the pupil stage start learning how to write Qur'ānic verses through the use of wooden slates (*allo*) and quill pen (*tawada da alkalami*). He will always be guided either by the malam or by some senior pupil in the school. Reading is continued with switch-over from allo to lose pages of the text of the Qur'ān up to the last chapter.[43]

The pupil continues until the next studentship level (or *gardi*) that leads to graduation. At this stage, the student is expected to at least be able to read the Qur'ān fluently, followed by its memorisation to earn the title of *alaramma* (or *hafiz*). Experienced students could acquire the title of *gangaran* by not only committing the Qur'ān to memory but also writing it down from memory.[44] This is between 22 years to the period when the student is expected to get married. After this stage, the student moves to the *zaure* or *ilmi* stages to acquire knowledge of Islam from different specialists; Qur'ān *tafsīr* (exegesis), hadith, *fiqh* (jurisprudence), Arabic grammar and literature, *tauhid*, *manṭiq* (logic), history and *sira*, etc.[45] Scholars such as Sheikh Mukhtari Adam,[46] a respected Sufi sheikh in Jos consider the *zaure/ilmi* system to be the best system in terms of the authenticity of Islamic knowledge because of its methodological qualities, such as the gradual process (i.e., going from one page to the other and one book to another) and interpersonal relationship between the student and teacher. Unlike secular universities that use a semester syllabus, Adam stressed that *zaure* is more rigorous and in-depth, each book is studied from cover to cover and the books are followed serially. For example, according to Sheikh

[43] Lawal, 'Innovative Approach to Qur'anic Education in Nigeria', 48.

[44] Writing the Qur'ān from memory is a popular achievement in northern Nigeria. An interesting feature of the hand-written Qur'ān in the region is its calligraphic design using colours, for example, writing the beginning of chapters in red and carpeted design in different colours to indicate the end of a chapter while the sides of the pages are full of rectangular marginal decorations in colours (Muazu, 'Islamic Art', 2016), 63.

[45] Lawal, 'Innovative Approach to Qur'anic Education in Nigeria', 48.

[46] Interview with Sheikh Mukhtari Adam, a renowned influential Sufi Muslim scholar in Jos, June 2021. Mukhtari Adam is also a traditional *ilmi* scholar who has a circle for students to come and learn and also conducts Ramadan *tafsīr* every year.

Adam, in the Maliki *fiqh*, a student starts from the book of *Qawā'id*, then moves to *Ahdhari*, *Ishmāwi*, *Iziyya*, *Risāla*, *Askari* and, finally, *Mukhtasar*. The student will read a sentence from the Arabic text then the teacher will translate and explain it into the Hausa language, what Sheikh Adamu Garko[47] describes as the best place to know the names of difficult Arabic items in the Hausa language as well as the cultural context. *Zaure* or *ilmi* studies of Islam go hand-in-hand with *tarbiya* (moral training). Students are train to be respectful and be morally upright. This is because traditional Muslim teachers in northern Nigeria are expected to impart knowledge that is embedded with 'moral values, customs, and behaviors to the youth and prepare them to be acceptable members of the Muslim community'.[48] Education according to Muslim understanding in Nigeria is to achieve two *maqāsid* (purposes): *maqāsid al-shar'ī'* (purpose of the creator) and *maqāsid al-mukallaf* (human purpose).

Therefore, university students and graduates of Islamic studies are seen in the same light and are expected to conform with the informal students in the society in northern Nigeria in order to become custodians of Islam.[49] The societal assumption is that a student or graduate of Islamic studies is not the same as graduates of professional courses such as medicine, pharmacy, nursing or engineering, who are considered to lacks a religious educational background and moral guidance. Graduates of Islamic Studies are expected to be the same symbol of morality as those students from an informal setting. Therefore, a knowledgeable person in Islamic Studies on assumption will fulfil God-consciousness, truthfulness, trustworthiness, justice, compassion and have good character,

[47] Interview with Sheikh Adamu Garko, a renowned traditional Muslim scholar in Kano State, June 2021. Garko studied in the *zaure* system under different Muslim scholars and he mentions many of them, which is the pride of anyone that studies in the *zaure/ilmi* school system.

[48] Quick Sheih Abdullah Hakim, *Advice to an Islamic School Teacher* (Cape Town: International Board of Educational Research and Resources (IBERR)) (2004), 64, available at: https://iou.edu.gm/instructors/test-user.

[49] Masooda Bano, 'Engage yet Disengage: Islamic Schools and the State in Kano, Nigeria', International Development Department Working Paper, 29, University of Birmingham, (2009), 3, available at: https://www.researchgate.net/publication/268381573_Engaged_yet_Disengaged_Islamic_Schools_and_the_State_in_Kano_Nigeria.

while these are also qualities befitting a believer.[50] Though the human purpose of a university degree is ultimately to secure employment, just as the human purpose of marriage is to find companionship while *maqāsid sharʿī* in marriage is procreation without neglecting other purposes. Lastly, Sheikh Mukhtari added that the *zaure* or *ilmi* studies emphasise the teacher–student relationship. The teacher will know the student very well and the student will hold the teacher in the same high regard as he would his father. For this category of teachers, there is no difference between worship and teaching.

The challenge of this type of traditional schooling is that it represents an old system of traditional education in northern Nigeria, which has become less attractive today especially among young Muslims. When such traditional *malam*s die, replacing them becomes quite challenging. The financial income of the *malam* according to some interlocutors who are either *malam*s themselves or are familiar with the system, such as Sheikh Adamu Garko, Sheikh Mukhtari Adam, Aliyu Ibrahim Yalwa, Usman Jibril Mika'il, depends on daily monetary contributions from their students, therefore it is difficult to get a young *malam* that is willing to accept sitting back and waiting for such daily contributions. Within the *zaure* system, there is no academic or scientific engagement with the teacher and literature as is the case in modern universities. The teacher is the sole authority. The act of criticising or arguing with the teacher is seen as disrespectful. The major issue in this form of teaching is in students understanding the translation of Arabic into the Hausa language and to understand the context of some rulings with the culture. Students that passed through this system from the beginning to the higher level are mostly constrained in terms of English language, except those that attend English schools. Another constraint is that students from these traditional schools do not acquire any recognisable certificate that will enable them to further their education in secular tertiary institutions in northern Nigeria or secure jobs with the secular state in Nigeria. It remains an informal system that has not been developed.

Another set of what I called hybrid local Muslim theologians in northern Nigeria are those that study in the Arab world, especially Saudi Arabia, Egypt and Sudan, or in institutions established in West Africa with strong Saudi

[50] Mohammad Hashim Kamali, 'Actualization (*Taf'il*) of the Higher Purposes (*Maqasid*) of Shari'a', *Islam and Civilisational Renewal* 8(3) (2017): 295–321 at 295.

Arabian influence such as the Islamic University in Niger Republic. Some these scholars have acquired an undergraduate certificate, some MAs and even PhDs before their return to Nigeria. Originally, according to Usman Jibril Mika'il,[51] they were trained as preachers (*du'at*, sing. *da'ī*) not as academics and they are good at preaching. The late 1980s and throughout the 1990s witnessed an influx of these scholars into northern Nigeria. They take preaching (*da'wa*) seriously and most of them have become religious authorities in their different localities in northern Nigeria. Most have mastered the Arabic language, and therefore established schools to teach Arabic and Islamic sciences to Muslim children and adults. This group is not a monolithic in its compassion, rather, every one seems to operate individually, yet they somehow cooperate with one another. Sheikh Adamu Garko stressed that 'graduates from Madina seem desperately to achieve relevance in the Muslim society in northern Nigeria'. Most have become imams of mosques in their localities or have joined Muslim organisations, especially the Izala B, to become local and national preachers. Subsequently, because they have somehow to survive with their families, the teaching of Arabic and Islamic Studies in tertiary institutions, especially secular universities in northern Nigeria, attract their attention as a convenient source of employment. Apart from teaching, they also see universities as an immoral environment, hence the need to change the situation in northern Nigeria. This is not without some challenges. Secular universities are English-language oriented, especially given that the official language in Nigeria is English, whereas their training and degree(s) are in Arabic, which makes their survival in these universities very difficult except those that acquired some English-language background earlier on. Another challenge is the syllabus used in Islamic Studies in secular universities. All my interlocutors that teach in different secular universities have expressed concern over the Islamic Studies syllabus there. For example, Shehu Abdurrahman Aboki,[52] a professor of Islamic Studies at the Usman Danfodio University, Sokoto, stressed that

[51] Interview with Usman Jibril Mika'il, a lecturer with the Islamic Studies Department, Federal University Kashere, Gombe State, June 2021.

[52] Interview with Shehu Abdurrahman Aboki, a professor at the Department of Islamic Studies, Usman Danfodio University, Sokoto, June 2021. Professor Aboki, has been teaching Islamic studies for about nineteen years.

the Department of Islamic Studies at Danfodio University has been making desperate efforts to revise the syllabus to what he called 'befitting Islamic studies'. Their constraint is that NUC has to approve any change they intend to include or exclude. Another major challenge is the kind of students that are admitted to the course and they are obliged to teach; some do not have any Arabic background or even an interest in studying Islamic Studies.[53] They were often allocated to the course instead of the one they applied to, but as getting admission into universities is difficult, they just have to accept it. For example, Aisha Abubakar,[54] a graduate of Islamic Studies narrated how she desperately sought admission to study medicine three times and had to accept Islamic Studies. Many students complained of lack of choice to study their preferred courses in universities in northern Nigeria. The main aim of most young people that enrol at university is to acquire a university degree for the purpose of obtaining a job, not because they want to specialise in any area. Sometimes it is parents that force their children into a particular course so that they can assist them when they graduate and get jobs. Though there are many that apply for Islamic Studies as their first choice. I organised a focus group interview in June 2021 with eight students of Islamic Studies from different levels. Three of them applied to read Islamic Studies, three were persuaded by family members and two were forced/convinced into Islamic studies either by their parents or husbands against their wishes.

[53] Many of my interlocutors from different universities have the same complaint about admission into Islamic Studies. For instance, the system is organised in such a way that students apply to a particular university through the Joint Admissions and Matriculation Board (JAMB), a body responsible for placing candidates in various universities in Nigeria to study specific courses. Names of successful candidates are forwarded to the academic office of every university. Sometimes courses and departments screen the names and reject them either because they lack certain basic requirements or there are too many candidates for the course in question. In such situations, the university will of its own volition send the candidates to departments that do not have enough applicants, and Islamic Studies is one of those that always receive such candidates, most of whom lack any Arabic background and or interest in studying Islam. Some write JAMB exams and apply to the department and course of their choice, while others that are desperate for the university certificate remain there until graduation.

[54] Interview with Aisha Abubakar, an MA student in Islamic Studies in one of the universities in northern Nigeria, June 2021.

## Competing for the Soul of Islamic Studies in Universities in Northern Nigeria

Four categories of lecturers are found in Islamic Studies in secular universities in northern Nigeria. First, there are professors/lecturers in Islamic Studies departments that have Islamic studies backgrounds from *Zaure/ilmi* and also acquire some English-language skills. This category are often grounded in theology and can read and translate Arabic, but lack oral Arabic, are divided into two, those with an English background can teach in English and write academic papers in English. Within academia, they are divided into two; those that adapt anthropological, historical or sociological methods to conduct research are few, and the second category lack the knowledge of research methodology according to Aliyu Ibrahim Musaddad.[55] The first category are very few in the universities, many assumed they know according to my discussion with many academics in Islamic Studies. Usman Jibril[56] was optimistic that the first category in this group is the kind of lecturers needed in Islamic Studies in Nigeria, while some academics have an entirely different view. The second group are more complex, they often lack a knowledge of Arabic and lack a concrete background in local Islamic knowledge, therefore, all their studies of Islam are from English background/sources. Majority of my interlocutors in Islamic Studies with an Arabic background constantly criticise those academics without an Arabic background, asking how would they acquire authentic Islamic knowledge from its source, that is, the Qurʾān and hadith, which are both in Arabic except for their translations and other important Arabic sources. This category of lecturers is a problem to Islamic

[55] Interview with Aliyu Ibrahim Musaddad, a lecturer in the Department of Islamic Studies, Nassarawa State University, Keffi. Aliyu studied Islamic Studies as a first choice right from undergraduate and MA. This is linked with his family background, his father being an influential Sufi sheikh in Jos. Presently, Aliyu is undertaking a PhD in Sudan.

[56] Interview with Usman Jibril Mikaʾil, a lecturer in Islamic Studies at the Federal University Kashere, Gombe State, June 2021. Jibril Mikaʾil is presently the imam of the Kashare University Mosque and a one-time chairman of the Muslim community and a member of the senior staff disciplinary committee. Usman Jibril recalls an incident where a graduate of Islamic Studies could not write *Surat al-Fātiha* (the opening sura of the Qurʾān) during an interview.

Studies according to Najib Auwal Abubakar.[57] Auwal stressed that it is meaningless for a lecturer to depend only on translated sources in teaching Islamic Studies. Some of these lecturers, according to Abdullahi Adamu Suleiman,[58] a professor of Islamic Studies at the Nassarawa State University, Keffi, are in Islamic Studies by accident just like some students. An interlocutor in one of the universities recounted how he always explained certain subjects to such people in his department before the other person starts to teach the students. While another interlocutor (now a lecturer in Islamic Studies) recounted how one of such lecturers at undergraduate level mispronounced an Arabic word *mushaf* as *mushāf* when they were students at one of the secular universities and later found that it was a wrong pronunciation. He concluded 'how can you learn Islam from such people'.[59] According to Usman Jibril, such lecturers can easily use Orientalists' publications to teach students, which could be damaging to a Muslim's understanding of Islam. Third, are those who graduated from the Arab world, especially the University of Madina, many of whom have acquired employment to teach Arabic and Islamic studies in most universities in northern Nigeria. The problem with this category, apart from the lack of an English-language background, is that, according to Usman Jibril, they are being indoctrinated with *aqīda* (creed)[60] from Saudi Arabian

[57] Interview with Najib Auwal Abubakar, an Islamic Studies lecturer at Bayero University, Kano, June 2021. Auwal Najib has a PhD, with background from the University of Madina, Saudi Arabia, where he obtained an undergraduate degree with specialisation in hadith.

[58] Interview with Abdullahi Adamu Suleiman, a lecturer at the Nassarawa State University, Keffi, June 2021. Adamu has been teaching Islamic studies for the twenty-six years at different institutions in Plateau and Nassarawa states. He is currently the director of academic planning, Nassarawa State University, Keffi. He is also the initiator of the Multi-Purpose Cooperative Society when he was the head of department, Department of Islamic Studies, Nassarawa State University, Keffi.

[59] Interview with Usman Jibril Mika'il, June 2021.

[60] The Salafi doctrine of *aqīda* or theology subjects other Muslims in northern Nigeria to the accusation of idolatry and *bid'a* (innovation). and are therefore seen as being less Muslim. According to Salafi theology, 'the worship of God depended on the act of ascribing unity to God (*tawhid*) and anything short of that is misleading' (Zachary Wright, 'Salaf Theology and Islamic Orthodoxy in West Africa', *Comparative Studies of South Asia, Africa and Middle East* 35(3) (2015): 647–56 at 653). The Salafi model of Islamic belief is based on imitating the Muslim forefather (*salaf al-sāleh*). Part of its core teachings is rejection of unlawful innovation (*bid'a*) (Abdoulaye, 'Salafi Revolution in West Africa', 1).

theology and they try to promote it within the society in northern Nigeria, including in secular universities. They mostly preach to their students. This group are also accused of lacking in-depth experience of the local situation in northern Nigeria. For example, Adamu Garko, a Muslim scholar accused some such graduates of having projected themselves into powerful/important sheikhs within their local community whereas they obtained only an undergraduate degree from Saudi Arabia, which is damaging to Islam. He gave an example from his encounter with an imam who graduated from Madina not long ago, indicating a total lack of understanding of local issues in the community.[61] Lastly, most graduates from Madina are also accused of looking down on local scholars and having a disregard for local knowledge, which often causes a lot of internal disputes among Muslims. Another category of academics in Islamic Studies are those that study in western countries or in non-Arabic Muslim-majority countries such as Malaysia. Those that study in the West (e.g., United States, United Kingdom and Germany) often return home with strong methodological and theoretical competency, but some of them are also somehow lacking in a strong Arabic-language background. According to the understanding of many academics in northern Nigeria, the West is not a place for Islamic Studies. Already, the West is categorised as being hostile to Muslims, therefore, any knowledge of Islam from them is seen as distorted. Secondly, most Muslims in northern Nigeria believe that 'authentic' knowledge of Islam can be obtained only from believers and that was the reason for the preference of the Arab world for Islamic studies. Some academics in Islamic Studies, especially those without an Arabic background

[61] Adamu Garko recalls his encounter with a graduate from the University of Madina over a *fiqh* issue. A family asked the imam about a complicated issue of a woman who has two female children that were married to different husbands and gave birth to a boy and a girl. The one that gave birth to a girl fell sick and brought her to her mother for suckling while the girl was only few months old. Later, when the girl and the boy matured, they fell in love. Is it possible for them to marry under Islamic ruling? The imam answered in affirmative. The family wanted a further confirmation, and therefore they contacted Adamu Garko who responded negatively, after which about eight highly renowned Muslim scholars were contacted, such as Shaykh Abdulwahab (*imamu ahlus sunna*), Dr Bashir Aliyu, Sheikh Aminu Daurawa, Sheikh Abdullahi Gadan Kaya, etc. They all disagreed with such a marriage providing further references from the Qur'ān and hadith.

often choose Malaysian universities for Islamic Studies, which also led to other challenges and are considered half-baked, neither here nor there in scientific academic research.[62]

The above academics in Islamic Studies in universities in northern Nigeria are divided on the issue of the conduct of research within the context of their area of specialisation. Conducting research and publication of findings is another major challenge. This is because scientific research requires methodological clarity and is usually situated within a particular theoretical context, which depends on academic area of specialisation or is borrowed and manipulated to conform with the area of research. From the interviews I conducted, it seems there is no clear methodology followed by those in Islamic Studies and a theoretical framework is a completely a new experience for both the academics and students in Islamic Studies as very few are exposed to that. For example, I interacted with some PhD fellows in Islamic Studies in one of the universities and three of them intend to use hundreds of questionnaires during fieldwork. I asked them how they intended to analyse the data from the questionnaire, and they had no idea on how to do that and were given no guidance. Some of the teachers in Islamic Studies explained that they use mix methods (qualitative and quantitative) to analyse research results, and when I asked them to explain it appeared to be a total confusion. Therefore, I examined some of the publications of the scholars in Islamic Studies; it is clear that about 95 per cent of the papers are published in local journals without proper editing, and the so-called international are mostly in predatory journals that accept articles and print them in the same month without language editing or review. For example, I enquired of three professors in Islamic Studies whether they have peer-reviewed international publications and they mentioned the countries and titles, so I googled them and all are in predatory journals probably targeted for promotion. What revealed more confusion is the topics/titles of the papers on which research was conducted. Most of the titles are theologically based and that is what they also

[62] These are the views of many interlocutors that teach in universities, including Aliyu Musaddad, Usman Jibril, Abdurrashid Abdurrazaq and Abdullahi Suleiman, etc.

teach their students. Scholars such as Najib Auwal Abubakar[63] emphasises that his publication are mostly in his area of specialisation, that is, hadith.

The syllabus and courses taught in Islamic Studies in these secular universities is designed by the secular state in Nigeria, therefore, any addition or revision has to be approved by the National Universities Commission (NUC). Every four years, the NUC send a team of accreditation to ensure that admission of students, teaching and research are done in accordance with state regulations. NUC also has the power to suspend a programme or close it completely if found wanting. Therefore, no individual or group of external people have any control over what is taught in the universities in Nigeria. Most Islamic Studies departments and units in these universities have maintained their syllabus from inception to date, teaching courses on Qurʾān and *tafsīr*, *tawḥīd* and Islamic theology, hadith science, brief history of Islam in Nigeria, Islamic law and jurisprudence, etc. Few universities revised or created new courses based on their experiences of the older universities with permission from the NUC. For example, Islamic Studies at the Federal University Kashere, according to Usman Jibril, added Islamic economics, Islam and gender, conflict management and resolution in Islam, human rights in Islam, etc.[64] While universities such as the Nassarawa State University, Keffi, created an informal system of contributing to society by creating a collective community service known as 'Advisory Committee', which settles family and land disputes, as well as advising on the choice of courses in the university for Muslim children in Keffi, etc.[65] Adamu Abdullahi emphasised that this committee was created so that Muslims will feel the impact of the Islamic Studies department in the whole of Keffi town.

From the overall analysis of the situation of Islamic Studies in northern Nigeria, we can ask, what is the principal focus of Islamic Studies in secular universities in northern Nigeria? Was it to train imams and theologians for Muslim societies in Nigeria who will issue fatwas within the Muslim society? Or to train scientific researchers that will conduct various researchers in different Muslim societies in northern Nigeria? Producing imams and theologians

[63] Interview with Dr Najib Auwal Abubakar, June 2021.

[64] Interview with Usman Jibril Mikaʾil, Federal University Kashere, Gombe State, June 2021.

[65] Interview with Abdullahi Adamu Suleiman, Nassarawa State University, Keffi, June 2021.

has been the wish of some lecturers that studied in Arab countries, especially Saudi Arabia. But Abdurrashid Abdulrazak seems to present a different view and challenges that notion of training *du'at* (preachers) from the secular university system, he said: 'the present university system is not meant to produce imams and theologians'.[66] Abdulrazak emphasised that it is not possible to train most of the students in Islamic Studies because they lack a background in Islamic Studies, and some were forced by the university's academic office to study Islamic Studies without having any background in Arabic, which according to him is like sending a person to study engineering who does not have background in mathematics.

Most of the students themselves are not ready to become imams and theologians in their different societies and that is why some of them do not want to reveal their identity as students of Islamic Studies. For example, one of the lecturers narrated an incident that happened to one of their graduates who was employed in the army as an imam. The graduate confessed that he accepted the position because it is difficult to secure employment, therefore, he requested to be redeployed to another department. A major challenge that confronts graduates of Islamic Studies from universities in northern Nigeria is the issue of employment after graduation. Having experienced years of teaching in a university in Nigeria, I have come to realise that what is important for most graduates and their families is the prospect of getting employment after graduation, which is contrary to the assumption of some people from traditional Islamic education backgrounds who think that students should be authorities on Islam in their different communities. Modern university education usually equips graduates with 'skills, attitudes and values which make them function properly in the society'.[67] Abdussamad Yahya, a 400-level student of Islamic Studies at a secular university stressed that: 'I have realized this type of university is not a place to acquire deep traditional knowledge of Islam contrary to my initial assumption when I came.'[68]

[66] Interview with Abdurrashid Abdulrazak, a lecturer in Islamic Studies at Gombe State University, June 2021. Abdulrazak acquired an undergraduate degree from the University of Madina.

[67] Luqman Adedeji, 'Islam, Education and Development: The Nigerian Experience', *British Journal of Arts and Social Sciences* 5(2) (2012): 273–82 at 277.

[68] Interview with Abdussamad Yahya, a 400-level student of Islamic Studies, June 2021.

The above discussion and considering the various interest groups competing to control Islamic Studies in the secular universities in northern Nigeria, one notices a confusion. This confusion has serious effect on students studying Islamic Studies at all levels. If Islamic Studies is to be studied in secular universities in Nigeria, there are urgent questions that needed to be given attention by the government: what criteria should be adapted that is suitable for it within the new environment? Who should teach Islamic studies and what should be taught? Lastly, what kind of students should be admitted to study Islamic studies?

## Conclusion

Islamic Studies in secular universities in northern Nigeria is confronted with numerous methodological challenges. The secular educational system imported from the West emphasises a scientific approach, while the centuries-old traditional method of Islamic Studies in northern Nigeria is embedded in theology and Muslim morality, which is promoted by traditional local scholars especially returnees from Saudi Arabia. This has produced not only competing actors for the soul of Islamic Studies in universities in northern Nigeria, but also forced the courses into confusion. Many questions are still not clear: who should teach or study Islam in secular universities and what approach should be used to study Islam? Should there be two approaches to studying Islamic Studies: modern, in secular universities, and traditional, at *zaure*? What role should the graduates of Islamic Studies from secular universities play in Muslim society in northern Nigeria? Whereas secular universities are an independent system funded and run by the Nigeria secular state, with less emphasis on religion, the traditional system runs independently. As many actors compete within and without the system, state policies on education conflict with external forces, which produce conflicting interest. These challenges and confusion have reduced the ability of Islamic Studies to meaningfully contribute to academia.

Students of Islamic Studies, on the other hand, are also challenged because most of them were not there to become Islamic authorities in their societies. The few that do aspire to acquire knowledge of Islam do so outside the system either in the *zaure/ilmi* system or even outside Nigeria from the Arab world. The major aim of most students of Islamic Studies in secular universities in northern Nigeria is to obtain a certificate that will enable them obtain employment either with the government or in the private sector. These students feel the effect of the complexity of the system and the many forces at work within it.

## Bibliography


Abdoulaye, Sounaye, 'Salafi Revolution in West Africa', Leibniz-Zentrum Moderner Orient Working Paper 19, 2017, available at: https://www.ssoar.info/ssoar/handle/document/54611.

Abou El Fadl, Khaled, *The Great Theft: Wrestling Islam from the Extremists*. San Francisco: HarperOne, 2005.

Adedeji, Luqman, 'Islam, Education and Development: The Nigerian Experience', *British Journal of Arts and Social Sciences* 5(2) (2012): 273–82.

Aiyebelehin, James Afebuameh. '"Add-my-name" as a Parody of Research Collaboration among Nigerian Researchers', *Journal of Accountability in Research* (2021): 1–10, available at: https://www.tandfonline.com/loi/gacr20.

Akilagpa, Sawyerr, 'Renewal of the African University', paper presentation on the Development of African Universities, 20 May 2006, Association of African Universities, Accra, available at: https://www.cedol.org/wp-content/uploads/2012/02/155-159-2007.pdf.

Alemika, E. O. Etanbi and Festus Okoye (eds), *Ethno-Religious Conflicts and Democracy in Nigeria: Challenges*. Kaduna: Human Rights Monitor, 2002.

Alubo, Ogoh, 'Ethnic Conflicts and Citizenship Crises in the Central Region', Programme on Ethnic and Federal Studies (PEFS), University of Ibadan, 2006.

Anzar, Uzma, 'Islamic Education: A Brief History of *Madrassas* with Comments on Curricula and Current Pedagogical Practices', (2003), available at: https://www.academia.edu/3218472/ Islamic_education_A_brief_history_of_madrassas_with_comments_on_curricula_and_current_pedagogical_practices.

Bano, Masooda, 'Engage yet Disengage: Islamic Schools and the State in Kano, Nigeria', International Development Department Working Paper, 29, University of Birmingham, 2009, available at: http://epapers.bham.ac.uk/1568.

Bollag, Burton, 'Improving Tertiary Education in Sub-Saharan Africa: Things that Work', Report of a Regional Training Conference, Accra, Ghana, 22–25 September 2003, 2004, available at: https://www.aau.org/wp-content/uploads/sites/9/2018/04/Improving-Tertiary-Education-in-SSA-Things-that-Work.pdf.

Britta, Frede, 'What does Traditional Islamic Education Mean? Examples from Nouakchott's Contemporary Female Learning Circles', in Ousmane Oumar

Kane (ed.), *Islamic Scholarship in Africa: New Directions and Global Contexts*. Woodbridge: Boydell & Brewer, 2021, 300–19.

Carayannis, Elias G. et al., 'Mode 3 Knowledge Production: Systems and Systems Theory, Clusters and Networks', *Journal of Innovation and Entrepreneurship* 5(17) (2016): 1–24.

Gari, Hussein Mohammed, *Islamic Trends in Northern Nigeria: Sufism, Salafism and Shiism*, 2017, available at: https://www.academia.edu/34244887/Islamic_Trends_in_Northern_Nigeria_Sufism_Salafism_and_Shiism.

Gibbons, Michael, *The New Production of Knowledge: The Dynamics of Science and Research in Contemporary Societies*. London: SAGE Publications, 2002.

Ghassib, Hisham, *A Theory of the Knowledge Production Industry*, 2011, available at: https://www.researchgate.net/publication/230750331_A_Theory_of_the_Knowledge_Industry.

Gunter, Helen M., 'Knowledge Production and Theory Development: The Case of Educational Administration', paper presented to the Political Studies Association Conference, Cardiff, March 2013.

Gustavsen, Bjørn, 'New Forms of Knowledge Production and the Role of Action Research', *Action Research* 1(2), (2003): 153–64.

Iddrisu, Abdulai, 'The Growth of Islamic Learning in Northern Ghana and Its Interaction with Western Secular Education', *Africa Development, Council for the Development of Social Science Research in Africa* 30(1/2) (2005): 53–67. http://dx.doi.org/10.4314/ad.v30i1.22212

Izama, Melina Platas, 'Muslim Education in Sub-Saharan Africa', paper presented at the AALIMS Graduate Student Workshop, 5 April 2013, available at: https://www.semanticscholar.org/paper/Muslim-Education-in-Sub-Saharan-Africa-Izama/b12ba0c4a9a3f586c3b21413096793489134a3f8.

Kamali, Mohammad Hashim, 'Actualization (*Taf'il*) of the Higher Purposes (*Maqasid*) of Shari'a', *Islam and Civilisational Renewal* 8(3) (2017): 295–321, see at: https://iiit.org/en/book/actualization-tafil-of-the-higher-purposes-maqasid-of-shariah.

Katsina, Misbahu Na'iya, 'A Discourse on the Intellectual Legacies of Some Pre-Jihad Scholars of Katsina', in Isma'ila A. Tsiga and Abdalla U. Adamu (eds), *Islam and the History of Learning in Katsina*. Ibadan: Spectrum Books, 1997.

Kooria, Mahmood, 'Cosmopolis of Law: Islamic Legal Texts and Ideas across the Indian Ocean and Eastern Mediterranean Worlds', PhD dissertation, University of Leiden, 2016.

Kragh, Helge, *Quantum Generations: A History of Physics in the 20th Century*. Princeton, NJ: Princeton University Press, 1999.

Lawal, Salihu, 'Education and Change in Katsina Kingdom', in Islma'ila Tsiga and Abdalla U. Adamu (eds), *Islam and the History of Learning in Katsina* (Ibadan: Spectrum Books, 1997).

Lawal, Salihu, 'Innovative Approach to Qur'anic Education in Nigeria: Reflections on the Development of Qur'anic Education in Katsina from Nigerian Independence to the Present', *Al-Maher Journal for Qur'anic Studies* (2016): 41–55.

Mamdani, Mahmood, Keynote Address to the 16th Conference of Commonwealth Education Ministers, Access to Quality Education: For the Good of All. Report of the Canadian Delegation, Cape Town, 2006, available at: https://www.cmec.ca/Publications/Lists/Publications/ Attachments/96/16ccem.countryreport.en.pdf.

Muazu, Rahina, 'Islamic Art: The West African Qur'an Manuscript', *Al-Maher Journal for Qur'anic Studies* (2016): 56–62.

Mutula, Stephen, 'Challenges of Doing Research in Sub-Saharan African Universities: Digital Scholarship Opportunities', *Inkanyisa Journal of Humanities and Social Sciences* 1 (1) (2009), available at: https://www.researchgate.net/publication/272453247Challenges_ of_doing_research_in_subSaharanAfrican_universities_digital_scholarship_opportunities.

Nkulu, L. Kiluba, *Serving the Common Good: A Postcolonial African Perspective on Higher Education*, Series of Society and Politics in Africa 15. New York: Peter Lang, 2005.

Ozohu-Suleiman, Abdulhamid and Mohammed Enesi Etudaiy, 'Clash of Cultures: The Interface between Islam and the West', *Global Journal of Politics and Law Research* 1(2) (2013): 7–26.

Paden, John, N., *Muslim Civic Cultures and Conflict Resolution: The Challenge of Democratic Federalism in Nigeria*. Washington, DC: Brookings Institution Press, 2005.

Quick, Sheikh Abdullah Hakim, *Advice to an Islamic School Teacher*. Cape Town: International Board of Educational Research and Resources (IBERR), 2004.

Sa-U, Samsoo, Nik Abd Rahman, Nik Suryani and Nordin Ahamad Sahari, 'Infusing Islamic Manners (*adāb*) in Secular Classroom: Its Relationship with Islamic Work Ethic and Organizational Commitment', paper presented at the International Conference on Teacher Education in Muslim World (ICTEM), Crown Princess Hotel, Kuala Lumpur, 2008, available at: http://www.academia.edu/516785/Infusing_Islamic_Manners_adab_in_secular_classroom_Its_relationship_with_Islamic_Work_Ethic_and_organizational_commitment.

Tanko, Peter Bauna, 'Ethnicity, Religion and the Survival of Democracy in Nigeria', in Etanbi E. O. Alemika and Festus Okoye (eds), *Ethno-Religious Conflicts and Democracy in Nigeria: Challenges*. Kaduna: Human Rights Monitor, 2002.

Ware, Rudolf, T., *The Walking Qur'an: Islamic Education, Embodied Knowledge, and History in West Africa*. Chapel Hill, NC: University of North Carolina Press, 2014.

Wright, Zachary, 'Salaf Theology and Islamic Orthodoxy in West Africa', *Comparative Studies of South Asia, Africa and Middle East* 35(3) (2015): 647–56.

Zougris, Konstantinos, 'Communities of Scholars: A Conceptual Scheme of Knowledge Production', *Societies* 8(4) (2018): 1–10.

# 10

# NARRATIVES FROM THE PERIPHERIES: AN INDIAN OCEAN PERSPECTIVE FOR THE STUDY OF ISLAM

ABDUL JALEEL P.K.M.

## Introduction

For last few decades, there have been strong calls to decentralise the studies on Islam and Muslims that have disproportionately converged on the Middle East despite the majority of Muslim communities living outside the region. Although being a constantly connected region proximate to the Arabian heartlands of Islam, Muslims in various regions of the Indian Ocean, their religious cultural manifestations and scholarly contributions did not gain adequate scholarly attention in the study of Islam and Muslim societies. Muslims of these littoral regions have constantly been contributing to the realms of Islamic disciplines. As they wanted to engage with non-Muslim polities in new host locations and faced unprecedented maritime ecological necessities, the community produced novel interpretations of the religion and its legal requirements. The significant scholarly contributions from the region highlighting these interesting trajectories of Islam in the Indian Ocean, the maritime ecological realities and littoral specificities are not reflected adequately in the recent studies of Islam.[1] Nor do we place correctly the littoral Islam in

[1] See, for example, Mahmood Kooria, 'Introduction', in Mahmood Kooria and Michael Naylor Pearson (eds), *Malabar in the Indian Ocean: Cosmopolitanism in a Maritime Historical Region* (New Delhi: Oxford University Press, 2018), xviii; The concern with littoral

the study of the Indian Ocean. However, there have been intense scholarly efforts during the last few decades to read coastal regions of the entire Indian Ocean as a coherent entity formed by similar ecological and historical experiences. The maritime routes did not merely bring economic goods but also stranded many cultural elements that invested these vast coastal regions with unique cultural and historical features. This oceanic uniformity model first introduced in the Mediterranean Sea by Fernand Braudel has exemplarily had vivid results once reformulated in the Indian Ocean.[2]

Religions especially Islam became one of the many crucial points in constructing this cultural uniformity in the Indian Ocean – a point historians such as Chaudhuri and Pearson pioneered decades ago.[3] Muslims in the region attempted to reframe the religion in a way that was viable in the maritime littoral contexts and produced large chunks of literature which remain hith-

specificities of Islam in the Indian Ocean has recently been advancing especially within the legal history of the region. Mahmood Kooria, 'Cosmopolis of Law: Islamic Legal Texts and Ideas across the Indian Ocean and Eastern Mediterranean Worlds', PhD dissertation, University of Leiden, 2016, 193; and see Sebastian R. Prange, *Monsoon Islam: Trade and Faith on the Medieval Malabar Coast* (Cambridge: Cambridge University Press, 2018), 116.

[2] Fernand Braudel, *The Mediterranean and the Mediterranean World under the Age of Philip II* (Berkeley: University of California Press, 1995). Among a corpus of pioneering works on the India Ocean, see, for example, Sugata Bose, *A Hundred Horizons: The Indian Ocean in the Age of Global Empire* (Cambridge, MA: Harvard University Press, 2006); Kirti N. Chaudhuri, *Trade and Civilisation in the Indian Ocean: History from the Rise of Islam to 1750* (Cambridge: Cambridge University Press, 1985); Kirti N. Chaudhuri, *Asia before Europe: Economy and Civilization of the Indian Ocean from the Rise of Islam to 1750* (Cambridge: Cambridge University Press, 1990); Ashin Das Gupta and Michael Pearson (eds), *India and the Indian Ocean, 1500–1800* (Calcutta: Oxford University Press, 1987); Kenneth McPherson, *The Indian Ocean: A History of People and the Sea* (Delhi: Oxford University Press, 1993); Michael Pearson, *The Indian Ocean* (London: Routledge, 2003); Michael Pearson, *The World of the Indian Ocean, 1500–1800: Studies in Economic, Social and Cultural History* (Burlington, VT: Ashgate, 2005).

[3] Chaudhuri, *Trade and Civilisation*, 46–51; Pearson, *Indian Ocean*, 62–112. Muslim diasporic communities in the region also gained scholarly attention for their diasporic and Sufi features, although some talked of the ecumenical Islam they brought. For example, Engseng Ho, *The Graves of Tarim: Genealogy and Mobility across the Indian Ocean* (Berkeley: University of California Press, 2006), 95–51; Anne K. Bang, *Sufis and Scholars of the Sea: Family Networks in East Africa, 1860–1925* (London: RoutledgeCurzon, 2003), 57–90.

erto unutilised. This literature assumes similar patterns and modes of interpretation throughout the Indian Ocean. However, neither did the historians nor the scholars of Islam galvanise earnestly the possibilities of an emerging Indian Ocean perspective to comprehend local religious contributions and socio-historical prospects that these embarrassingly divergent Muslim societies in the region engendered. The present chapter discusses the prospects of having a nuanced Indian Ocean perspective to study Islam and Muslim societies and its culturally vibrant scholarly productions in the region.

Since Islam in the Indian Ocean has ever been a by-product of the long-distance east–west trade that existed before the advent of Islam, traders and trading activities were prime reasons for bringing this epochal cultural change and social uniformity across the region.[4] Traders often became preachers and conversion often provided a way to the success of trading activities in the Indian Ocean.[5] On many occasions traders returned as scholars, Sufis and jurists as they settled and integrated as part of host societies. Unlike many of the land histories of Islam where warriors were harbingers of the religion, the Indian Ocean witnessed a smooth and very tranquil expansion of Islam across oceans. For these emerging Muslim communities in the Indian Ocean, these new littoral regions often with amicable non-Muslim polities induced certain legal and cultural ambiguities and they earnestly addressed these local questions in new scholarly texts. Approaching such historical, legal, cultural and religious nuances emerged in local contexts of the Indian Ocean as a coherent spectrum, as this chapter argues, would help to provide us more insightful understanding of Islam and Muslims in the region.

As this chapter signifies an Indian Ocean perspective for studying Islam in the region, certain questions may be relevant for further appraisal: what features make Indian Ocean Islam so unique that we really require a perspective that obviously projects the littoral Islam of the Indian Ocean as a separate entity

[4] Despite a plethora of literature on Islamisation of various regions of the Indian Ocean that are mentioned below, from trade to syncretic forms, Prange has sufficiently exposed the role of humdrum traders in the Islamisation of Malabar, south India. See Prange, *Monsoon Islam*, 25–91.

[5] Patricia Risso, *Merchants and Faith: Muslim Commerce and Culture in the Indian Ocean* (Oxford: Oxford West View Press, 1995), 5–6.

different from Islam in deserts or land-based polities? What kind of differences did this trader-oriented Islam in the Indian Ocean have from Islam in the lands? How did the long trade reflect in the making of Islamic communities in the region? What tools do we need to study the littoral and syncretic nature of Islam and matrilineal Muslim systems in Indian Ocean Islam? How were legal points being adopted and reformulated according to the non-Islamic political establishments in the region? How did these traders adapt to a Hindu political system and agree upon becoming a minority in a Hindu majoritarian society, giving legitimacy to such a political system? How did Sufis incorporate maritime notions of Islam in the coastal regions they settled? An attempt to understand these questions related to Islam in the Indian Ocean, the local interpretations of Islamic legal political and cultural realms, as well as the tools and perspectives in facilitating the process will be explained in the following.

## Islam in the Indian Ocean World

That the process of Islamisation in the Indian Ocean is historically owed to the monsoon trade advocates us to consider seriously maritime features and oceanic perspectives and its historical engagements with Islam in the region.[6] The long east–west trade that existed historically in the Indian Ocean has induced Islamisation in various ways. First, it left many progenies of sojourning

[6] To mention a few among growing analysis of Islamisation in southeast Asia, see M. T. Osman, 'Islamization of the Malays', in A. Ibrahim et al. (eds), *Readings on Islam in Southeast Asia* (Singapore: Institute of Southeast Asia Studies, 1985), 46; Anthony Reid, 'Islamization and Christianization in Southeast Asia: The Critical Phase, 1559–1650', in Anthony Reid (ed.), *Southeast Asia in the Early Modern Era: Trade, Power and Belief* (Ithaca, NY: Cornell University Press, 1993), 151–79; Anthony Reid, 'Islamization in Southeast Asia: Reflections and Reconsiderations with Special Reference to the Role of Sufism', *Southeast Asian Studies* 31(1) (1993): 43–61; R. M. Feener and M. F. Laffan, 'Sufi Scents across the Indian Ocean: Yemeni Hagiography and the Earliest History of Southeast Asian Islam', *Archipel* 70 (2005): 185–208; M. C. Ricklefs, *Mystic Synthesis in Java: A History of Islamization from the Fourteenth to the Early Nineteenth Centuries* (Norwalk, CT: EastBridge, 2006). On Islamisation in south India where trade, marriages of local women, and local caste practices played, see Sheikh Zayn al-Dīn bin Abd al-ʿAzīz bin Zayn al-Dīn bin ʿAlī al-Maʿbarī, *Tuḥfat al-Mujāhidīn fī Baʿḍi Akhbār al-Burtughāliyyīn* (Hyderabad: Maṭbaʿ al-Tārīkh, 1931), 13–20; Prange, *Monsoon Islam*, 166.

foreign Muslims in all coastal belts in the region, as these traders occasionally married indigenous women and left for their home town with the 'return monsoon' leaving their family back in coastal towns. Secondly, inspired by a more codified and elaborated law of economic transactions in Islam, traders in these regions preferred conversion as it boosted trade prospects, and many foreign merchants preferred trade with fellow believers. Thirdly, conversion evoked upward mobility in many of emerging Muslims polities in the Indian Ocean and enabled them access to high profiles. Fourthly, and most importantly, many natives found Islam and its mystical orders as the lone way to achieve direct salvation and proximity to God.[7]

These processes that brought Islam into coastal regions of the Indian Ocean at least since the last millennium left a very vibrant religious community whose living experiences with Islam were different from those of the arid lands of Arabia. For instance, Muslim societies in some of these regions of Malabar unprecedentedly had to accede to local non-Muslim socio-polities unlike Muslims in the Middle East where Islam made structural socio-political changes. Their simultaneous attempts to meet religious legal requirements of Islam necessitated refashioning them in a way suitable to multi-religious socio-political contexts. The maritime ecologies as well as non-Muslim contexts demanded fresh attention to established judgements made in the context of the arid lands of Arabia. Such engagements were not totally inventive, but were attempts to meaningfully revisit legal and textual interpretations held by preceding Muslims in Arabia and elsewhere. A number of texts produced in Malabar in the sixteenth century raised such interesting questions related to the region to scholars in Arabia and elsewhere in order to gain universal legitimacy. For example, *Ajwiba al-'Ajība*, a sixteenth-century text written by Sheikh Zayn al-Dīn al-Makhdūm al-Ṣaghīr of Malabar, asked opinions of scholars in Mecca, Cairo and elsewhere, and it brought answers given by

[7] Chiara Formichi, *Islam and Asia: A History* (New York: Cambridge University Press, 2020), 30–4; Risso, *Merchants and Faith*, 5–6; André Wink, *Al-Hind: The Making of the Indo-Islamic World, Vol. 1: Early Medieval and Expansion of Islam 7th–11th Centuries* (Leiden: Brill, 1990), 184–97, 206–20.

these scholars.[8] These novel reinterpretations left so many possibilities for expanding Islam's maritime littoral scope in these places, most of which are totally discarded in the study of Islam and Muslims.

Islam conveyed by maritime traders to the Indian Ocean is well explained in many historical narratives of Asian and European travellers. One of the early documents on the coming of Islam in the region, *Qiṣṣa Shakrawatī Farmād* informs how trade and religious activities were inextricably interlinked in the region.[9] *Qiṣṣa* shows that the coastal trade centres across Malabar, from Batkal in the north to Kollam in the south, were crucial in founding strong Muslim settlements in the region.[10] The inclusion of names of port leaders (*Shābanders*) along with Qadis (religious judges), as well as the description of endowments related to these founding mosques have often been raised as an evidence for early formation of a religious class inspired from trade activities in the region.[11] That the port leaders also were appointed by these religious heads in Malabar records the intrinsic influence that foreign religious delegates in Malabar had retained in trade activities.[12] Although *Qiṣṣa* does not promisingly provide a broader socio-cultural context of the local host society, the littoral context of spreading the message of Islam through sea trade evokes interesting insights for studying Islam in the Indian Ocean. These questions related to the littoral context grew as Islam expanded its influence, and many versions of Sufi legal traditions prospered in the region.

[8] *Ajwiba* is written by the famous scholar and historian of sixteenth-century Malabar, Sheikh Aḥmad Zayn al-Dīn al-Makhdūm al-Malibārī al-Ṣaghīr, *Al-Ajwiba al-ʿAjība ʿalā al-ʾAsʾila al-Gharība* (n.p.: Kunhi Muhammad al-Kodanchery and V.K Mūsān Kutty Musliyār, n.d).

[9] Copies of this manuscript are available at various locations in Malabar. The copy utilised here is from the personal library of Nellikuth Muhammad Musliyar, Nellikuth. Anonymous, *Qiṣṣa Shakrwatī Farmāḍ*, Manuscript, no. number (Nellikuth: Muhammad Ali Musliyār Personal Library, n.d.). Copies of the manuscript are available at the Library of Islāḥ al-ʿulūm Arabic College, Tanur and at the personal library of Calicut Qadi, Sayyid Shihāb al-Dīn Imbichikoya Tangal.

[10] Anonymous, *Qiṣṣa*, 12–18.

[11] Prange, *Monsoon Islam*, 93–102.

[12] Y. Friedmann, 'Qiṣṣat Shakarwatī Farmāḍ: A Tradition Concerning the Introduction of Islām to Malabar', *Israel Oriental Studies* 5 (1975): 233–58; Prange, *Monsoon Islam*, 101–2.

A number of royal chronicles such as the Rasulids in the thirteenth century indicate that the religious class across the coasts of Malabar was politically and religiously prominent, as the royal court in Yemen distributed stipends in 1290s CE to scholars in distant port cities of Malabar.[13] And the Qadi of Calicut sent a letter in 1393 CE to the court of Sultan Ashraf II requesting the right to honour their *Minbar* (podium in mosques for Friday sermons) with the sultan's name.[14] Simultaneous to rampant trade networks, a silent but deep expansion of Islam coincided across the Indian Ocean especially after the fall of Abbasid Baghdad in 1258 in the wake of the Mongol onslaught. By the time, Muslim traders and Sufis could set up new polities and they expanded the reach of Sufi Islamic hospices into distant littoral regions. A great number of Sufi orders, such as Qādiriyya, Ḥaydariyya and Kāzarūniyya that were founded rebuking the lust for power shown by Muslim political elites in the caliphate cities such as Baghdad, became successful in building strong networks at major port cities in the Indian Ocean. Quite often even maritime trade leaders were being called by the name of the Sufi order they pursued, as Ibn Battuta mentions.[15] Alms and votive offerings by sailors were prominently made to the Sufi hospices like that of al-Kāzarūnī and other mosques built by Sufi merchants across port towns. Thus, an Islam of Sufi nature with the Shāfiʿī legal school connected the distant regions of the Indian Ocean by the fourteenth century, and Muslim societies in the region articulated littoral Sufi manifestations of religion and its legal aspects in negotiation with earlier interpretations here and elsewhere.

Being himself a religious scholar and a judge and affiliated with many ruling echelons in the region, Ibn Battuta was able to record the minuscule details of people he met in the Indian Ocean in the early half of the fourteenth century. His interesting analysis helps to draw a detailed picture of Islam in the Indian Ocean. At Cambay of Gujarat, he mentions huge mansions and mosques were

[13] Muḥammad ʿAbd al-Raḥīm Jāzim (ed.), *Nūr al-maʿārif fī nuẓum wa-qawānīn wa-aʿrāf al-yaman fī al-ʿahd al-muẓaffarī al-wārif*, 2 vols (Sanaʿa: Centre Français d'Archaéologie et de Sciences Sociales de Sanaa, 2003–5), 516–18.

[14] Sheikh ʿAlī bin al-Ḥasan al-Khazrajī, *al-ʿUqūd al-Luʾluʾiyya fī Tārīkh al-Dawla al-Rasūliyya*, ed. Sheikh Muhammad Basyūnī ʿAsal (Miṣr: Matbaʿa al-Hilā, 1914), 2:244–7.

[15] Ibn Battuta, Abū ʿAbd Allah bin Muhammad al-llawāttī, *Riḥla ibn Baṭūṭa ʿAjāʾb al-Amsār wa Gharāʾib al-Asfār* (Miṣr: al-Maṭbaʿ al-Khayriyya, 1905), 137–41.

built by foreign traders, such as the mosque built by the king of Kāzarūnī merchants.[16] The merchant Kwāja Isḥāq was another Sufi he met at Cambay, who supported travellers, spent for them and hosted them at his hospice. The farther Ibn Battuta moved to the next port towns the more vivid his description of Sufi hospices and mosques built by foreign traders became. At most of the places in the Indian Ocean from Cambay to Guhangzu, Muslim quarters were visible, and some of them, according to him, had practiced very correctly while others very lackadaisically. Across coasts, Ibn Battuta was keen to note a number of mosque-based learning centres for teaching Islamic studies and colleges run exclusively for girls.[17] It is clear from his description that trading communities in the region had always wholeheartedly supported mosques, Sufi hospices, as well as religious learning centres. At Eli, the mosque was basically funded by sea travellers with their donations, and Calicut had boasted of its beautiful mosque built by the famous merchant, Nākhuda Mithqāl.[18] Many Kāzarūnī hospices were run by votive offerings made mainly by sailors irrespective of their religion.[19] So the Sufi informed Shāfiʿī School of jurisprudence was connecting traders and Sufis in most of the regions that Ibn Battuta travelled in the Indian Ocean.

As we read from Ibn Battuta's experiences, Sufis and their hospices were one of the strongest symbols that united Islam in the entire Indian Ocean. Although the Sufi *modus operandi* does not aspire to systematic missionary activities, Sufis were very successful in propagating the message of Islam to the hinterlands of the region. The littoral metaphors and oceanic symbols are exuberant in many Sufi writings of the region as we see in the poems of Ḥamza Fansūrī (d. 1527) of west Sumatra, who tried to render Sufi thoughts in Malay.

[16] Ibn Battuta, *Riḥla ibn Baṭūṭa*, 128–9.

[17] Ibn Battuta, *Riḥla ibn Baṭūṭa*, 137.

[18] Ibn Battuta, *Riḥla ibn Baṭūṭa*, 139. See also Mehrdad Shokoohy, *Muslim Architecture of South India: The Sultanate of Maʿbar and the Tradition of the Maritime Settlers on the Malabar and Coromandel Coasts (Tamil Nadu, Kerala and Goa)* (London: Routledge Curzon, 2003), 131–294.

[19] Ibn Battuta, *Riḥla ibn Baṭūṭa*, 139.

Listen, young reciter of the Quran,
Do not look too far afield
Passing by the water unwittingly . . .
The whale is casting about
In the ocean in search of water.
Yet the sea is clearly manifest
To the pious and the profligate.[20]

As a local expression of eulogy on the famous Sufi figure of Baghdad, Sheikh ʿAbd al-Qādir al-Jīlānī, we find a very popular Sufi text *Muḥyiddīn Māla*, written in Malabar by Qadi Muhammad (d. 1616) in vernacular Arabic Malayalam language. In another Sufi litany, *Adhkiyā'*, Zayn al-Dīn al-Makhdūm al-Kabīr introduces three important aspects of Islam, *sharīʿa*, *ṭarīqa* and *ḥaqīqa* utilising the metaphor of a voyage: *sharīʿa* is like a ship where *ṭarīqa* is the ocean and *ḥaqīqa* are very precious pearls, for which one has to board a ship and dive in the ocean.[21] It has recently been argued that the metaphoric usage of ship for human body and sailing for human life has been quite common in Sufi texts of southeast Asia and south India.[22] By the sixteenth century, this much omnipresence of Muslim societies and their Sufi religious symbols across the coasts had embarrassed the Portuguese Christian sailors. Barbosa writes that if the king of Portugal had not discovered India, 'this country would have a Moorish king: because many of the gentiles turned Moors'.[23] Many times, mosques and Islamic learning centres

[20] G. W. J. Drewes and L. F. Brakel (eds), *The Poems of Hamzah Fansuri* (Foris: Dordrecht, 1986); Malay text, p. 140. Cf. Michael Feener, 'South-East Asian Localisations of Islam and Participation within a Global Umma C. 1500–1800', in David O. Morgan and Anthony Reid (eds), *The New Cambridge History of Islam* (Cambridge: Cambridge University Press, 2010), 472.

[21] The concise meaning of the fifth and ninth lines of the litany are given. See al-Kabīr, *Adhkiyā'*, Zayn al-Dīn al-Kabīr, MS No. 432 (Tanur: Valiyakulangara Palli, n.d.).

[22] Jahfar Shareef Pokkanali, 'Sailing across Duniyav: Sufi Ship–Body Symbolism from the Malabar Coast, South India', *South Asian Studies* 41 (2018): 1–14; Vladimir Braginsky, 'Sufi Boat Symbolism: Problems of Origin and Symbolism', *Indonesia and the Malay World* 26 (1998): 50–64.

[23] Duarte Barbosa, *Description of the Coasts of East Africa and Malabar in the Beginning of the Sixteenth Century* (London: Hakluyt Society, 1866), 146.

also became targets of Portuguese attacks as happened to the Mithqāl mosque in Calicut and the Jami mosque in Ponnani.[24]

Muslims in the region displayed no hesitation in assuming the architectural styles of local Hindu temples and Buddhist pagodas for their new mosques built in south India, Java and southern China.[25] While these syncretic cultures and architectures raised eyebrows of scholars from heartlands, it was a beautiful reflection of local Islam being capable of adapting to local cultures and yet not losing its universal forms in these places. This process of assuming local art and architecture without losing its universal religious contents leaves a distinctive feature of Islam in the Indian Ocean.

Non-Muslim political systems in the port cities of the Indian Ocean such as Calicut were often strongly supported by indigenous Muslim communities, contrary to legal recommendations practiced in heartlands.[26] Although most of the polities in southeast Asia and elsewhere became successfully Islamised, important ports of Malabar and nearby regions remained under non-Muslim control. Local scholars such as Zayn al-Dīn Makdhūm al-Ṣaghīr

[24] Shokoohy, *Muslim Architecture,* 154; Sheikh Zayn al-Din bin 'Abd al-ʿAzīz bin Zayn al-Dīn bin ʿAlī al-Maʿbarī, *Tuḥfat al-Mujāhidīn fī Baʿḍi Akhbār al-Burtughāliyyīn,* ed. Shams Allah al-Qādirī (Hyderabad: Maṭbaʿ al-Tārīkh, 1931), 71; S. Muhammad Husayn Nainar, *Shaykh Zainuddin Makhdum's Tuḥfatul Mujāḥidīn: A Historical Epic of the Sixteenth Century,* trans. S. Muhammad Husayn Nainar (Calicut: Other Books, 2005), 130.

[25] See for an excellent analysis of south India and its Muslim architecture, Shokoohy, *Muslim Architecture.* The Pagoda architecture is explicit from 'the first mosque in Huaisheng Mosque in Guangzhou, which is claimed to date to 627, to the Grand Mosque in Xi'an, built in the early Ming era'. Formichi, *Islam and Asia,* 54.

[26] Muslim support for the Hindu Zamorin is historically visible in the Arabic texts and others as *Tuḥfa al-Mujāhidīn* and *Fatḥ al-Mubīn,* written by indigenous scholars such as Makhdum al-Ṣaghīr. Al-Maʿbarī, *Tuḥfat al-Mujāhidīn,* 22; Nainar, *Shaykh Zainuddin Makhdum's Tuḥfatul Mujāḥidīn,* 15; al-Kālikūtī, *Qaṣīda Fatḥ al-Mubīn.* Legal opinions on the participation of Muslims in non-Muslim polities and demarcations of lands into abodes of Islam, *Ḥarb* (war), *ʿAhd* (treaty) and *daʿwa* (preaching) evolved historically. Contrary to the earlier position in Muslim centres of Arabia, Shafiʿis reached a position of retaining the status of abode of Islam for Baghdad even after its conquest by non-Muslims in the wake of the Mongol invasion. See Khaled Ab al-Fadhl, 'Islamic Law and Muslim Minorities:The Juristic Discourse on Muslim Minorities from the Second/Eighth to the Eleventh/Seventeenth Centuries', *Islamic Law and Society* 1(2) (1994): 183–5.

were not only pleasantly accepting of the political leadership of Hindu kings, but also argued for the legitimacy of the judges appointed by non-Muslim rulers. Al-Ṣaghīr recorded in the sixteenth century that 'if a Sultan, even if he is a non-Muslim, appoints an ineligible judge it would be legal'.[27] The Muslims wholeheartedly joined the Hindu Nayar army in the fight against the Portuguese to reconquer the Chaliyam fort in the 1570s. The sixteenth-century poem, *Fatḥ al-Mubīn*, written by Qadi Muhammad of Calicut, was written to praise Zamorin who loved Muslims. The poem exalts that Qadis and renowned Sufi figures such as Sheikh Mamukoya al-Ḥimsī were also present to support the fight for the Hindu king, Zamorin, against the Portuguese.[28] So the Muslim leaders in the region were contributing to local political and economic realms irrespective of religious differences, while often such a stand was not fully accepted well elsewhere.

The matrilineal political system also was indigestible for most foreign scholars, while indigenous Muslims adopted and legitimised the practice utilising textual and legal recommendations of *sharīʿa*. In the Maldives, we see Ibn Battuta agreed to serve under the female political leadership as a Qadi.[29] A later Javanese scholar, Abd al-Raʾūf al-Singkilī (d. 1693), in his *Mirʾat al-Ṭullāb* also legitimates the female leadership for the Muslim state.[30] The discursive analysis of female political leadership as being Islamic might differ from the usual patrilineal political system in land-based political centres of Islam. A matrilineal political system was elevated as conforming to *sharīʿa* and meeting the requirements of a maritime system that often left women alone at home. This religious uniformity that existed in coastal regions of the Indian Ocean was also reflected in the peaceable mercantile transactions,

[27] Aḥmad Shaykh Zayn al-Dīn bin ʿAbd al-ʿAzīz al-Maʿbarī al-Malaybārī al-Fonnānī al-Shāfiʿī, *Fatḥ al-Muʿīn bisharaḥ Qurrat al-ʿAyn bi Muhimmāt al-Dīn* (Calicut: Tirūrangādi Book Stall, 2006), 215.

[28] Qāḍī Muḥammad ibn Qāḍī ʿAbd al-ʿAzīz al-Kālikūtī, *Qaṣīda Fatḥ al-Mubīn li al-Sāmirī al-ladhī Yuḥibbu al-Muslimīn*, Manuscript No. 85 (Chaliyam: Dār al-Iftāʾ al-Azhariyya, n.d.).

[29] Ibn Battuta, *Rihla*, 142.

[30] Amirul Hadi, *Islam and State in Sumatra: A Study of Seventeenth-Century Aceh* (Leiden: Brill, 2004), 60.

which were broken by the coming of the Portuguese who introduced trade with the artillery fitted guns and broke the unwritten law of peaceable trade in the region.[31] The provocation against the Arab trading guilds in various ports from Malabar to Malacca induced Muslim polities to seek assistance from far distant maritime players such as the Ottomans.[32]

## Legal Questions from Malabar and Universalising Attempts

Muslim societies in various regions of the Indian Ocean attempted to provide meaning to the cultural practices that existed among them and to legitimise them as 'being Islamic'. They found ways to incorporate non-Muslim political systems and locally derived ritual practices. Local scholarly writings, such as Makhdum al-Ṣaghīr's *Fatḥ al-Muʿīn* from Malabar and Abdal-Raʾūf al-Singkilī's (d. 1699) *Mirʾāt al-Ṭullāb* from Java, are examples of such local scholarly productions.[33] Abdal-Raʾūf al-Singkilī argued on the basis of *sharīʿa* for the legitimacy of a female ruler, Sulṭāna Ṣafiyyat al-Dīn, as the head of the Muslim state in Aceh and a deputy of God, who was succeeded by three female sultanas in the seventeenth century.[34] While foreign Muslim scholars often questioned many such practices upheld among Indian Ocean Muslim societies, the scholars in the region mostly argued for legitimising their version of rituals and practices.[35]

Similar writings addressing particular issues of matrilineal systems, non-Muslim polities and littoral contexts of the Indian Ocean have constantly been produced from many coastal places such as Malabar. Particular legal questions were raised to renowned scholars of Mecca and Cairo for reaching a scholarly consensus. Some of the questions raised by renowned scholars of Malabar, as Sheikh Zayn al-Dīn al-Makhdūm al-Ṣaghīr recorded in his sixteenth-century text, *Ajwiba al-Ajība*, are as follows:

[31] Ashin Das Gupta, 'Malabar in c. 1740', in Uma Das Gupta (ed.), *The World of the Indian Ocean Merchant 1500–1800* (New Delhi: Oxford University Press, 2001), 423.

[32] Al-Maʿbarī, *Tuhfa*, 41; Nainar, *Shaykh Zaynuddeen*, 78.

[33] Al-Shāfiʾī, *Fatḥ al-Muʿīn*, 215.

[34] Hadi, *Islam and State in Sumatra*, 60.

[35] See for example, Ibn Battuta's initial disdain towards certain practices among Muslims of the region, Ibn Battuta, *Rihla*, 150–1, 159–60.

> One of the *ḥarbīs* is owed an amount to a Muslim and the custom among non-Muslims of Malabar is that they inherit property through the matrilineal side, from aunts to children of sisters. Is it allowed for this Muslim to incur the debt from such inheritors and to procure it by force or not? If it is allowable, is the creditor eligible to demand an oath if they would deny leaving any inheritance by the demised debtor?[36]
>
> I was asked about one guardian who set out to sea intending for more than two *marḥalas* (distance covered a day) and there is a strong wind in his travel direction if the governor can conduct marriage of his girl, considering the immense chance for her guardian's travel beyond the two *maraḥalas*, or should he wait for confirming his travel for that distance by witness?[37]
>
> This question is about excreta of fleas with more legs and found in coconut leaves used for thatching the roofs of houses. They cannot clean it until these coconut leaves are changed, which they usually do after three months. The question is whether its excreta [that] falls in water or places of worship can be pardoned off or not.[38]
>
> An Arab women entered Cochin with her husband and he divorced her. She eventually was remarried by her first husband after she informed that she got *Taḥallul* (a permission for remarrying after a second marriage, intercourse, divorce and observation of mandatory *'Idda*) and her period of *'Idda* has expired. As they fought later, she argued that the *Muḥallil* has not penetrated but he has owned her. The question was raised to a local scholar and he ordered that the second marriage of the husband was invalid for the above two matters. So, I was asked and replied that her claim after the second *Nikāḥ* that the process of *Taḥallul* has not happened will not be accepted.[39]

Among various issues raised and addressed in the textual sources produced by indigenous scholars in the region, there are questions related to political, social, cultural, ecological and legal matters, including matrilineal inheritance in the region, syncretic architectures, non-Muslim polities, littoral characters, the ecological and maritime nature of the religion here. These above questions raised to scholars in Mecca, Cairo, Yemen and other places indicate

[36] Al-Saghir, *al-Ajwiba*, 60–1.

[37] Al-Saghir, *al-Ajwiba*, 74.

[38] Al-Saghir, *al-Ajwiba*, 3.

[39] Al-Saghir, *al-Ajwiba*, 68–9.

attempts by the scholars of Malabar to engage some of littoral and ecological issues with legal and textual sources of Islam. They found it useful to gain further legitimacy from scholars of Arabia for accepting issues as Islamic in its interpretative engagements with the sources of Islam. The indigenous scholars such as al-Makhdūm al-Ṣaghīr were able to find solutions for issues raised specifically in the region. The question about the Arab lady in Cochin, as al-Saghīr makes it clear, has unequivocally been answered by him. He raised the same question for further legitimacy from scholars of Hejaz and elsewhere. So attempts were made to earn reaffirmation from the heartlands and acquire universal legitimacy for the legal adjudications already declared in littoral places. Such attempts also indicate that the indigenous legal productions were not totally detached from local contexts of Islam or many Islams.[40]

It is equally important to examine how this maritime Indian Ocean Islam would sustain its relations with universal Islam through such attempts to gain legitimacy from scholars of Arabia. Such legitimating answers from Arab lands would bring them together under the umbrella of a single religious community of Muslim Umma. So, it is interesting to ask how the universal and local aspects of religion work out in the case of Indian Ocean Islam. Do Hodgsonian demarcations of 'Islamic' and 'Islamicate' render justice as it denies most social and cultural expressions of Islam in the region?[41] The local versions of Islam or 'many Islams' school had engendered interesting scholarly debates in the study of Muslim societies. It was Greetz's definition of the religion as a complex cultural system of meanings expressed in symbols and signs that attracted loud enthusiasm in anthropological and methodological debates.[42]

Although Geertz has succeeded in signifying meanings in religious cultural systems, his failure to explain the meaning-making process in the lives of Muslims and his complete disregard of textual as well as extra-textual

[40] Daniel Martin Varisco, *Islam Obscured: The Rhetoric of Anthropological Representation* (New York: Palgrave Macmillan, 2005); Abdul Hamid El-Zein, 'Beyond Ideology and Theology: The Search for the Anthropology of Islam', *Annual Review of Anthropology* 6 (1977): 227–52.

[41] Marshall Hodgson, *The Venture of Islam: Conscience and History in a World Civilization, Volume 1: The Classical Age of Islam* (Chicago: University of Chicago Press, 1974), 57–9.

[42] Clifford Geertz, *The Interpretation of Cultures* (New York: Basic Books, 1973), 89.

traditions in Muslim societies called forth severe criticism.[43] The cultural system of meaning Geertz articulated, therefore, could not explain how meanings are formulated in connection with earlier textual sources of Islam.[44] Asad's solution was to approach Islam as a discursive tradition: 'If one wants to write an anthropology of Islam one should begin, as Muslims do, from the concept of a discursive tradition that includes . . . texts of the Qurʾān and the Hadith.'[45] Although very promising, Asad's definition, according to Ahmed, ended up in orthodoxy and fails to consider many explorative realms of Sufism and Islamic philosophy.[46]

The maritime Indian Ocean perspective does not mean that we need to abandon universal contents of Islam to adopt such local varieties of Islams or 'Islams approach'.[47] Ahmed's critique that these approaches fail to consider how local Muslim societies earnestly attempt to figure out and sustain their universal content of Islam is extremely valuable.[48] The meaningful engagements with textual and pre-textual sources of Islam articulated through scholarly writings in the region were potent enough to connect these communities with the universal Muslim society. Ahmed's definition of 'being Islamic' as a meaningful engagement with the revelation matrix (Text, Pre-Text and Con-Text) helps to encompass both explorative realms and normative legalistic realms in the region, in contrast to the legalistic orthodox position that Asad has finally ended up with.

As we saw above, many aspects of Sufi explorative realms of Islam as well as legal contributions produced in the Indian Ocean, it is very clear that there were continuous attempts from the region as questions of fatwas and other scholarly productions to engage maritime specificities with normative as well as explorative prospects of universal Islam. Thus, linguistic, legal, Sufi

[43] See for the critique of his approach Shahab Ahmed, *What is Islam: The importance of Being Islamic* (Princeton, NJ: Princeton University Press, 2016), 129–40.

[44] Clifford Geertz, *Islam Observed: Religious Development in Morocco and Indonesia* (New Haven, CT: Yale University Press, 1968); Geertz, *Interpretation of Cultures*, 87–90.

[45] Talal Asad, *The Idea of an Anthropology of Islam* (Washington, DC: Center for Contemporary Arab Studies, Georgetown University, 1986), 14.

[46] Ahmed, *What is Islam?*, 270–4.

[47] Varisco, *Islam Obscured*; El-Zein, 'Search for Anthropology', 227–52.

[48] Ahmed, *What is Islam?*, 129–40.

and political aspects of Islam that were formulated in littoral contexts of the Indian Ocean fostered a very maritime-specific Islam distinct from earlier forms, and Muslims in the region always attempted to engage it with the revelation matrix of textual, pre-textual as well as con-textual sources. Such aspects become visible only if we bring Ahmed's revelation matrix approach with a perspective that is well informed with socio-political, historical as well as ecological specificities of the Indian Ocean.

## An Indian Ocean Perspective in the Study of Islam

The application of the Braudelian method in the study of the Indian Ocean brought clear insights to approach the entire region as a world system unified by many historical, ecological, as well as cultural factors.[49] As the long east–west trade was the primary channel through which such a unified system was processed, earlier studies focused mainly on commercial activities in the Indian Ocean. Non-commercial cultural exchanges, including the expansion of communities of scholars and Sufis, later became a matter of serious investigation, at least since the last few decades.[50] Islam propagated by humdrum traders and peaceful sailors in the Indian Ocean was as much conspicuous and

[49] To mention a few works that followed the Braudelian model in the Indian Ocean, see, for example, the works of Bose, *A Hundred Horizons*; Chaudhuri, *Trade and Civilisation*; Chaudhuri, *Asia before Europe*; Ashin Das Gupta and Michael Pearson (eds), *India and the Indian Ocean, 1500–1800* (Calcutta: Oxford University Press, 1987); McPherson, *The Indian Ocean*; Pearson, *The Indian Ocean*; Pearson, *The World of the Indian Ocean.*

[50] A wide array of literature has recently been published on communities of commercial and non-commercial nature, such as Hadramis. For example, on Hadramis of the Indian Ocean, see Ulrike Freitag and William G. Clarence-Smith (eds), *Hadhrami Traders, Scholars and Statesmen in the Indian Ocean 1750s–1960s* (Leiden: Brill, 1997); Natalie Mobini-Kesheh, *The Hadrami Awakening: Community and Identity in the Netherlands East Indies, 1900–1942* (New York: Cornell University Press, 1999); Linda Boxberger, *On the Edge of Empire: Hadhramawt, Emigration and the Indian Ocean, 1880s–1930s* (New York: State University of New York Press, 2002); Ulrike Freitag, *Indian Ocean Migrants and State Formation in Hadhramaut: Reforming the Homeland* (Leiden: Brill, 2003); Bang, *Sufis and Scholars*; Ho, *Graves of Tarim*; Engseng Ho, 'Two Arms of Cambay: Diasporic Texts of Ecumenical Islam in the Indian Ocean', *Journal of Economic and Social History of the Orient* 50(2/3) (2007): 347–61.

uniform across coastal regions to be called 'Monsoon Islam'.[51] Such cultural and religious expansions through sea routes also led to an Arabic linguistic cosmopolis where the Arabic became a lingua franca and the main component in linguistic syncretic forms across the region.[52] Arabic interacted with indigenous languages giving Arabic scripts to vernacular languages, including Malayalam, Tamil, Java, etc. On similar lines, a legal cosmopolis of the Shāfiʿī School of jurisprudence is claimed to have existed in the region.[53]

These studies on the Indian Ocean, which have recently flourished over the last few decades, shed light on various aspects of the region. This new research provides us with an overview to comprehend this historical complexity of economic, socio-political, Sufi and legal aspects of Islam in the littoral world. An Indian Ocean perspective basically provides an understanding of the Indian Ocean as a historically and culturally unified territory. This perspective enables scholars of Islam and Muslim societies to have a comprehensive understanding of what we may call 'Monsoon Islam' preached mainly by traders, sojourning and diasporic communities. A comparative analysis of the historical accounts of an Islam that was conveyed very peacefully to maritime port cities in southern Arabia, east Africa, south India, southeast Asia and south China has to be guided by this maritime perspective. Interactions of Islam with these local socio-political contexts, cultural etiquettes and regional economies made distinctive experiences for emerging Muslim societies in these regions for diverse

51 Prange, *Monsoon Islam*, 3. It has been widely acclaimed that the Asian trade in the Indian Ocean before the advent of the Portuguese was relatively peaceable, see Chaudhuri *Trade and Civilisation*, 64; Janet L. Abu-Lughod, *Before European Hegemony* (New York: Oxford University Press, 1989), 276; Engseng Ho, 'Empire through Diasporic Eyes: A View from the Other Boat', *Comparative Studies in Society and History* 46, (2004): 217. However, Margariti has turned attention to how Indian Ocean states and merchant guilds were involved in adversarial and sometimes open conflict and competition though not challenging the relative peace that existed in the ocean. See Roxani Eleni Margariti, 'Mercantile Networks, Port Cities and "Pirate States": Conflict and Competition in the Indian Ocean World of Trade before the Sixteenth Century', *Journal of Economic and Social History of the Orient* 51(4) (2008), 543–77.

52 Ronit Ricci, *Islam Translated: Literature, Conversion and the Arabic Cosmopolis of South and Southeast Asia* (Chicago: University of Chicago Press, 2011).

53 Kooria, Mahmood, 'Cosmopolis of Law: Islamic Legal Texts and Ideas across the Indian Ocean and Eastern Mediterranean Worlds', PhD dissertation, University of Leiden, 2016.

engagements with textual as well as pre-textual (normative and explorative) realms of Islam. This highly complex process that Islam made through interactions with local cultures is comprehensible mainly by scholars focusing on Islam and its various explorative and normative sciences, rather than by historians who focus on legal, economic, socio-political and other aspects of history of Muslims in the Indian Ocean. Certain insights that an Indian Ocean perspective would shed light upon studies of Islam and Muslim societies in the region may be outlined as follows:

First, the Indian Ocean perspective helps to view comparatively how the religion was successful in engaging with local contexts and producing indigenous narratives in various locations of the region. Islam in almost all these coastal regions was able to cope with a number of challenges unprecedented in other land-based Muslim polities. In Java, for example, Islam has incorporated the traditional usage of shadow puppets (*wayang*) in Javanese music as 'categories of God's creatures' in Sufi cosmology.[54] Muslims in the region almost tried to incorporate and reinterpret their local contexts according to the textual and pre-textual recommendations of Islam. Conspicuous in the process is the very syncretic architectural styles of mosques in south India, Java and elsewhere, which adopted styles of Hindu and Buddhist religious structures but were able to survive as centres of Islam in these coastal towns. Although such cultural give and take is not exclusive to the littoral spaces, the traditional-style mosques across the coastal regions with multi-tiered extensive superstructure that allowed the passage of coastal breezes accorded to the very humid and rainy climates in these littoral places and enabled these mosques to work as learning centres as well as temporary accommodation for traders. As Ahmed explains in his definition of being Islamic as a meaning-making process, indigenous scholars in these regions were successful in finding meanings for these syncretic religious forms with Text, Pre-Text and Con-Text of Islam.[55]

[54] Petrus Josephus Zoetmulder, *Pantheism and Monism in Suluk Literature: Islamic and Indian Mysticism in an Indonesian Setting*, ed. and trans. M. C. Ricklefs (Leiden: KITLV Press, 1995), 245.

[55] Ahmed, *What is Islam?*, ch. 6.

Secondly, an Indian Ocean perspective will require us to see why matrilineal family inheritance as well as matriarchal political authority was equally legitimised in almost all societies across the region. Since male members of these littoral societies mostly leave for seafaring and maritime activities, their female members retained influential positions and even sometimes assumed political authority. Thus, most of the local scholarly writings in these regions legitimised matrilineal systems and foreign religious scholars, as Ibn Battuta also agreed to assume the position of Qadi under a female ruler in Maldives.[56] Similar questions attributed to matrilineal and matriarchal systems in littoral societies were addressed in most of these coastal centres of the Indian Ocean.

Thirdly, the religious uniformity of Islam in the Indian Ocean that is called forth by many of the Sufi orders and legal schools such as the Shāfiʿī School becomes clear with an overarching oceanic perspective that proposes a method of multi-sited ethnography. It informs that Sufi orders along with the Shāfiʿī School were successful in providing a uniformity for Islam in the region. Many of the Sufi texts have adopted local oceanic and littoral metaphors in the region. For example, we see Hamza Fansuri (d. 1527) and Zayn al-Dīn Makhdūm al-Kabīr (d. 1522) introduced Sufi thoughts that emerged in the Middle East into symbolic maritime metaphors such as whales in oceanic water and pearls as the experiences in the journey seeking the ultimate truth of Allah.[57]

Fourthly, approaching the diasporic communities sojourned and settled in these regions, who played a large part in shaping religious societies in the region with an Indian Ocean perspective, would unveil many political aspects that led to centuries of political as well as religious struggles in the region. A number of immigrant communities such as Hadramis were very much active in the socio-political realms and led anti-colonial struggles throughout the region, while a number of them could access the political echelons of the host society.[58] The rise of Arabs as Hadramis in southeast Asian polities led 'to incorporation of Islamic elements in the symbols of political power

[56] Ibn Battuta, *Rihala*, 142.

[57] Feener, 'South-East Asian Localisations of Islam', 472; al-Kabir, *Adhkiya*, 1–2.

[58] Ho, 'Empire through Diasporic Eyes', 567–91.

in Southeast Asian states'.[59] The political as well as religious influences that these societies adopted in the region such as their anti-colonial stand assuming influential political positions and their Sufi religious activities across the region become clear once we adopt an approach that helps to perceive the entire region as a coherent unit.

Fifthly, the linguistic cosmopolis such as the Arabic that works as a lingua franca and maintains a common thread connecting many vernacular linguistic expressions in the region also could be explored better through this perspective.[60] There has been a great trend of translation of Arabic scholarly texts and reproductions in the local language as well as localisation of ritual litanies especially since the sixteenth century, when indigenous scholars such as Qadi Muhammad in Calicut produced Sufi texts in Arabic–Malayalam and ʿAbdal Raʾūf al-Singkilī (d. 1693) in Aceh brought Qurʾānic interpretation as *Tarjumān al-Mustafid* in Malay.[61] Such vernacular productions of Islamic texts in east African, south Asian as well as southeast Asian languages and the role of Islam and its Arabic medium have to be approached with a coherent maritime perspective. Understanding Islam and its various vernacular literary productions in a connected littoral sphere of the Indian Ocean will help to comprehend not only the history of the region in novel ways but also the socio-political and religious contributions of Muslims in the region to Islam and Islamic sciences.

The scholarly contributions made in these regions to re-articulate certain legal as well as spiritual realms of Islam in maritime regional contexts would also be advanced with a unified Indian Ocean perspective. These scholarly productions, as Ahmed argued, are attempts to engage with the matrix of Text, Pre-Text and Con-Text. The maritime moment in the Con-Text engages with previous land-based interpretations as well as maritime explorations and helped Muslim societies in the Indian Ocean further their meaningful engagements with the littoral form of Islam. An Indian Ocean perspective will be

[59] Feener, 'South-East Asian Localisation', 495.

[60] Ricci, *Arabic Cosmpolis.*

[61] See Qadi Muhammad al-Kalikuti, *Muhyiddīn Māla*, manuscript not numbered, preserved at the Library of Shihāb al-Dīn Imbichi Koya Tangal, Calicut, not dated; Feener, 'South-East Asian Localisations of Islam', 492.

highly useful for understanding this much diversity as well as the unity that this vast littoral area of Asia provides for understanding of Islam and Muslims in general.

Ahmed's request to engage with both explorative and normative aspects of the religion becomes really crucial once we study Islam in the Indian Ocean.[62] Because, the process of Islamisation in the entire region was largely carried out through maritime activities and the establishment of Muslim polities where religious people such as the Sayyids, mosques and Sufi spiritual hospices played greater roles. The Sufi philosophical as well as artistic and aesthetic realms excelled in the region as the legal normative aspects. Likewise, since scholarly productions of Islam in the region exalted both the explorative Sufi ways and normative legal aspects of the religion in a uniform way across the entire Indian Ocean, Ahmed's insights are really promising in an Indian Ocean perspective that focuses the entire region. The larger framework of a unified Indian Ocean region enables the historical assessment of the process of Islamisation and scholarly contributions in a much-interconnected form.

## Conclusion

Islam in the Indian Ocean provides immense opportunities to decentralise studies of Islam and Muslims from the Middle East and its colonial Orientalist baggage. The socio-cultural patterns of Islam and Islamisation via traders in the region were distinctively unique from the spread of the religion elsewhere. While normative legal forms determine the nature of the religion in most of studies on Islam and Muslims, the Indian Ocean with its ample socio-cultural, Sufi artistic, aesthetic and other explorative realms provide ample opportunities to challenge the normative legal partiality in determining what Islam is. Unlike the legal obsession that carried along with the land-based polities of Islamic heartlands, Islam conveyed through common maritime actors not patronised by polities have paved the way for Sufi explorative realms in the region. Thus, the religion in the Indian Ocean is a big promising account to not only decentralise studies on Islam from the Middle East but also from the legalistic determinism.

[62] Al-Kalikuti, *Muhyiddīn Māla*, ch. 5.

It is also regrettably true that very rich and diverse scholarly contributions made from the region to both explorative and normative forms of Islamic disciplines have not gained adequate attention, despite some of the historically informed writings from the region. These scholarly texts written in various regions of the Indian Ocean were products of a necessity to connect their local contexts with the universal ideas of Islam, as some of the above examples of fatwas showed. Approaching such texts with a coherent Indian Ocean perspective would enable us to perceive how Islam engaged with vast littoral regions and its diverse cultural moorings. The matrilineal systems and syncretic institutions attached to the littoral aspects of the society in the region would have to be explored in the light of indigenous, hitherto unutilised, sources. As the studies of the Indian Ocean have been leaping ahead for the last few decades, more historical aspects of economic and non-economic interactions in the region have been revealed. A larger chunk of diverse scholarly contributions in various studies of Islam has been left totally to students of Islam. It is our duty as researchers of Islam and Muslims in the Indian Ocean to utilise emerging insights of the Indian Ocean perspective to locate Indian Ocean Islam in the larger studies of Islam and Muslims.

## Bibliography

Abou El Fadl, Khaled, 'Islamic Law and Muslim Minorities: The Juristic Discourse on Muslim Minorities from the Second/Eighth to the Eleventh/Seventeenth Centuries', *Islamic Law and Society* 1(2) (1994): 141–87.

Abu-Lughod, Janet L., *Before European Hegemony*. New York: Oxford University Press, 1989.

Ahmed, Shahab, *What is Islam?: The Importance of Being Islamic*. Princeton, NJ: Princeton University Press, 2016.

al-Kabīr, Zayn al-Dīn, *Adhkiyā'*. MS No. 432. Tanur: Valiyakulangara Palli, n.d.

al-Kālikūtī, Qāḍī Muḥammad ibn Qāḍī ʿAbd al-ʿAzīz, *Qaṣīda. Fatḥ al-Mubīn li al-Sāmirī al-ladhī Yuḥibbu al-Muslimīn*. Manuscript No. 85. Chaliyam: Dār al-Iftā' al-Azhariyya, n.d.

al-Khazrajī, Sheikh ʿAlī bin al-Ḥasan, *al-ʿUqūd al-Lu'lu'iyya fi Tārīkh al-Dawla al-Rasūliyya*, ed. Sheikh Muhammad Basyūnī ʿAsal, 2 vols. Miṣr: Matbaʿa al-Hilāl, 1914.

al-Maʿbarī, Sheikh Zayn al-Dīn bin Abd al-ʿAzīz bin Zayn al-Dīn bin ʿAlī, *Tuḥfa al-Mujāhidīn fi Baʿḍi Akhbār al-Burtughāliyyīn*. Hyderabad: Maṭbaʿ al-Tārīkh, 1931.

al- Maʿbarī, ʿAbd al-ʿAzīz bin Zayn bin ʿAlī bin Zayn al-Dīn Aḥmad, *Maslak al-Atqiyā' wa Manhaj al-Aṣfiyā' fī Sharaḥ Hidaya al-Adhkiya Ila Ṭarīqa al-Awliyā'*. Calicut: Tirurangadi Books, n.d.

al-Ṣaghīr, Sheikh Aḥmad Zayn al-Dīn al-Makhdūm al-Malibārī, *Al-Ajwiba al-ʿAjība ʿalā al-ʾAsʾila al-Gharība*. n.p.: Kunhi Muhammad al-Kodanchery and V. K Mūsān Kutty Musliyār, n.d.

al-Shāfiʿī, Aḥmad Shaykh Zayn al-Dīn bin ʿAbd al-ʿAzīz al-Maʿbarī al-Malaybārī al-Fonnānī, Muhammad al-Ghazālī, *Fatḥ al-Muʿīn bisharaḥ Qurrat al-ʿAyn bi Muhimmāt al-Dīn*. Calicut: Tirūrangādi Book Stall, 2006.

Anonymous, *Qiṣṣat Shakrwatī Farmāḍ*. Manuscript not numbered. Nellikuth: Muhammad Ali Musliyār Personal Library, n.d.

Asad, Talal, *The Idea of an Anthropology of Islam*. Washington, DC: Center for Contemporary Arab Studies, Georgetown University, 1986.

Asad, Talal, *Genealogies of Religion: Discipline and Reasons of Power in Christianity and Islam*. Baltimore, MD: Johns Hopkins University Press, 1993.

Bang, Anne K., *Sufis and Scholars of the Sea: Family Networks in East Africa, 1860–1925*. London: RoutledgeCurzon, 2003.

Barbosa, Duarte, *Description of the Coasts of East Africa and Malabar in the Beginning of the Sixteenth Century*. London: Hakluyt Society, 1866.

Bose, Sugata, *A Hundred Horizons: The Indian Ocean in the Age of Global Empire*. Cambridge, MA: Harvard University Press, 2006.

Bouchon, Genevieve, 'Sixteenth-Century Malabar and the Indian Ocean', in Ashin Das Gupta and M. N. Pearson (eds), *India and the Indian Ocean 1500–1800*. Calcutta: Oxford University Press, 1987, 71–93.

Braginsky, Vladimir, 'Sufi Boat Symbolism: Problems of Origin and Symbolism', *Indonesia and the Malay World* 26 (1998): 50–64.

Braudel, Fernand, *The Mediterranean and the Mediterranean World under the Age of Philip II*. Berkeley: University of California Press, 1995.

Chandra, Satish (ed.) *The Indian Ocean: Explorations in History, Commerce and Politics*. New Delhi: Sage Publications, 1987.

Chaudhuri, K. N., *Trade and Civilization in the Indian Ocean: An Economic History from the Rise of Islam to 1750*. Cambridge: Cambridge University Press, 1985.

Chaudhuri, Kirti N., *Asia before Europe: Economy and Civilization of the Indian Ocean from the Rise of Islam to 1750*. Cambridge: Cambridge University Press, 1990.

Dasgupta, Uma (ed.), *The World of the Indian Ocean Merchant 1500–1800: Collected Essays of Ashin Das Gupta*. New Delhi: Oxford University Press, 2001.

Drewes, G. W. J. and L. F. Brakel (eds), *The Poems of Hamzah Fansuri*. Foris: Dordrecht, 1986.

Eickelman, Dale F. and James Piscatori (eds), *Muslim Travellers: Pilgrimage, Migration, and the Religious Imagination*. Berkeley: University of California Press, 1990.

El-Zein, Abdul Hamid, 'Beyond Ideology and Theology: The Search for the Anthropology of Islam', *Annual Review of Anthropology* 6 (1977): 227–52.

Feener, Michael, 'Abd al-Samad in Arabia: The Yemeni Years of a Shaykh from Sumatra', *Southeast Asian Studies* 4 (2015): 259–77.

Feener, Michael, 'South-East Asian Localisation of Islam and Participation within a Global Umma C. 1500–1800', in David O. Morgan and Anthony Reid (eds), *The New Cambridge History of Islam*. Cambridge: Cambridge University Press, 2010.

Feener, R. M. and M. F. Laffan, 'Sufi Scents across the Indian Ocean: Yemeni Hagiography and the Earliest History of Southeast Asian Islam', *Archipel* 70 (2005): 185–208.

Formichi, Chiara, *Islam and Asia: A History*. New York: Cambridge University Press, 2020.

Friedmann, Y., 'Qiṣṣat Shakarwatī Farmāḍ: A Tradition Concerning the Introduction of Islām to Malabar', *Israel Oriental Studies* 5 (1975): 233–58.

Geertz, Clifford, *Islam Observed: Religious Development in Morocco and Indonesia*. New Haven, CT: Yale University Press, 1968.

Geertz, Clifford, *The Interpretation of Cultures*. New York: Basic Books, 1973.

Green, Nile, *Making Space: Sufis and Settlers in Early Modern India*. New Delhi: Oxford University Press, 2012.

Gupta, Ashin Das, 'Malabar in c. 1740', in Uma Das Gupta (ed.), *The World of the Indian Ocean Merchant 1500–1800*. New Delhi: Oxford University Press, 2001, 421–56.

Gupta, Ashin Das and M. N. Pearson (eds), *India and the Indian Ocean 1500–1800*. Calcutta: Oxford University Press, 1987.

Ho, Engseng, 'Empire through Diasporic Eyes: A View from the Other Boat', *Comparative Studies in Society and History* 46 (2004): 210–46.

Ho, Engseng, *The Graves of Tarim: Genealogy and Mobility across the Indian Ocean*. Berkeley: University of California Press, 2006.

Ho, Engseng, 'Two Arms of Cambay: Diasporic Texts of Ecumenical Islam in the Indian Ocean', *Journal of Economic and Social History of the Orient* 50(2/3) (2007): 347–61.

Hodgson, Marshall G. S., *The Venture of Islam: Conscience and History in a World Civilization, Vol. 1: The Classical Age of Islam*. Chicago: University of Chicago Press, 1974.

Hodgson, Marshall G. S., *The Venture of Islam: Conscience and History in a World Civilization, Vol. 2: The Expansion of Islam in the Middle Periods*. Chicago: University of Chicago Press, 1974.

Ibn Battuta, Abu Abd Allah bin Muhammad al-Lawāttī, *Riḥla ibn Baṭūṭa ʿAjāib al-Amsār wa Gharā'ib al-Asfār*. Miṣr: al-Maṭbaʿ al-Khayriyya, 1905.

Kathirithamby-Wells, J., '"Strangers" and "Stranger-kings": The Sayyid in Eighteenth-Century Maritime Southeast Asia', *Journal of Southeast Asian Studies* 40(3) (2009): 567–91.

Kooria, Mahmood and Michael N. Pearson (eds), *Malabar in the Indian Ocean: Cosmopolitanism in a Maritime Historical Region*. New Delhi: Oxford University Press, 2018.

Lombard, Denys and Jean Aubin (eds), *Asian Merchants and Businessmen in the Indian Ocean and the China Sea*. New Delhi: Oxford University Press, 2000.

Margariti, Roxani Eleni, 'Mercantile Networks, Port Cities and "Pirate States": Conflict and Competition in the Indian Ocean World of Trade before the Sixteenth Century', *Journal of Economic and Social History of the Orient* 51(4) (2008): 543–77.

McPherson, Kenneth, *The Indian Ocean: A History of People and the Sea*. Delhi: Oxford University Press, 1993.

Mukherjee, Rudrangshu and Lakshmi Subramanian (eds), *Politics and Trade in the Indian Ocean: Essays in Honour of Ashin Das Gupta*. Delhi: Oxford University Press, 1999.

Nainar, S. Muhammad Husayn, *Shaykh Zainuddin Makhdum's Tuḥfatul Mujāḥidīn: A Historical Epic of the Sixteenth Century*, trans. from Arabic with annotation by S. Muhammad Husayn Nainar. Calicut: Other Books, 2005.

Osman, M. T., 'Islamization of the Malays', in A. Ibrahim et al. (eds), *Readings on Islam in Southeast Asia*. Singapore: Institute of Southeast Asia Studies, 1985.

Panikkar, K. M., *Malabar and the Portuguese*. New Delhi: Voice of India, 1997.

Pearson, Michael, *Pious Passengers: The Hajj in Earlier Times*. New Delhi: Sterling Publishers, 1994.

Pearson, Michael, *The Indian Ocean*. London: Routledge, 2003.

Pearson, Michael, *The World of the Indian Ocean, 1500–1800: Studies in Economic, Social and Cultural History*. Burlington, VT: Ashgate, 2005.

Pokkanali, Jahfar Shareef, 'Sailing across Duniyav: Sufi Ship–Body Symbolism from the Malabar Coast, South India', *South Asian Studies* 41 (2018): 1–14.

Pollock, Sheldon, *The Language of the Gods in the World of Men: Sanskrit, Culture, and Power in Premodern India*. Berkeley: University of California Press, 2006.

Prange, Sebastian R., *Monsoon Islam: Trade and Faith on the Medieval Malabar Coast*. Cambridge: Cambridge University Press, 2018.

Reid, Anthony, 'Islamization and Christianization in Southeast Asia: The Critical Phase, 1559–1650', in Anthony Reid (ed.), *Southeast Asia in the Early Modern Era: Trade, Power and Belief*. Ithaca, NY: Cornell University Press, 1993, 151–79.

Reid, Anthony, 'Islamization in Southeast Asia: Reflections and Reconsiderations with Special Reference to the Role of Sufism', *Southeast Asian Studies* 31(1) (1993): 43–61.

Ricklefs M. C., *Mystic Synthesis in Java: A History of Islamization from the Fourteenth to the Early Nineteenth Centuries*. Norwalk, CT: EastBridge, 2006.

Risso, Patricia, *Merchants and Faith: Muslim Commerce and Culture in the Indian Ocean*. Oxford: Oxford West View Press, 1995.

Shokoohy, Mehrdad, *Muslim Architecture of South India: The Sultanate of Maʿbar and the Tradition of the Maritime Settlers on the Malabar and Coromandel Coasts (Tamil Nadu, Kerala and Goa)*, London: Routledge Curzon, 2003.

Varisco, Daniel Martin, *Islam Obscured: The Rhetoric of Anthropological Representation*. New York: Palgrave Macmillan, 2005.

Wink, André, *Al-Hind: The Making of the Indo-Islamic World, Vol. 1: Early Medieval and Expansion of Islam 7th–11th Centuries*. Leiden: Brill, 1990.

Zoetmulder, Petrus Josephus, *Pantheism and Monism in Suluk Literature: Islamic and Indian Mysticism in an Indonesian Setting*, ed. and trans. M. C. Ricklefs. Leiden: KITLV Press, 1995.

# 11

# INCLUDING LOCALISED ISLAMIC CONCEPTS IN THE STUDY OF ISLAM

CLAUDIA SEISE

## Introduction

Islam, as a revealed religion, has its roots in the Hijaz, a region in the west of present-day Saudi Arabia. From there it spread to all parts of the Middle East, central and south Asia, southeast Asia, and the rest of the world. From the very beginning, translocal contact and connections[1] within the *umma* (the Muslim community) was maintained and strengthened through the main centre, the common *qibla* or direction of prayer in Mecca, home of the Kaʿba and destination of the hajj. This contact was also strengthened and maintained through various intellectual centres that were established over time in the Middle East and other regions. Despite being centred on the Hijaz, the Muslim world has always been polycentric and highly interconnected on different spatial scales. Although ritually Mecca is considered the centre of the Muslim world, different views on Islamic space do exist.[2]

[1] On translocality, see Ulrike Freitag and Achim von Oppen, *Translocality: The Study of Globalising Processes from a Southern Perspective* (Leiden: Brill, 2010), 1–21.

[2] Dale F. Eickelman and James Piscatori, 'Social Theory in the Study of Muslim Societies', in *Muslim Travellers: Pilgrimage, Migration and the Religious Imagination* (London: University of California Press, 1990), 12–15.

Situated at a geographical distance of the so-called 'central lands' of the Islamicate civilisation in the Middle East[3] and on the geographic extremities of the Muslim world.[4] Indonesia is often perceived as being located on the periphery by the rest of the Muslim world;[5] however, Indonesia is nevertheless seen as a major centre of Islamic knowledge by many Indonesian Muslims.[6] Scattered references in Chinese court chronicles and epigraphic evidence from the region hint at the presence of Muslims in the ports of the Indonesian archipelago since the first centuries of Islamic history. However, according to Feener, only at the end of the thirteenth century, did quantitatively significant local conversions to Islam take place.[7] From the seventeenth century onwards, various local Islamic Nusantara[8] scholars have been known beyond present-day Indonesia and Malaysia, especially in the established centres of Islamic thought in Mecca and Cairo.[9] The opening of the Suez

[3] Michael R. Feener, 'South-East Asian Localisations of Islam and Participation within a Global Umma, c. 1500–1800', in D. O. Morgan and A. Reid (eds), *The New Cambridge History of Islam* (Cambridge: Cambridge University Press, 2010), 470.

[4] Christopher M. Joll, 'Local and Global Islams in Southeast Asia: Historical and Anthropological Perspectives', in Z. Ibrahim (ed.), *Social Science and Knowledge in a Globalising World* (Selangor: PSSM/SIRDC, 2012), 237.

[5] Eickelman, and Piscatori, 'Social Theory in the Study of Muslim Societies', 12–14; Joll, 'Local and Global Islams', 219–21.

[6] Ronald Lukens-Bull, *A Peaceful Jihad: Negotiating Identity and Modernity in Muslim Java* (London: Palgrave Macmillan, 2005), 1–152; Mark R. Woodward, 'The Slametan: Textual Knowledge and Ritual Performance in Yogyakarta', in Mark R.Woodward (ed.), *Java, Indonesia and Islam* (Berlin: Springer, 2011), 113–36; E. Srimuliyani, *Women from Traditional Islamic Educational Institutions in Indonesia: Negotiating Public Space* (Amsterdam: Amsterdam University Press, 2012), 36–62; Claudia Seise, *Religioscapes in Muslim Indonesia: Personalities, Institutions and Practices* (Berlin: Regiospectra, 2017), 1–293.

[7] Feener, 'South-East Asian Localisations of Islam', 471. He further remarks that only the political and mercantile elites of select maritime entrepôts converted to Islam at the end of the thirteenth century.

[8] When I use the term Nusantara, I refer to the Muslim archipelago of southeast Asia, including Indonesia, Malaysia, Singapore, Brunei Darussalam and arguably south Thailand.

[9] Azyumardi Azra, *The Origins of Islamic Reformism in Southeast Asia Networks of Malay–Indonesian and Middle Eastern 'Ulamā' in the Seventeenth and Eighteenth Centuries* (Malbourne: Asian Studies Assn. of Australia in assoc. with Allen & Unwin, 2004), 8–108; Michael Laffan, *The Makings of Indonesian Islam: Orientalism and the Narration of a Sufi Past*

Canal in 1869 and the introduction of modern steamers in the decades that followed made travel and exchange of ideas between Nusantara and the Middle East more frequent. Islamic knowledge in Indonesia is transmitted and learned in the thousands of local boarding schools (*pesantren*)[10] and, similar to other parts of the Muslim world, in informal study circles and the family.

Scholars of southeast Asian studies have given some attention to the study of Islam in the region. However, many scholars share the perception that Muslim southeast Asia is located on the Muslim periphery, both geographically as well as religiously. In my view, part of this scholarship has established and contributed to the notion that Islam in southeast Asia is qualitatively different and somewhat 'less Islamic' than the Islam found in the Arabic-speaking world due to 'ahistorical and essentialized understandings of "Islam" conceptualized in relation to a rather limited range of modern reformist conceptions that persist across various academic fields, as well as in popular perceptions.'[11] This narrative is also echoed in contemporary transnational Islamic movements that can be counted as belonging to the Salafi–Wahhabi School of thought and strongly criticise different localised Islamic practices as being syncretic and unlawful innovations (*bid'a sayyi'a*). Different religious groups in the region of Nusantara that ascribe to Salafi–Wahhabi thought

(Princeton, NJ: Princeton University Press, 2011), 3–39; Joll, 'Local and Global Islams', 221–8. There exists proof of a Sufi sheikh with a connection to southeast Asia that is dated as early as the late thirteenth century. For a detailed discussion, see Feener, 'South-East Asian Localisations of Islam', 471.

10 See, for example, Nurcholis Madjid, 'Merumuskan Kembali Tujuan Pendidikan Pesantren', in D.M. Rahardjo (ed.), *Pergulatan Dunia Pesantren: Membangun Dari Bawah* (Jakarta: Perhimpunan Pengembangan Pesantren dan Masyarakat, 1985); Martin van Bruinessen, 'Pesantren and Kitab Kuning: Maintenance and Continuation of a Tradition of Religious Learning', in W. Marshall (ed.), *Texts from the Islands: Oral and Written Traditions of Indonesia and the Malay World* (Bern: University of Bern, 1994), 121–45; Martin van Bruinessen, 'Traditionalist and Islamist Pesantren in Contemporary Indonesia', in A.N. Farish (ed.), *The Madrasa in Asia: Political Activism and Transnational Linkages* (Amsterdam: Amsterdam University Press, 2008), 217–47; Ivan A. Hadar, *Bildung in Indonesien: Krise und Kontinuität: Das Beispiel Pesantren* (Frankfurt: IKO-Verlag für Interkulturelle Kommunikation, 1999); Lukens-Bull, *A Peaceful Jihad*; Srimuliyani, *Women from Traditional Islamic Educational Institutions.*

11 Feener, 'South-East Asian Localisations of Islam', 470.

oppose all forms of traditional, localised Islamic practices such as the ritual reading of sura Yasin after a person's death, which, according to their point of view, are not rooted firmly in the *sunna* of the Prophet Muḥammad.[12]

The issue above can also be observed in the discussion about the global and the local with regard to Islam in Indonesia.[13] However, I suggest that these terms should not be understood hierarchically; global Islam should not be considered as being superior in terms of piety and purity and local Islam as being adulterated with pre-Islamic or non-Islamic rituals. In addition, local forms of Islam should not be assumed to contradict the so-called scriptural or normative Islam.[14] In this context, Hefner argues that Muslim societies in southeast Asia suffer a dual marginalisation at the hands of both

[12] Claudia Seise, 'The Transformational Power of Barokah and Silaturahmi in Muslim Indonesia', *International Journal of Islam in Asia* 1 (2021): 1–21. The following critique has been put forward in anti-Wahhabi circles since the eighteenth century: the Wahhabis interpret the Qur'ān according to personal opinion, they disrespect the Prophet, they do not respect the views of authoritative *'ulamā'*, and they consider only those believers who agree with them (David Commins, *The Wahhabi Mission and Saudi Arabia* (London: I. B. Tauris, 2006), 136.

[13] Redfield proposed specifically local variants or 'little' traditions to occur alongside globally normative 'great' traditions (Robert Redfield, *Peasant Society and Culture* (Chicago: University of Chicago Press, 1956), 72). Geertz put forward the conception of Javanese Islam as being a cultural complex consisting of an *abangan* substratum onto which Hindu, then Islamic, structures were built. He described three distinct traditions: those of the village *abangan* (non- or little practising Muslims); the practising Muslims or *santri*; and the *prijaji* who were the elites and practised Javanese syncretism (Clifford Geertz, *The Religion of Java* (Chicago: University of Chicago Press, 1960), 5–7). Geertz also noted that both in Java and in Morocco, Islamic mysticism was more susceptible to particularisation than what he termed 'scripturalist' Islam (Clifford Geertz, *Islam Observed* (New Haven, CT: Yale University Press, 1968), 11–13). Joll remarked that the most enduring criticisms of Geertz are his exaggerated Hindu–Buddhist influences, oversimplified Islamic ones and his preference to speak in terms of a split – rather than pluralism – existing within Islamic traditions (Joll, 'Local and Global Islams', 219–42). See also Mark R. Woodward, *Islam in Java: Normative Piety and Mysticism in the Sultanate of Yogyakarta* (Tucson: University of Arizona Press, 1989), 1–311; Martin van Bruinessen, 'Global and Local in Indonesian Islam', *Southeast Asian Studies* 37(2) (1999): 158–75.

[14] Andre Möller, *Ramadan in Java: The Joy and Jihad of Ritual Fasting* (Lund: University of Lund, 2005), 23.

anthropologists and religious historians.[15] The latter perceive Islam as an intrusive cultural force or an ill-fitting and improperly worn outer garment, which led to the former privileging the local over the global, while making only occasional reference to Islam. Neglect by historians permits accusations of the peripheral nature of Islam in southeast Asia where Islamic faith and practice are more 'diluted' than in the Middle East, which is still considered the centre of the Muslim world.[16] This point has also been stressed by Feener, a trained historian, who argued that it would be mistaken to assume religious texts and traditions of the southeast Asian region are 'necessarily "less Islamic" than those of Muslim societies in the Middle East, or that Islam was merely a "thin, flaking veneer" upon more solid foundations of Indic and local cultures.'[17] To consolidate the above discussion, it is useful to understand that Islam was spread in a lateral manner. Local customs and traditions (Ind. *adat*) were negotiated, adopted, Islamised, kept or discarded and influenced how Islamic teachings were appropriated and localised.[18]

Writing about localised Islamic concepts and local concepts connected to Islam, I aim to provide a non-hierarchical perspective of Islamic perceptions and practices (as opposed to Redfield's conceptualisation of little and great tradition) that provides a unique Islamic perspective situated in the region of Nusantara and modern-day Indonesia. Rather than focusing on the distinctively local Muslim ritual complexes, something critically observed by Bowen among anthropologists studying Islam, I wish to also highlight the commonalities, certain rituals and practices shared with Muslim orthodoxy

[15] Robert W. Hefner, 'Islam in an Era of Nation-States: Politics and Religious Renewal in Muslim Southeast Asia', in H. W. Robert and P. Horvatich (eds), *Islam in an Era of Nation-States: Politics and Religious Renewal in Muslim Southeast Asia* (Honolulu: University of Hawaii Press, 1997), 3–40.

[16] In Joll, 'Local and Global Islams', 219. Additional binaries to local and global Islam include official/normative/universalist/formal/scholarly Islam versus popular/local/received/informal/folk Islam (230). Other categories describing Muslims in post-colonial Indonesia include *santri* versus *abangan*, traditionalist versus modernist, political versus cultural Muslim, fundamentalist versus liberal, great tradition versus little tradition, and local versus global Islam (Muhamad Ali, 'Categorizing Muslims in Postcolonial Indonesia', *Moussons* 11 (2007): 22–62.

[17] Feener, 'South-East Asian Localisations of Islam', 470.

[18] I thank Vincent Houben for drawing my attention to this point.

and orthopraxy in other geographical areas.[19] Furthermore, while analysing localised Islamic concepts and local concepts connected to Islam, I aim to address the creative tensions that exist between the above mentioned binary terminologies that try to fit a lived reality into certain pre-perceived perceptions.[20] At the same time, my analysis has the potential to add an alternative interpretation and perspective to the different regional socio-religious phenomena observed.

## Localised Islamic Concepts from the Perspective of New Area Studies

Southeast Asian area studies occupy a clear-cut epistemological terrain, focusing on human world-making within the geographical region conventionally labelled southeast Asia. Area in this context is defined as a location from which perspectives on the world emerge that are different from those in other areas of the world.[21] This is also applicable to Islamic concepts and practices and their unique localisation or situatedness in the Indonesian *religioscape*[22] as well as local concepts connected to Islam. I argue that the concept of *religioscapes* and their unique character within the area reflect the historically cultivated plural

[19] John R. Bowen, *Muslims through Discourse: Religion and Ritual in Gayo Society* (Princeton, NJ: Princeton University Press, 1993), 4.

[20] Möller, *Ramadan in Java*, 53.

[21] 'Following up on current debates in the field of geography, area should be understood in the chronotopical sense, as a temporal–spatial constellation within which various time dimensions and spatial scales, ranging from local to global, intersect. This idea of area is open to human mobility as well as translocal and transregional dimensions.' (Vincent Houben, 'New Area Studies as an Emerging Discipline: The Way Ahead for Southeast Asian Studies', *International Quarterly for Asian Studies* 51(3/4) (2020): 53).

[22] My definition of *religioscapes* reads as follows: 'Religioscapes are dynamic social spaces where one religious practice and/or religious interpretation is predominant. Religioscapes are neither purely static nor entirely fluid. Cultivated historically, they include movement, change, and transformation, as well as continuity and stability of religious practices and interpretations. Religioscapes are influenced by individuals and influence individuals. This constitutes a mutual process. Religioscapes can extend and shrink depending on the individuals' preference, influence and connections within it. Different religioscapes can exist within one geographical region and several religioscapes can overlap. Religioscapes allow for an analysis and understanding about relations and dynamics between different spatial scales ranging from the local to the global' (Seise, *Religioscapes*, 30–1).

character of Islamic practices in Indonesia and point to an ongoing pluriformity of Islamic interpretations, teachings and practices in the present day. However, individual *religioscapes*, besides reflecting a unique singular religious landscape surrounding a person, have in common certain markers that point to the same specific situatedness of a geographical area. Localised Islamic concepts and local concepts connected to Islam form such common markers.[23] For the area of Nusantara and especially Indonesia, I refer to *silaturahmi* (brotherly bond), *barokah* (blessing), *rasa* (feeling) and the quest for harmony as common markers for a plurality of different *religioscapes* in the region.[24]

Concerning the local, Baumann stresses that the question about what the local is needs to be specified with regard to each individual research interest. Local in my research includes the greater region of Nusantara, with strong focus on Yogyakarta in central Java and Palembang in south Sumatra. To use Baumann's words, I was emplaced in the 'here' of the local as opposed to seeing the local as 'there'.[25]

When analysing localised Islamic concepts and local concepts within the framework of New Area Studies[26] it is important to understand that their theory is not based upon a singular discipline from humanities or social sciences, but is rather considered to be a cross-disciplinary,[27] or an interdisciplinary,

[23] In Indonesia there also exist normative Islamic values that are universally understood and applied in the daily life of any practising Indonesian Muslim include *taqwā* (piety), *tawakkul* (trusting in Allah's plans), *ḥayā'* (sense of shame; modesty), *iḥsān* (excellence of behaviour; doing good deeds), and a relational connectedness to fellow Muslims also referred to as *ukhuwwa islāmiyya* (for further discussion, see Seise, Religioscapes, 192–202).

[24] *Rasa* is a concept more prevalent in Javanese culture.

[25] Benjamin Baumann et al., '"Small Places, Large Issues" Revisited: Reflections on an Ethnographically Founded Vision of New Area Studies', *International Quarterly for Asian Studies* 51(3/4) (2020): 8.

[26] At the core of New Area Studies theory and methodology lies 'the aim of finding relational spatiotemporal outcomes instead of making static, singular and generalized claims of truth. The main subject matter, focusing on processes of world-making within a perspectival time-space constellation called "area", puts human agency and positionality at the centre of the scientific effort.' The adoption of a kaleidoscopic dialectic is the principle of generating knowledge with a comparative perspective. (Houben, 'Emerging Discipline', 56).

[27] Peter A. Jackson, 'South East Asian Area Studies beyond Anglo-America: Geopolitical Transitions, the Neoliberal Academy and Spatialized Regimes of Knowledge', *South East Asia Research* 27(1) (2019): 50.

endeavour, allowing for 'new' knowledge to emerge.[28] Trained in area studies with focus on southeast Asia, I have adopted the practice of incorporating local concepts into my theoretical and analytical framework. During my doctoral research, local and localised concepts and values became an additional focus. Thus, the arguments put forward in this chapter reflect a continuous pondering on how local and localised concepts have influenced and shaped Islam in Indonesia. My use of different methods is reflected in the situational analysis as developed by Clarke.[29] In addition, I make use of the research methods specific to area studies.[30] Taking a view from the inside, emic or local concepts constitute an important part of area study findings. These local concepts must be translated and used to analyse and further explain the research findings. Local and localised concepts can best be analysed with an area studies' perspective that has a certain space instead of a particular thematic field as a venture point rather than using preconceived knowledge, including aims and methods, as its point of departure.[31]

This chapter is an attempt to analyse and translate local and localised concepts with different spaces in Indonesia as venture points. *Silaturahmi* and *barokah*[32] are two concepts that can both be viewed as local concepts as well as localised Islamic concepts, depending on our perspective. As localised Islamic concepts and local concepts they are unique to Indonesia and the

[28] Houben, 'Emerging Discipline', 54.

[29] Adele A. Clarke, *Situational Analysis in Practice: Mapping Research with Grounded Theory* (London: SAGE Publishing, 2005), 1–347. Situational analysis ultimately aims at the production of situated knowledge, marked by place, time and circumstance. The aim is not to separate object from subject, micro from macro, individual from society, but rather to show the ways in which these are intertwined (Aleah Connley, 'Politicising Piety in Provincial Indonesia: Towards a Theory of the Dynamics of Local Politics and Islam', PhD dissertation,. Institute for Asian and African Studies, Humboldt University, 2019, 72–80; as in Houben, 'New Area Studies', 56).

[30] Vincent Houben, 'The New Area Studies and Southeast Asian History', *Dorisea Working Paper* 4 (2013): 3.

[31] Houben, 'The New Area Studies and Southeast Asian History', 3.

[32] From the Arabic word *baraka*, which means 'blessing' and is recognised as such by Muslims worldwide. The Indonesian transliteration *barokah* used in this text refers to the concept as understood by Indonesian Muslims.

greater Nusantara region in their specific use and significance. However, they do not exist by and of themselves; instead, they consist of a multitude of relations that are situated not at the level of totality but at the level of specificity.[33] This point reflects back to connections within the wider Muslim community and their specific localisations of Islamic concepts, rituals and practices. In this sense, analysing localised Islamic concepts and local concepts connected to Islam is a form of uncovering (opening up) structured differences[34] in Islamic understandings and practices within the particular region of Nusantara and Indonesia. Furthermore, using the term localised Islamic concepts means that I acknowledge the fact that Indonesia, as a majority-Muslim country, has contributed to the knowledge world[35] of Islam, although located on the periphery of the Muslim world. More Muslims live in the region of southeast Asia than in the Middle East, making it ever more important to pay close attention to local formations of localised concepts grounded in orthodox Islamic teachings.

Concerning the localisation of Islam in Indonesia, Feener argues that the early history of translating Islamic teachings into the Javanese cultural milieu 'can be seen in surviving manuscripts that contain religious texts in Arabic, accompanied by interlinear glosses in Javanese. It is texts of this type that provide some of our best evidence for the early stages of the "Islamization" of Java, and the "localization of Islam" there.'[36] Early examples of Islamic religious texts in Arabic that were translated and adapted into southeast Asian languages, especially Malay, include the creed of al-Nasafi (d. 1142), and the 'Mantle' poem (*qaṣīda al-burda*) in praise of the Prophet by al-Buṣīrī (d. 1296). One of the oldest translations in Javanese is strongly influenced by the

[33] Boike Rehbein, *Critical Theory after the Rise of the Global South: Kaleidoscopic Dialectic* (Abingdon: Routledge, 2015), 1–17.

[34] Elucidating structured differences is part of the aim of mid-range concepts that area studies are engaged with (Houben, 'New Area Studies and Southeast Asian History', 9).

[35] Liam C. Kelley introduced the term 'knowledge worlds' in his keynote speech, Liam C. Kelley, '"Localization" and "Knowledge Worlds" in the Southeast Asian Past and Present', keynote speech presented at the 3rd Engaging with Vietnam: An Interdisciplinary Dialogue Conference, Vietnam National University, Hanoi, 4 December 2011.

[36] Feener, 'South-East Asian Localisations of Islam', 475.

works of al-Ghazālī (d. 1111).[37] Historically, local forms of art and literary expressions like poetry (*syair* in Malay and *suluk* in Javanese), music, shadow-puppet theatre (*wayang kulit*) or dance were used to transmit Islamic teachings. It is these different expressions that are often mentioned when referring to localised Islam. Rather than being passive recipients of what is referred to as global or normative Islam, van Bruinessen argues that southeast Asian Muslims have incorporated Islam into their existing religious and cultural traditions through the process of negotiation and modification. These processes of negotiation and modification can also be referred to as localisation.[38]

When I use the term localised Islamic concepts, I talk about concepts that are rooted in the orthodox Islamic tradition and that can be found in the Qurʾān or the *sunna*, transmitted practices and sayings, of the Prophet Muḥammad. These orthodox Islamic concepts were then adapted to the specific situatedness of the Nusantara region and especially present-day Indonesia. This includes the adaption of concepts to the traditional epistemological framework of the region.[39] Through the process of situated adaption and embodiment, these localised concepts then received an additional layer of meaning and orthopraxy as will become clearer in the discussion below. I see local concepts connected to Islam like *rasa* and the quest for harmony as native to a particular geographical region that were then appropriated within an Islamic context.

By analysing and discussing localised Islamic concepts, I aim to show that certain orthodox Islamic teachings were developed within Muslim southeast Asia, and especially in Indonesia, that have the potential to contribute to a

[37] Feener, 'South-East Asian Localisations of Islam', 473.

[38] Bruinessen, 'Global and Local in Indonesian Islam', 163–4.

[39] Examples of this epistemological framework include a strong tendency to structure reality according to a binary worldview of male and female, in which created entities are thought of as having male and female qualities. Another example is Javanese cosmology that teaches that humanity is the youngest of creation and therefore needs to learn from the other and older creation. The relationship between humanity and other created things is that of being brethren (Javanese: *sedulur*). This local epistemological framework influences how new concepts are appropriated and localised. I will not provide a deeper analysis of the epistemological framework and its relation in this chapter since this would go beyond the topic under discussion.

deeper understanding of these teachings. Localised Islamic concepts form a specific expression and embodiment of Islam in a particular situatedness of knowledge and have the potential to contribute to the greater discourse of understanding, interpreting and negotiating Islamic concepts and teaching.[40] Furthermore, local concepts connected to Islam provide us with an additional layer of understanding how Islam in a particular locality or area is practiced and enriched with local wisdom and traditions. Analysing and understanding both localised Islamic concepts as well as local concepts connected to Islam are done in relation to place and time while taking into account concrete practices connected to these concepts. Focusing on localised Islamic concepts and local concepts connected to Islam is inspired by the idea of developing a 'view from within'.[41] To arrive at such a view an acquisition of 'thick knowledge' is a prerequisite and can be acquired only through the mastery of the language and an emersion in the locality through long-term field research. Thick knowledge can be obtained only if the researcher understands what Wittgenstein referred to as language games.[42] According to Wittgenstein, we are able to understand the meaning of a word only if we are accustomed to its associated practice.[43] This resonates strongly with my aim to analyse and understand localised Islamic practices and local practices connected to Islam in the specific situatedness of Indonesia. The examples of localised Islamic and local concepts connected to Islam discussed in this chapter emerged during my long-term research stays in Indonesia between 2010 and 2019. It was during these stays that I engaged in a process that historians refer to as an 'explaining kind of Verstehen'.[44] In this sense, intercultural *Verstehen* (understanding) requires 'reflexive conditioning, in the sense that cognition of the other presupposes reflection of the self, and also

[40] Katja Mielke and Anna-Katharina Hornige, *Area Studies at the Crossroads: Knowledge Production after the Mobility Turn* (London: Palgrave Macmillan, 2017), 19.

[41] Houben, 'New Area Studies, Translation', 202.

[42] Ludwig Wittgenstein, *Philosophische Untersuchungen – Philosophical Investigations*, trans. G. E. M. Anscombe, 2nd edn (Oxford: Oxford University Press, 1999).

[43] Boike Rehbein and Gernot Saalmann (eds), *Verstehen* (Konstanz: UVK, 2009), 53.

[44] Ulrich Muhlack, 'Verstehen', in H-J. Goertz (ed.), *Geschichte. Ein Grundkur* (Berlin: Rowohlt, 2007), as cited in Houben, 'New Area Studies and Southeast Asian History', 6.

entails a rejection of essentializing strategies which reduces the complexity of the other'.[45] As a Muslim researcher, I engaged deeply in the 'explaining kind of Verstehen' of the concepts discussed here. I did this to the point that I embodied the concepts I had encountered to the extent that I was able to arrive at an understanding that encompassed the interior of these concepts as they were becoming a part of my own lived reality in the local here. Connected to this last point, it is necessary to make some additional remarks concerning my identity as a Muslim researcher, which were part of an article about reflections on insider and outsider research.[46] My religion is attached to me; similar as not-believing is attached to other researchers. My religion influences the topics I choose for research, the way I conduct research, the way I talk to my informants, the way I analyse my data and the way I eventually write about my research. Here, the religious or believing researcher is not different to the atheist or agnostic researcher. True believing or not believing as it is, is something very personal. These considerations also echo Edward Said: 'No one has ever devised a method for detaching the scholar from the circumstances of life, from the fact of his involvement (conscious or unconscious) with a class, a set of beliefs, a social position, or from the mere activity of being a member of society.'[47] Therefore, my religion is attached to me; similarly as not-believing is attached to other researchers. The researcher cannot be detached from circumstances of life, and for the current case especially religion.

Discovering and understanding localised Islamic concepts, however, does not presuppose the assumption that local actors are aware of the unique localisation of the Islamic concepts they use, embody and interact with on a daily basis. Rather, the concepts introduced and discussed in this chapter are mostly naturalised in such a profound way that they are viewed as authentic Islamic teachings. This means that local actors oftentimes are not aware of the translocal root and character of the concepts they apply in everyday life, and

[45] Rehbein and Saalmann, *Verstehen*, as cited in Houben, 'New Area Studies and Southeast Asian History', 6.

[46] Claudia Seise, 'The Muslim Researcher: Reflections on Insider/ Outsider Research in Indonesia', *Journal of Islam in Asia* 16(1) (2019): 306–7.

[47] Edward Said, *Orientalism* (London: Routledge & Kegan Paul, 1978), 18.

also that the local or localised is viewed as orthodox Islam. The naturalisation of localised concepts and local concepts connected to Islam mainly occurs through repeated action and embodiment, which in turn shapes their world-making.[48] In the following section I will briefly outline the above-mentioned concepts.

## Understanding Localised Islamic Concepts and Local Concepts Connected to Islam

*Silaturahmi* constitutes a central value, concept and practice that can be observed all over Indonesia and the wider Nusantara area, including Malaysia. In its localised formation it is unique to the region and to Indonesia in particular. However, as the word itself reveals, *silaturahmi* is rooted in the Islamic tradition. Although grounded in a hadith, its practice, use and meaning in everyday language among Indonesian Muslims is unique to Indonesia. However, it is also through the social reality of Indonesian communal life that is based on the group rather than the individual that *silaturahmi* has been adapted to the Indonesian context and has become such a basic concept of important value for Indonesian Muslims.

My understanding of *silaturahmi* in the Indonesian context is that it is a religiously motivated form of social interaction (practice) through which – consciously or unconsciously – translocal relations are maintained on various scales from the local to the global and on different societal levels, including kinship, educational, economic and religious connections. *Silaturahmi* is also an intention (Ind., *niat*) that can serve as a religious motivator, as well as a reminder, and is mostly, although not exclusively, used among Indonesian Muslims. In addition, it is important to stress that *silaturahmi* is accompanied by what I refer to as transformational power. By practising *silaturahmi*, a person can be exposed to new or different ways of living, interpreting and practicing Islam. I will return to this point later. Examples of applied *silaturahmi* in the Indonesian context are annual religious events like Halal Bi Halal in the Islamic month of Shawwal, which can take place in different settings and communities. *Silaturahmi* (not the Indonesian word *berkunjung*) is also

[48] I thank Vincent Houben for vocalising this important point that had occupied me thinking how to properly include it in the discussion.

used when visiting friends and family members, but also for official purposes such as alumni gatherings or meetings of people, organisations or communities with a common goal, agenda, political view or religious motivation.[49]

A second important concept and value for understanding the local expression of Islamic piety and Islamic practices and interpretation is the idea of *barokah* or *berkah*, often translated as 'divine blessing' but actually encompassing a whole set of interdependent components, as will be shown below. *Barokah* as a spiritual reality is usually felt by an individual or group in their daily activities through the interaction with or usage of certain media connected to Islam. In the narrations about the Prophet Muḥammad's life, we can find many instances where the Prophet asked for *baraka* (in its original and general context) to be bestowed upon food or drink. *Baraka* has been discussed in different contexts and geographical regions.[50] The recitation of the Qur'ān is also considered as a source of blessing.[51] According to my own observations, *barokah* is a concept that motivates Indonesian Muslims to follow certain rituals, personalities or practices because they hope and expect that they will receive special divine blessings, which are a power in themselves and capable of bringing about positive change. During my research, I found that *barokah*, as a localised Islamic concept, is mostly found among non-reformist and non-modernist Indonesian Muslims. I found that mostly

[49] For a detailed discussion, see Seise, *Religioscapes*; Seise, 'The Transformational Power of Barokah'.

[50] Julia Day Howell, 'Sufism and the Indonesian Islamic Revival', *Journal of Asian Studies* 60(3) (2001): 701–29; Möller, *Ramadan in Java*; P.G. Pinto, 'The Sufi Ritual of the Darb al-Shish and the Ethnography of Religious Experience', in B. Dupret et al. (eds), *Ethnographies of Islam: Ritual Performances and Everyday Practices* (Edinburgh: Edinburgh University Press, 2012), 63–5; K. Lange, '"There Used To Be Terrible Disbelief": Mourning and Social Change in Northern Syria', in B. Dupret et al. (eds), *Ethnographies of Islam: Ritual Performances and Everyday Practices* (Edinburgh: Edinburgh University Press, 2012), 34.

[51] 'This too is a Book which We have revealed; full of blessing, confirming what was revealed before it so that you might warn the people of the Mother of Cities (Mecca) and those around it. Those who believe in the Hereafter believe in it, and are ever-mindful of their Prayers' (Q 6:92). Other verses mention the reality of *baraka*: 'If the people of the towns had but believed and feared Allah, We should indeed have opened out to them (All kinds of) blessings from heaven and earth; but they rejected (the truth), and We brought them to book for their misdeeds' (Q 7:96).

sympathisers of the Nahdlatul Ulama (NU),[52] or members and followers of the ʿAlawiyin, the direct descendants of Prophet Muḥammad,[53] have the idea of *barokah* deeply instilled in their lives. *Barokah* is part of their spiritual reality and something to look and strive for. However, other groups, commonly described as reformist or modernist, also refer to *barokah* but rarely tie it to specific individuals as its source. To understand *barokah* within the particular situatedness of Indonesia and as a common marker for Indonesian *religioscapes* enables us to obtain a broader understanding of the concept of *baraka* in its original and general context as used in Qurʾān and hadith. At the same time, we are able to appreciate a possible additional nuance or colour to the 'normative' understanding. Furthermore, as I will explain in the following part, identifying *barokah* as a localised form of *baraka* has the potential to discover certain socio-religious phenomena connected to it.

*Rasa* and the quest for harmony form two local concepts connected to Indonesian Islam. *Rasa* constitutes the basis for achieving harmony, be it social, individual or religious and spiritual harmony. At the same time, *rasa* guides all social and religious or spiritual actions. The person that has a well-developed sense of *rasa* is looked up to and held in high esteem and respect in Javanese society. A person who has an underdeveloped sense of *rasa*, on the other hand, is seen as not being a real Javanese.[54]

The concept of *rasa* includes more than feeling or emotion. On the social level, *rasa* also incorporates intuition, knowledge of the proper way to behave, knowledge of correct emotions, and also knowledge of how to suppress improper emotions. If one does not have this knowledge, *rasa* means being able to intuitively wait and observe the situation without acting spontaneously or impulsively, learning from this observation and deducing the

[52] Largest Muslim organisation in Indonesia. Founded in 1926 to defend traditionalist Islamic practices according to the Shafiʿi School of law.

[53] The ʿAlawiyin are descendants of Hadhrami migrants, who claim to be descendants of the Prophet Muḥammad. Large-scale migration from east-central Yemen started in the middle of the eighteenth century, which came to a halt with the emergence of nation-states (Martin Slama, 'Indonesian Hadhramis and the Hadhramaut: An Old Diaspora and Its New Connections', *Antropologi Indonesia* 29(2) (2005): 109). Until today, the Islamic practices and teachings observed by the ʿAlawiyin are very similar to the Islamic practices found in Yemen.

[54] Interview with Pak Herjaka, 29 August 2013.

proper kind of behaviour. It also means to feel empathy and to understand symbols easily.[55] In Javanese, this level of *rasa* is referred to as *lantip* and it is this part of *rasa* that is of direct importance for my discussion. *Lantip* can be achieved through social learning and interaction. A traditional Javanese proverb reflects the meaning and realisation of *rasa* in everyday life in a symbolic way: '*Ngono Ya Ngono Ning Aja Ngono*' ('Do whatever you want, but don't overdo it; meaning: do not let differences undermine group harmony'[56]). It is this stress on 'group harmony' that is prevalent in Yogyakarta and central Java. This integration, however, does not include the individual's religious beliefs. A Christian can be just as good a Javanese as a Muslim, Hindu or Buddhist.

On the religious and spiritual level, *rasa* can refer to a person's relationship with the divine and is usually called *eling* (to remember). To be able to achieve this level of *rasa* called *eling* one needs to master *lantip*, in addition to practising *laku* – certain individual spiritual practices also referred to as *amaliyah*.[57] The ultimate goal is to improve one's relationship with the divine, to draw closer to God and to control and overcome one's *nafs* (ego; lower desires).[58] Only through the *rasa* level of *lantip* can social harmony be created and prevail. And only through *eling* can an individual feel harmony with oneself and the Creator or the divine in general and improve one's relationship with the surroundings. *Rasa* also serves as a personal and subjective epistemological instrument when faced with the divine.[59]

It is the deep prevailing social concept of *rasa* and its different levels, the tendency to see and explain the world through symbols, and an aversion towards straightforward, direct and crude forms of social interaction and approaches towards life in general, as well as a deep love and

[55] Interview with Kyai Muhaimin, August 2013.

[56] Translated by Christopher Torchia, *Indonesian Idioms and Expression: Colloquial Indonesian at Work* (North Clarendon: Tuttle Publishing, 2007), 119.

[57] *Laku* can include a wide range of practices, from walking long distances without talking, to abstaining from certain foods (e.g., sugar and salt over the course of a lifetime), fasting, *dzkir*, among other things.

[58] There exist other levels connected to the concept of *rasa* that will not be discussed here, for example, *waskita*, which refers to the supranatural.

[59] For a more detailed discussion, see Seise, *Religioscapes*.

need for harmony (Ind., *kerukunan*) that seems to have contributed to a unique localisation of Islam in Nusantara and Java in particular. The need to maintain and preserve social and religious/spiritual harmony is especially reflected in traditional Javanese practices that are often referred to as syncretistic Islamic practices, and even condemned as being *syirik* (Arab., *shirk*) or *bid'a* by certain Islamic groups like the Muhammadiyah[60] and other reformist-orientated groups. These practices include preparing what is commonly referred to as ritual offerings (Ind., *sesajen*), preparing *tumpeng* (a special rice dish for religious rituals) or commemorative gatherings held after a person's death. I will return to some of these practices in the next part.

## Enriching the Study of Islam by Understanding Localised Islamic Concepts

Understanding how localised Islamic concepts work within a particular situatedness has the potential of an alternative or more nuanced understanding of certain socio-religious phenomena that have mainly been understood within a political framework. I made this point clear in my article[61] where I argue that there exist localised Islamic concepts and practices that can be applied to arrive at a more nuanced understanding of Islam in Indonesia in general, and Islamic dynamics and movements in particular. Analysing examples from my own ethnographic field research, I found that *barokah* and *silaturahmi* within the geographical area of Indonesia have transformational power attached to them that can change a person's understanding of Islam. In Indonesia, studying at a certain *pesantren* or joining a certain *pengajian* (religious lecture) to obtain *barokah* has the potential to change a person's understanding of Islam. The same is true for practising *silaturahmi*. The act and intention to engage in *silaturahmi* has attached to it a potential for transformation. Long-term field research and the mastery of *Bahasa Indonesia*, including language games, enabled me to arrive at this nuanced understanding of the local formation of

[60] The reformist Muhammadiyah is the second largest Muslim organisation in Indonesia and was founded in 1912 by Ahmad Dahlan.

[61] Claudia Seise, 'The Transformational Power of Barokah', *International Journal of Islam in Asia* 1 (2021): 5–11.

*silaturahmi* and *barokah*. Therefore, I argue that these localised Islamic concepts, as common markers of the diverse *religioscapes* of Indonesia, should be taken into account when analysing Islamic movements and religious change in Indonesia.

The 212 movement in Indonesia,[62] led by Habib Rizieq Shihab, serves as a recent example of how searching for *barokah* has the potential for individual and societal transformation on a significant level. I propose that viewing this movement through the lens of *barokah* as a kind of transformational power can provide an additional layer of understanding to this particular case.[63] As indicated by his title 'Habib', Habib Rizieq claims to be a direct descendant (*sayyid*) of the Prophet Muḥammad, and being connected to a descendant of the Prophet Muḥammad is seen by traditional Indonesian Muslims as carrying *barokah*.[64] In addition to political arguments,[65] I suggest that many followers of the 212 movement took part in order to gain the *barokah*, which they believe to be connected to Habib Rizieq. In this sense, seeking the *barokah* of the person Habib Rizieq has attached to it the power of transforming individuals and society at large. The annual mass gatherings for singing praises on the Prophet Muḥammad led by Habib Syech in Java are attended by thousands of Indonesian Muslims. These gatherings have a similar potential for change that is driven by the wish to gain the *barokah* of a descendant of the Prophet Muḥammad.

[62] On 4 November and 2 December 2016, the largest demonstrations since the *reformasi* movement took place in Indonesia. However, the protestors did not demand more democracy and liberty, instead they called for the imprisonment of the Christian governor of Jakarta, Basukri Tjahaja Purnama ('Ahok') whom they accused of blasphemy.

[63] Seise, 'The Transformational Power of Barokah', 14–15.

[64] Ho also mentions that blessings are attached to the descendants of the Prophet Muḥammad in Tarim (Engseng Ho, *The Graves of Tarim: Genealogy and Mobility across the Indian Ocean* (Berkeley: University of California Press, 2006), 69, 84).

[65] Mohamed Nawab Osman and Prashant Waikar, 'Fear and Loathing: Uncivil Islamism and Indonesia's Anti-Ahok Movement', *Indonesia* 106(1) (2018): 89–109; M.F. Pramono, 'Phenomena of Habib Muhammad Rizieq Shihab in Islamic Leadership Politics in Indonesia', working paper, University of Darussalam, Gontor, 2018, 843–54; Khusna M. Amal, 'Explaining Islamic Populism in Southeast Asia: An Indonesian Muslim Intellectual's Perspective', *Journal of Critical Reviews* 7(5) (2020): 583–8.

On a similar note, the concept of *silaturahmi* has been utilised by several Islamic groups in Indonesia. For example, during my field research on the Islamic political organisation Muslimah Hizbut Tahir, the women's wing of Hizbut Tahrir Indonesia (HTI), in Yogyakarta 2008–9, I noticed the extensive use of *silaturahmi* in their language discourse to recruit supporters and sympathisers for their cause. Muslim scholars, public figures, politicians and even military personnel were invited in the name of maintaining or establishing *silaturahmi* ties with their fellow Muslims from HTI. Since all Indonesian Muslims feel obliged to follow the call to keep or establish *silaturahmi* relations, even the more traditionally inclined scholars and politicians from all parts of the spectrum had followed their call and attended events organised by HTI. At the same time, HTI was strongly criticised and warned against by local Islamic authorities. There are several other examples from my field research that can illustrate the transformational power attached to the concept and practice of *silaturahmi* in Indonesia, ranging from interreligious dialogue forums to family gatherings or meetings between Muslim scholars from different schools of thought.[66] For the study of Islam in other regions of the Muslim world, it can be worthwhile to explore whether a similar transformational power is attached to certain localised Islamic concepts and practices, and how paying attention to these can provide a different or more nuanced perspective on the socio-political issues observed.

Analysing local concepts connected to Islam like *rasa* and the quest for harmony also aid us to arrive at a deeper understanding of the socio-religious dynamics at work in a certain *religioscape* and situatedness. Interreligious dialogue formats are important institutionalised tools to maintain and keep interreligious harmony in Indonesia. Furthermore, attempting to understand *rasa* in the Indonesian context helps us to arrive at an alternative way of viewing and contextualising historical processes and developments. In my new research project, I aim to show how this can be the case in understanding the *dakwah* strategies of the Walisongo (also written as Wali Sanga), the nine saints that are believed to have made a major impact in spreading Islam in Java from the fifteenth century onwards. According to my informant who is a teacher of traditional Javanese singing and long-term

[66] See Seise, 'The Transformational Power of Barokah', 15–16.

student of Javanese culture and spirituality, the Walisongo had perfectly understood how the soul of the Javanese people perceives the divine and had adopted their *dakwah* strategies accordingly. In my point of view, this assumed understanding on the side of the Walisongo is closely connected to understanding the importance of certain local concepts of the Javanese culture and tradition. Their understanding and internalisation of these local concepts enabled the Walisongo to use, apply and embody these concepts and attract the Javanese people to Islam. I argue that through comprehending local concepts connected to Islam like *rasa* and the quest for harmony, one can appreciate a different possible reading of the specific formation of Islam and Islamic practices that, in the Nusantara context, have often been regarded by modern scholarship of Islam as an exceptional case, and discussions have tended to focus on issues such as syncretism.[67]

*Rasa* and the quest for harmony presuppose the necessity to maintain and establish harmony on different levels in society because of a heightened sense of *rasa*. Furthermore, establishing and maintaining harmony in nature has at its core the belief that all creation is created by the divine, which results in the belief that every created thing has a spirit (Ind., *roh*) of its own that needs to be respected in order to achieve harmony. This respect of the spirit of a created being or object does not necessitate worshipping it. In this sense, as a researcher, whether working with qualitative research methods or analysing historical texts, it is necessary to understand the importance of local concepts in order to avoid misinterpretation that can lead to false or only partly true conclusions. The cosmological framework of seeing creation as brethren (Javanese, *sedulur*) to mankind mentioned above needs to be kept in mind. An interesting example in this regard is the 'dressing' of the banyan tree (*Ficus benjamina*; Ind., *pohon beringin*) with cloth – sarong – in parts of Java. This

[67] Feener, 'South-East Asian Localisations of Islam', 13. One example of this is Bubalo and Fealy, who argue that southeast Asian Muslims have been selective in their appropriation and application of Islam brought from the Middle East. These, according to the authors, include non-Islamic features of local religious practices. This selective appropriation and indigenisation led to southeast Asian forms of Islam resembling their Middle Eastern antecedents but with some distinguishing features (Anthony Bubalo and Gregory Fealy, *Joining the Caravan?: The Middle East, Islamism and Indonesia* (Sydney: Lowy Institute for International Policy, 2005), 16.

practice is commonly interpreted as a form of worshipping the tree (*menyembah pohon*), the spirits or spiritual forces residing in the tree and linked to animism or pre-Islamic beliefs.[68]

However, my informant on Javanese Islamic spirituality suggests a different reading of this practice. According to her, Javanese cosmology teaches that the banyan tree, as a creation older than humanity, should be respected by human beings as being a brethren older and more experienced than humans. Therefore, 'when you respect someone, you robe them. It is not worshipping trees.'[69] According to this reading of robing the banyan tree, the practice is rooted in the respect for the tree as a brethren, not as a creation that is worshipped. Here, I see the concept of *rasa* and the subsequent need to preserve harmony with creation as a driving force in maintaining this often as un-Islamic perceived practice. From the perspective of the Islamic worldview, the practice of robing the tree can be understood as a situated understanding of respecting and preserving the environment as part of the God-given responsibility to man as God's vicegerent (*khalīfa*) on earth.

Another example of a Javanese ritual that allows for multiple and opposing interpretations is the offering of *sesajen* (ritual offerings) by Muslims around Java. In Yogyakarta[70] and other places around Java, one can find these small offerings at crossroads or watercourses. These gifts, prepared with attention to detail, are offered on a piece of banana leaf that is approximately 5 × 5 cm in size. Yellow rice, desiccated coconut and small pieces of meat are usually found on the leaf, in addition to various pieces of flowers. This form of offering can be found to a much larger extent on the predominantly Hindu island of Bali. In Yogyakarta, these offerings are mostly associated with the Javanese tradition and mysticism (*kejawen*) and are referred to by

[68] R. Kahane, 'Modern Interpretation of Animistic Metaphors: An Example from Indonesia', *Sojourn: Journal of Social Issues in Southeast Asia* 8(1) (1993): 11–34; Merle Calvin Ricklefs, *Mystic Synthesis in Java: A History of Islamization from the Fourteenth to the Early Nineteenth Centuries* (Norwalk, CT: EastBridge, 2006); Merle Calvin Ricklefs, *Polarising Javanese Society: Islamic and Other Visions* (c. 1830–1930) (Honolulu: University of Hawaii Press, 2007), 1–12.

[69] Participatory observation via Zoom class, March 2021.

[70] A major part of my field study between 2013 and 2014 was conducted in Yogyakarta, a city in central Java.

modernist Muslims as syncretistic rituals. It is argued that these offerings go against the principle of belief in one God (*tawḥīd*) and thus cannot be linked to the orthodox Islamic belief. Connected to this interpretation of the *sesajen* is the interpretation that these offerings are intended to pacify or ask something from jinn, another creation that is believed to be made of fire and shares this world with human beings but in a different realm. In orthodox Islamic belief, it is stressed that the realms of the jinn and humans should be separated, and both creations should not mingle with one another. Since the world of jinn and human beings should be separated and people should only worship Allah and seek Him for protection, pacifying the jinn in the form of sacrifices is seen as a form of polytheism (Ind., *syirik*). It is argued that Muslims who give offerings to the jinn on paths, along rivers or in front of houses have not fully internalised the concept of *tawḥīd* and still adhere to pre-Islamic rituals. However, my informant Mas Herman, a Muslim, Javanese mystic and local historian, disagrees with this interpretation. He defends Muslims who make so-called offerings to the jinn. Because, as he explained to me in an interview, it is about what kind of intention (Ind., *niat*) a person has when making an offering. He went on to explain that in pre-Islamic times these offerings were made to pacify the jinn but most Muslims nowadays know that this is not allowed in Islam. However, according to Mas Herman, the Islamic religion attaches great importance to donations (Ind., *sedeqah*) and generosity, and therefore the small offerings are brought to the jinn as donations. From the perspective of the local concepts of *rasa* and the quest for harmony, Mas Herman's explanation adds an alternative interpretation to contemporary *sesajen* given in Java. In addition to interpreting this ritual as reminiscence of syncretic believes, it can also be understood as serving to preserve harmony with one's surroundings because of a heightened sense of *rasa*.

In addition, the framework of localised Islamic concepts also has the potential to add a local Islamic component to the methodological framework of the integration of knowledge (or the Islamisation of human knowledge) developed by different scholars connected to the International Islamic University Malaysia. Integrating Islamic concepts into human sciences as a form of enriching human sciences with religious wisdom and values forms an approach to return knowledge to the realm of values. Here, integration of knowledge, as developed by Kamal Hassan, differs slightly to what has been referred to as the Islamisation of human knowledge. The methodology of the integration of knowledge aims to 'purify' human knowledge from un-Islamic influences or traits that are not in line with the Islamic worldview.[71] Enrichment with relevant references or concepts from Qur'ān and *sunna* forms the second important element used in Hassan's method. Both methods have in common that they aim to de-secularise human sciences and (re)-connect knowledge and Islam.

I propose to broaden the framework of the Islamisation of human sciences to also include localised Islamic concepts such as *silaturahmi*. In my point of view, the way certain Islamic concepts have been localised has the potential to adding an extra layer of wisdom to the original concept found in Islamic scriptures. In my article[72] I try to illustrate this point using the example of *silaturahmi*. I argue that in the case of Islamic diplomacy in Indonesia, for example, the local context and wisdom of the region needs to be taken into account in order to be able to extract the greatest benefit of the theme under discussion. As such, localised Islamic concepts can be included in the category of 'Islamic legacy' in the methodological framework of 'integrated knowledge' that is applied to enhance or 'beautify' bodies of secular knowledge.

During my long-term qualitative field research in Indonesia, I observed that *silaturahmi* in its localised form has attached to it a diplomatic component. This observation inspired me to propose that the socio-religious concept of *silaturahmi* can enrich the field of diplomacy. As already described above, *silaturahmi* is a socio-religious concept and practice deeply engrained in the people of Indonesia. It is referred to and prevalent in different social

[71] Abdelaziz Berghout (ed.), *Introduction to the Islamic Worldview: Study of Selected Essentials* (Kuala Lumpur: IIUM Press, 2009), 1–35; Abdul Hamid Abu Sulayman, *The Qur'anic Worldview: A Springboard for Cultural Reform* (London: IIIT, 2011), 1–30; Malik Badri, *The Dilemma of Muslim Psychologists* (Petaling Jaya: Islamic Book Trust, 2016), 1–3; Abdulaziz Berghout, 'Understanding Worldview: Islamic Perspective', in *The Islamic Worldview: Selected Essays* (Kuala Lumpur: IIIT & IIUM, 2017), 51–71.

[72] Claudia Seise, 'The Potential of Localized Islamic Concepts: The Example of *Silaturahmi* for the Field of Diplomacy', *Nusantara: An International Journal of Humanities and Social Sciences* 3(2) (2021): 38–56.

and religious spheres. According to my observations, the motivation to please God and seek reward is part of having the intention of practising *silaturahmi*. Understanding that diplomacy is a reflection of the values of nations and peoples, their cultural and civilisational specificities and their religious precepts and traditions[73] including *silaturahmi* as part of Indonesia's framework of diplomacy, forms an important step towards creating a uniquely coloured Indonesian diplomacy. At the same time, the concept of *silaturahmi* enhances the idealist framework of international relations and should be added to the tool kit of soft power diplomacy. My example of *silaturahmi* as an enrichment tool in diplomacy illustrates how understanding localised Islamic concepts can enrich the study of Islam from the perspective of the methodological framework of the integration of knowledge discussed above.

## Conclusion

I have shown that including in the study of Islam localised Islamic concepts as well as local concepts connected to Islam allows us to arrive at a deeper, more nuanced or even alternative understanding of socio-religious dynamics at work in a certain *religioscape*. In addition, we can obtain situated knowledge of orthodox Islamic concepts. The localised Islamic concepts introduced in this chapter, although grounded in orthodox Islamic teachings or connected to Islam, are unique to a particular geographical area. However, when considering the inclusion of these concepts in the theoretical and methodological framework of the study of Islam, one should acknowledge the fact that each geographical region is likely to possess its own unique localised Islamic concepts. The same holds true for local concepts connected to Islam as discussed above. To discover these concepts within a certain situatedness will enable scholars of Islam to appreciate an additional perspective of how Islamic concepts and local concepts connected to Islam are embedded in a particular geographical region, culture and tradition. This can be achieved by applying the methodological framework from New Area Studies, which includes the mastery of the local language and a long-term immersion in qualitative field research by being in the local here and arriving in the field without preconceived aims, methods and knowledge

[73] Iqbal Dar Arshid and Sayed Jamsheed, 'Diplomacy in Islam', *Asian Journal of Science and Technology* 8(9) (2017): 5616–18.

from a particular thematic field of study or discipline. The importance of this approach is grounded in the fact that regions other than the so-called heartland of the Muslim world, like the area of Nusantara and especially present-day Indonesia, have historically contributed to the knowledge world of Islam and continue to do so until today.

## Bibliography

Abu Sulayman, Abdul Hamid, *The Qur'anic Worldview: A Springboard for Cultural Reform*. London: IIIT, 2011.

Ali, Muhamad, 'Categorizing Muslims in Postcolonial Indonesia', *Moussons* 11 (2007): 22–62.

Amal, Khusna M., 'Explaining Islamic Populism in Southeast Asia: An Indonesian Muslim Intellectual's Perspective', *Journal of Critical Reviews* 7(5) (2020): 583–8.

Arshid, Iqbal Dar and Jamsheed Sayed, 'Diplomacy in Islam', *Asian Journal of Science and Technology* 8(9) (2017): 5616–18.

Azra, Azyumardi, *The Origins of Islamic Reformism in Southeast Asia Networks of Malay–Indonesian and Middle Eastern 'Ulamā' in the Seventeenth and Eighteenth Centuries*. Melbourne: Asian Studies Assn. of Australia in assoc. with Allen & Unwin, 2004.

Badri, Malik, *The Dilemma of Muslim Psychologists*. Petaling Jaya: Islamic Book Trust, 2016.

Baumann, Benjamin, Danny Kretschmer, Johannes von Plato, Jona Pomerance and Tim Rössig, '"Small Places, Large Issues" Revisited: Reflections on an Ethnographically Founded Vision of New Area Studies', *International Quarterly for Asian Studies* 51(3/4) (2020): 1–33.

Berghout, Abdelaziz (ed.), *Introduction to the Islamic Worldview: Study of Selected Essentials*. Kuala Lumpur: IIUM Press, 2009.

Berghout, Abdulaziz, 'Understanding Worldview: Islamic Perspective', in *The Islamic Worldview: Selected Essays*. Kuala Lumpur: IIIT & IIUM (2017), 3–51.

Bowen, John R., *Muslims through Discourse: Religion and Ritual in Gayo Society*. Princeton, NJ: Princeton University Press, 1993.

Bruinessen, van, Martin, 'Pesantren and Kitab Kuning: Maintenance and Continuation of a Tradition of Religious Learning', in W. Marshall (ed.), *Texts from the Islands: Oral and Written Traditions of Indonesia and the Malay World*. Bern: University of Bern, 1994, 121–45.

Bruinessen van, Martin, 'Global and Local in Indonesian Islam', *Southeast Asian Studies, Kyoto University* 37(2) (1999): 158–75.

Bruinessen, van, Martin, 'Traditionalist and Islamist Pesantren in Contemporary Indonesia', in A. N. Farish (ed.), *The Madrasa in Asia: Political Activism and Transnational Linkages*. Amsterdam: Amsterdam University Press, 2008, 217–47.

Bubalo, Anthony and Gregory Fealy, *Joining the Caravan?: The Middle East, Islamism and Indonesia*. Sydney: Lowy Institute for International Policy, 2005, 1–149.

Clarke, Adele E., *Situational Analysis in Practice: Mapping Research with Grounded Theory*. London: SAGE Publishing, 2005.

Commins, David, *The Wahhabi Mission and Saudi Arabia*. London: I. B. Tauris, 2006.

Connley, Aleah, 'Politicising Piety in Provincial Indonesia. Towards a Theory of the Dynamics of Local Politics and Islam', PhD dissertation, Institute for Asian and African Studies, Humboldt University, 2019.

Day Howell, Julia, 'Sufism and the Indonesian Islamic Revival', *Journal of Asian Studies* 60(3) (2001): 701–29.

Eickelman, Dale F. and James Piscatori, 'Social Theory in the Study of Muslim Societies', in *Muslim Travellers: Pilgrimage, Migration and the Religious Imagination*. London: University of California Press, 1990, 3–29.

Feener, Michael R., 'South-East Asian Localisations of Islam and Participation within a Global Umma, c. 1500–1800', in D.O. Morgan and A. Reid (eds), *The New Cambridge History of Islam*. Cambridge: Cambridge University Press, 2010, 470–503.

Freitag, Ulrike and Achim von Oppen, *Translocality: The Study of Globalising Processes from a Southern Perspective*. Leiden: Brill, 2010.

Geertz, Clifford, *The Religion of Java*. Chicago: University of Chicago Press, 1960.

Geertz, Clifford, *Islam Observed*. New Haven, CT: Yale University Press, 1968.

Hadar, Ivan A., *Bildung in Indonesien: Krise und Kontinuität: Das Beispiel Pesantren*. Frankfurt: IKO-Verlag für Interkulturelle Kommunikation, 1999.

Hefner, Robert W., 'Islam in an Era of Nation-States: Politics and Religious Renewal in Muslim Southeast Asia', in H.W. Robert and P. Horvatich (eds), *Islam in an Era of Nation-States: Politics and Religious Renewal in Muslim Southeast Asia*. Honolulu: University of Hawaii Press, 1997, 3–40.

Ho, Engseng, *The Graves of Tarim: Genealogy and Mobility across the Indian Ocean*. Berkeley: University of California Press, 2006.

Houben, Vincent, 'The New Area Studies and Southeast Asian History', *Dorisea Working Paper* 4 (2013), 1–10.

Houben, Vincent, 'New Area Studies, Translation and Mid-Range Concepts', in K. Mielke and A.-K. Hornige (eds), *Area Studies at the Crossroads. Knowledge Production after the Mobility Turn*. London: Palgrave Macmillan, 2017, 195–211.

Houben, Vincent, 'New Area Studies as an Emerging Discipline: The Way Ahead for Southeast Asian Studies', *International Quarterly for Asian Studies* 51(3/4) (2020): 51–64.

Jackson, Peter A., 'South East Asian Area Studies beyond Anglo-America: Geopolitical Transitions, the Neoliberal Academy and Spatialized Regimes of Knowledge', *South East Asia Research* 27(1) (2019): 49–73.

Joll, Christopher M., 'Local and Global Islams in Southeast Asia: Historical and Anthropological Perspectives', in Z. Ibrahim (ed.), *Social Science and Knowledge in a Globalising World.* Selangor: PSSM/SIRDC, 2012, 219–42.

Kahane, R., 'Modern Interpretation of Animistic Metaphors: An Example from Indonesia', *Sojourn: Journal of Social Issues in Southeast Asia* 8(1) (1993): 11–34.

Kelley, Liam C., '"Localization" and "Knowledge Worlds" in the Southeast Asian Past and Present', Keynote speech presented at the 3rd Engaging with Vietnam: An Interdisciplinary Dialogue Conference, Vietnam National University, Hanoi, 4 December 2011.

Laffan, Michael, *The Makings of Indonesian Islam: Orientalism and the Narration of a Sufi Past.* Princeton, NJ: Princeton University Press, 2011.

Lange, K., '"There Used To Be Terrible Disbelief": Mourning and Social Change in Northern Syria', in B. Dupret et al. (eds), *Ethnographies of Islam: Ritual Performances and Everyday Practices.* Edinburgh: Edinburgh University Press, 2012, 31–40.

Lukens-Bull, Ronald, *A Peaceful Jihad: Negotiating Identity and Modernity in Muslim Java.* London: Palgrave Macmillan, 2005.

Muhlack, Ulrich, 'Verstehen', in by H-J. Goertz (ed.), *Geschichte. Ein Grundkurs.* Berlin: Rowohlt, 2007, 104–35.

Madjid, Nurcholis, 'Merumuskan Kembali Tujuan Pendidikan Pesantren', in D. M. Rahardjo (ed.), *Pergulatan Dunia Pesantren: Membangun Dari Bawah.* Jakarta: Perhimpunan Pengembangan Pesantren dan Masyarakat, 1985, 3–16.

Mielke, Katja and Anna-Katharina Hornige, *Area Studies at the Crossroads: Knowledge Production after the Mobility Turn.* London: Palgrave Macmillan, 2017.

Möller, Andre, *Ramadan in Java: The Joy and Jihad of Ritual Fasting.* Lund: University of Lund, 2005.

Osman, Mohamed Nawab Mohamed and Prashant Waikar, 'Fear and Loathing: Uncivil Islamism and Indonesia's Anti-Ahok Movement', *Indonesia* 106(1) (2018): 89–109.

Pinto, P. G., 'The Sufi Ritual of the Darb al-Shish and the Ethnography of Religious Experience', in B. Dupret et al. (eds), *Ethnographies of Islam: Ritual Performances and Everyday Practices.* Edinburgh: Edinburgh University Press, 2012, 62–71.

Pramono, M. F., 'Phenomena of Habib Muhammad Rizieq Shihab in Islamic Leadership Politics in Indonesia', Working Papers of the University of Darussalam Gontor. Gontor: University of Darussalam, 2018, 843–54.

Redfield, Robert, *Peasant Society and Culture*. Chicago: University of Chicago Press, 1956.

Rehbein, Boike, 'Verstehen in den Sozialwissenschaften', in Boike Rehbein and Gernot Saalmann (eds), *Verstehen*. Konstanz: UVK, 2009, 43–60.

Rehbein, Boike, *Critical Theory after the Rise of the Global South: Kaleidoscopic Dialectic*. Abington: Routledge, 2015.

Rehbein, Boike and Gernot Saalmann (eds), *Verstehen*. Konstanz: UVK, 2009.

Ricklefs, Merle Calvin, *Mystic Synthesis in Java: A History of Islamization from the Fourteenth to the Early Nineteenth Centuries*. Norwalk, CT: EastBridge, 2006.

Ricklefs, Merle Calvin, *Polarising Javanese Society: Islamic and Other Visions (c. 1830–1930)*. Honolulu: University of Hawaii Press, 2007.

Seise, Claudia, *Religioscapes in Muslim Indonesia: Personalities, Institutions and Practices*. Berlin: Regiospectra, 2017.

Seise, Claudia, 'The Muslim Researcher: Reflections on Insider/Outsider Research in Indonesia', *Journal of Islam in Asia* 16(1) (2019): 297–324.

Seise, Claudia, 'The Potential of Localized Islamic Concepts: The Example of Silaturahmi for the Field of Diplomacy', *Nusantara: An International Journal of Humanities and Social Sciences* 3(2) (2021): 38–56.

Seise, Claudia, 'The Transformational Power of Barokah and Silaturahmi in Muslim Indonesia', *International Journal of Islam in Asia* 1 (2021): 1–20.

Slama, Martin, 'Indonesian Hadhramis and the Hadhramaut: An Old Diaspora and Its New Connections', *Antropologi Indonesia* 29(2) (2005): 107–13.

Srimuliyani, E., *Women from Traditional Islamic Educational Institutions in Indonesia: Negotiating Public Space*. Amsterdam: Amsterdam University Press, 2012.

Torchia, Christopher, *Indonesian Idioms and Expression: Colloquial Indonesian at Work*. North Clarendon: Tuttle Publishing, 2007.

Wittgenstein, Ludwig, *Philosophische Untersuchungen – Philosophical Investigations*, trans. G. E. M. Anscombe, 2nd edn. Oxford: Oxford University Press, 1999.

Woodward, Mark R., *Islam in Java: Normative Piety and Mysticism in the Sultanate of Yogyakarta*. Tucson: University of Arizona Press, 1989.

Woodward, Mark R., 'The Slametan: Textual Knowledge and Ritual Performance in Yogyakarta', in Mark R. Woodward (ed.), *Java, Indonesia and Islam*. Berlin: Springer, 2011, 113–36.

# 12

# BODIES, THINGS, DOINGS: A PRACTICE THEORY APPROACH TO THE STUDY OF ISLAM

AYŞE ALMILA AKCA, EYAD ABUALI AND AYDIN SÜER

## Introduction

The study of Islamic texts, mainly in the Arabic language, has traditionally shaped and demarcated the field of Islamic Studies and Theologies in the academy. Scholarly approaches to Islamic texts, however, have largely focused on socio-political and intellectual history in the fields of law, theology, politics, philosophy and Sufism. This focus traditionally constituted, and to some extent still constitutes, the field of Islamic Studies. Research on contemporary Islam also draws primarily on texts in the form of speeches, interviews and treatises in order to elucidate the ideas and positions of Muslim intellectuals and authorities. Despite the necessity of these works, however, this has led to the neglect of a variety of sources such as ritual texts, dream interpretations, prayer books and other manuals of worship (*ʿibāda*), devotional literature, ethnographic observations in ordinary settings and in everyday life, as well as audio and video material, to name a few. However, the textual approach is not problematic per se, but quite often the essentialist reading of texts produces a particular normative notion of Islam. Consequently, a myriad of phenomena that constitutes the Islamic will be excluded, as Talal Asad has pointed out in his important analysis of textual approaches that have been hegemonic in the academy for a long time.[1] This has led to the development of a canon of texts, topics and authors within the field that has excluded those that do not conform to a specific idea of what texts *should do* so to speak. Since Asad's significant contributions on the pitfalls of the study of an anthropology of Islam,[2] decontextualised positivistic approaches to Islamic knowledge have been challenged by several scholars who have drawn attention to discourses, practices and social contexts and settings, through which ideas come to life. This chapter aims to demonstrate the value of an interdisciplinary methodology for the study of Islam and Muslims, both in the past and the present, by drawing on a broad range of practice theories.

In recent studies, scholars of Islamic texts have attempted to address these gaps in the study of Islam by extending the boundaries of the field of textual research while broadening the analytical tools of ethnographic analysis. Kevin Reinhart, for example, has noted that textual scholars struggle to engage with ritual and *fiqh* texts, ultimately ignoring writings on rituals that attempt to inform Muslim behaviour.[3] He argues that the textual representation of rituals must be taken seriously for their own sake.[4] This moves us some way towards avoiding interpreting rituals as symbols in order to grasp at their supposedly hidden meanings, or identifying the descriptions in the text as the real practice of Muslims. Neither approach allows us to fully understand what a text on rituals is *truly* saying. He suggests that textual studies of ritual require the study of the acts and activities of bodies in rituals, including bodily moods, sentiments and emotions.[5] In addition, Shahzad Bashir has highlighted how hagiographical literature has been considered unimportant for historical research

[1] Talal Asad, *The Idea of an Anthropology of Islam* (Washington, DC: Center for Contemporary Arab Studies, Georgetown University, 1986).

[2] Asad, *The Idea of an Anthropology of Islam*; Talal Asad, 'Anthropological Conceptions of Religion: Reflections on Geertz', *Man* NS 18(2) (1983): 237–59.

[3] A. Kevin Reinhart, 'What to do with Ritual Texts: Islamic Fiqh Texts and the Study of Islamic Ritual', in Leon Buskens and Annemarie van Sandwijk (eds), *Islamic Studies in the Twenty-First Century* (Amsterdam: Amsterdam University Press, 2016).

[4] Reinhart, 'What to do with Ritual Texts', 74.

[5] Reinhart, 'What to do with Ritual Texts', 84.

due to what has been seen as its ahistorical nature.[6] Yet, as Bashir shows, such texts are in fact extraordinarily valuable for the study of Islamic history. He suggests that approaching these texts through the lens of embodiment allows us to think of these sources 'not as static representations of the way things were in the past, but as elements of a dynamic process embedded within them'.[7] In other words, approaching the study of texts through the lens of the body allows us to understand the text itself as part of these processes, rather than simply representing these processes to the historian. Bashir points us in a fruitful direction. Considering Islamic texts from the perspective of the body forces us to bridge this gap between texts that more explicitly detail intellectual and political historical processes, on one hand, and ritual, devotional and practical texts, on the other. When considering the body however, an array of theories can be drawn upon, from sensory studies,[8] emotions,[9] materiality,[10] as well as theories of embodiment and habitus.[11] Texts themselves are objects after all, and are a type of media, and as Birgit Meyer has noted, such media may act as bodies that are 'incorporated by, and at the same time form their beholders and shape their habitus', shaping the sensory regimes of a particular community.[12] For Monique Scheer, drawing on Bourdieu's concept of habitus, emotions are a form of embodied practice that is deeply socialised, and involves 'language, material artefacts, the environment, and other people'.[13]

6 Shahzad Bashir, *Sufi Bodies* (New York: Columbia University Press, 2011), 2.

7 Bashir, *Sufi Bodies*, 18.

8 Birgit Meyer, 'Picturing the Invisible: Visual Culture and the Study of Religion', *Method & Theory in the Study of Religion* 27(4/5) (2015): 335; David Howes, 'Multisensory Anthropology', *Annual Review of Anthropology* 48 (2019): 20.

9 Monique Scheer, 'Are Emotions a Kind of Practice (and is that What Makes Them Have a History)? A Bourdieuian Approach to Understanding Emotions', *History and Theory* 51(2) (2012): 193–220.

10 Martha L. Finch, 'Rehabilitating Materiality: Bodies, Gods, and Religion', *Religion* 42(4) (2012): 625–31; Dick Houtman and Birgit Meyer (eds), *Things: Religion and the Question of Materiality* (New York: Fordham University Press, 2012).

11 Pierre Bourdieu, *The Logic of Practice* (Stanford: Stanford University Press, 1990).

12 Meyer, 'Picturing the Invisible', 345.

13 Scheer, 'Are Emotions a Kind of Practice and is that What Makes Them Have a History?' 193.

Therefore, Scheer suggests that the body is embedded in society, trained and, consequently, has historicity.[14]

The analytical focus within studies on contemporary Islam has also been challenged in recent years, accompanying a shift from focusing on treatises of Muslim authorities and religiously conscious actors to everyday practices of ordinary, often non-organised, Muslims. According to Samuli Schielke 'ethnographies about the religious lives of Muslims often privilege people who consciously present themselves as pious, committed Muslims'.[15] In addition, studies that focus on what are considered deviant, mystical or demotic practices have also been hegemonic within the academy for a long time, often represented as manifestations of religiosity that are not truly Islamic.[16] Both of these focuses can be nuanced and complicated by paying attention to the constitution of the Islamic as it is negotiated in everyday settings. A shift towards a 'Lived Islam' or 'Everyday Islam'[17] grants insights into the distinctive practices of women and youth, in public and private spaces, for example. The recent turn to the everyday is therefore very welcome. But as Nadia Fadil and Mayanthi Fernando have pointed out, the close relationship between Islamic norms and Islamic practices often remains unproblematised in these studies, which often 'conceptualize normative doctrine and everyday practice as unconnected'.[18] The notion that a practice is not – or not sufficiently – involved in shaping norms also leads to the idea that practices do not have an impact on how norms are negotiated in everyday settings. Consequently, we ask that attention be paid to how practices play a part in constructing norms and vice versa.

[14] Scheer, 'Are Emotions a Kind of Practice and is that What Makes Them Have a History?' 219–20.

[15] Samuli Schielke, 'Second Thoughts about the Anthropology of Islam, or How to Make Sense of Grand Schemes in Everyday Life', ZMO Working Papers 2, 2010, 2.

[16] Reinhart, 'What to do with Ritual Texts', 67.

[17] Nathal M. Dessing et al. (eds), *Everyday Lived Islam in Europe* (Farnham: Ashgate, 2013); Erkan Toguslu (ed.), *Everyday Life Practices of Muslims in Europe* (Leuven: Leuven University Press, 2015).

[18] Nadia Fadil and Fernando Mayanthi, 'Rediscovering the "Everyday" Muslim: Notes on an Anthropological Divide', *Hau: Journal of Ethnographic Theory* 5(2) (2015): 70.

Another concern involves the methods used to gather data in ethnographic studies that focus on Muslims: interviews are often conducted instead of focusing on textual treatises, replacing one text with another. This, of course, differs substantially but not structurally. Participant observation still mostly focuses on oral expressions rather than actions, bodies, materials or spaces. Interviews are in many ways insufficient:[19] they refer to rational reflection and can give a glimpse into the motivations, postures and reasons for certain practices. These statements however are not the practice itself but are in fact representations of practices. We therefore require different methodological tools to analyse the actions, objects and spaces in certain situations. In our attempt to rethink the normative and how it is constituted in Islamic societies, this chapter explores the importance of activities and actions, the body and embodiment, and the material aspect of religious practices. In doing so, it highlights the value of practice theory for the study of Islamic societies past and present, allowing us to reconsider how to move beyond the once dominant essentialist approaches to the study of Islam.

## Practice: Focus on Activities in Actions

What we have referred to so far encompasses the study of bodies, habitus, emotions, affects, material aspects of religion, space, action or behaviour informed by a scholarly move towards the study of practice (the practical turn). Practice theory is not a single homogeneous body of theories but rather covers various elements and strands of scholarship, providing a broad analytical framework and epistemological vocabulary. Although practice theories evolved within cultural studies and sociology as theoretical frameworks for the analysis of the social in the present by Pierre Bourdieu,[20] Theodore Schatzki,[21] Andreas Reckwitz,[22] to

[19] Various studies have discussed the shortcomings of interviews, for example, David Silverman, 'How was it for You? The Interview Society and the Irresistible Rise of the (Poorly) Analyzed Interview', *Qualitative Research* 17(2) (2017): 144–58.

[20] Bourdieu, *The Logic of Practice*.

[21] Theodore R. Schatzki, *The Site of the Social: A Philosophical Account of the Constitution of Social Life and Change* (University Park, PA: Pennsylvania State University Press, 2002).

[22] Andreas Reckwitz, 'Toward a Theory of Social Practices: A Development in Culturalist Theorizing', *European Journal of Social Theory* 5(2) (2002): 245–65; Andreas Reckwitz, 'Praktiken und Diskurse: Eine sozialtheoretische und methodologische Relation', in Herbert Kalthoff, Stefan Hirschauer and Gesa Lindemann (eds), *Theoretische Empirie: Zur Relevanz qualitativer Forschung* (Frankfurt a. M.: Suhrkamp, 2008), 188–209.

name just the most fundamental authors, these theories have also proven to be useful for historical approaches based on textual and/or material sources as historians have shown.[23] Practice theories reveal that the social is the product of social practices that are constituted by people, bodies, objects and discourses. They draw our attention to the array of doings and sayings, to bodies and embodiment, to acts and activities, to artefacts, and performances in particular spatial and temporal settings. In other words: they concentrate on socialised bodies, spaces and materials. When we consider these observations for the study of Islam and Muslims, we are compelled to conclude that the Islamic is also constituted in practical execution at a particular place in a particular time. It is our view that this execution should gain more scholarly interest within the field of Islamic studies.[24]

Theoretical frameworks that prioritise practice supplement investigations of religious texts and speeches as well as studies of attitudes, intentions, motivations and objectives in Muslims' actions, by analysing the performance of Muslim life in both quotidian and exceptional moments: 'Alongside actors' statements, discourses and textually imparted knowledge, concrete meaning can be attributed to the actors' embodied knowledge.'[25] Practice is what individuals habituate as 'practical knowledge, an ability, a savoir-faire, a conglomeration of everyday techniques, a practical understanding in the sense of "knowing one's way around something"'.[26] Practical knowledge is conceived as an incorporated knowledge, often not-yet-reflected upon, grounded in experience, and cultivated through bodily routines that generate practical abilities, and/or demonstrated in intuitive relationships to materiality. Analysis of statements of actors in interviews, books or speeches, or of essays on legal, ethical

[23] Arndt Brendecke (ed.), *Praktiken der frühen Neuzeit: Akteure – Handlungen – Artefakte* (Cologne: Böhlau Verlag, 2015); Marian Füssel, *Gelehrtenkultur als symbolische Praxis: Rang, Ritual und Konflikt an der Universität der frühen Neuzeit* (Münster: Wissenschaftliche Buchgesellschaft, 2004); Rieske Haasis (ed.), *Historische Praxeologie: Dimensionen vergangenen Handelns* (Paderborn: Ferdinand Schöningh, 2015).

[24] Ayşe Almıla Akca, *Moscheeleben in Deutschland: Eine Ethnographie zu islamischem Wissen, Tradition und religiöser Autorität* (Bielefeld: transcript Verlag, 2020), 42–5.

[25] Akca, *Moscheeleben in Deutschland*, 43.

[26] Andreas Reckwitz, 'Grundelemente einer Theorie sozialer Praktiken: Eine sozialtheoretische Perspektive', *Zeitschrift für Soziologie* 32(4) (2003): 289.

or political issues (past and present) sometimes tend to an essentialisation of Islam and Muslims. The approach of practice theories does underline that Muslims' quotidian and non-quotidian lives are pervaded by bodily experiences, routines, rituals, emotions, harmonised behaviour patterns, disruption and fracture, knowledge of appropriate and inappropriate forms of clothing, communality, celebrating, praying, greeting, mourning, shopping, working, doing politics, etc. This vantage point permits scholars to investigate questions about ways of life in general; about forms of community; about gendering situations; about feeling and sensing; about environmental, social and bioethical valuing and behaving from an empirical point of view. Existing research on normative taxonomies should be complemented by considering these aspects' diverse interconnections. We argue that practices are not simply derived from their underlying moral attitudes, dispositions or norms, but that embodied practices have relational impacts.[27]

An instance from an ethnographic fieldwork in Germany[28] shows the importance of shifting our gaze from a presupposed normative Islamic to Muslims' actions: a mosque was hosting a contest (best muezzin and khutbah lecturer) among young men of a certain region in its main *masjid* room, led by the middle-aged theology-trained Turkish imam of that particular mosque. The ethnic background of the approximately 200 mosque attendees was mainly Sunni Turkish, both first-generation immigrants and German-born Muslims. At the beginning of the event women and men were gender-separated in a women's section and the main *masjid* room, respectively. After the initial ritual prayer shortly before the start of the contest the imam then invited the women to the main *masjid* room in order to let them participate directly and not only through speakers. The visual and audible appearance of women in the formerly male-only main *masjid* room is worth describing: first, the men finished their greetings and conversations in the mosque courtyard before entering the *masjid* and then adopted a particular devotional posture inside the *masjid*, maintaining silence, sitting at the walls, and with stooped body postures. In contrast,

[27] Akca, *Moscheeleben in Deutschland*, 112.

[28] The fieldwork was conducted between 2012 and 2016 by Ayşe Almıla Akca as part of research on processes of Islamic knowledge production in German mosque associations. The main results can be found in the monography of Akca (2020), *Moscheeleben in Deutschland*.

the women entered the women's section immediately when they arrived at the mosque without chatting and greetings in the outside courtyard. Their conversations took place inside the women's section and their interactions were quite noisy even when the *salah* prayer began. When the women entered the main *masjid* after prayer, where the men had already taken their positions, the volume of the women's speech did not lessen. The women behaved in the same manner as they had behaved in their own section without considering the dominant postures in the main *masjid* adopted by men. The new situation displeased some men obviously. These men gave disapproving looks during the ceremony and made negative comments regarding the women's attendance in the main *masjid* afterwards. At the end of the contest, some men were complaining to each other about the women's attendance, others raised no objection to the appearance of the women. None of the women engaged in an argument with the men in attendance. Secondly, without exception all the women chose to sit down in the rear part of the *masjid* without any discussion. The mostly young men there were prompted to sit in the front part of the *masjid* by elderly men without saying anything but with bodily gestures. No women came to the front of the *masjid* nor did they intend to do so. With their bodily positioning both men and women *gender-separated* the *masjid* of their own accord. Thirdly, during the imam-led contest among the young men preaching a khutbah and reciting the call to prayer, most men and women remained in their former bodily moods. While most men were silent, without children, and with an adopted devotional attitude, most women audibly commented on the candidates and looked after the children. Lastly, when the women were about to enter the main *masjid* some men in the outside courtyard rebuked the women, telling them that this is not the women's entrance. By referring to the invitation of the imam some women insisted that the *masjid* is 'not male property' and ignored these interventions. Against the background of practice theory some observations and remarks on gender can be made:

People engage with each other by distinguishing 'between regular and irregular, competent and incompetent actions' and by '[sanctioning] those actions that are at odds with the common game'.[29] With their practices, they

[29] Thomas Alkemeyer, 'Körperwissen', in Anina Engelhardt and Laura Kajetzke (eds), *Handbuch Wissensgesellschaft: Theorien, Themen und Probleme* (Bielefeld: transcript Verlag, 2010), 299.

demonstrate what it means to act equitably and appropriately with regard to a particular social position. It is the material and symbolic familiarity with the practices, that is, with all verbal and non-verbal expressions and actions in the events themselves that are termed 'tact, skill, dexterity, delicacy or savoir-faire, all names for practical sense'.[30] The behaviour of the men and women in the gendered *masjid* rooms in the example above shows this familiarity and how it is challenged by a novel situation (the attendance of women in the main *masjid* room) both for men and for women. This familiarity derives from habitualisations or embodiments of certain practices by socialisation, experiences and education, giving *practical sense*[31] for bodies. Habitualisations must not be understood only in cognitive terms, but in physical terms, in other words, embodiments. The men stopped their conversations before entering the *masjid* and adopted a certain bodily posture that they have trained for years which was alien for women entering their own section of the mosque. In recurring gestures, attitudes, and ways of speaking and behaving, such field-specific orders materialise and thus manifest themselves in public. Therefore, the spatial change did not cause any difference in their behaviour from the female space to the male *masjid*, at least not for most of them. The negative comments on their entering the male-only area of the mosque by some men even before they entered indicates that their attendance was challenged. Embodiment and practical meaning are crucial for either the production or reproduction of a certain practice. Practical knowledge should not be viewed as isolated, individual or selective; neither is it merely the outcome of normative knowledge, inherent to Muslimness or predetermined by written sources and religious norms. Instead, practices should be defined as comprehensive and socially shared, held together by implicit, methodological and interpretive knowledge. To sum up, enacted in a certain practice are discursive, material, and symbolic chains of processes and politics that organise specific knowledge: production, dissemination, circulation, reception, impact, (de-)legitimisation, (de-)canonisation and signification. But what is also at stake is rejection, marginalisation and exclusion. The very brief description

[30] Bourdieu, *The Logic of Practice*, 80.

[31] Pierre Bourdieu, *Practical Reason: On the Theory of Action* (Stanford: Stanford University Press, 1998), 25.

and analysis of this particular field note on gender separation and women's attendance of mosques[32] shows how the scholarly debate on gender issues in Islam can be enriched when we consider acts including moving, talking, sitting, feeling, the spatial ordering and dis-ordering of practices, and the practical knowledge on appropriate and non-appropriate behaviour. Considering the practical logic of a practice demonstrates that analysing discursive knowledge alone is insufficient for the study of Islam and Muslims.

In order to comprehend an action's rationale and its practical meaning, a research method that analyses the detailed description of actions and the social settings in which they take place can help to avoid superficially rationalising or 'Islamising' them. People act, and whether their actions occur directly as a result of religious motivation cannot be directly ascertained – especially not by the people themselves. Of course, people's own explanations must be included in the analysis, but without conceiving of them as normative or viewing them as the sole causes of their actions. Ethical motivations, for example, may give a glimpse of the context in which certain practices could be embedded. Also, the intentions and reflections on a certain behaviour, driven by norms, should be considered. But one should avoid focusing solely on the ethical justifications or normative regulations and forgetting the context in which these practices occur. Previous experiences, skills and socialisation, that is, the cultural and social habitus, shape people's perceptions, understandings and interpretations. By adopting such a perspective, researchers can explore social patterns of action without having to immediately incorporate them into normative or unifying patterns of interpretation. Given these considerations, we must identify the habits underlying a practice.

## Embodiment and Emotions

Identifying these habits in historical settings presents a particular challenge given that our access to them is mediated by texts. Of course, what shapes the study of Islam is a matter that is continually evolving. The debates surrounding which languages and cultures should constitute a definitive curriculum and canon for understanding Islam seem to have gathered pace in

32 A larger description of the field note and a broader discussion of its analysis can be found in Akca, *Moscheeleben in Deutschland*, 191–218.

recent years. Historical and philological approaches, however, still seem to occupy an essential place in the study of Islam. When it comes to the study of text and Islamic history, attempts to move beyond the construction of the Islamic through a particular canon of sources and particular methodological approaches have begun in earnest only recently in comparison with similar developments in the study of European history. There has been a tendency to sideline certain textual traditions,[33] those of ritual and hagiography, for example. Such texts appear to have been viewed as either too mundane or too fantastical, respectively, and therefore deemed unworthy of the attention of historians. Yet there is no doubt that such texts make up part of the historical culture that we can study. The ways in which bodies are represented in these sources, for example, tell us much about Islam in the past. The body itself provides a link between nature and the culturally constructed. As Walker-Bynum has noted, though in studies of medieval Christianity, 'what we study – what we can study – is culturally constructed. But we know we are more than culture. We are body.'[34] Both the seemingly mundane and fantastical then are useful sources to engage with the question of where the body ends and the culturally constructed begins in Islamic contexts.

Yet even when we read Islamic texts that are far more theoretical and seemingly abstract, it becomes apparent that the authors of these texts themselves had concerns about the interconnection between the body and its role in what constitutes the cultural. To take one example, a common oft-recurring discussion in Sufi texts considers whether Sufis should consciously behave as if they are experiencing ecstatic states even if they do not truly 'feel' them. Sufi opinions on the subject vary, but many encourage the practice, especially if it means that Sufis in attendance at a musical ceremony imitate the behaviour of their fellow Sufis.[35] Our medieval authors themselves therefore clearly grappled with questions of authentic and constructed bodily expressions of emotions. They had clear ideas about the benefits, or dangers, of collective

33 Bashir, 'Sufi Bodies', 2–4; Reinhart, 'What to do with Ritual Texts', 68.

34 Caroline Walker-Bynum, *Fragmentation and Redemption: Essays on Gender and the Human Body in Medieval Religion* (New York: Zone Books, 1992), 20.

35 See, for example, Abū Naṣr al-Sarrāj, *Kitāb Al-Lumaʿ* (Cairo: Dar al-Kotob al-Haditha, 1960), 247; ʿAlī Al-Hujwīrī, *Kashf Al-Maḥjūb*, trans. Reynold A. Nicholson (Leiden: Brill, 1911), 418.

bodily disciplines, but their discussions reflect that these behaviours occurred independently of their theorisations on the topic and likely preceded them. Hence, to approach texts through practice theory is not to simply impose a theoretical lens onto our medieval authors, but to engage with their concerns, and in some cases to be guided by texts that have been influenced by popular practice. The scholar of Islamic texts can therefore find the tools to engage with these texts through methodologies that centre the body, senses, emotions or ritual.

These approaches can also help us to appreciate texts by considering their dynamic nature. They not only represent a certain process in the history of Islamic thought and society, they also construct them. When approached through these theoretical lenses they also tell us something about the lived experiences of Muslims, their cultural history and the history of the body itself. For example, Muḥammad Ibn al-Munawwar, in his hagiographical *Asrār al-tawḥīd* (the secret of God's oneness) relates a story whereby a dervish from a mountain village enters the Sufi sheikh Abū Saʿīd ibn Abī al-Khayr's mosque but does not adhere to the proper etiquettes. He speaks loudly, wears noisy shoes, and moves in such a way as to cause excessive noise. The sheikh then sends him on a journey where he encounters a dragon or large serpent. He returns from the experience shaken and in a state of dread and awe, he removes his shoes on his journey back and remains quiet from then on, both in speech and bodily posture.[36] Whether this episode of the hagiography is to be believed or not, it reveals to the reader the behaviour and disposition that was expected in the medieval mosque, namely refinement and silence from pious worshipers. It also associates these bodily postures with certain affective states such as awe and dread. These hagiographical stories were also most probably read aloud and disseminated orally in the form of sermons and storytelling. Hence, they themselves would have been involved in shaping the behaviours and emotional repertoires of medieval Muslims. We may say then that the text does not only represent something about the habitus of medieval Muslims but shapes them as well. By paying attention to what practice theories reveal regarding the embodied experiences of people, they allow us to

[36] Muhammad ibn al-Munawwar, *Asrār al-Tawḥīd fī Maqāmāt al-Shaykh Abū Saʿīd* (Tehran: Chapkhaneh-ye Fardin va Baradar, 1896), 80–2.

see how Muslim communities in the past were constituted by shared bodily practices, emotions and sensory regimes. This moves us beyond the notion of a normative Islam that is constructed by elites to reveal an interaction between theory, community and practice that has historically constituted the Islamic in a relational manner.

## Materiality

One of the essential features of practice theories is that they highlight the material dimension of all social life.[37] Since practice theories also reject 'thinking about religion as if it is unlike everything else that people do',[38] they presuppose that there can be no such thing as an *immaterial* religion either. This means that practice theories first and foremost challenge the notion that religion can be conceptualised in terms of belief or affiliation alone. Religion never occurs without the presence of things and artefacts. Hence, analysing it requires engagement with theories of materiality.[39]

Islam, in this sense, is no exception to the rule. When we look at Islamic rituals, for instance, we can easily observe the involvement of physical objects: prayer rugs, beads, items of clothing, evening meals in the rite of breaking fast, the circumambulation of the Kaaba, the stoning of the devil during Hajj, mosque buildings and many more.

So, if the materiality of religious practices is so obvious, why is it then that – save for a few exceptions – it has been largely neglected in the study of Islam so far? One of the reasons certainly lies in the prevalent modern misconception of Islam as a religion with an alleged universal essence defined by a core set of principles and beliefs.[40] Along with the 'longstanding materiophobia'[41] in the study

[37] Theodore R. Schatzki, *Social Change in a Material World* (London: Routledge, 2019), 51–77; Andreas Reckwitz, 'The Status of the "Material" in Theories of Culture: From "Social Structure" to "Artefacts"', *Journal for the Theory of Social Behaviour* 32(2) (2002): 207–14.

[38] Robert Wuthnow, *What Happens When We Practice Religion? Textures of Devotion in Ordinary Life* (Princeton, NJ: Princeton University Press, 2020), ix.

[39] Birgit Meyer et al., 'The Origin and Mission of Material Religion', *Religion* 40(3) (2010): 210.

[40] Shahab Ahmed, *What Is Islam? The Importance of Being Islamic* (Princeton, NJ: Princeton University Press, 2016), 132.

[41] Birgit Meyer, '"Material Approaches to Religion" Meet "New Materialism": Resonances and Dissonances', *Material Religion* 15(5) (2019): 620.

of religion in general, Islam, too, has been addressed according to a belief-centred view on religion, privileging its mental and spiritual dimensions and thus being mainly concerned with interiority, meaning and consciousness. This view not only de-materialises religion but also, as Sonia Hazard puts it, denigrates external religious phenomena as mere 'manifestations of prior beliefs or ideas that enjoy more complete expression in discursive forms such as doctrines, scriptures, and confessions'.[42] Having its origin in anti-Catholic polemics of historical Protestantism which emphasised 'that true religion is essentially immaterial',[43] this notion was adopted not only by the modern discipline of the study of religion but also in modern Islamic discourse. As Abdulkader Tayob states, there seemed no need for early Muslim scholars 'to represent Islam as a cohesive and comprehensive set of beliefs'.[44] Thus, the scholarly perspective and conceptualisation of Islam had to make it into a religion in this modern sense of the term,[45] privileging belief as the guiding concept when investigating it.

Representatives of the cultural turn of the 1960s disagree with this treatment of religion as if it were an abstract entity unrelated to the context of behaviour, practice or, for that matter, materiality. In his much-cited article on 'Religion as a Cultural System', Clifford Geertz calls for a *social* analysis of religious *activities*, that is, for the engagement in ethnographic research rather than in mentalistic worlds or in speculative philosophy.[46] Although Geertz himself defines religion as 'a system of symbols' which formulates 'conceptions of a general order of existence', he asserts that religion also 'projects images of cosmic order onto the plane of human experience'.[47] Following this, religion cannot be narrowed to an impalpable worldview but needs to be investigated in the lived experiences of people where symbols are staged in religious practices and rituals. Departing

[42] Sonia Hazard, 'The Material Turn in the Study of Religion', *Religion and Society* 4(1) (2013): 58.

[43] Peter J. Bräunlein, 'Thinking Religion Through Things: Reflections on the Material Turn in the Scientific Study of Religions', *Method & Theory in the Study of Religion* 28(4/5) (2016): 370.

[44] Abdulkader Tayob, *Religion in Modern Islamic Discourse* (London: Hurst, 2009), 12.

[45] Tayob, *Religion in Modern Islamic Discourse*, 9.

[46] Clifford Geertz, 'Religion as a Cultural System', in *The Interpretation of Cultures: Selected Essays* (New York: Basic Books, 1973), 91.

[47] 'Geertz, 'Religion as a Cultural System', 90.

from lived experiences instead of whatever is deemed their cosmological premise may, however, be challenging when it comes to capturing religious experiences. For the mere observation of a religious practice does not enable the researcher to penetrate the believers' inner mental and affective lives. Yet it is not the intimate experiences of the sacred, nor the subjective interpretations of the participants on which practice theories put their main focus. As a matter of fact, starting from the notion of practice implies that subjectivity itself does not precede but is produced in situated practices.

When it comes to materiality, however, practice theory differs fundamentally from Geertz's and other cultural theorists' assertions. First, for them it is the symbol that takes precedence, not practice. This means that material objects for cultural theorists are nothing more than representations of cultural codes, that is, patterns of classification, and hence are ascribed no independent explanatory force. Material entities exist only insofar as they are carriers of meaning. This decreases their status to being mere objects of knowledge – or objects of interpretation – within a collective meaning structure.[48] They serve as vessels for ideas of cosmic order. In other words, cultural theorists conceptualise material objects as embodiments of 'something else taken to be religion's blueprint or true essence – something presumed to be primary, irreducible, and independent, something ideational, that is to say immaterial, such as beliefs and meanings'.[49] Studying religion from this point of view therefore means decoding symbols or reading them as if they were texts first – and this includes practices and objects – in order to eventually get at the cosmology which is understood to be the *actual* religion hidden behind its material manifestations. Even though religion is something observable here, as Geertz himself emphasises,[50] its material dimension, however, is just the projection of an envisaged and ontologically predominant transcendental reality. Here, material culture is reduced to a quasi-linguistic sign where its physical properties are devoid of all but highly abstracted meanings.[51]

48 Reckwitz, 'The Status of the "Material" in Theories of Culture', 202.

49 Hazard, 'The Material Turn in the Study of Religion', 60.

50 Geertz, 'Religion as a Cultural System', 91.

51 Nicole Boivin, 'Grasping the Elusive and Unknowable: Material Culture in Ritual Practice', *Material Religion* 5(3) (2009): 271–2.

Practice theories deem these kinds of representationalist conceptions of the material world as insufficient with respect to understanding human activities. For them, objects are more than the content of their cultural representations and thus cannot be read as texts. They are used and have effects in their specific materiality without which practices would simply not unfold.[52] Following Bruno Latour,[53] practice theorists challenge the modern binary distinctions between nature and culture, subject and object, and, ultimately, facts of the world and human constructions. Differing from constructivist approaches in general, they do not regard the relation between discourse and materiality as unidirectional. That is to say, that matter is not a passive product of discursive practices. This 'anthropocentric exceptionalism'[54] needs to be overcome by dismantling the dichotomies mentioned above and making allowance to a materiality that is not reducible to the discursive. Otherwise, constructivist orientations to social analysis – as Geertz demands it – will remain inadequate for thinking about matter and materiality.[55]

Coming back to religion, its material practices are not to be conceptualised as reflections of a pre-existing social, cultural, cognitive or cosmological framework either. For it is not only human beings that form the components of practices. Non-human artefacts are just as equal participants in and hence constitutive elements of them. As materiality is not some element added to a culture that is already complete in itself,[56] 'things, their use, their valuation, and their appeal are not something *added* to a religion, but rather inextricable from it'.[57] So, according to practice theorists there is a need for a remateri-

[52] Reckwitz, 'The Status of the "Material" in Theories of Culture', 209; see also Karin Knorr Cetina, 'Objectual Practice', in Theodore R. Schatzki, Karin Knorr Cetina and Eike von Savigny (eds), *The Practice Turn in Contemporary Theory* (London: Routledge, 2001), 184–97.

[53] Bruno Latour, *We Have Never Been Modern* (Cambridge, MA: Harvard University Press, 1993).

[54] Manuel A. Vásquez, *More Than Belief: A Materialist Theory of Religion* (Oxford: Oxford University Press, 2011), 197.

[55] Diana Coole and Samantha Frost, 'Introducing the New Materialisms', in Diana Coole and Samantha Frost (eds), *New Materialisms: Ontology, Agency, and Politics* (Durham, NC: Duke University Press, 2010), 6.

[56] Reckwitz, 'The Status of the "Material" in Theories of Culture', 195.

[57] Meyer et al., 'The Origin and Mission of Material Religion', 209 (emphasis in original).

alisation of religious studies. Needless to say that this also refers to the study of Islam. This does not mean, however, that the materiality of religious practices should now gain priority over discursivity. As George Ioannides puts it, 'both are intra-actively inseparable and inseparably constitutive of/in the world. Neither matter nor discourse precedes the emergence of the material-discursive, and neither precedes the other in onto-epistemological processes; *relations* constitute matter-discourse. When applied to the study of religion, such a directive yields the rich insight that religions are material-discursive practices that create and comprise the phenomena of the world.'[58]

How, then, does religion happen materially? First, practice theories recognise the fact that all practice is enabled by physicality – be it human bodies or things and artefacts that are involved. This means that practices evolve only insofar as human bodies and objects interrelate with each other. The temporal and spatial relevance of those objects are facilitated by what practice theorists call *affordances*.[59] These are (physical) properties of objects such as size, substance and surface that provide for or make possible certain usages. As James J. Gibson, who coined the term *affordance*, puts it, things can appear as being 'stand-on-able', 'sit-on-able', 'bump-into-able', 'get-underneath-able', 'climb-on-able' or 'fall-off-able',[60] and hence contribute to the constitution and structuration of particular practices. The concept of affordance does not, however, just designate the qualities of objects in and of themselves, but highlights their interdependence with other bodies and objects. Affordance therefore is a relational concept that encompasses both the embeddedness of things and bodies in situations and the establishment of their meaning within practices that take place in those situations. Yet meaning in this sense is practical and therefore to be distinguished from social constructivist and

[58] George Ioannides, 'The Matter of Meaning and the Meaning of Matter: Explorations for the Material and Discursive Study of Religion', in Frans Wijsen and Kocku von Stuckrad (eds), *Making Religion: Theory and Practice in the Discursive Study of Religion* (Leiden: Brill, 2016), 68–9 (emphasis in original); see also Reckwitz, 'Praktiken und Diskurse'.

[59] Joseph Rouse, 'Practice Theory', in Stephen P. Turner and Mark W. Risjord (eds), *Philosophy of Anthropology and Sociology* (Amsterdam: Elsevier, 2007), 676.

[60] James J. Gibson, 'The Theory of Affordances', in Robert Shaw and John Bransford (eds), *Perceiving, Acting, and Knowing: Toward an Ecological Psychology* (Hillsdale, NJ: Lawrence Erlbaum, 1977), 68.

representationalist notions described earlier. For practice theory starts its investigation of religion with material practices and not beliefs.[61]

## Conclusion

As this chapter has shown, the theoretical rematerialisation of religion ascribes significance to things and artefacts without referring to verbal expressions of doctrine or symbolism. The question of how religion happens materially is thus not to be confused with asking 'the much less helpful question of how religion is *expressed* in material form'.[62] Consequently, a practice theoretical study of religion emphasises a bottom-up approach where the situational and the particular become methodological entry points, challenging the notion that religion can be assessed in terms of predefined categories such as belief or affiliation.[63] A focus on bodies, materials and doings undermines the idea of an 'Islam' that is constituted in a top-down manner, by over-emphasising the representative relationship between texts and historical or societal processes.

Accordingly, religion is not to be found solely in texts, statements, or discourses, but is constituted and – in the truest sense of the word – materialised via practices that evolve in situational settings of interrelated bodies and objects. Here, practice theory joins other materialist theories by focusing on configurations of human bodies and non-human entities and by remaining 'humbly agnostic about "the supernatural" sources of religion'.[64] Acknowledging the fact that practices, and likewise religion, are observable phenomena, it approaches religion, as Manuel A. Vásquez avers, 'as it is lived by human beings, not by angels'.[65] The questions practice theorists ask with regard to Islam then need to be: how are things involved in practices that constitute what we indicate as being Islamic? How are we to identify the specific constellations of things and bodies in Islamic religious practices? To

[61] Webb Keane, 'The Evidence of the Senses and the Materiality of Religion', *Journal of the Royal Anthropological Institute* 14(S1) (2008): 117.

[62] Meyer et al., 'The Origin and Mission of Material Religion', 209 (emphasis in original).

[63] Wuthnow, *What Happens When We Practice Religion?*, 1; Bräunlein, 'Thinking Religion Through Things', 373.

[64] Vásquez, *More Than Belief*, 5.

[65] Vásquez, *More Than Belief*, 5.

what extent do things that are embedded in practical settings invoke Islamic religious sentiments and feelings?

Taken together, practice theoretical approaches to Islam with their rivet on materiality could perhaps even contribute to a fundamental critique of mentalistic stances and belief-centred views that underpin Eurocentric presumed universalisms such as *religion*.[66]

## Bibliography


Ahmed, Shahab, *What Is Islam? The Importance of Being Islamic*. Princeton, NJ: Princeton University Press, 2016.

Akca, Ayşe Almıla, *Moscheeleben in Deutschland: Eine Ethnographie zu islamischem Wissen, Tradition und religiöser Autorität*. Bielefeld: transcript Verlag, 2020.

Al-Hujwīrī, ʿAlī. *Kashf Al-Maḥjūb*. Leiden: Brill, 1911.

Alkemeyer, Thomas, 'Körperwissen', in Anina Engelhardt and Laura Kajetzke (eds), *Handbuch Wissensgesellschaft: Theorien, Themen und Probleme*. Bielefeld: transcript Verlag, 2010, 293–308.

al-Sarrāj, Abū Naṣr, *Kitāb Al-Lumaʿ*. Cairo: Dar al-Kotob al-Haditha, 1960.

Asad, Talal, 'Anthropological Conceptions of Religion: Reflections on Geertz', *Man* NS 18(2) (1983): 237–59.

Asad, Talal, *The Idea of an Anthropology of Islam*. Washington, DC: Center for Contemporary Arab Studies, Georgetown University, 1986.

Bashir, Shahzad, *Sufi Bodies*. New York: Columbia University Press, 2011.

Boivin, Nicole, 'Grasping the Elusive and Unknowable: Material Culture in Ritual Practice', *Material Religion* 5(3) (2009): 266–87.

Bourdieu, Pierre, *The Logic of Practice*. Stanford: Stanford University Press, 1990.

Bourdieu, Pierre, *Practical Reason: On the Theory of Action*. Stanford: Stanford University Press, 1998.

Bräunlein, Peter J., 'Thinking Religion Through Things: Reflections on the Material Turn in the Scientific Study of Religions', *Method & Theory in the Study of Religion* 28(4/5) (2016): 365–99.

Brendecke, Arndt (ed.), *Praktiken der frühen Neuzeit: Akteure – Handlungen – Artefakte*. Cologne: Böhlau Verlag, 2015.

Coole, Diana and Samantha Frost, 'Introducing the New Materialisms', in Diana Coole and Samantha Frost (eds), *New Materialisms: Ontology, Agency, and Politics*. Durham, NC: Duke University Press, 2010, 1–43.


[66] Meyer, '"Material Approaches to Religion" Meet "New Materialism"', 620.

Dessing, Nathal M., Nadia Jeldtoft, Jørgen S. Nielsen and Linda Woodhead (eds), *Everyday Lived Islam in Europe*. Farnham: Ashgate, 2013.

Fadil, Nadia and Fernando Mayanthi, 'Rediscovering the "Everyday" Muslim: Notes on an Anthropological Divide', *Hau: Journal of Ethnographic Theory* 5(2) (2015): 59–88.

Finch, Martha L., 'Rehabilitating Materiality: Bodies, Gods, and Religion', *Religion* 42(4) (2012): 625–31.

Füssel, Marian, *Gelehrtenkultur als symbolische Praxis: Rang, Ritual und Konflikt an der Universität der frühen Neuzeit*. Münster: Wissenschaftliche Buchgesellschaft, 2004.

Geertz, Clifford, 'Religion as a Cultural System', in *The Interpretation of Cultures: Selected Essays*. New York: Basic Books, 1973, 87–125.

Gibson, James J., 'The Theory of Affordances', in Robert Shaw and John Bransford *Perceiving, Acting, and Knowing: Toward an Ecological Psychology*. Hillsdale, NJ: Lawrence Erlbaum, 1977, 67–82.

Haasis, Rieske (ed.), *Historische Praxeologie: Dimensionen vergangenen Handelns*. Paderborn: Ferdinand Schöningh, 2015.

Hazard, Sonia, 'The Material Turn in the Study of Religion', *Religion and Society* 4(1) (2013): 58–78.

Houtman, Dick and Birgit Meyer (eds), *Things: Religion and the Question of Materiality*. New York: Fordham University Press, 2012.

Howes, David, 'Multisensory Anthropology', *Annual Review of Anthropology* 48 (2019): 17–28.

Ioannides, George, 'The Matter of Meaning and the Meaning of Matter: Explorations for the Material and Discursive Study of Religion', in Frans Wijsen and Kocku von Stuckrad (eds), *Making Religion: Theory and Practice in the Discursive Study of Religion*. Leiden: Brill, 2016, 51–73.

Keane, Webb, 'The Evidence of the Senses and the Materiality of Religion', *Journal of the Royal Anthropological Institute* 14(S1) (2008): 110–27.

Knorr Cetina, Karin, 'Objectual Practice', in Theodore R. Schatzki, Karin Knorr Cetina and Eike von Savigny (eds), *The Practice Turn in Contemporary Theory*. London: Routledge, 2001, 184–97.

Latour, Bruno, *We Have Never Been Modern*. Cambridge, MA: Harvard University Press, 1993.

Meyer, Birgit, 'Picturing the Invisible: Visual Culture and the Study of Religion', *Method & Theory in the Study of Religion* 27(4/5) (2015): 333–60.

Meyer, Birgit, '"Material Approaches to Religion" Meet "New Materialism": Resonances and Dissonances', *Material Religion* 15(5) (2019): 620–1.

Meyer, Birgit, David Morgan, Crispin Paine and S. Brent Plate, 'The Origin and Mission of Material Religion', *Religion* 40(3) (2010): 207–11.

Reckwitz, Andreas, 'The Status of the "Material" in Theories of Culture: From "Social Structure" to "Artefacts"', *Journal for the Theory of Social Behaviour* 32(2) (2002): 195–217.

Reckwitz, Andreas, 'Toward a Theory of Social Practices: A Development in Culturalist Theorizing', *European Journal of Social Theory* 5(2) (2002): 245–65.

Reckwitz, Andreas, 'Grundelemente einer Theorie sozialer Praktiken: Eine sozialtheoretische Perspektive', *Zeitschrift für Soziologie* 32(4) (2003): 282–301.

Reckwitz, Andreas, 'Praktiken und Diskurse: Eine sozialtheoretische und methodologische Relation', in Herbert Kalthoff, Stefan Hirschauer and Gesa Lindemann (eds), *Theoretische Empirie: Zur Relevanz qualitativer Forschung*. Frankfurt a. M.: Suhrkamp, 2008, 188–209.

Reinhart, A. Kevin, 'What to Do with Ritual Texts: Islamic Fiqh Texts and the Study of Islamic Ritual', in Leon Buskens and Annemarie van Sandwijk (eds), *Islamic Studies in the Twenty-First Century*. Amsterdam: Amsterdam University Press, 2016, 67–86.

Rouse, Joseph, 'Practice Theory', in Stephen P. Turner and Mark W. Risjord (eds), *Philosophy of Anthropology and Sociology*. Amsterdam: Elsevier, 2007, 639–81.

Schatzki, Theodore R., *The Site of the Social: A Philosophical Account of the Constitution of Social Life and Change*. University Park, PA: Pennsylvania State University Press, 2002.

Schatzki, Theodore R., *Social Change in a Material World*. London: Routledge, 2019.

Scheer, Monique, 'Are Emotions a Kind of Practice (and is that What Makes Them Have a History)? A Bourdieuian Approach to Understanding Emotions', *History and Theory* 51(2) (2012): 193–220.

Schielke, Samuli, 'Second Thoughts About the Anthropology of Islam, or How to Make Sense of Grand Schemes in Everyday Life', ZMO Working Papers 2, 2010.

Silverman, David, 'How was it for You? The Interview Society and the Irresistible Rise of the (Poorly) Analyzed Interview', *Qualitative Research* 17(2) (2017): 144–58.

Tayob, Abdulkader, *Religion in Modern Islamic Discourse*. London: Hurst, 2009.

Toguslu, Erkan (ed.), *Everyday Life Practices of Muslims in Europe*. Leuven: Leuven University Press, 2015.

Vásquez, Manuel A., *More Than Belief: A Materialist Theory of Religion*. Oxford: Oxford University Press, 2011.

Walker-Bynum, Caroline, *Fragmentation and Redemption: Essays on Gender and the Human Body in Medieval Religion*. New York: Zone Books, 1992.
Wuthnow, Robert, *What Happens When We Practice Religion? Textures of Devotion in Ordinary Life*. Princeton, NJ: Princeton University Press, 2020.

# INDEX

EU Authorised Representative:
Easy Access System Europe Mustamäe tee 50, 10621 Tallinn, Estonia
gpsr.requests@easproject.com

Printed and bound by CPI Group (UK) Ltd, Croydon, CR0 4YY
26/05/2025
01882744-0005